OIL, GOD, AND GOLD

Anthony Cave Brown

OIL, GOD, AND GOLD

The Story of Aramco and the Saudi Kings

A Marc Jaffe Book

HOUGHTON MIFFLIN COMPANY

BOSTON • NEW YORK

1999

For information about permission to reproduce
selections from this book, write to
Permissions, Houghton Mifflin Company,
215 Park Avenue South, New York,
New York 10003.

Library of Congress Cataloging-in-Publication Data
Brown, Anthony Cave.
Oil, God, and gold : the story of Aramco and the
Saudi kings / Anthony Cave Brown.
p.   cm.
"A Marc Jaffe book."
Includes bibliographical references and index.
ISBN 0-395-59220-8
1. Arabian American Oil Company.   2. Petroleum
industry and trade — Saudi Arabia.   I. Title.
HD9576.S33B76 1999
338.7'6223382'09538 — dc21   98-39654 CIP

Printed in the United States of America

Book design by Robert Overholtzer

QUM 10 9 8 7 6 5 4 3 2 1

The author is grateful for permission to quote from "American
Perspectives of Aramco, the Saudi-Arabian Oil-Producing Company, 1930s to 1980s," an oral history conducted 1992–1993,
Regional Oral History Office, The Bancroft Library, University
of California, Berkeley, 1995. Used by permission of the University of California, Berkeley. Excerpts are taken from the oral histo-
ries of Frank Jungers, Paul and Elizabeth Arnot, Baldo Marinovic,
William L. Owen, R. W. "Brock" Powers, Peter Speers, Ellen Speers.

Far are the shades of Arabia,
Where the Princes ride at noon
'mid the verduous vales and thickets,
Under the ghost of the moon. . . .
They haunt me — her lutes and her forests;
No beauty on earth I see
But shadowed with that dream recalls
Her loveliness to me:
Still eyes look coldly upon me,
'He is crazed with the spell of Arabia,
They have stolen his wits away.'

— WALTER DE LA MARE

CONTENTS

OIL, GOD, AND GOLD

PROLOGUE

T HE ARABIAN AMERICAN OIL Company (Aramco), the origin and the fount of American power in the Middle East, was the creation of an unusual complex of forces — Anglo-American great power rivalries, including the pursuit of world dominion — that attended World War I. At the center of the complex were three remarkable men. One was a young Arab prince known as Ibn Saud, of whom a British intelligence officer wrote in a description of him that has not been bettered:

> He is a man of splendid physique, standing well over six feet, and carrying himself with the air of one accustomed to command. Though he is more impressively built than the typical nomad shaikh, he has the characteristics of the well-bred Arab, the strongly-marked aquiline profile, full-flesh nostrils, prominent lips and a long narrow chin accentuated by a pointed beard. His hands are fine, with slender fingers, a trait almost universal among the tribes of pure Arab blood, and, in spite of his great height and breadth of shoulder, he conveys the impression, common enough in the desert, of an indefinable lassitude, not individual but racial, the secular weariness of an ancient and self-contained people, which has made heavy drafts on its vital forces and borrowed little from beyond its own forbidding frontiers. His deliberate movements, his slow sweet smile and the contemplative glance of his heavy lidded eyes, though they add to his dignity and charm, do not accord with the western conception of a vigorous personality. Nevertheless, report credits him with the powers of physical endurance rare even in hard-bitten Arabia. Among men bred in the camel saddle he is said to have few rivals as a tireless rider. As a leader of irregular forces he is of proved daring, and he combines with his qualities as a soldier that grasp of statecraft which is yet more highly prized by the tribesmen. . . . Politician, ruler and raider, Ibn Saud illustrates a historic

type. Such men as he are the exception in any community, but they are thrown up persistently by the Arab race.[1]

In the tumult created by World War I in Arabia and in the Persian Gulf and Southwest Asia (the Germans and the Turks were allied against the British Empire), the British government saw in Ibn Saud the possibility of an alliance, if only because his vast desert domain might possess oil. In December 1915, therefore, a British agent signed with him a pledge that he would not, now and forever, be "antagonistic to the British Government in any war," and that he would "refrain from entering into any correspondence, agreement, or treaty, with any Foreign Nation or Power, and further to give immediate notice to the Political Authorities of the British Government of any other power to interfere in" Ibn Saud's domain.[2] By this parchment Ibn Saud was bound to recognize Britain's interest in whatever treasure lay under the deserts. In return, Ibn Saud received a pension from the British government for arms and £5,000 gold yearly.

Then, in December 1917, a British political agent, Harry St. John Bridger Philby, landed on the Gulf coast of Ibn Saud's dominion. Born in British Ceylon, the son of a tea planter, Philby was a member of a leading family of soldiers and civil servants in the British Empire. He had been an administrator in the Punjabi and Kashmir provinces of British India. There he had shown himself to be a unique individual of a type spawned by the special culture of the nineteenth-century British Empire — young, fit, ambitious, a scholar and linguist in Asian and European languages, personable, and well known as a good man in a tight spot. The world came to know him in later years as the father of Kim Philby, who became a high officer of the British Secret Service and, at the same time, Stalin's principal spy in England during World War II. There was a very strong streak of the contrarian in both father and son.

St. John Philby's mission to Arabia was to ensure that Ibn Saud did not attack his enemy, Hussein, sherif of Mecca, using British arms and gold to do so. For one thing, Hussein was another British ally in Arabia; for another, his tribes, under the command of Lawrence of Arabia, were engaging large numbers of Germans and Turks; and for a third, it was Britain's desire to end the war as the principal power in the Arabian Peninsula, and for that purpose it would be essential that Ibn Saud remain an ally of Britain. His other task was military; he was to induce Ibn Saud to annihilate the regime of the sherif of Hail, a dynasty in northwestern Arabia that was in alliance with the Turks against both Ibn Saud and the British government.

On his arrival by camel in Riyadh, Ibn Saud's capital in the Nejd region of the central Arabian Peninsula, Philby was well received by the prince. In the ten days they spent together in Ibn Saud's fortress-palace, their talks were warm, and indeed, they established a close friendship that was to last for the next thirty-five years. Such was their friendship that to an important extent it led to the outcome that the United States, not Great Britain, obtained what was later called by the U.S. State Department "the greatest commercial prize of the planet."[3] Like son, like father: St. John Philby was to betray the British government in favor of Standard Oil.

The third man, John Davison Rockefeller, the founder of the Standard Oil Company, had become one of the richest and the most powerful men in the United States. Until the U.S. government in 1909 decided that Rockefeller had become too powerful, Rockefeller had gained control of up to 95 percent of the oil industry of the United States. When the government broke up Rockefeller's monopoly, Rockefeller's lawyers formed the "Standard Oil Group," which included Standard Oil of California (Socal), Standard Oil of New Jersey (Exxon), and Standard Oil of New York (Mobil). And of this new tremendous union of industrial, financial, and political power, Anthony Sampson, the British oil historian, would write,

> These three daughters of Rockefeller, Exxon, Mobil and Socal, were all for years afterwards . . . accused by their many enemies of acting in unison. The suspicion was hardly surprising; they all sold their oil at the same price, under the same Standard name, their directors were old Standard men, and their principal shareholder was still John D. Rockefeller. In later years . . . these three sisters were to come together in their many operations abroad — linking hands, now in one place, now in another, as in an intricate square dance. The indignant denials of collusion were not very credible after the record of mendacity and secrecy of their ugly parent.[4]

But was the ugly parent guilty of more than mendacity, of a conspiracy, or a common understanding of the harsh facts of world oil? That was the "recurring question." It was clear from their origins "that they had grown up outside any traditional field, whether of government, banking or earlier industry. They were deeply distrusted, with some reason, and the men who ran them were cut off behind high walls from the rest of society."[5] Certainly, Standard Oil of New Jersey and Standard Oil of California came under suspicion and were investigated by the U.S. Federal Trade Commission and the Monopolies Subcommittee of the U.S. Senate. But if the government was looking for conspiracy, it failed to find one. That investigation, however, produced important evidence of how, and why, the Standard Oil Group decided to challenge that most powerful government, that of the British Empire, for control of Persian Gulf oil. The group's decision was both relentlessly pursued and most daring, the more so since the common opinion of the Arab nation was not complimentary. Especially its religion, which pervaded all aspects of life in Arabia, was frowned upon. Colston's *Geography*, the authoritative New York geopolitical study of those days, expressed the view, widely held, that

> Mohammedism or Islamism is the religion taught by Mohammed, an impostor who recorded his doctrines in a book called the Koran. It consists of a confused mixture of grossly false ideas and precepts with the Judaism and Christianity [*sic*]. . . . Most systems of religion, while professing to cultivate virtue, often encourage vice; and thus injure both spiritual and worldly interests. Christianity is the only system which elevates man to a true sense of his moral relations, and adds to his happiness.[6]

Throughout this period of evolution in the American oil industry, the grand strategists of Whitehall in London were confronted by a basic fact: the British Empire, dependent for its security on the Royal Navy, was forced to seek reliable supplies of fuel oil for the fleet from foreign companies. The only other major oil power was the United States. But only rarely during the 1800s had the United States shown itself well disposed toward Great Britain, and therefore an alternative source of oil must be found. Since the American invasion of Canada in 1812, there had been several American threats against what was called the British North American Colonial Territories; and during the American Civil War, President Lincoln had come close to a declaration of war against the British Empire over the Trent Affair of 1861, carrying with it, as it did, the possibility that Britain might abandon its position of neutrality in the Civil War and throw its power behind the South. Shortly thereafter occurred the *Alabama* incident, in which the Confederate cruiser *Alabama*, built in England and used against the Union as a commerce destroyer, captured, sank, or burned sixty-eight ships in twenty-two months before being sunk by the USS *Kearsarge* off Cherbourg in June 1864. Along with several other ships, the *Alabama* was built or fitted out privately on British territory and put to sea despite the belated intervention of the British government. To avoid further deterioration of Anglo-American relations, on May 8, 1871, the parties signed the Treaty of Washington in which Great Britain expressed official regret over the *Alabama* matter. It was settled finally when Britain paid the United States damages of $15 million in gold.

But then disputes ensued between the Republic and the Empire over Samoa, Togo, and Hawaii — minute entities, but important to U.S. naval power in the Pacific. This was followed by an Anglo-American dispute over the boundaries between British Guiana and Venezuela, which sparked more talk of war.

Thus, considering that war might break out between Britain and Germany, Whitehall concluded it would be prudent for Britain to find supplies of oil free from the influence of foreign powers. They began to look in the Persian Gulf, Turkish Ottoman lands over which Britain had much influence. It had been known for centuries that there was plentiful oil in the states of Persia (Iran); Mesopotamia (Iraq); the Midian, "the land of Moses," adjoining the Gulf of Aqaba; and in the Arabian province of Hasa on the Persian Gulf coast of Arabia. As early as 1877 and again in 1878, Sir Richard Burton, the English Orientalist, was commissioned by the Egyptian ruler Khedive Ismail to examine and report on the mineral possibilities of the Midian. Burton's enthusiastic report and his recommendation that full-scale prospection and exploitation should begin immediately attracted the attention of the government of the Turkish Ottoman Empire and the British government.

The Admiralty, responsible for the political control of the British navy, then the most powerful in the world, was interested in converting its warships from coal- to oil-burning engines, and two British admirals, Edmund Commerell and Henry Woods Pasha (pasha is a Turkish Ottoman title for a man of high rank or office) examined the Midian prospect. A shadowy British corporation called the XY Prospecting and Developing Syndicate, Limited, of 15 Angel Court in the City of London, was established with the object of entering "into a partnership agreement with the Imperial Ottoman Government to develop the mineral wealth of the Land of the Midian."[7] Woods Pasha, who held a high appointment in the Admiralty and in Cairo and was thought to be the managing director of XY, and a small group of Turkish notables entered into a joint Anglo-Turkish agreement to exploit the region. The contract between them gave XY sole prospecting rights for ten years; it would pay annual rent of $5 an acre for gold and silver and $1 an acre for oil, and the concession would last for fifty years. This was followed up with immediate formation of an entity called the Dead Sea Oil Company. The fact that it was capitalized at £1 million ($5 million) suggests the Admiralty's involvement.

The group's intention was to work the area around Sodom and Gomorrah, those sinful cities in the Book of Genesis. The estimate was that the "evidence of the Dead Sea area" was "all in favor of producing oil at a profit." A prominent British peer, Cowdray, was associated with the enterprise. He knew whereof he spoke, having been involved in developing the petroleum industry in Mexico. And as he remarked, indicating something of the speed with which the importance of oil was taking hold in London, "The demand for fuel oil is growing day by day: the more assured the supply becomes, the greater the demand." And in a company paper he quoted Burton: "'The tale of these mining cities reads like a leaf from The Arabian Nights, yet it is the sober truth. . . . My assertions are borne out by the report of the mineralogists officially appointed by the Viceroy [of Egypt].'" So positive were the British reports of major oil prospects throughout the Middle East that the British prime minister, H. H. Asquith, had declared that "should the war lead to the breaking up of the Turkish Empire," as it would, then "the province of the Hijaz," in which the Midian concession was then situated, would "come under the special consideration of the British Government."[8]

Thus, in Whitehall, Middle Eastern and Persian Gulf oil became a matter of the highest strategic and political importance. As Anthony Sampson recorded, "The British, from the beginning, were acutely conscious of their vulnerability in the new age of oil," one that "acquired from the beginning an association with national survival and diplomacy, and oil soon seemed part of the empire itself." A powerful destroyer squadron of sixteen warships was positioned at Bahrein Island, and an intricate network of political agents, high commissioners, consuls, and vice consuls was stationed in and around the Gulf, to prevent the intrusion of foreigners — especially Americans — into the British hegemony. Treaties were signed with every state and tribal leader of consequence, binding them in perpetuity to the British crown. In May 1903 the British foreign secretary, Lord Lansdowne, made the historic warning that the British government would "regard the establishment of a naval base or of a naval fortified port in the Persian Gulf by any other power as a very grave menace to British interests, and we should certainly resist it with all the means at our disposal."[9]

Like the Mediterranean, the Indian Ocean, and all other approaches to the Arabian Peninsula and India, the Persian Gulf became a British lake. And when Germany displayed imperial ambitions by making an alliance with the caliph of Islam, Lansdowne's warning was fulfilled. General war broke out in Europe in August 1914, and soon World War I spread to the Middle East. In October the Muslim Ottoman Empire declared for Germany. Arabs in Ottoman-controlled areas pledged a jihad against Germany's enemies.

The British imperial strategists at Simla, the summer capital of India high in the Himalayan foothills, stood to arms. The attitude of the Arabs to the call to jihad greatly concerned Western imperial powers — especially Great Britain, whose empire enclosed more Muslims than any other political entity did. Would the Muslim populations of the British Empire — seventy million in British India, sixteen million in the Anglo-Egyptian Sudan, twenty million in French North Africa, and a like number in the Imperial Russian Caucasus and Central Asia — rise against the Grand Alliance? German and Turkish agents working in concert in San Francisco, British Columbia, and Lahore in the Punjab did succeed in raising jihad against Britain in the Punjab, but it proved to be much ado about nothing. German agents in Persia sought to raise anti-British elements to sabotage Anglo-Persian oil installations and murder employees. The plot was detected and the Germans involved were hanged.

But for Britain the danger was greater than jihad. Through their hold on Syria and Mesopotamia, the Turks threatened British interests at two vital points: the Suez Canal, through which the imperial route ran to the Orient and beyond, and the Anglo-Persian oil fields, the Royal Navy's sole source of oil in British hands. The Turks attacked the British defenses of the Suez Canal; the effort misfired through Turkish incompetence. Britain responded by annexing the Turkish island of Cyprus, deposing the pro-Turk viceroy of Egypt, and declaring Egypt to be a British protectorate, a diplomatic status in which Egypt surrendered to Great Britain all major functions of state, especially in the realm of foreign relations. Then, to protect the Anglo-Persian Oil Company and its refinery at Abadan, the Raj in India launched an Anglo-Indian army to capture the enemy's main port on the Gulf, Basra. The world's first oil war had begun. It was called the Mesopotamian Campaign, and it lasted for four years. The British imperial forces lost 252,000 men, dead, wounded, and taken prisoner, in one of the nastiest little conflicts of the century, demonstrating how important the British regarded the Gulf and its oil.

[1]

THE SETTING AND
THE STAGE

AT THE END OF World War I, two economic colossi bestrode the
world: the United States and the British Empire. Their relations,
an important factor in the looming struggle for Persian Gulf oil,
were poor and, on occasions, hostile. The mercantile rivalry between them was frequently intense. To compare their positions in the
world, the United States had become the paramount industrial power,
and the British, the paramount political power. Through its position as
victor after World War I, Great Britain had attached the Middle East to
its world empire.

Britain's principal allies remaining at the end of the war — America,
France, and Italy — had contributed little if any military assistance to
the British in the Middle East; and Whitehall's paramountcy there was
reinforced when, at the San Remo Conference on the Italian Riviera in
April 1920 (a conference largely between the British and the French
governments, and one from which the Americans complained they
had been excluded), Germany's 23.75 percent interest in the Iraqi
oil fields was awarded to the French as part compensation for the war
damage inflicted on them by the Germans. Britain alone retained
its prewar majority shareholding in Persian oil. The conference also
awarded the new state of Iraq, in which a monarchy was being established under the auspices of the British government, a 20 percent
interest in any private petroleum company set up there. Shortly, the
British established the Iraq Petroleum Company, and that company
took over the assets of the Turkish Petroleum Company (the weakened
Ottoman Empire had come to an end at the war's conclusion).

Thus Great Britain emerged as the principal oil power in the Middle East — indeed, the only one. Its position was reinforced further when the San Remo agreement awarded mandates — the legal right to administer former Ottoman possessions in the Middle East judged to be unready or incapable of self-government. Britain was awarded the mandates for Iraq and Palestine, and the French received those for Syria and Lebanon. Thus the victors completed their carving up of the region — or so it seemed.

But Britain's absolute primacy in the Middle East was to be severely challenged by the United States. This conflict began when the British and their historical allies, the Dutch, refused to permit Standard Oil of New Jersey to send oil exploration parties into British India with the explanation that "it is not desired by [British] Indian Government to introduce any of the American oil companies, or their subsidiary companies, into India."[1] When the American companies applied directly for exploration rights in India, Burma, and Assam, a U.S. Senate paper later asserted, they received the advice from India that the "cardinal principle" of Anglo-Indian policy was that "the licensees shall be and remain British or state subjects under British or state control."[2] The British government then awarded a British company, Burmah Oil (owned partly by the Anglo-Persian Oil Company in the Persian Gulf), a monopoly for the production of crude oil in India. Through the merger of the British company Shell with Royal Dutch before World War I, all production and marketing facilities were reserved to Anglo-Dutch interests, notably the Royal Dutch–Shell combine. Throughout the Anglo-Dutch empires, similar restrictions existed to keep the United States out, partly to prevent Americans from propagating American republicanism on British territory, and partly, of course, to maintain the immense profits that derived to the British and the Dutch from their monopolies in Europe, the Middle East, and much of Asia. But the U.S. State Department had begun to press the British government to open the door to Standard Oil of New Jersey. Although the Foreign Office was resisting with all the means at its disposal, the American assault on the Gulf, Britain's most important imperial prize after India, had already begun.

In 1921 the U.S. government entered the fray when Secretary of Commerce Herbert Hoover and Secretary of State Charles Evans Hughes encouraged seven oil companies to form an American group, led by Standard Oil of New Jersey, to seek a share of Iraqi oil. The battle between the U.S. and British governments for primacy in the region was thus joined.[3] The Americans sought an "open door" policy from the British. Its important provisions were (1) that nationals of all nations be subject, in all mandated territories, to equal treatment in law; (2) that no economic concessions in any mandated region be so large as to be exclusive; and (3) that no monopolistic concession relating to any commodity be granted. The State Department urged, too, that the Allies had fought and won the war together and that consequently, any benefit, whether in oil or otherwise, should be available to the nationals of all the Allies, and should not be seized by "those of any one particular power,"[4] in this case, Great Britain.

According to the British point of view, British nationals had "acquired rights" — oil concessions — that must be respected. Although the United States had been an ally of Britain's, that fact alone gave its nationals no right to trespass upon "acquired rights." The fact was, the British argued, the "acquired rights" here in question belonged to the British government through the Anglo-Persian Oil Company and the Iraq Petroleum Company, and they had been purchased and exploited by legal contract, in many cases long before the war.

Both positions had merit, but not much. Nonetheless, by 1927, when Big Oil was first discovered in Iraq, the State Department had won. The Near East Development Corporation was formed, led by the American group. It obtained full partnership in the Iraq Petroleum Company along with the British Anglo-Persian Oil Company, the French Compagnie des Pétroles, and the Anglo-Dutch Shell. The reasons for the Anglo-Dutch-French surrender were several. First, Britain had overextended its military power through its control of the Middle East and feared that in the event of another major war, it would lose the empire unless it won American support. Since Britain had more oil than it knew what to do with, it would actually lose no essential resources in such an arrangement with the United States, but would gain leverage with an important ally in the event of another war with Germany and Russia, either separately or, as seemed possible at that time, in combination.

Second, the U.S. State Department had proposed a plan for worldwide Anglo-American oil "reciprocity." Shorn of its diplomatic obscurity, this term meant an Anglo-American world oil "combination," that term of ill repute during the Rockefeller era that meant, plainly and simply, a cartel, a term defined in the United States, where such entities were abhorrent, as "a combination of independent commercial or industrial enterprises designed to limit competition or fix prices."[5] Despite the inconsistency with internal U.S. policy against cartels, need for oil drove the attempt to obtain through diplomacy what the

United States had failed to get through the treaties of San Remo and
Sèvres — entry into Middle East oil. This arrangement suited the British. Though it ceded some of its oil riches to the United States, such a
cartel would allow Britain to retain a great deal of power over this
important resource.

A third factor in Britain's decision was the possibility of American
retaliation for being excluded from the Middle East, the nature of
which was never specified. Also, experiencing "the too vast orbit of her
fate," Britain had troubles with Arab and Persian nationalists, the Turks
and the Persians in combination, and the conflicts between Arabs and
Jews in Palestine. The agreement with the United States seemed to
hold out the promise of stabilizing the region.

But there was a sting in the tail of these large accommodations to the
United States in its "oil shortage" (an assertion uttered from time to
time by Standard Oil of New Jersey, the most ambitious of the American majors and an adept at the craft of creating imaginary emergen-
cies). In this combine, the leading American and British oil companies
were for the first time united in one operation. The name of the
company was the Iraq Petroleum Company (IPC).

But now the old specter of a cartel reappeared, in the shape of
Standard Oil of New Jersey and one of the two British majors in an
alliance against the rest of the world oil industry. Article 10 in the
agreement obliged the majors to sign a pact that became known as
the "Red Line Agreement." Originally proposed by the French, vigorously supported by the British — and by the Americans too when the
benefits became evident — the agreement specified that each company was not to seek oil concessions in a large area of the old Ottoman
Empire without the agreement of all the partners. This placed all the
known potential and actual oil fields in the Persian Gulf, Arabia, and
Bahrein — a vast and immense prize — within the Red Line Agreement. As the American members of the Near East Development Corporation (NEDC) declared in committee, "The board of [NEDC] expressed their full approval of the new arrangement."[6]

The Senate committee defined the situation as "a striking illustra-
tion of the evolution of joint control through common ownership."
By such control "the major international companies were able effectively to restrain competition"[7] and control prices — and that was a
grave offense in law. The committee reaffirmed that "the basic philosophy of the United States" was "to oppose vast concentrations of economic power," in this case those of the international oil industry. "Practically alone among the great nations of the world, the United States —

through fact-finding and through enforcement of the anti-trust laws — endeavors to hold in check the power of giant organizations." For whether "privately or publicly owned, such organizations carry with them the inherent possibility that their overwhelming power may be abused to the detriment of the people."[8]

It was against that background that an American "outsider" company, Standard Oil of California, originally a member of the Rockefeller combine, smashed the Anglo-American combination dominating the Gulf oil industry.

Fred Alexander Davies, lately of the small market town of Aberdeen, South Dakota, arrived in Bahrein in the Persian Gulf in 1929. An oil engineer who had graduated from the University of Minnesota, class of 1916, Davies was in his late thirties or early forties. A photograph of him at this time shows that he was tall, well over six feet, muscular and slim, ungainly and good-humored. He was described as a man who combined "hunch and slog" when he was looking for oil. He wore a pith helmet, a white shirt with rolled-up sleeves, long-legged Bermuda-style shorts, white ankle socks, and black shoes. He had a degree in mining engineering, and he was now employed by Standard Oil of California, one of the more gentlemanly of the old Standard Oil companies. Davies was looking for oil and was particularly interested in a peculiarity of the Arabian coastline that came to be called "the Dammam dome."

Here Davies encountered Major Frank Holmes, a portly man who posed as "a traveler in the Persian Gulf for the good of his health" — the Gulf having perhaps the worst climate in the world. Born on a sheep farm in New Zealand in 1874, Holmes had been a quartermaster with the British army during its march on Jerusalem and Damascus, and while buying beef in Abyssinia he had heard rumors of oil seepages in both the Persian Gulf and Red Sea coasts of Arabia. A rival who knew Holmes well — St. John Philby — described him as "a man of considerable personal charm, with a bluff, breezy, blustering, buccaneering way about him."[9] After World War I, Holmes had established the Eastern and General Syndicate to develop business in the Middle East, had begun to travel extensively in the Gulf states, and was soon being described in official dispatches as a troublemaker. He secured the concession from Ibn Saud to prospect oil in Hasa, an eastern region of Arabia; he established his headquarters in Bahrein, and when the ruler showed no interest in the oil deposits there, only in water wells, Holmes found water for the sheikh. In return, the ruler rewarded him in 1925 with the concession to mine oil there as well. He also obtained the concession to the Burgan oil field in Kuwait, which would prove to be a supergiant. Despite his great success in obtaining concessions (developing any one of them would have made him an exceedingly rich man), he was forced to abandon the Hasa concession and to sell the Kuwait concessions to Gulf Oil, owned by the Mellon banking family of Pittsburgh, because Holmes had never been able to raise capital to develop the fields of which he was concessionaire. Then he met Davies and sold the Bahrein concession to Standard Oil of California through Davies. But Davies was not interested only in the Bahrein field. He was interested, too, in the Dammam dome on the Arabian coast; and Holmes knew more than anyone about that dome. After all, he had once owned the concession to it.

Holmes still owed a debt of £6,000 to Ibn Saud when Holmes met Davies in Bahrein. Holmes claimed, however, that he was well and favorably known to the king and offered to act as an intermediary between Davies and the king. Davies thereupon authorized Holmes to approach Ibn Saud in 1922 and establish whether the king would consider making an agreement to permit Standard Oil of California to explore Hasa for oil and whether Ibn Saud would agree to make Standard Oil the concessionaire if the company's findings were favorable. The Holmes connection did not prosper. He did send several cables to the king at his palace in the capital of central Arabia, Riyadh, but the prospect foundered not on the rock of Holmes's debt but upon the intercession of India House in London. The British government ministry, responsible politically for India and the Persian Gulf, is said to have prevailed upon Holmes's company, the Eastern and General Syndicate, not to promote the interests of any American company in the Gulf. Plainly Holmes's license to prospect for oil in the Persian Gulf, issued by the British high commission in Baghdad, had been placed at risk by his association with an American company, and Holmes felt it prudent to comply with the wishes of so powerful a ministry. Thus, the Holmes connection petered out, but only for the moment. Furthermore, the telegrams from Holmes alerted Ibn Saud to the fact that Standard Oil of California was interested in Hasa, the king's easternmost province on the Gulf, and that discovery had consequences of high importance. As Davies wrote of his arrival in the British protectorate off the Arabian coast:

> From the day we first set foot on Bahrain, we had a strong desire to examine the geology of the mainland in Arabia, not only because of its bearing on what might be expected below the surface on Bahrain, but

also because it was thought that there might well be oil possibilities in the vastly larger area of the mainland.[10]

By the spring of 1930, King Ibn Saud had emerged as monarch of Arabia after four years of warring with his earlier supporters, the Ikhwan, who wished to return to the "pure Islam" of the Prophet. They constituted the strictest group within the Islamic Wahhabi sect, opposing all Western influences and recognizable by their distinctive appearance — the men wore pointed beards and white robes, and they smeared black antimony paste around their eyes. The Ikhwan had been defeated at the Battle of Sibilla near the Iraqi frontier, a battle that had brought British bombers and armored car forces into the fray. Although they did not gain political control of the region, the Ikhwan would continue to exert considerable influence on Arabian society.

With his throne secure, the king visited Jidda, his kingdom's main port on the Red Sea, and he met with St. John Philby, who had left British government service. They had matters of moment to talk about, including whether or not the world was flat, which was what Ibn Saud believed. It seems certain, too, that Philby raised the question of his possible conversion to the Muslim faith, a step deemed necessary if Philby was to remain a close confidant and adviser. The king agreed that he should take that step. Philby recorded in his diary that on two occasions Ibn Saud referred to the proposal. During conversation he remarked upon "'how nice it would be for me when I became a Muslim and could have four wives.'" The other occasion was on May 3 when, just before his departure, the king asked: "'Are you coming to the pilgrimage?'" Philby replied, "'Just as you wish.'"[11]

Ibn Saud wished Philby to become a convert for reasons of his own. He was in serious financial trouble, he wished to establish diplomatic relations with the United States, and he wanted Philby in his privy council, the group at the palace that resembled a cabinet in its functions, so that Philby could help him meet his financial and diplomatic goals. Ibn Saud consulted the group before taking action in temporal affairs, but he alone made the final decision, for he alone ruled the state. Yet Ibn Saud never trusted the privy council, largely because it was mainly Syrian and conversed in their own dialect of Arabic, which Ibn Saud, being a Nejdi, could not understand. Philby could speak the Syrian dialect, and Ibn Saud believed Philby would be loyal to him personally, as he had proved to be so often in the past. Ibn Saud could trust none in his privy council except his finance minister, Abdullah

Suleiman. Whether Philby believed that the existence of God was or was not intellectually possible, if Philby was to serve him at court, then he must become a convert. In August 1930, therefore, Philby wrote the following letter, so that the king would have something to show to the divines proving that he was sincere in his desire to convert. It was a masterpiece of artifice:

> Peace, Mercy and the Blessing of Allah be upon you. I have already had the honour to submit to your Majesty's consideration my desire to become a Moslem and to abandon other religions.
>
> Now I once more beg to state to Your Majesty that Allah has rejoiced my heart to accept Islam and has shown me the right way to follow this religion with firm belief and perfect conscious satisfaction.
>
> I therefore bear witness that "there is no God but Allah and that Mohammad is His slave and Messenger," and I believe in all that is mentioned in the "Book of Allah," in the tradition of His Messenger and in what the good ancestors did.
>
> I also wish to express that I am convinced that all is true and that I desire to follow the same; and as regards the details that I desire to follow all that is written in the books of the good ancestors and more especially the statements of Shaikh Mohammed Ibn Abdul Wahhab, may God have mercy on him and all other Moslems.
>
> I beg you to accept my conversion to Islam which springs in me from grounds of belief, reflection, wisdom and good intention. Allah the Almighty guides me to the right path.[12]

The king responded to Philby's letter by telephone on August 7, 1930. It was an order, a royal command. He wished Philby to join him at Taif, the summer hill resort in the mountains of the Hima above Jidda. But first he must go to Mecca "for a ceremony." Could Philby come to Mecca that very night? He said yes. He penned a note to his wife, Dora, in London. "I have only a quarter of an hour to get ready," he told her. Otherwise he had "too long decided on this step to feel the least excited by it, but I dare say I shall have worked up the right sort of feeling as I approach the walls of Mecca."[13] Then he left Jidda just after dark, his driver in attendance, and was driven up the pilgrims' trail to Bahra, about halfway along the trail to Mecca. There he was met by Abdullah Suleiman, the finance minister and the most important figure in Ibn Saud's government, together with the second most important figure, Fuad Bey Hamza, the acting foreign minister of Arabia. Under their scrutiny, Philby, the man who had once declared that the existence of God was "intellectually incredible," entered into the sacred state necessary before accepting the faith. He performed the Ihram, the ritual cleansing of his person, and donned the pilgrim's habit, white winding sheets around his upper and lower body, and leather sandals for his feet. He forswore, for the period of his sanctification, sexual relations, shaving, and cutting his nails. Following the prescribed sequence, he began the rites by walking seven times around the sacred shrine of the Kaaba in the Grand Mosque, declaring as he did so, "At your service, O Lord, at your service." He kissed the Black Stone of the Kaaba, and he prayed twice in the direction of the holy stone and the Kaaba. He prostrated himself at Abraham's Station and drank from the holy well of Zamzam. At sunrise he faced the east and uttered the sacred oath: "I testify there is no god but God; and that Mohammed is His Servant and Prophet." And having cast seven stones at Satan, Philby became a Wahhab. Now he could place his many abilities at the service of the king and Islam. Later, at Abdullah Suleiman's house in Mecca, he completed the rites with the shaving of the crown of his head, the cutting of his nails, and the trimming of his beard. Then he breakfasted on a melon.

On the day after his conversion, Philby was driven to the king's palace at Taif. He and Ibn Saud kissed foreheads and, it emerged, the king had indeed had misgivings about Philby's sincerity. The king therefore felt the need to make a speech to his court. He explained that Philby had "sacrificed a great deal for Arabia," that he had disagreed with his own government and had resigned his post because the British would not back Ibn Saud. The king added that Philby had "never taken a salary for his services to the Arabs." He also asked Philby publicly to write an article for the official Arabian newspaper, *Umm al Qura,* giving his reasons for adopting Islam. Philby penned this brief statement: "Allah has opened my heart to the acceptance of Islam and has guided me to accept this religion in the rooted belief and full conviction of my conscience."[14] The article further stated that Philby would take no government post and that a theologian would complete his religious instruction.

Ibn Saud bestowed on Philby the Arabic name "Abdullah, Slave of God." It was announced, too, that Philby had agreed to serve Arabia unofficially as a privy councilor. Since his conversion was news overseas, he sent explanatory articles to the socialist *Daily Herald* in London and to the *Egyptian Gazette* in Cairo. These dwelt upon the ethical rather than the spiritual reasons that had caused him to adopt an alien faith. He compared Ibn Saud with Oliver Cromwell, the Puritan English general and parliamentarian who in the seventeenth century helped restore England's status to that of a leading European power from its decline since the death of Queen Elizabeth I. The allusion was not errant, and the king was greatly pleased to be so compared. Philby's statement of loyalty to Islam could hardly have been stronger:

> Similarly, I believe that the present Arabian puritan movement harbingers an epoch of future political greatness based on strong moral and spiritual foundations. Also I regard the Islamic ethical system as a real democratic fraternity, and the general conduct of life, including marriage, divorce and the unjust stigma of bastardy, resulting in a high standard of Arabian public morality, as definitely superior to the European ethical code based on Christianity. . . . I consider an open declaration of my sympathy with Arabian religion and political ideals as the best methods of assisting the development of Arabian greatness.[15]

Most Wahhabs did not accept Philby as a sincere convert. Abdullah Suleiman, the finance minister, Yusuf Yassin, the king's political secretary, Fuad Bey Hamza, the acting foreign minister, Khalid Gargani, a political and commercial adviser, and others disliked this British intruder into the pious and powerful circle around the king.

Having been made aware of American interest in oil, and becoming ever more desperate for money, Ibn Saud directed his acting foreign minister, Fuad Bey Hamza, to write formally to the secretary of state in Washington to open the question of diplomatic relations between the United States and his kingdom. That was done with the advice and assistance of Philby. In 1930, Cloyce K. Huston, vice consul of the United States at Aden, the British port on the southwestern tip of Arabia, received a letter in a strange hand. It was plainly an instrument of state and written by someone with an elegant pen. The envelope had been sealed by a blob of red sealing wax and stamped with the Arabian coat of arms — two crossed scimitars, a palm tree, and the words in Arabic: "There is no God but God and Muhhamad is His Prophet." This letter would prove to be one of the most important in the annals of U.S. diplomacy, although few could foresee that.

The letter began with the declaration that "the Government of the Kingdom of the Hejaz and Nejd and its Dependencies considers the moment particularly opportune to approach Your Excellency's Government with a view to an arrangement for the exchange of diplomatic instruments of mutual recognition." The writer, Fuad Bey Hamza, proceeded to advise the American consul that "I am accordingly charged by my august sovereign His Majesty the King of the Hejaz and Najd to seek, through the good offices of your Excellency, the formal recognition of the Kingdom of the Hejaz and Najd and its Dependencies by the Government of the United States of America." There followed a brief survey of the dual monarchy, a short history of the house of Saud, the form of government, its commercial prospects, and the nature of the theocracy over which Ibn Saud presided. In all, the writer presented a picture of a young state that was secure, serene, progressive, and, above all, worth investing in. It ended with a salutation: "Please accept the expression of my highest consideration for your Excellency" — worthy of the style set for diplomatic intercourse by the Congress of Vienna.[16]

Attached to the letter was another, from Philby, whom Huston knew. As Huston advised his superiors: "He is English and has had many years of experience in Arabia, engaging in travel and exploration as well as many business ventures, and is considered by many to be a very good authority on Arabian questions." As Philby's letter stated, "The Hedjaz has made great strides in a progressive direction," and "formal recognition by your government would be a great help to this country in a general way and, apart from that, it would perhaps open the door to such things as concessions, etc." Philby had in mind Arabian mineral rights — gold in the mountains of Arabia between Mecca and Medina, oil perhaps in Hasa, iron ore in the Hejaz. To persuade his reader that under Ibn Saud, Arabia had become a stable and humane country worthy of consideration for entry into the community of nations and where foreign capital might be invested safely and profitably, Philby noted that a politically prominent American multimillionaire, Charles R. Crane, a friend of U.S. presidents, had visited Jidda in 1926 and had felt safe enough to remain for a week, lodging at the mansion of the leading Arabian divine and Islamic philosopher, Sheikh Nassif. So, Philby wrote further, "I should be glad to see your country and countrymen take a more active interest in Arabian affairs and I think that is to be strongly recommended in the interests of your commerce alone."[17]

Philby had certainly benefited personally through his association with the Arabian monarch, although not nearly to the extent he suggested. He represented the Standard Oil Company of New York, the Ford Motor Company, the Singer Manufacturing Company, and the Franklin Motor Company. Philby had therefore "very good reason to know that the Government here would welcome the advent of an American consul at Jidda." Dealing with that most difficult of problems, the tendency of the Muslim divines to regard Christians as infidels, people not fit to talk to, let alone to eat with, people no better than dogs, Philby advised Mr. Huston that the king's attitude toward "foreigners in general and consuls in particular is perfectly correct and even cordial, and all they ask of foreigners is to respect the laws of the

land and not to seek refuge from them under consular protection."
Philby had "no doubt whatever that the Kingdom of Hedjaz and Najd is
a permanent institution capable of great things in the future and indeed likely to take some day the lead in Islam which Turkey once
enjoyed but has now relinquished." Philby had written that the consuls in Jidda "enjoy all the immunities of ordinary diplomatic usage
throughout the world and in some to have a diplomatic status which is
not to be found elsewhere." The general restriction on importations of
goods such as whiskey and tobacco, the anathema of the Prophet, "is
waived in their favor by courtesy." In fact, "the Hedjaz Government is
definitely to be numbered among the civilized governments of the
world and all it needs is an acceleration of the economic development
which is already well launched."[18] There were few consuls in Jidda who
would have agreed with the letter, and Huston must have known this —
hence his statement that he was forwarding it without comment.

After the correspondence reached Washington, and perhaps because of it, Huston received a request for a report on the relationship
between Philby and Ibn Saud. He replied that the intimacy between
the king and Philby "is fairly close" but that

> it is, of course, an intimacy between an occidental and an oriental,
> between a nominal Christian and a puritan Mohammedan, between a
> merchant and a king; but it is to be remembered that they were host
> and guest over a long period, they have dined and sipped coffee to-
> gether a very great number of times and they have traveled together
> over considerable distances in Arabia, they have exchanged presents,
> suggestions, comment, and advice on various subjects, and they have
> discussed at various times such questions as Arabian politics, religion,
> the social order, and others. Mr. Philby professes to discern a great
> future leader in Ibn Saud. . . . Ibn Saud, on the other hand, has always
> given the appearance of respecting and esteeming Mr. Philby very
> highly.[19]

But, Huston continued,

> No one but Ibn Saud himself actually knows the amount of confi-
> dence now extended to Mr. Philby. Mr. Philby believes, or at least
> claims, that it is a great deal, and many, including British officers,
> complain that he has become so pro-Arabian and pro–Ibn Saud that
> he is anti-British in many Anglo-Arab questions of today. It is, indeed,
> probably true that he is closer to Ibn Saud than any other white man
> and he does enjoy an unusual amount of confidence, but the heart of a
> shrewd and intelligent Arab who is playing a game of politics on the
> Arabian chessboard can rarely be read or understood.[20]

After Huston's reports and letters were received, the Department
of Near Eastern Affairs put together an extensive document entitled

"Memorandum on King Abdul Aziz [Ibn Saud]." This contained much more information about Ibn Saud and his adviser, Philby, acquired by the American ministry at Cairo through Philby's rather frequent calls there during the late 1920s. The first visit concerned the treaty that Ibn Saud had signed with the British government in 1915 in return for a subsidy of £60,000 in gold and some machine guns. In 1927, with Philby advising him, Ibn Saud had signed the Treaty of Jidda with a Foreign Office representative. In this, "bondage clauses" were removed, and Arabia was in law free of treaty obligations. The way was open for the American oil barons to engage in commerce with the Arabian government if they wished to do so.

As to Ibn Saud, the State Department report found him to be "about fifty" and intelligent, energetic, and warlike. As the writer noted, "All the persons I have met who have come into contact with him have been extremely favorably impressed." Undoubtedly, the king was "picturesque, and that he has ability and imagination is amply proved by his rise from a refugee princeling at Kuwait in 1900 to the most powerful potentate in the Arabian peninsula." On the other hand, it could not be claimed that Ibn Saud's kingdom had "commercial importance or that it will [do so] in the near future. The country has few economic resources and is of such a nature that it can be but little developed." The importance of Ibn Saud was political and religious. The Hejaz could not be ignored, embracing as it did the cities of Mecca, where the Prophet Muhammad was born, and Medina, where he died. Both were considered holy cities by a large number of the earth's population. Further, "the political importance of Ibn Saud himself could be readily realized when it is considered that he is frequently acknowledged as the most powerful and unifying force in Arabia since the Prophet. The mere fact that he holds the holy cities and that he has succeeded to a remarkable degree in extending his authority over a large part of Arabia makes him an important figure in the Muslim World." The writer continued, weighing whether the United States should recognize Ibn Saud: "The question of Ibn Saud's formal recognition by the United States is open to discussion. His country is of little commercial importance and one in which the United States has few interests; it is improbable that our relations with the Hejaz will increase to a noticeable extent; and it might be argued that recognition would lead to more unpleasant entanglements than real benefits."[21] Only recently one of these "unpleasant entanglements" had occurred to cast doubt on Philby's claim that Arabia was a stable country in which capital could be safely and profitably invested.

In the cool season of 1928–29, while Ibn Saud was fighting his last and decisive battle with Sheikh Dawish of the Ikhwan at Sibilla, not far away an American missionary, the Reverend Henry Bilkert, was riding with Charles R. Crane, the American multimillionaire and philanthropist whom Philby had mentioned in his letter to Huston. They were motoring along the camel track from Kuwait to Riyadh to call on Ibn Saud — more to satisfy Crane's curiosity than for any official purpose. Just short of the Hamsa Ridge they were ambushed by Ikhwan, the "Soldiers of God" of the Wahhabi theocracy. Bilkert was shot dead. There was no doubt who the marauders were, for they were close enough for the other travelers to see that they wore the traditional Ikhwan white headdresses with black tassels, that black paste of antimony had been painted around their eyes, and that they wore their henna-dyed beards in the manner of the Prophet, jutting outward.[22]

After the Bilkert incident, and because of it, Crane abandoned any further thought of attempting to see Ibn Saud for the time being. The question of U.S. recognition of the king was suspended indefinitely, largely, Philby believed, on Crane's advice. But the State Department kept a foot in the door to Arabia. It advised Fuad Bey Hamza that the secretary of state had read the correspondence with appreciation and, though he found it impossible to reply at that moment, believed that eventually Fuad Bey Hamza's request would receive the secretary's considerate attention. Meanwhile the secretary of state sent cordial greetings and good wishes to him.

But for the time being, because of its religious, tribal, and frontier wars, the opaque nature of Arabian society, and the oppressive authority of the Islamic divines, Arabia, as far as the State Department was concerned, could remain a Lost Horizon. Why should it be otherwise? For all his abilities, Ibn Saud had little to offer the United States; he was no more than a small potentate ruling a country from which sensible people stayed clear.

By 1931 it became evident to Philby that the king's financial state had worsened to the point where he might not be able to maintain the security of his realm, and he wrote that the atmosphere at court was "one of gloom and depression. The world economic crisis had set in with a vengeance, and Arabia was in for a lean time. Ibn Saud had relied on revenues from the thousands who each year took part in the Muslim pilgrimage to Mecca, to replenish the royal coffers — and to keep up the lavish lifestyle of his household and harem. But the prospects of the next pilgrimage visitation were somewhat grim, as the agricultural communities of India and the Far East had been badly affected by the slump in the prices of their products."[23] Most pilgrims typically came from those parts of the world, and now they lacked money to make the long and expensive journey.

> The King and his ministers became glum; and the talk at Taif and Mecca had turned largely on ways and means of meeting the expected shortage of funds. . . . I became inevitably involved in the lugubrious debate. . . . The general line I took was that the Government . . . could not hope for security or stability unless it could find more reliable sources of steady revenue than the precarious pilgrimage, on which it had hitherto almost depended. The country obviously had hidden minerals which could only be developed with the cooperation of foreign experts, while the policy of the Government precluded the participation of foreigners in their discovery and development. The King, in view of his recent troubles with the more fanatical leaders of the Wahhabi movement, was reluctant to open his country to the infidel. But the Finance Minister, Abdullah Sulaiman, had a more open mind on the subject, to say nothing of his personal responsibility to keep the country solvent. . . . Suffice it to say, for the moment, the idea of foreign participation in the development of the country had its advocates, who knew full well that everything depended on the attitude of the King.[24]

A crisis arose when the pilgrimage dropped from an average of one hundred thousand pilgrims in 1930 to twenty thousand in 1933. Philby became aware, too, that he could not help the king through his presence on the privy council, for the council was itself too incompetent and corrupt to deal with matters of state finance. He was left with the pessimistic feeling that, apart from the king himself, who for all his faults was a colossus, there was nobody in the Wahhabi government with the combined will and ability to render conspicuous service in the Arab cause. At length, Philby decided that if the king would not help himself, he would have to help the king. The opportunity arose one afternoon when Ibn Saud and Philby were alone in the palace Hudson automobile, visiting the Atna date gardens just outside Riyadh. Philby "made bold to say that the king and his people were like folk sleeping over a vast buried treasure, but without the will or energy to search under their beds." He ventured a Koranic quotation for the king's consideration: "God changeth not that which is in people unless they change what is in themselves." Ibn Saud exclaimed: "O! Philby! if anyone would offer me a million pounds. I would give him all the concessions he wants." Philby replied that "no one would give him anything at all without having reasonable ground for believing that the minerals were there" and "he would win far more than the sum he mentioned if they did in fact exist and were intelligently exploited." He must over-rule the divines and allow infidels into the Hima to see what was there. Yes, said the king, although he disliked strangers at the gate.[25]

Philby met the king again and said he knew a man who was in a position to help. That man proved to be Charles R. Crane, the American multimillionaire and philanthropist who had made two attempts to speak with the king, once in 1926 and again in 1928–29. After the murder of Bilkert, it seemed unlikely that Crane would make any further attempt, although Philby continued to correspond with him at his home in Woods Hole on Cape Cod, Massachusetts. Crane remained interested in Arabia, and in September 1930 he advised Philby that he would visit Egypt in the new year. Crane was already known to Ibn Saud as "the darling of the Arabs" for his work on the King-Crane Commission in 1919. Appointed to the commission at the request of President Woodrow Wilson during the Paris Peace Conference of 1919, his task had been to determine the attitudes of the inhabitants of Syria and Palestine toward the post–World War I settlement of their territories. Crane visited Syria and Palestine June 10–July 21, 1919, and found that a vast majority of Arabs favored an independent Syria, free of any French mandate, and that, of 1,875 petitions received, 72 percent were hostile to the Zionist plan for a Jewish national home in Palestine. Such findings, coupled with Zionist talk of dispossession of the Arabs, led the commission to advise a serious modification of the Zionist immigration program. Moreover, Crane became known as "the Golden Peril" for the subsidies he had paid out of his own pocket to various Balkan and Arab potentates to enable them to shed their dependence upon the European imperial powers.

Thus when Philby asked Ibn Saud if he would permit him to invite Crane to make a state visit to Jidda early in 1931, Ibn Saud again agreed. Philby duly made the invitation, and Crane replied that he would arrive in Jidda in six weeks' time, by the Egyptian steamer *Taif* on February 25, 1931. So, a few days before that date Ibn Saud did something he did only rarely, and always with reluctance. He disliked the airless Jidda, with its stench of stale human and animal waste, yet he, the princes, and a selection of his wives, concubines, courtiers, and divines set out for Jidda. The royal party journeyed across the wet, cold hills and made their way down to the coastal plain to meet Crane.

When the Egyptian steamer *Taif* arrived in Jidda's lagoon on the appointed date, motorboats drew up alongside it. A group of Arab notables boarded the ship and made their way to the saloon, with its beaded curtains and whirring fans. Sheikh Muhammad Nassif, the leading Wahhabi philosopher, led the way. Philby was there, too, in a sheikh's robes, and they greeted a tall, lanky figure with a white-speckled goatee, wearing a well-cut suit and carrying a sun helmet. Born in 1888 into the family of Richard Teller Crane, an industrialist in Chicago, Charles Crane had inherited some $70 million from his father's estate and lived in great style at Woods Hole and on Fifth Avenue in New York City. He was said to have saved the *New York Times* from bankruptcy and to have acted as a private adviser in foreign affairs to each president between William Taft and Franklin D. Roosevelt. He had been particularly close to President Wilson (at Wilson's request in 1919, Crane visited Russia to report on the Bolshevik Revolution, and then he was sent to China as the American minister). By occupation a philanthropist, Crane had heightened his stature with the Arabs by vigorously opposing the League of Nations' mandates in the Near East and by funding an expensive translation of the Koran into English. Crane's sympathy with Arab causes had been reinforced by time; between 1921 and 1930 he made numerous journeys throughout the Middle East in his "pursuit of knowledge." Each journey was carefully planned so that he might take his own political soundings, and inevitably he took an interest in Big Oil, although not for his own profit or for the profit of his family and friends. He did, however, have an important connection with Big Oil in the Persian Gulf. A son, Richard, had married into the family of Andrew W. Mellon, of the Gulf Oil Company, which had recently purchased Major Holmes's concession at Kuwait. And when Crane bought Westover Plantation in Virginia as a country home for his son, the Mellons and the Cranes became neighbors. Crane may well have recommended Ibn Saud as a ruler with whom Mellon could do business. But there is no evidence of this. Nor is there any evidence that Crane was interested in Arabia for any reason other than his pursuit of knowledge. Certainly Crane seems to have been much more interested in giving money away sensibly than in making it.

Sheikh Nassif formally welcomed Crane to the kingdom on the king's behalf. After the speeches of welcome, the blind cantor of the mosque at Jidda, Sheikh Ahmad Zahra, chanted some verses from the Koran. Then the party left for the shore where Crane was to lodge during his four days in Jidda at Sheikh Nassif's mansion. There, Crane was given luncheon and invited to rest and prepare for his audience with the king, which was to take place at the king's lodge at four o'clock that afternoon. At the appointed time, a short line of Fords and Hudsons from the royal garage moved off through the crowded, narrow streets of beaten earth and arrived at exactly the right time at the two-story palace, which was built from bricks of red mud in the handsome style of classical Arab architecture. Here, the king's bodyguard, in brocade and red robes, admitted Crane's party to the audience room. There was a pause. The bodyguard brought rose water and perfumed oils so that Crane and his party might refresh themselves. Then there was a stir.

Ibn Saud emerged from the shadows. He was in the pink of good humor and charm when he greeted Crane, for he hoped for much from his visitor — £1 million, no less. A Palestinian scribe, George Antonius, the representative of Crane's private intelligence service in the Levant and a man known to the Near East section of the State Department, kept Crane's diary of the visit. He recorded this of Crane's reception:

> The King welcomed Mr. Crane who, after an exchange of greetings, said that he was particularly pleased to find that his long-felt desire to meet the King in person had at last been realised. . . . He had followed the King's career with close interest for some years, and his interest was all the keener as he knew that His Majesty was all the time working, and working successfully, for the welfare of Islam.[26]

The elaborate courtesies had begun. Ibn Saud replied that he greatly appreciated Mr. Crane's remarks and the interest he displayed. He had known Mr. Crane by name for several years and was aware that his interest and sympathy for the Arabs were real and genuine. He was delighted to make his acquaintance and to see him looking so well. The audience lasted for forty-five minutes and ended when the time approached for sunset prayers. It had been no more than an elaborate, cordial Arab reception, and it ended with Crane and his party withdrawing backwards and bowing thrice. The meeting was judged to have been a great success. Indeed, not since Ibn Saud's coronation in Jidda as King of the Nejd and the Hejaz had there been such a grand meeting of the king, the royal family, the court, and the leaders of Hejazi rank and fashion.

Over the next five days Ibn Saud and Charles Crane discussed many subjects, including the king's experiments in settling the Ikhwan in agricultural communes in order to give them an interest in life other than war, the work of the American missionaries at Bahrein, the strength of Ibn Saud's armed forces, and how to improve sanitation and water supplies. The king discussed what was required to modernize Jidda. But Charles Crane did not rise to this bait, if it was bait. Certainly he enjoyed his visit, for, as he wrote to a son, John Crane, on March 6, 1931, the King was all that I could possibly have wished. He is a magnificent man, six feet three or four, powerful in every way but of great charm. While he plays a strong uncompromising role, he is most generous to his former enemies. . . . To me he is most kind, open, friendly, frank and informing. He tried with great care to answer my questions in the fullest, clearest way.[27]

But so far as is known there was no mention of the £1 million that Ibn Saud needed. But Ibn Saud did make one odd suggestion to his illustrious visitor. Would Mr. Crane accept an honorary post, that of the chief muezzin at the Kaaba in Mecca? All Mr. Crane would have to do would be to state publicly: "Allah is most great. There is no God but Allah." Given the Wahhab's fear and even hatred for infidels, this was an extraordinary offer, for no Christian had ever been permitted to enter the Grand Mosque, let alone be associated with the Black Stone of the Kaaba. So it does appear that an attempt was being made to induce Crane to convert to the Muslim faith. But Crane was a confirmed Christian, and as such he was forbidden to make any such commitment. When his party returned to the home of Sheikh Nassif, the cantor Sheikh Shaibi was waiting. Crane wrote home, "For about an hour we listened to his beautiful chanting of that passage in the Koran which relates to the birth of Christ." Sheikh Shaibi, a leading divine, repeated that all Crane had to do was to make "a brief confession in public and I will get him the job." All Crane had to do was to "utter one word — Mohammed — and the job is yours."[28] Crane's conversion to Wahhabism would have been a political prize indeed. But it was not to be. Crane did not utter the name of the Prophet.

At his last meeting with Ibn Saud, Crane demonstrated views similar to those of Philby — if the king needed help, he must first help himself. He dwelt on "scientific farming" or "dry farming," his experiments at his ranch in California. These included production of "very successful" dates and, in a memorable moment, given the large sum of money Ibn Saud was hoping to extract from his visitor in order to save his kingdom, Crane instead produced a box of his California-grown dates and handed it to Ibn Saud. As Philby remembered, "It was like bringing coals of a poor quality to Newcastle, and the king was not greatly impressed. When the king withdrew, he asked me whether I liked dates (!) and gave me the box with a caution against my telling Crane that he had done so."[29]

Perhaps the king's disappointment had to do with his gifts to Crane — two white horses from the royal stables, a prize Arab stallion, and a mare for Crane's own stables in America. Also, Ibn Saud had given

Crane a set of Arabian day robes, complete with a bejeweled dagger. A box of dates may have seemed niggardly by comparison. But the gift was richly symbolic. Allah helped those who helped themselves. The date palm, cultivated and prized from remotest antiquity, certainly signified self-sufficiency. Its fruit was the staple food in Arabia; all parts of the date palm yielded products of economic value. Its trunk furnished timber; the leaves supplied material for crates and furniture; the leaflets, for basketry; the leaf bases, for fuel; the fruit stalks, for rope and fuel; and the fiber, for cordage and packing material. The seeds were sometimes ground and used as stock feed. Syrup, alcohol, vinegar, and a strong liquor were derived from the fruit. The sap was used as a beverage, and when a palm was cut down, its bud was eaten as a salad.

The discussion continued at tea that afternoon in Philby's mansion, the Beit Baghdadi. Crane told Ibn Saud that his sole means of irrigation on his desert estate was water drawn from two artesian wells. Crane suggested, in the context of water, not oil, that if His Majesty was agreeable, he would instruct Karl S. Twitchell, a mining engineer from Vermont whom he had sent to the Yemen to build a road and a bridge for the imam, to visit Arabia. Arrangements could be made for Twitchell to visit Jidda on his way back to the United States soon and give further advice on dry farming. Did His Majesty agree? Ibn Saud accepted readily and asked whether Twitchell might look for water near Jidda, where there was little except for the water from the occasional rainstorms and the drinking water brought by steamer once a fortnight from Egypt. All other water was being produced at an insufficient rate of 135 tons a day at the town's desalting plant. Crane assented, stating that Twitchell was capable and trustworthy. He was also under a five-year contract to Crane so that Twitchell would place no burden on the king's treasury, except the need to provide him with protection against footpads and the Ikhwan.

Crane's visit ended on March 3, 1931. Attended by a guard of honor of Hejazi troops drawn up at the watergate, along with many officials and notables, Crane went aboard the *Taif* when it arrived from Port Sudan, bound for Suez. Ibn Saud had made a profound impression on Crane, who wrote this to President Franklin Roosevelt:

> Ibn Saud is the most important man who has appeared in Arabia since the time of Mohammed. He is severely orthodox, manages his affairs, his life and his government as nearly as possible as Mohammed would have done. He was now the supreme power in the peninsula. He has always been guided by the old desert doctrine of *Hilm,* which Moham-

med emphasized so much, of doing everything possible, in the most affectionate manner, to reconcile his enemies once he has conquered them.[30]

Twitchell arrived at Jidda on April 15, 1932, to be received by the king, the finance minister, and Philby. A tall, slight, youngish man, his high forehead, intense and hollow eyes, and spade-shaped beard made him look like a holy man. Twitchell was the first American to work in Arabia, except for the missionaries from Bahrein and Kuwait. From the first, his relationship with Ibn Saud personally was good, and that ensured that his relationship with Philby would be poor. Philby regarded Arabia and the king as his private preserve, one that he guarded so closely that when the American anthropologist Carleton Coon landed at Jidda without permission, he was very severely beaten and forced aboard a boat that dumped him at Port Sudan across the Red Sea. Coon reported later to the U.S. government that Philby was "an insanely jealous man" who has "any number of Arabs to do his dirty work for him."[31] When Twitchell called at the Beit Baghdadi to leave his card, Philby took his time calling off the baboons on guard (a familiar practice in this primitive city) at his front door. The king deputed another member of the privy council, Khalid Gargani, as his interpreter and his fixer. Twitchell described him with respect as Ibn Saud's special representative, though it was later to emerge that he was a German spy and Hitler's agent of influence at Ibn Saud's court.

Twitchell began well. Accompanied by Gargani, first he rode out to Wadi Fatima, about six miles from the tomb of Eve, wife of Adam and therefore, in Judeo-Christian and Islamic traditions, the original human couple. In some good years perhaps 125,000 men, women, and children landed at Jidda from all parts of the world, to make the pilgrimage across the forty-three miles of parched desert and through the high mountains to Mecca. To make the pilgrimage was the supreme moment in any Muslim's life, and so powerful was the prospect of Paradise if they made it and their desire to place the title of Hajji, "one who has made the pilgrimage," before their names after they had made it, that they would run any risk to do so. So many died of dehydration and disease before reaching Mecca that some sixty years earlier, the Turks had sought and found water at Ain Wazira, about seven miles outside Jidda, and had laid terra-cotta pipes from the spring to Jidda. This system had fallen into disrepair. Twitchell found the spring, repaired the pipes, and then, to improve the volume, cabled to Crane in New York for a sixteen-foot windmill and an engine complete with pump equipment and new pipes to help regulate the flow of the water to Jidda. Crane paid the bill, £168. That modest but important transaction became America's first contribution to the well-being of Arabia.

After that, Twitchell and his wife, still accompanied by Gargani and some thirty of Ibn Saud's cameleers, set out on an expedition through the Hejaz to examine its mineral resources. He found oil seepages and examined what he believed to be King Solomon's gold mines in the mountains near Medina. Then he traveled across from the Red Sea side of Arabia to Hasa on the Persian Gulf, and his work there did "intensify the interest aroused by the discovery of oil in Bahrain."[32] In all, however, Twitchell's survey was most notable for his success with Ibn Saud, Abdullah Suleiman, and Khalid Gargani. With, he claimed, the king's permission to exploit his findings commercially, Twitchell set out from Jidda for New York, where he arrived in July 1932 to seek capital for an oil exploration in Hasa and for mining King Solomon's gold mines. He could not have selected a worse time to look for financing, for the Depression had severely damaged the capital markets, there was a worldwide glut of oil, and Texas oil was fetching only a dime a gallon.

Yet despite Philby's important role in the intrigue and manipulation concerning the oil concession, he was much more interested in achieving a personal goal that had tantalized him for years — exploring the Empty Quarter, the great desert of South Arabia. When this opportunity came, he casually left the question of the oil concession unresolved in order to pursue this passion. For years he had been nagging the king for permission to do so. But the desert was in the Hima, the holy land of the Arabian Peninsula, and the divines would not give their assent because of their suspicion that, even though Philby had become a Wahhab, he would revert to being a Christian the moment he left Arabia. Philby wanted to be recognized as the region's first explorer, knowing that simply enduring the arduous trek would result in his public adulation as a hero. It was unlikely that he wanted to examine the region for oil and other prospects, but that may have been the case. Nobody knew what was there (later it would emerge that vast oil fields indeed existed there). The Empty Quarter covered about 250,000 square miles in a basin lying mainly in southeastern Saudi Arabia, with lesser portions in present-day Yemen, Oman, and the United Arab Emirates. It is the largest desert in the world, occupying more than one quarter of Saudi Arabia.

Certainly Philby was bitterly disappointed when, while the king continued to resist Philby's plans, a younger assistant of former times, Bertram Thomas, political adviser to the sultan of Muscat, succeeded in crossing part of the desert in February 1931, thereby becoming the first Occidental to explore part of that region. "Curse!" Philby exclaimed in his diary when he heard the news. "There is nothing to do but drain the dregs of disappointment with a bitter heart." His attitude produced the first known row between himself and Ibn Saud. "*Uskut!* — Shut up!" Ibn Saud hurled at him in public when Philby complained. And as Philby wailed in a letter to his wife, Dora, "Alas! Alas! So the sword of Damocles has at last fallen on my hapless head and Thomas has borne off the laurels of the [Empty Quarter]!"[33]

Philby was at a loss to know why the monarch whom he loved so deeply had prevented him from garnering "the Blue Riband of modern exploration," the more so since Ibn Saud owed him £30,000 for the automobiles he had taken delivery of from Philby's company, Sharquieh, but had not paid for. He complained vigorously that "Ibn Saud has let me down in spite of all my entreaties and his promises and my very clear warning that Thomas would certainly be trying the venture at the very time I wanted to do it."[34] Such was the depth of his anger that, for the first time, he contemplated leaving Arabia and taking up a political career in Parliament.

The king was assuredly concerned by Philby's disenchantment and sent him a royal girl, Miriam bint Abdullah al Hasan, "by way of solacing me for my great disappointment." But her presence could not "solace the woe of my defeat. Time alone can do that. Damn and blast Ibn Saud and Thomas!" He had made arrangements to go to England "on leave" when good news arrived from the palace. The king acted to keep his faithful friend at his side. In 1932 he agreed that Philby could now explore the Empty Quarter, and, more, that the Civil List would pay the costs — for the escort, guides, camels, provisions — although there was precious little left in the treasury even to pay the modest sums involved. His expedition would easily dwarf Thomas's feat. "Starting! Love everybody!" he cabled to the family in London.[35] Then he vanished into the desert.

Meanwhile, Twitchell had been to New York, trying to raise interest and capital for his gold and oil prospects. He may have used Charles Crane's name without his consent. True or false, Crane wrote to Twitchell sharply, stating "emphatically that he did not wish and would not accept participation in any company, or companies, which might be formed for this work" and that he "did not wish a statement ever to appear to the effect that there were ulterior commercial motives behind his philanthropic activities in Arabia."[36] When Twitchell sought to interest American oil companies in Ibn Saud, they offered Crane a 10

percent interest in Arabian oil if it was found. Crane remained adamant; he would not profit from Arabia. In that moment, Crane passed
up an opportunity that would have made him one of the world's richest
men. He wrote to Ibn Saud with his assessment of the situation:

> Although I am hesitant about offering advice on any particular project
> . . . I do feel that in general it is better for a nation to develop its own
> resources with its own talent and money, or, if those are inadequate,
> with a minimum of such aid from abroad. Certainly the granting to
> aliens of monopolies or extensive concessions not infrequently leads to
> both internal and external difficulties.[37]

Twitchell's search for American backing became daunting. Potential
backers asked endless questions: Where the hell is Hasa? Where the
hell is Arabia? What is its stratigraphy? Who is this fellow Ibn Saud?
Have we not more than enough oil much closer to home? Who go
halfway round the world to find more? At last Twitchell met Maurice
E. Lombardi of Standard Oil of California, a company that was at once
efficient, bold, and rich, with a board staffed by the San Franciscan
variety of swells, gentlemanly in appearance but as tough as Rockefeller
under the polish. The company had not been doing well recently:
in 1930 its staff had drilled some thirty-seven wells in six foreign countries and had explored twelve countries without any substantial reward
to show for the investment. Yet Lombardi, a director of Standard Oil
of California, was interested in Hasa, for the good reason that Ibn
Saud was free to negotiate without involving the British, and the signs
that oil might be there were good to excellent. Doubtless the board
had Fred Davies's reports from Bahrein in front of them, and their
technical advisers had noted the Dammam dome as a horse worth
backing. Perhaps Twitchell had said that he had seen the dome and
had formed the opinion that if there was oil on the Arabian coast, it was
at Dammam.

At length Standard Oil decided to retain Twitchell's services, according to Dr. Glenn Brown (the geologist who later discovered much of
Riyadh's water and thereby enabled the expansion of Ibn Saud's capital into a large modern city), and as compensation Twitchell was offered a relatively small retainer and an interesting percentage in royalties, should oil be discovered. But Twitchell rejected this proposal.[38]
The company then offered him a lump sum of $75,000, a very large
sum in gamble money by Depression standards, and one made "as
a technical adviser," mainly because of his connections to Ibn Saud
and the privy councilors Suleiman and Gargani. The offer satisfied
Twitchell, who now had the seed money he needed to develop the King

Solomon's gold mines project. He accepted and in that moment he, too, lost the chance to become an exceedingly rich man.

As Twitchell did so, Standard Oil separately made contact with Philby in London. Philby had arrived there in May 1932, basking in the fame of having made the first east–west traverse of the Empty Quarter and having spent fifty-five days without water (drinking only the sap of plants and camels' milk) in that vast terra incognita. All the world now knew of his tremendous feat of endurance, and this, combined with Philby's exotic reputation as the grand vizier of Ibn Saud, caught the imagination of the public, whose only entertainment that year was the Great Depression. He was received as the hero of the hour. In London, the Royal Geographical Society gave a dinner in his honor, and Philby lectured afterward to an illustrious audience. The Royal Central Asian Society booked him for a lecture, the BBC asked him to talk, newspapers commissioned articles, and a publisher wanted him to write a book. The British Museum wanted to know more about the birds, animals, and insects he had seen.

Then came the letter, at the end of May 1932.

Philby was pottering about the British Museum, preparing talks about the birds and geological specimens he had collected while on the march, and making maps. He was unaware that Standard Oil had struck oil on Bahrein in paying quantities in May 1932 at a depth of 2,000 feet, and in circumstances that reinforced the engineers' belief that the Bahrein structure was part of that large arc of sedimentary conditions that began in the Caucasus of South Russia and extended, so it seemed, through Iraq and Iran. The question before Standard Oil of California was whether the arc continued under the Persian Gulf to Bahrein, and if so, did it extend into Arabia? The engineer in Bahrein, Fred A. Davies, thought it likely, and he had reported his finding to Standard Oil at their headquarters in San Francisco. At that point a decision was taken to ask for the help of the State Department in finding Philby, and Philby in London learned that his correspondent was the U.S. consul general in London, Albert Halstead. The letter said, in the gracious style of that period,

Please permit me to introduce to you The Honorable Francis B. Loomis, formerly Under Secretary of State, and a gentleman whom I have known most favorably for many years. Mr. Loomis has been impressed with your work in the desert of Arabia, and would like to meet you. Would you kindly address Mr. Loomis at this Consulate General . . . and inform him when it would be possible to meet you? . . . With apologies for this intrusion, and thanks in advance.[39]

Philby agreed to see Mr. Loomis — the promise of an excellent lunch at Simpson's no doubt had its attractions. There they lunched on July 7, 1932. Loomis, a courtly figure who had been an undersecretary of state in the government of President Theodore Roosevelt, proved to be the counsel to Standard Oil in San Francisco. He came to the point quickly. His company was interested in exploring Hasa for oil and wished to obtain the concession to do so. Aware of Ibn Saud's dire need of money and the fact that he had received nothing from Crane except a box of dates, Philby replied "positively," provided that concession would involve "a satisfactory arrangement regarding the price to be paid for the privilege." Loomis then said that he would have to consult with his colleagues in San Francisco "before committing himself to anything definite, but that he would be glad of my cooperation in the event of the company being desirous of proceeding with the business." Philby told him that he "would be glad to help in any scheme which would contribute to the prosperity of Arabia." There the matter rested until the beginning of September when Philby again met with Loomis, who stated that he was still "deeply interested" in the oil but that he was still unable to commit his company, although he proposed to stay in contact. Philby gave Loomis an idea of his immediate plans: he intended to return to Arabia at the end of the year by automobile and in the manner of the Grand Tour — Ypres, Leiden, Osnabruck, Hamburg, Berlin, Prague, Vienna, Budapest, Belgrade, Sofia, and Adrianople (Edirne, Western Turkey). Thus he and Dora left London in his brand new blue and silver Ford Phaeton, a graceful open carriage "built for gentlemen." He gave little thought to oil, he spent a good deal of time working on his book about his ride across the Empty Quarter, and, as he wrote, he had "not a care in the world, having achieved the peak of my ambition."[40] Nor did a telegram from Loomis just before he set out cause him to change his plans. Loomis cabled this message:

> We are now considering certain pertinent plans, and hope to cable you on arrival, asking if you will not be good enough, on behalf of our company, to inform His Majesty that we are about to submit to him a formal request for permission to make a careful geological survey of Hasa . . . areas, in order to furnish him and ourselves with dependable scientific data concerning the probable occurrence of commercial petroleum in these areas. Should we make this request and obtain desired permission, and if our survey develops favorable results, we shall hope, with your assistance, to enter into practical working contract for development of petroleum. Will communicate with you on your arrival Jidda giving details. . . . Loomis.[41]

[2]

PAX ARAMCO

P HILBY AND HIS ENGLISH wife, Dora, reached Jidda from England on December 3, 1932, to find two more telegrams awaiting him from Standard Oil of California, each more urgent in
tone. A third arrived as he resumed his work in Arabia at his
mansion, the Beit Baghdadi, a place so fly-ridden that Philby could
work only in darkened rooms. The second telegram was the most important. It was from Loomis at the headquarters of Standard Oil of
California, and it advised that

> our company is now desirous of making geological investigations in
> Arabia. In particular we would like to obtain exclusive right to exam-
> ine Hasa and Neutral Territories lying between Kuwait and Qatar pen-
> insula, and the territory lying inland adjacent hereto. Then, if geologi-
> cal indications seem favorable to us, we contemplate a concession for
> exploration for petroleum, to be followed by lease for producing pe-
> troleum, if found in sufficient quantities. Will you not kindly ascertain
> His Majesty's reaction to this proposal; and, if favorable, we desire
> your suggestions as to what steps we should take to obtain permission
> to do this preliminary geological work and your assistance in carrying
> them out.[1]

The third telegram, dated November 28, 1932, was still more urgent
in tone: "Owing to recent developments, earnest desire as early as
possible answer to my preceding cable. This is very urgent."[2] Plainly
this advice had to do with the possibility of the intervention of the
Anglo-Persian Oil Company and its affiliate, the Anglo-Iraq Oil Company. By now able to advise Loomis of the king's terms, Philby telegraphed them directly to San Francisco from Mecca. He felt able to
arrange the desired concession in Standard Oil's favor, he announced,

but "only on the basis of reasonable quid pro quo which is essential. Owing to economic conditions, Government unable to pay debts and urgently needs funds. It has however potentially valuable mineral resources, and requires guarantee *bona fide* exploitation of territory as soon as possible, in order to derive advantage of the power of the money."[3]

How Philby felt able to communicate the assurance that there might be "potentially valuable mineral resources" in Arabia is nowhere stated, then or later. It was known that the Arabian desert contained some gold, some water, and possibly valuable deposits of iron ore, but unless Philby knew more about the oil resources than he had revealed so far, his statement must be regarded as bait. As he ended his reply, the government's terms were "firstly, lease of required area, including protection, *et cetera*, £5,000 gold per annum in advance; secondly Government to have thirty per cent of profits of enterprise; thirdly, your company should loan to Government £100,000 gold recoverable from these payments due to it, or repayable in installments in event of surrendering concession."[4]

Loomis's reply arrived on December 28, 1932, thanking Philby most courteously for his "efforts on our behalf" but stressing that "our information concerning His Majesty's terrain is very meager" and that, therefore, his terms "seem quite burdensome." Philby's reaction to this telegram was to reveal the American interest in the Hasa concession to the two other parties that would be most interested in the concession themselves.

One was Sir Andrew Ryan, the British minister in Jidda. Ryan was one of the ablest men in Islamic affairs in the Foreign Office. The dragoman at the British embassy at Constantinople for many years before and after World War I, he was the official who had arranged affairs so that Britain, not Turkey's ally, Germany, won the Mesopotamian oil concession in 1914. Now he was minister in Jidda, responsible for guarding Britain's interests in Arabia. By now his knowledge and experience of Islam had become endless. And he was said to know more about Ibn Saud than Ibn Saud knew about himself. He never regarded Arabia's charms as being any greater than, as he himself described the steamy port of Jidda, "a place with only holiness to export."[5]

Aware that Ryan's mission was to keep the American oil companies out of the Persian Gulf region in general and Arabia in particular, at a personal meeting Philby assured Ryan that he would keep the minister informed of the American interest as it evolved, and Ryan duly informed the Foreign Office in London of Philby's assurance. "Philby," the minister announced, "will be my main informant."[6] That, of course, was an untruth. Philby intended to double-cross Ryan if he could; his objective was to wreck British control of the Middle East, and this depended upon American entry into the Middle East through the "open door" policy.

The second to receive the information had been a close friend of Philby's since their days together as Scholars of Trinity College, Cambridge — Martin Lees. He was now the chief geologist with Anglo-Persian and its affiliate in Iraq. These companies controlled both the Iranian and the Iraqi oil fields and were immensely powerful, therefore, in the British politico-commercial spectrum. It was Winston Churchill, as first lord of the Admiralty, who arranged his government's purchase of a 51 percent interest in Anglo-Persian as a source of oil for the British navy just before World War I. As to Iraqi oil, the British army had undertaken a major military campaign to eject the Turks from Iraq during that war and to establish its control over the great oil fields there. Anglo-Persian was reckoned to be the largest and the richest oil company in the world at that time and, accordingly, Philby's secret intention was to work against its interests while appearing to promote them. This was a measure of his cunning and perhaps, also, his foolhardiness. As he informed Lees by cable over a system wholly controlled by a British company,

> Lest there should be any misapprehension in the matter in connection with the appreciation of my efforts acknowledged by Mr. Loomis above, I should perhaps explain that, at this stage, my association with [Standard] is a purely platonic one. . . . I was in no way "retained" and received no remuneration for my services. Indeed I regarded myself as primarily responsible, also in a purely honorary capacity, for getting the best possible terms for the Government. The Finance Minister had impressed on me his expectation that I would work on these lines; and later on . . . expressed his conviction that I would give priority to the interests of the Government. I assured them both that I would do just that; and all concerned will probably agree that I did.[7]

From that time forward, Philby played the two parties, Standard Oil of California and the Anglo-Persian Oil Company, in the interests of the middle, Ibn Saud. He did inform his own trading company in Jidda, Sharquieh, but they displayed no interest, perhaps because Philby had advised them earlier that the prospect of oil in Arabia was "much ado about nothing." In a letter to Martin Lees of Anglo-Persian he announced that

in return for your anticipated services in [the negotiations] I can pass
on for your private ear a piece of information anent a territory . . . I
have been approached by an American concern to apply to the Government for a concession of the exploration and exploitation rights in
the Hasa province. I am not in any way committed to serve the interest
of said company; but I am generally disposed to help anyone practically interested in such matters, and capable of being useful to the
Government. I have accordingly ascertained that the Government, for
financial reasons, is prepared to consider the grant of a concession to
any reputable concern able to help it in its present difficulties.[8]

Philby set down the terms recently offered to Loomis but with the
caveat that "this information is strictly private, of course, between you
and me; but, if your people are interested, there is nothing to prevent
them communicating with me, with a view to placing a definite offer
before the Government."[9] As he had done in his telegram to Standard
Oil, he noted that the concession would not be given except for a
substantial quid pro quo; but

the Government is right up against a serious economic situation, and
would be bound to accept a reasonable offer. I am of course informing
the American concern of the position, and must retain my liberty to act
for them, if they swallow the bait. I am similarly at liberty to work for
your friends in the same circumstances, as my main object is to get the
concession going in the interests of the Government. I have not asked
for or received any personal remuneration, and I am quite prepared to
leave that matter to the conscience of anyone getting what he wants
through me. I know you will handle the matter discreetly, and will say
no more.[10]

He stressed, too, that there was no time to lose, as Ibn Saud was eager to
sell the concession.

As Philby sought to create a bargaining position between the king
and the American and British oil companies, he stressed the king's
indigence in unmistakable terms. "The main point," he advised Standard, "is that Ibn Saud's government owes a good deal of money, and
has to default on its payments to its creditors. Its only hope of being
able to pay them now depends on the mortgaging of its potential resources; and I don't think it will change its policy in the immediate
future."[11] The ability of the king's administration to survive depended
upon the outcome of the negotiations. For some reason, Philby supposed that Standard would be more generous and more caring about
giving the king money than would the British. On occasion during the
negotiations, Philby did allude to a proposal from an Indian group for
the establishment of an Anglo-Saudi bank and a railroad between Jidda

and Mecca, and said that the Indians were prepared to put up £75,000 to get things started. If this was true, then, Philby figured, if Standard Oil did not meet Ibn Saud's demands, then the Saudi government might well obtain from the Indians the gold it needed to satisfy its creditors.

Then Philby received the very unwelcome news that Karl Twitchell, the American engineer proposed to Ibn Saud by Charles Crane, was on his way to Jidda with a Standard official and that Twitchell would represent Standard Oil of California in its negotiations with the government. On January 26, 1933, Philby received a cable from Maurice Lombardi, a director of Standard, announcing that Twitchell and Lloyd N. Hamilton, a lawyer employed by Standard Oil, would arrive at Jidda on February 15, "for the purpose of conferring with you and discussing with the Arabian Government the terms," and Lombardi hoped that "they can have your continued support."[12] Philby of course had no intention of working with Twitchell. Philby quickly managed to exclude his rival from the forthcoming negotiations, and Twitchell, having been paid his $75,000 and cashed the check, seems to have vanished from the scene, probably to begin work on the King Solomon's gold mines project.

Almost immediately after that cable, Philby received a letter from his friend Martin Lees, announcing that his company, Anglo-Persian, was "definitely in the bidding for Hasa" and that Philby would be hearing shortly from the sister company, Anglo-Iraq, which was sending its agent to discuss matters personally with Philby. But, Lees warned, whether Anglo-Iraq would meet the king's demand for an important quid pro quo was a sticking point. Philby replied to Lees's communication immediately, revealing what he knew about Standard's intentions and something of his dissatisfaction with the way he was being treated. The "California Company," Philby responded, was sending Twitchell and "a man named Hamilton: and they would arrive at Jidda on February 15." Philby revealed that he was not "quite sure where I stand in the business." The Americans seemed not to really need his assistance unless it was "to prevent my helping some other party." At the moment he was not pledged to any party and therefore he would be "glad to know as soon as possible to what extent your people mean serious business." Philby then applied the squeeze. "Let me know pretty soon," he wrote to Lees, "and I will similarly let you know what is happening, so long as I remain morally free to do so."[13]

As to his own attitude, Philby recorded that "in the event of both parties being willing to go all the way, and in so far as my advice might be of any avail with the Government, I should, for purely political reasons, have been inclined to favor the Americans, whose record is entirely free of any imperialistic implications." Politically, Ibn Saud's position seemed to be the reverse, although his statements were possibly a gambit to placate Ryan. He said he wished the British to get the concession, provided their price was right. Philby wrote in a memorial on the negotiations, "Ibn Saud, strangely enough like a bird mesmerized by a snake, was known to be personally desirous of giving the Hasa concession to a British company, if only he could get something solid in return."[14] But the king, too, was fully capable of playing everyone except Philby against his own interests.

The character and personality of Ryan, and his relationship with Philby, now became of high importance in the outcome of the negotiations, and not only in regard to oil. Whitehall might have accepted the American demand that it recognize the "open door" policy in the Middle East, but Ryan, while having to accept the Foreign Office's instructions, had no intention of opening the door for the Americans, unless he had to. The British oil companies might have all the oil they needed, but, Ryan decided, if there was oil in the Arabian Peninsula, they should have it anyway.

On learning that the British had elevated the consulate to a legation, Philby wrote a personal letter to the parliamentary undersecretary of state at the Foreign Office, assuring him that "all my knowledge and efforts will be unreservedly at [Ryan's disposal]." In a day when a man's word in official matters was regarded as his bond, that assurance, when the undersecretary informed Ryan, did much to assure Ryan that Philby would be a friend in the negotiations, the more so when Philby offered his services as an informant. Ryan would have been prudent had he paid more attention to the reception that Philby gave him when Ryan arrived in Jidda's harbor. Philby, having declined an invitation to the reception given Ryan on board the warship that brought him, appeared at the stern of the ship with a loud hailer. Knowing that Ryan was a poet of note, he broadcast to the new minister a poem in Latin, written by himself, that was, in Philby's subtle fashion, far from being a true welcome. In English, the poem read:

> Our greetings warm receive, Sir Andrew Ryan,
>   A poet thou, 'tis said, from poetaster's hands.
>   Hail! worthy envoy of the British lion!
>   Hail! harbinger of peace to Arab lands
> After long discord and dissension! Fie on
>   Those so long denied that Arab sands
>   Could yet produce a really worthy scion

Of that great chivalry that still commands
The admiration of the world! But why on
Earth should we suppose that impious rebel bands
Of Hashim's rivalry or greedy Zion
Could cut inexorable Fate's sure strands
Wove on the loom of Wahab's creed. Orion
Himself, with belt and buckler girt, forth stands
To warn with dire destruction all who's try on
The game of war with one whose doughty hands
Have wrought an empire, though he oft die lie on
An exile's bed, forlorn, near coral strands
Of Parsic Gulf far off. Amphitryon
Of the seas' lords, of Briton's sons demands
To leave henceforth the Arabs to rely on
One who has clearly strewn that his commands
Within his sphere of rule on lamb and lion
Alike impose the peace, that British hands
Alone were wont to guard, though they might die on
Far paynim shore, relieving robber bands
Of smuggled arms and captive slaves that cry on
Their God or England's might. She reprimands
All evil-doers her roaming sailors pry on;
But God decrees: the torch to other hands
Must pass; 'tis time and thou, Sir Andrew Ryan,
Art come to land the "white man's burden" on these sands
And win Arabian love and thanks for Albion.[15]

For all its elegance, the poem was a warning to Ryan to respect Ibn Saud's sovereignty. But Ryan may have misjudged its import and other dynamics of the Arabian court, for as he wrote of Philby in his memoir: "The most notable member of our self-contained society was H. St. John Philby. . . . He hated British policy in the East and was suspect in many official circles at home. He was credited in the English press with a tremendous influence in Ibn Saud's entourage. This legend was greatly exaggerated. . . . He was much more remarkable as an explorer than as a politician, and his adhesion to Islam greatly enlarged his opportunities for travel in the remoter parts of Arabia. . . . Whatever his peculiarities of character and outlook, he was far and away the most conversable person in our circle, and my wife and I were on the best of terms with him and his very attractive wife, who remained a non-Moslem."[16]

When Philby became a Wahhab, Ryan joined his name, pronounced "Sinjun" in English, to that of Allah, and so, to Ryan, he became known thereafter as "Sinjallah." If Ryan looked at Philby's file at the Foreign Office before leaving London, as he must have done, he would have found much that was worrisome about Philby's career. While acting as the political agent to Jordan, he was suspected of having stolen the Foreign Office file on the arrangements that led to the Arab Revolt against the Turks in 1916, and to have given it to Ibn Saud. There was evidence that, at that same time, he had engaged in an unauthorized correspondence with Ibn Saud, suggesting that he had undertaken espionage in the interests of Ibn Saud against the British crown.

As to Philby's friend and patron, Ibn Saud, Ryan remembered: "He was very shrewd and very difficult in negotiation." Ryan believed that at heart Ibn Saud was hostile to all Western influences, including Britain's. Ryan did not unreservedly admire Ibn Saud, as did most Western- ers and almost all the Americans who had business with him when he was at the height of his powers. Ryan had had the "misfortune to have to dun the government, and sometimes the King himself, for certain moneys, and it was hard to secure payment even . . . when it was prom- ised. I did what I could to carry out my instructions from home, but I always felt that it could only appear to an Arab ruler somewhat ungen- tlemanly to make so much of money matters between friends. In other respects Ibn Saud was a man of his word, however difficult it might be to extract it in political matters."[17]

In the scenario forming around the oil negotiations, Ryan would prove to have little influence as an individual. He was part of a formida- ble and efficient system established to defend the imperial interest in the Middle East against the designs of foreigners. But events were hinting at the huge changes to come. The Foreign Office reported to Ryan that an American oil company was becoming interested in Saudi Arabia, a country that Britain considered to be in its sphere of influ- ence. Although Ibn Saud had united the Nejd, the Hejaz, and other regions in the kingdom of Saudi Arabia in 1932, it was, like most of the Arabian Peninsula, still a protectorate of Great Britain. Earlier, on December 25, 1932, a telegram from the British political agent at Bahrein had advised Ryan and the British government in Whitehall that the Americans had begun to try to force the "open door" policy still further, thus threatening to further erode Great Britain's control of the region. On January 3, 1933, a second such telegram arrived on Ryan's desk at Jidda. Displaying the quasi-official relationship between the Anglo-Persian Oil Company and the British government, the mes- sage advised Ryan that the staff at Anglo-Persian's headquarters at the Abadan refinery in the Gulf had been instructed to approach Ibn Saud with a view to purchasing an option on the rights to prospect for oil in Hasa. If the king agreed to a meeting, then Anglo-Persian would send a small party of its agents to a place nominated by him.[18] These two telegrams make clear that the Anglo-Persian Oil Company and its partner, the Iraq Petroleum Company, had directed Ryan to alert the king that they wished to enter the negotiations. The culminating match in this great game of Big Oil in the Middle East thus began.

Unlike the British oil companies, the American agents of Standard Oil of California acted independently, without the involvement of the U.S. government. This was partly by choice — at the time, Big Oil in the United States had as little to do with the government as possible. Nor, at first at least, did the State Department wish to become involved. America's representation in the Middle East was minimal, reflecting its lack of interest in the region. Moreover, when Loomis of Standard Oil asked the State Department what protection Standard Oil could expect "in case of disorders in Arabia or in case the present government is overthrown and its successor were disposed to break our contract without just cause," Secretary of State Henry L. Stimson's response was discouraging. The "State Department," he advised, "was unable to indicate in advance the nature of protection, if any, which it could afford in the event of the contingencies" mentioned by Standard Oil. The United States did not intend to establish diplomatic or consular representation in the near future in Jidda, and such representation would depend on "the character and growth of American interests in the Arabian Kingdom."[19]

Meanwhile, all parties mysteriously accepted Jidda as the venue for negotiations. It was the worst possible place to conduct high-stakes business. Jidda seemed to be in a perpetual state of suspended animation, where nothing seemed to work and success of any kind seemed improbable. The Hejaz, the region in which the city was located, had a bad reputation for health and hygiene, and anyone who completed the pilgrimage there and then traveled to other destinations was liable to end up in quarantine stations. During the pilgrimage the two desalting stations in Jidda were overworked and often produced brackish water. Rates of exchange could fluctuate greatly as the shroffs robbed the poor. Sick and dying pilgrims were often found in the streets and squares. And as the Dutch consul noted: "They could have been taken to the hospital, but that then was a place of despair and feared by every pilgrim not on the point of death. I shall never forget those hospital wards full of dying patients who had been picked up in the streets."[20] And the negotiations were indeed scheduled to take place during the pilgrimage.

The weather in the region was invariably hostile. Winter chills and rainstorms were followed by high humidity in the spring. As Lawrence of Arabia wrote of the climate in Jidda, "The heat of Arabia came out like a drawn sword and struck us speechless." He spoke of "the oppressive alley of the food market" where "many squadrons of flies like particles of dust danced up and down the sunshafts" from "the men to the dates and back to the meat." "The atmosphere," he wrote, "was like a bath."[21]

Anywhere — Cairo, Beirut, Alexandria, or Constantinople — would have provided a more congenial venue. In Jidda there was only one hotel, The Egyptian, and it was a small lodging at the end of a narrow alley that stank of urine. The hotel had a telephone, but it rarely worked. Its lavatories consisted only of sand closets and zinc sponge baths. Since Westerners rarely went to Jidda and those that did stayed usually at one of the legations, the hotel had considered it unnecessary to add Western-style amenities. Certainly no tourists lodged there. Water was always scarce and therefore expensive — $25 for a bath, it was said. There was no air conditioning, and the fans often malfunctioned because of the antiquated electrical system. The hotel had no room service and barely a rudimentary kitchen; taxis were few and far between and, in any case, they could not drive through the narrow alley to the hotel door. And if anyone was taken ill, a frequent occurrence in that rotting hole, it was useless to expect quick medical attention. Only Ryan's legation or the Soviet Russian legation could provide medical help. There was only one cablehead; there were no restaurants or cafés; the single bank in Jidda tended to deal only with financial abstractions such as the price of gold at Bombay. Even Ibn Saud found the town so uncongenial that he never went there if he could avoid the place. Worst of all, it was infested by the "street eyes" of the religious police, the Ikhwan, the pietists of Wahhabism who detested Occidentals. They forbade alcohol, tobacco, music of any description, and the cinema. And though visitors did enjoy a certain immunity from the attention of the religious police, who were identifiable by their heavy beards, white robes, long canes, and the black antimony around their eyes, it was unwise for Occidental women to appear in the streets in Western clothes. And when the men attended official meetings and functions, the women often found themselves confined to the harem — Dora Philby was a case in point. Why therefore were the negotiations conducted in Jidda? Possibly Philby arranged matters so that he, with the help of the "street eyes," could keep the visitors under surveillance, watching what they were doing, whom they were seeing, and even what messages they were sending by cable.

Wearing wrinkled white duck suits and that most imperial of sun helmets, that of the Cawnpore Tent Club pattern worn by the British Raj in India almost as a badge of office, the Hamiltons and the Twitchells arrived in the Egyptian passenger steamer *Talodi* on February 15, 1933. They were expected to take up residence at The Egyptian, which had been tarted up by the viceroyalty of the Hejaz for the comfort of its illustrious Western visitors. The Hamiltons took one look at The Egyptian and moved in with the Philbys, St. John and Dora, at the Beit Baghdadi. Sir Andrew Ryan and her ladyship gave a Sunday afternoon tea for them at the legation. All attended in their Red Sea evening dress kit — whites with black cummerbund, without tie. Ryan recalled that "they were on quite friendly terms, but the rivalry was keen. The Saudi Government were in the happy position of having an unknown quantity to sell, and the question for them was which party would pay the largest sum down for it."[22]

The earliest development after the Hamiltons and the Twitchells arrived served to reinforce Philby's view about the state of Standard's knowledge. Hamilton advised Philby that Standard accepted in principle the necessity of making a substantial loan to the government. The government had asked for a down payment of £100,000, and Hamilton offered £10,000 gold (about $250,000), being prepared to improve on it if pressed by competition.

Second, much to Philby's relief, Hamilton invited Philby to work as adviser on behalf of Standard Oil in return for a fee of £1,000 (about $5,000) a month for a minimum period of six months, with what he called "substantial bonuses on the signing of the concession, and of the discovery of oil in commercial quantities." And as Dora Philby remarked on hearing the news, her husband was "a different man as he was beginning to get very jumpy about the money problem."[23] The terms were substantial, but Philby kept them a secret. Elizabeth Monroe, Philby's biographer, was able to publish what they were: $1,000 a month backdated to January, $10,000 if Standard Oil won the concession, a further $25,000 if commercial oil was found, and a royalty of fifty cents per ton exported until a second $25,000 was reached. Philby was in the chips at last. Only Dora Philby knew, for she did the confidential typing. It is not clear how long his monthly paycheck would last and whether Philby withdrew from his association with Martin Lees of Anglo-Persian. That company's agent was not aware of Philby's commitment to Lees's main rival and continued to trust and confide in Philby throughout the negotiations; and certainly the British minister, Ryan, did not know this until the negotiations had ended and Philby himself told him. Philby continued to advise him of the negotiations, duplicitously emphasizing that the information was Ryan's exclusively. He double-crossed Ryan, as Philby stated afterwards, because Ryan was a conservative imperialist, and such persons were his anathema. Philby's biographer related that "Philby concealed from everybody except the discreet Dora that he was already being paid a retainer by [Standard Oil]. He went to and fro disclosing tit-bits to the various people interested. . . . Philby also kept Hamilton primed . . . and Ibn Saud au courant with the lot. He vastly enjoyed his resultant sense of importance, as well as the assurances that he got from the King of the confidence placed in him."[24]

The agent of Anglo-Persian and its sister company, the Iraq Petroleum Company, then joined the party. He was Stephen Longrigg, a former governor of the major northern Iraqi oil center at Mosul. An Oxford man of the imperial school, Longrigg disembarked from the *Taif* complete with sun helmet and monocle. As he was to tell a Persian princess of his acquaintance, "The chief mistake I made was that I did not believe there was paying oil in Hasa."[25] He made one other mistake: his trust and confidence in Philby. He was at a serious disadvantage in every way; he lacked power to match and beat other offers because his company had a more limited goal: to keep Standard Oil out of Arabia. At the most, Anglo-Persian was willing to pay only a modest token sum and nothing more until geologists had had a chance to examine the ground. Longrigg and his colleagues mainly aimed to prevent anyone from obtaining the concession within Britain's sphere of influence (notwithstanding the British government's grant to Arabia of full sovereignty in 1927). Longrigg, who was aware of Ryan's view that there was not the slightest evidence of oil in Hasa and that any oil in Arabia would be found on the Red Sea coast, made a starting offer — a derisory £200 gold per month — in return for the exclusive right to explore Hasa for oil, the size of the concession payment depending upon his geologists' reports. Philby felt that this offer, though it was fully backed by the British legation, was preposterous and quite unacceptable.

Meanwhile, Philby continued to assist Standard Oil of California in its bid for the concession. The intricacies of Muslim law were an object of concern. Although Philby was not a lawyer, he had had much experience of Muslim law while serving with the Raj in the largely Muslim Indian province of the Punjab. This became useful when Hamilton sought to establish whether a contract for sixty years, which was what Standard wanted in order to protect its heavy capital investment, would really be worth anything in, say, five or ten years. Even if Ibn Saud remained in power, would the contract be binding on his heirs and successors? Would it survive a change of government? Philby's response was to point out several statements in the Koran, which Muslims regarded as being the word of God himself and thereby bound them to honor earthly pledges and agreements. The Koranic principles that applied to the Standard contract were these:

> *Sura V. Verse 1:* "Oh ye who believe, fulfill your pledges."
> *Sura V. Verse 91:* "Honor your covenant with God, when ye
>   enter into covenant with Him; and violate not your oaths,
>   after ratification thereof, since you have made God a
>   witness over you. Verily God knoweth that which ye do."
> *Sura XVI. Verse 94:* "And take not your oaths to practice
>   deception between yourselves."
> *Sura IX. Verse 4:* "So fulfill your engagements with them to
>   the end of their term: for God loveth righteousness."[26]

The Arabian minister of finance, Abdullah Suleiman, insisted that any contract be acceptable in Islamic courts, and Hamilton insisted that they be recognizable in the Western courts. But, as Philby advised Hamilton, a contract that appeared binding in Ibn Saud's world was perhaps more reliable than a binding contract in a Western society, for in the East, it was thought that to break such agreements would incur the wrath of God. But where were the legal and political safeguards? Could foreign concessionary companies enjoy the protection of international law? Was a contract concluded between an Eastern sovereign and an alien foreigner, an "infidel," binding under international law? Later, when the worth of the contract was challenged before the World Court, Hamilton sought the opinion of the professor of Muslim law at Cairo University, the leading Islamic authority on such contracts. He responded in writing, invoking the name of God:

> By the grace of God, I shall answer these questions seeking for the truth for its own sake and motivated by the desire to be fair and just in what I say, for such are the objectives established by Islam. The laws and commandments of Islam are the same for all men. They do not discriminate between friend and foe. Almighty God says in the Coran [*sic*]: "Your extreme hatred of a people should not lead you to be unjust. Be fair and just in your dealings, for such are the dictates of piety."[27]

As Philby observed to Hamilton, they could be confident that Ibn Saud, the leader of Islam in temporal affairs and a profound believer, was not likely to disobey and break the law of God. In fact, in all his dealings with the company over the coming twenty years until his death in 1953, not once did he compromise his covenant, even on those occasions when he was sure that he had been tricked by the infidel. Not often in earthly affairs, and especially in the affairs of Big Oil, could a Western company have greater confidence in the word of a sovereign.

But what of Abdullah Suleiman? Philby was concerned about him because he drank whiskey, which was forbidden in Islamic law, and he had been known to cream a little of the privy purse for himself. These breaches of conduct, though relatively minor, did not inspire complete confidence in his reliability, though he was a competent negotiator, even by Western standards. He was apt to break off talks, even at the most complicated moments. Five times each day during the one hundred days or so of the negotiations, he would go to a corner of the room, bow toward Mecca, and say his prayers. When tendering his agreement on each point discussed, he would always add the conditional remark *"Inshallah"* — "God willing" — as if each agreement he made was subject to a higher law. The spirit of the warranties in the Koran hung over every point in the scores of agreements made, especially those concerning matters for which Standard Oil of California required assurances. Would the government agree not to interfere if the company introduced aircraft into the Holy Land? Would it permit the aircraft to operate? Would it allow the use of radios and telephones, although their use had been proscribed by the ulema, the council of Muslim scholars and divines that decided whether the use of certain devices would constitute an affront to God? Many such matters, including the company workers' importation of alcohol, pork products, and any goods with an asterisk upon them (the asterisk was thought to resemble the Star of David) raised concern. Philby warned Hamilton that Suleiman might resemble a mere slip of a boy, but was nonetheless like everyone in official circles in Arabia. "The idiosyncrasies of this country and its people," Philby wrote, "are indeed like nobody on earth!"[28]

As the parties haggled, Major Frank Holmes reappeared on the scene. Philby and Holmes knew each other. After the war, Philby had briefly thought about joining forces with Holmes in business endeavors.[29] As the Jidda negotiations between Philby and Hamilton began in March 1933, and at a time when they seemed deadlocked over the king's demand for £100,000 gold on signature, Philby learned that Holmes had telegraphed Ibn Saud "asking him not to conclude any negotiation till he arrived, as he had some very important proposals to make." Holmes duly arrived on the steamer *Taif* on April 10, 1933, and he barreled into Philby's office. As bluff and breezy as ever, without referring in any way to the fact that he still owed Ibn Saud £6,000 gold, he "opened his guns" on Philby:

> What is all this nonsense about, Philby. Here we are, three competitors for the right of exploring the country in search of the oil that will make it rich, if it exists. Can't they [Ibn Saud's administration] see that the best way of ensuring discovery is to get us all on the job together, instead of setting us all at cutting each other's throats. Obviously their best course is to divide the whole territory concerned into a series of triple strips: giving each one of us in each district, without payment except for escorts, protection, etc., to operate for the ultimate benefit of the Government itself, which would get better terms in the end, if the oil were proved to exist. Certainly no one is going to offer them large sums of money, just for the privilege of providing the Government with valuable knowledge of the resources of the country.[30]

Holmes did not reveal in any way whom he represented. Philby listened patiently until he realized that Holmes "had no proposal to make involving any payment. . . . I took up the cudgels of argument: 'All that you say, Holmes, may be perfectly true; but what you don't seem to realize is that the Government is desperately in need of money and intends firmly to remedy that need through these negotiations. . . . Unquestionably the concession will go to the highest bidder, provided his bid is reasonably near the Government's target of £100,000 gold.'"[31] Holmes scoffed at the very idea that anyone would pay so much for such a pig in the poke. So Philby continued:

> "After all, Holmes, you had this very concession ten years ago on very easy terms; and it was not the fault of the Government that you still owe the Government something, a matter of about £6000 gold. . . . I think that Abdullah Sulaiman will insist on you paying that outstanding debt before being permitted at all to negotiate in the present case. You have given them reason to doubt whether you will, or can, fulfill your engagements." That shaft went right home![32]

The *Taif* was due the next day at Jidda from Port Sudan on its way back to Suez, and Philby made sure that Major Holmes was on the passenger list. Philby was at the wharf to see the gallant major off; thus he dispatched one of the three contenders for the concession. Holmes's visit to Jidda was apparently a deft attempt by Philby to force the company to deal only with him. Philby concluded his account with scholarly understatement: "The gallant Major undoubtedly had the faculty of impressing people; and he undoubtedly had achieved some striking successes. But I never thought he had a chance of securing the Hasa concession for the second time, and for a song."[33]

The negotiations now entered a prolonged period of intricate offer
and counteroffer. Philby became ever more nimble as he worked all
sides against the middle, the interests of Ibn Saud. To increase the
discomfort and the exasperation caused by Abdullah Suleiman's way
of doing business, in March tens of thousands of pilgrims arrived to
throng Jidda's narrow streets, bringing with them cholera and cerebro-
spinal infections. In April the dead heat of summer brought with it the
need to change clothes three or even four times each day. The Hamiltons went off to Cairo, and Longrigg took the steamer across the Red
Sea to buy a Cawnpore sun helmet and summer kit — just as Abdullah
Suleiman announced that his government had decided to reduce its
demand to £50,000 gold plus an annual rent of £5,000 gold for a
concession covering all of Hasa as far as the Dahna sandbelt, a great arc
of reddish sandy desert in central Arabia that, over eight hundred
miles, linked the Nafud desert to the northwestern borders of the
Empty Quarter. The government wanted, too, a hefty royalty of four
shillings, or about a dollar, for each ton of oil produced. And to make
the negotiations still more problematic, on April 19, 1933, President
Roosevelt, during a panic over bank failures in the United States, pro-
hibited the export of gold. That meant that, unless gold could be
bought outside the United States, Standard Oil of California would not
be able to pay Ibn Saud in the golden sovereigns he required. It would
have to pay in dollar paper currency, and Abdullah Suleiman would
not countenance that on the grounds that paper money disintegrated
quickly when it was passed from one sweaty palm to another.

When the parties returned, the negotiations resumed. Philby invited
Longrigg to dine, an invitation that the Briton accepted. While the
other guests played bridge, Longrigg said to Philby that he was anxious
to return to his work at Haifa as soon as possible. Would Philby take
over the negotiations for the Iraq Petroleum Company? Philby replied
that such a suggestion was rather late in the day, and, as Philby reported to Hamilton, he reminded Longrigg that the king

> had asked me to work for the Government as soon as [Longrigg]
> arrived to open negotiations, adding that my main object in any case
> must always be to secure a good deal for the Government. [Longrigg]
> tried to persuade me that I could in fact best serve the Government's
> interest by acting for the [British] side. I seized the opportunity of
> saying that, so far as I had gathered, their point of view was too far from
> that of the Government to make it possible for me to act for them. I
> eased the situation by suggesting that, in any case, he would no doubt
> be staying on for some time yet, and that the necessity for a decision on
> my part might therefore be delayed until he had had an opportunity of

judging how near his people would come to the Government point of view, which I understood to be an uncompromising demand for £100,000 gold [$500,000]. He answered that, in that case, [the Iraq Petroleum Company] would simply pack up, but that in the meantime he must lose no time in finding someone else to represent his Company. I left the matter at that, and I think he realised that I was definitely unwilling to commit myself to holding their brief. Undoubtedly Longrigg was seeking to appeal to that most powerful instinct in most Britons abroad, to see to it that the British causes prevailed.[34]

Equally, perhaps, Longrigg dangled the prospect that Philby might obtain something that was, despite his affection for the Wahhabs and their king, truly his heart's desire — a knighthood, a peerage, or perhaps a governor-generalship in the crown service somewhere on the frontiers of the empire. Only recently Philby had remarked to a friend and high authority at the Foreign Office that he might return to the fold if he was offered a title. Still, Philby did not budge for Longrigg.

At length, Hamilton returned from his Cairo sojourn and talked with Philby at the Beit Baghdadi. He had received new terms from San Francisco, which were to be considered Standard's last offer. It was "a very liberal one," according to Loomis, and "an improvement over any of the previous offers." Loomis felt he had pushed "my company to the limit in my sincere attempt to reconcile two different points of view; and I feel that the enclosed proposal not only imposes a very heavy set of obligations on my company (a set of obligations which few companies in the world would be able to meet), but it also protects adequately your Government's interests."[35]

Philby, who believed there was always a better deal just around the corner, recorded that Standard's offer was now "a great advance in the right direction, and promised great possibilities of progress. The contingent monetary inducements proposed went far beyond anything I had ever contemplated, much less suggested. The fundamental factor in the whole business was its immediate money aspect." He presented the document on April 22, 1933, at a meeting in Mecca with Prince Faisal, one of Ibn Saud's sons and the viceroy of the Hejaz, and the finance minister, Suleiman. They were, Philby told Hamilton over the telephone between Mecca and Jidda, "a little disappointed." Faisal and Suleiman had repeated the king's demand for £50,000 as the immediate up-front payment. Therefore the financial terms of Standard's final offer committed the company to loans totaling £50,000, yearly rentals of £5,000, and a royalty of four shillings gold per ton of oil produced. It also undertook to provide the government with free supplies of gasoline and kerosene once oil was found in commercial quantities. From

the government's standpoint, of equal importance were provisions calling for an immediate start of exploration, for drilling to begin as soon
as a suitable structure was found (in any case, no later than September
1936), and for construction of a refinery after oil was discovered. Many
more details were stipulated governing the nature and extent of the
relationship between the company and the government, for the concession was intended to act as "a Bible." Philby remarked that his impression was that the government would accept the terms if Longrigg
did not offer something better. Philby reminded Hamilton that Iraq
Petroleum Company had more oil in Persia and Iraq than it knew what
to do with, and that therefore its executives "do not really want the
concession at all, but are seriously interested to stop the exploitation of
the area."[36] For that reason he said he felt Longrigg might offer the
£50,000 gold. But if he did not, then, Philby said, Standard would
probably get the concession.

And so it was. Longrigg could offer only a trifling sum, and agreement was reached between Hamilton and Abdullah Suleiman on May
8, 1933. When Abdullah Suleiman declined to accept £50,000, Hamilton responded with an offer to pay £35,000, and the deal was done.

Philby attributed the British defeat to, among several reasons, its
overconfidence in the "known friendship of Ibn Saud towards Britain."
But, though gratified by the British defeat — it struck him as a just
reward to the Americans for their anti-imperialism and a punishment
to the British for, according to Philby's judgment, their sharp practice
in Arabia in the past — Philby was not pleased at the price, and he
recorded later that "one of the most valuable oil concessions in the
world" had been sold "for what we now know to have been a bargain
price." The agreement consisted of fourteen foolscap pages containing
thirty-seven articles. Two were of an importance higher than commerce. Article 1 gave to Standard the exclusive right, for a period of
sixty years, "to explore, prospect, drill for, extract, treat, manufacture,
transport, deal with, carry away and export petroleum, asphalt, naph-
tha, natural greases, ozokerite, and other hydrocarbons, and the de-
rivatives of all such products." Article 35, the "anti-imperial clause,"
unusual in such contracts, specified that "to avoid any doubt on the
point, it is distinctly understood that the Company or anyone connected with it shall have no right to interfere with the administrative,
political, or religious affairs within Arabia."[37]

The signatories for the agreement were to be Hamilton for Standard
Oil and Sheikh Suleiman for the Arabian government. Before the
signing, at the palace Abdullah Suleiman read aloud the document,

clause by clause. As the proceedings lengthened, Philby noticed, Ibn Saud grew drowsy and then fell asleep. They were then adjourned until the next morning, when the council reassembled at the palace in Jidda to hear the rest of the text. As Suleiman droned on, again Ibn Saud fell asleep, to wake with a start when the reading ended.

"Must have been asleep!" he exclaimed. "What do you think about it?"

All expressed their satisfaction. Philby noted his "pleasure at the successful termination of negotiations, which seemed to spell great prosperity for his people."

"Very well!" said the king, turning to Suleiman. "Put your trust in God, and sign." The document was signed. The party then devoted itself to what Philby called "a long and interesting discussion of women and their ways: the King did not sleep on this occasion, and was the life and soul of the party."[38]

The history of the kingdom of Saudi Arabia properly began from this moment for immediately afterward the king and his privy council dealt with matters of constitutional importance, including the matter of Ibn Saud's heir and successor. He wished that Prince Saud should be his successor. But his wish could not be a command. Ibn Saud therefore requested, as the unwritten constitution required, that the decision be taken by the Council of Deputies, the Consultative Council, and the ulema, the council of Wahhabi clerics. They deliberated and decided that Saud was the appropriate choice.

The president of both councils, Prince Faisal, the viceroy of the Hejaz, then signed the decree recognizing his half brother, Saud, as the heir to the throne. At some stage, it was decided also that when Saud succeeded, he, Faisal, would become his crown prince. After signing, Faisal formally presented the decree to Saud at a ceremony in the Grand Mosque at Mecca. (Faisal was to regret bitterly his oath of allegiance to his half brother, for in due course the "exceptional qualities" that were thought to reside in the crown prince were to be found sadly defective.)

It was now necessary, "as a matter of courtesy," to advise Sir Andrew Ryan, the British minister, of these matters. Ryan approved and recorded that "by the end of 1934 Ibn Saud was as comfortably situated as any self-made monarch could wish. He was at peace with his neighbors. He had done everything within his power to consolidate the future of his dynasty by making his eldest son heir apparent and by ensuring his recognition in that capacity by all the rest of the family. . . . There was talk of giving the country some sort of modern constitution, but this was not pursued. He remained an autocrat and made no secret of it."[39]

Philby wrote that the oil concession and the establishment of a dynasty constituted an *annus mirabilis* in the history of Saudi Arabia. Yet even as the concession document was readied for ratification, the kingdom's future with the Americans again seemed to become problematic. When President Roosevelt forbade the export of gold in April in order to meet the emergency created by the closing of so many banks, Standard Oil of California applied to the U.S. Treasury for a special permit to export the sum of $170,327.50 in gold, that sum being the £35,000 gold loan when changed into dollars. At the same time, Hamilton negotiated by telegram to buy the £35,000 gold in London. His move proved wise, for on July 28, 1933, the company received word that the undersecretary of the Treasury, Dean Acheson, had denied Standard Oil's request. The London gold, which was in sovereigns, was purchased and then shipped to Jidda on August 4. It arrived in wooden boxes at Jidda on about August 25 and was delivered to the Dutch merchant bank in the port. There it was counted by Twitchell under the eyes of Abdullah Suleiman, who gave a receipt to Twitchell for the sovereigns received.

Philby was invited to become a permanent adviser to the business entity that would eventually come to be known as the Arabian American Oil Company (Aramco) at an honorarium in perpetuity of £1,000 ($5,000) a year, backdated to January 1933. That sum was in addition to a payment of $10,000 if Standard got the contract, and another $25,000 if commercial exploitation followed, plus fifty cents per ton of oil exported until a second $25,000 was reached. There was also a reward from Ibn Saud: Philby gained the virtual monopoly of the right to provide motor vehicles for an operation by which pilgrims would ride, rather than walk, the forty-three miles between Jidda and Mecca. The king, too, celebrated by launching a little war against Yemen, the country on the Red Sea between Ibn Saud's southwesterly province of Asir and the British crown colony at Aden. The king had wanted that war for years, but had not been able to find an arms manufacturer who would give him credit to purchase the weapons he would need. Now Philby had no difficulty in getting and supplying arms on tick to the king.

Ibn Saud's debts were now very large: £40,000 to Philby's company, Sharquieh, mainly for automobiles; £17,000 to Marconi for wireless stations; and £30,000 to the Polish firm of Sepewe for rifles, machine guns, and ammunition. The debt to Philby was not settled until 1943, when the king began to receive money from the United States under the Lend-Lease Act. The Polish debt was never settled, despite the Poles' strenuous efforts through their official mission in Cairo. Marconi also had to wait until lend-lease funds were available.

Otherwise Philby's trade as a general merchant boomed during 1934–35; he obtained large quantities of medicines for the palace, Czech matches, British bicycles, British water pumps, and cranes for Jidda's dockyard. In all Philby sold 1,450 cars to the king in six years, which increased Arabia's debt to Sharquieh to £140,000 — but it did result in the Ford monopoly being granted to Philby for all automobile sales in Arabia. Philby complained that "all Sharquieh's capital and profits were locked up in the government debt and there is nothing in it for me or the shareholders." As for the king, Philby wrote to Dora in September 1934 that "things at present are in a frightful muddle and everyone seems to be robbing the king and the government just as fast as they can and the King is helping them splendidly. . . . He can't bear to be argued with and he always smothers anything that anyone else may have to say in a torrent of words."[40] Philby, and many others, benefited from the king's heavy-spending ways — when they managed to collect the debts he owed them.

Many factors had contributed to the victory of Standard Oil of California, in a region that the British government regarded as its own preserve. The speed with which the company conducted business and its willingness to pay Ibn Saud in gold stood it well. At a desperate time in world finances, Standard's executives showed themselves willing to take risks, although they may have known more about the geological structure of the Dammam dome than they let on.

Yet the clincher that enabled Hamilton to make the final play was Philby's double-cross of Ryan. Far from acting as Ryan's informant, Philby withheld from him the most crucial piece of intelligence — that Ibn Saud was about to accept Hamilton's offer of payment in gold. Thereby Philby ensured that the representatives of Iraq Petroleum Company would not raise the stakes, which they might have done if they had realized how close Standard Oil was to closing the deal.

Some have attributed the spineless performance of Longrigg and the board of Anglo-Persian, the parent company of Iraq Petroleum Company, not to the mishandling of a delicate situation, but to the intentional effort of the British government to help establish an American presence in Arabia. Britain, already overburdened by its global commitments, may have viewed American involvement in the Middle

East as a stabilizing influence, particularly with Hitler in power in Germany, Mussolini in Italy, and Stalin in Russia. There is no evidence that this was true in the early 1930s, but later in the decade, as will be seen, the British chiefs of staff certainly desired to embrangle the United States on Britain's side in the Middle East.

Whatever the truth of such a suggestion in 1933, Sir Andrew Ryan was discomfited by the Standard Oil agreement. He had been sure that Philby would so arrange matters that the concession would go to a British company. But, as Philby recorded of his meeting with Ryan after the deal was done,

> we talked about everything under the Arabian sun; but it was when I got up to take my leave that I said to him: "I suppose you have heard that the Americans have got the concession." He was thunderstruck, and his face darkened with anger and disappointment. . . . Our final leave taking was somewhat strained.[41]

[3]

ON DAMMAM DOME

FRED A. DAVIES, PREVIOUSLY the camp boss at Standard Oil of California's operation in Bahrein, landed in Hasa soon after the concession was signed to establish a base and begin exploration. In 1932 he had found the discovery well on the island that led him to the conclusion that the Dammam dome might be a hot property. This accounted, in part at least, for the determination with which Standard Oil, even in hard times, went after the eastern Arabian oil concession. It accounted also for the great success that attended Davies in his career with Standard Oil, most of which he spent in looking for and developing Arab oil, and then in heading the company's immense enterprise established to extract, transport, and market it. The company named the new enterprise the California Arabian Standard Oil Company (Casoc), but the name proved to be too cumbersome and inconsistent with the company's desire to make the entity appear to be a joint Saudi-American enterprise. Davies was made president of Casoc and he renamed it the Arabian American Oil Company (Aramco). And when Standard Oil built its first supertanker in the 1960s — a ship of about 120,000 tons deadweight — the company named it the *Fred A. Davies*.

The world Davies found himself working in was very strange. As he wrote, it could not have changed much since the days of the Prophet, who visited these parts in the seventh century. Saudi Arabia was "just emerging as a nation under the leadership of King Ibn Saud. Order and stability of Government had been established but the Government's only [financial] resources were . . . a modest income from customs and the Muslim pilgrimage to the holy cities of western Arabia." The country had little to sell, and over "vast areas of rock and sandy wastes, a nomadic society depended on the scant and uncertain provision of the desert. The culture — tribal, patriarchal, and Islamic — was ancient."[1]

Some foreign trade took place near the holy cities of Mecca, where the Prophet was born, and Medina, where he died and ascended into Paradise. Otherwise trade, mainly the export of dates, fish, and pearls, was confined to the settlements adjacent to the Persian Gulf. But

> contact with the outside world was slight and the amenities and opportunities of the western world . . . almost entirely lacking. Even the basic requirements of human life — food, clothing, and the simplest household and agrarian implements — were in short supply and had to be supplemented from abroad if progress and tranquillity were to be maintained.[2]

Few Saudi Arabs spoke English, fewer still knew anything of Americans or even that America existed, and they generally believed that it could not exist because the world was flat. They were suspicious of Westerners; they were difficult to deal with; they were quick to take offense. Many were religious fanatics, some were hostile and even dangerous, and there was no way to tell which was which except by the direction in which they pointed their rifles. Above all, the religion and the code of behavior by which the Arabs lived were very austere.

On arriving, Davies visited the governor of Hasa, Abdullah ibn Jiluwi, Ibn Saud's cousin and therefore a member of the house of Saud, the ruling dynasty of Saudi Arabia. A devoted servant of the king, Jiluwi was one of the men who had helped reestablish the Saud dynasty in Arabia in 1903. In appearance he was "a grizzled-bearded figure with a grim look and hawk eyes of an Old Testament prophet." He ruled his province according to the Koran, the doctrine of the Wahhabs, and the edict of his royal overlord. His justice was swift and harsh, administered with the sword, the knife, and the palm-stem.[3] He lived in splendor in his palace at Hofuf, the great oasis and capital of Hasa — Hofuf was sometimes said to be the greenest place in all Arabia. Davies's main business with Jiluwi concerned obtaining land at Dhahran to build the camp and establish equipment yards; other issues included the law and the strict Muslim code of behavior in Saudi Arabia, a much more complex problem.

As a colleague would record, Davies faced a basic problem that would last as long as there were Americans in Saudi Arabia: "How could Americans reared in the permissive Western world live under the strict rules established over thirteen hundred years ago by the Prophet to deal with conditions encountered at that time in this desert land?"[4]

The need to conform — or at least to not offend — extended into every dimension of life for the Americans in Saudi Arabia. Ibn Saud had declined to grant the company extraterritoriality, protection from Saudi law and its courts. As long as company workers lived in Arabia, they must abide by not only their own laws, but also Saudi customs, as laid down in the Koran. The Koranic body of law was known as the shariah, and it was, by Western standards, most burdensome. Woe betide the American who offended the code. And of all the offenses an American could commit, the worst was to be seen or known to be drinking beer, wine, or spirits. Although some Saudis were known to partake (Abdullah Suleiman, the finance minister, perhaps the most bibulous of the officials Davies had to deal with, was especially fond of Scotch whisky), the prohibition laws were enforced by Ibn Saud's religious police. They were posted everywhere to ensure that the laws, the religion, and the customs of Arabia were obeyed. They were very visible — wearing pure white robes and headdresses and carrying long canes with which to administer lashes. And as Dan van der Meulen, the Dutch consul at Jidda, wrote of them when they appeared in Jidda after Ibn Saud captured the port in 1926, they

> did not laugh. They were deadly serious. Their law was the divine command, directly taken from Allah's revelation to the Prophet. Strict obedience would be the only rule in the country singled out by God as His Holy Land. So life from now on was to be hard. The five daily prayers were to be strictly performed. . . . Smoking tobacco, drinking alcohol, dressing up in fine attire: all that would belong to the past. Music was banned. Men would no longer shave but have beards like the Prophet. Disobedience would be followed by the punishments laid down in the Prophet's own book, the Qur'an. Thus, a new, and hitherto remote, fear lay on the town: the fear of the Wahhabi.[5]

This state of affairs continued throughout the many years that U.S. employees of Aramco lived in Saudi Arabia.

To protect the American community from the attentions of the religious police (among much else besides), the company established an enclave. Inside, anything except beer, wine, and spirits was tolerated *so long as the Americans' conduct was seemly.* But outside the enclave, for example, on the beach at al-Khobar, woe betide the Americans who drank, danced, or played raucous music. The man who drank too much ran the risk of being arrested, jailed, fined, and then handed over to the company for deportation. So burdensome did prohibition of alcohol become that a Standard Oil lawyer and researchers were directed to search the body of laws for an actual statement by the

Prophet that alcohol was forbidden. They found nothing definitive —
only a statement that wine might have a negative effect on one's overall
prosperity:

> I have tried to find a text in God's Book . . . which forbids alcoholic
> beverages as clearly as idolatry, murder, adultery, usury, pork, etc.,
> are forbidden, but was unable to do so. . . . Neither these nor other
> texts contain any references to prohibiting alcoholic beverages unlike
> other things considered abominations. He stipulates death for a mur-
> derer, amputation of the hand of a thief, a hundred lashes for a forni-
> cator, eighty lashes for whoever slanders a married woman, and other
> similar penalties. No, the most that the Quran says of alcohol is "O ye
> who believe, verily, wine, gambling, idols, and the use of arrows in
> drawing lots are the work of Satan; avoid them in order that ye may
> prosper."[6]

The students asserted that the first divine to prohibit alcohol was the
second caliph of Islam, Umar, in the books of jurisprudence (*fiqh*), but
it was not clear that the *fiqh* was part of the shariah. The company then
submitted the finding to a second authority. He found, too, that the
caliph Umar, not the Prophet, was the first to administer punishment
for drinking alcoholic beverages.[7]

Although it did not seem to offend against the letter of Islamic law,
the Saudi divines ruled against the consumption of alcohol. But there
were some sneaky ways to partake, without incurring the wrath of the
religious police. Some workers (perhaps all except higher management) in the camp used homemade stills to brew what they called "blue
lightning." The favored spirit was in fact pink, made from raspberries
and brewed in a large crock at the main camp. The berries came from
the camp store, they were put into the crock with sugar and water, and
the mixture was allowed to ferment. When it was ready, the solids
would sink to the bottom and the clear red liquid could be drawn off
the top. The brew was known as "slob." They also brewed beer, which
came to be known as Grobut, Tuborg spelled backward.

Although the king, his administration, and his heirs and successors
would not authorize the consumption of alcohol, occasionally some
dispensation was accorded to the import of beer, most often as reward
for good work. In 1938 and early 1939, management formally asked
Ibn Saud to permit Americans to import beer. But even as the American official sought the beer permit,

> a group of Americans had returned from Bahrein, well liquored and
> loving everyone. After they landed [at Dhahran] one of the group

passed a bottle to a Saudi who drank from it, with results that might
have been expected. Word of that action passed through government
channels to Riyadh . . . and delayed the granting of the beer permit for
many months.[8]

In the autumn of 1934, Floyd W. Ohliger arrived at the camp from San
Francisco, his main task to handle government relations for Davies.
A graduate in petroleum engineering at the University of Pittsburgh,
class of 1925, Ohliger had worked for Standard Oil in Venezuela, Colombia, and the United States. He was a member of a small group
especially selected for their training and previous experience with oil
exploration in sparsely settled non-English-speaking countries.[9] He
acted as Standard's political liaison officer to the king and his administration. Whereas Davies was to become the most remarkable of the
first generation of the company's executives, Ohliger became an adept
maneuverer in the intricate machinations of Ibn Saud's court and
administration. He both represented his company well and took an
interest in the well-being of Saudi Arabia. It was said that he dearly
loved the king and his princes.

Between 1934 and 1951, he became, in turn, Aramco's assistant
resident manager, resident manager, general manager, vice president,
and senior resident in residence. He "directed or personally handled
liaison activity and discussions with the Saudi Arab Government at all
levels." He interpreted the government's oil policy and its attitudes
toward the company, thus ensuring that the two parties worked together as smoothly as possible. In this way he had a hand in shaping
company policy, particularly as it related to the Saudi Arabian government. He claimed to enjoy "the confidence of ranking Ministers of
His Majesty's Government, and of representatives of the United States
Government, including those of Cabinet level and Special Envoys of
American Presidents."[10]

He claimed, too, that a personal friendship existed between Ibn
Saud and himself, one that was "especially close for an Occidental,"
and that he enjoyed an "intimate friendship with the Crown Prince,
Saud." It became his "vocation and avocation" to "bring about the
industrial and social advancement of Saudi Arabia through the oil
development." Toward this end he devoted

much time in study and discussion with members of the Saudi Arab
Government and in acquainting non-Saudis, such as industrialists, officials and representatives of the United States Government, with the
needs, potentialities and aspirations of the Saudi Arab Government, in

the interests of gaining political and financial support for the Saudi
Arab Government.[11]

But balancing the interests of the U.S. oil company and Ibn Saud often
seemed as potentially explosive as wartime diplomacy, and a false move
always carried the threat of disaster. Despite his skills and good intentions, it proved to be an exceptionally hard row to hoe for Ohliger.

Ohliger was quite effective in his relations with the king, but he
made the gross mistake of believing that Ibn Saud was his friend. Everybody believed that, for the king had winning ways. But his only Western
friend was Philby. The king was really interested in money, preferably
in the form of gold. And if he did not get it, or the promise of it, he
could be most treacherous in his associations. Ohliger could not have
absolute faith in the words of Yusuf Yassin and Abdullah Suleiman, for
their statements would change according to the king's moods. The
king was always ready to terminate the concession immediately if he
did not get what he wanted. The only restraint was, of course, the king's
omnipresent need for money.[12]

A particular challenge for Ohliger involved his contact with Yusuf
Yassin, who with his Syrian friends was weaving large-scale intrigues at
court. The nature of those intrigues would reveal much about Ibn
Saud's attitude toward the Western powers as related to the growing
Arab-Jewish conflict in Palestine. Though at first Ohliger's problems
with the Saudi administration were confined to domestic, rather minor
matters, he soon confronted his first major difficulty.

The problem concerned the company's right to operate an aircraft
for purposes of mapmaking and geological exploration. Recognizing
that use of an aircraft was essential to keeping to the schedule of
operations laid down in the concession agreement, Davies assumed
that the king would permit it. Article 22 of the concession agreement
in fact stated that

> it is understood, of course, that the Company has the right to use all
> means and facilities it may deem necessary or advisable in order to
> exercise the rights granted under this contract, so as to carry out the
> purpose of this enterprise, including, among other things, the right to
> construct and use roads, camps, buildings, structures and all systems of
> communications.[13]

This article also included the right to the use of "all forms of communications," even those still proscribed by the divines, as well as the use
of "all forms of transportation." But, as the concession provided, "the
use of aeroplanes within the country shall be the subject of a separate
agreement."[14]

A separate letter dealt with this question:

> One purpose of the present letter is to set forth the agreement as to [the use of an aircraft]. . . . The Government will undertake to provide, at the request and at the expense of the Company, such aeroplane service as the Company may consider advisable for the purpose of its operations within the area covered by the Saudi Arab Concession. Such service shall be limited to the purposes of the enterprise. If any aeroplane photographs should be taken for geological or mapping purposes, the Government and the Company shall each receive copies, also at the expense of the Company.[15]

This letter proved to be a masterpiece of obfuscation. The king's aircraft were all new British de Havilland 9 fighters, Ibn Saud's first major purchase after the signing of the concession. But when Ohliger discussed the question with the authorities, he discovered that the aircraft had come with British personnel to fly and maintain them. None of the aircraft had the radio or photographic reconnaissance equipment that the company needed and, in any case, Davies could not permit the use of aircraft operated by the British government for missions to collect confidential data, especially since, at best, the British were considered a main rival in gaining such information. At worst, they were thought to be a potential enemy that might wrest the concession from Standard Oil at any opportune moment.

But on the other hand, it was evident that the king was not opposed to having Americans fly over the Hima, the holy land. Davies had a Fairchild aircraft from the United States waiting in Egypt, where it had been unloaded from the ship that had transported it and where it had been assembled and prepared for the flight to Dhahran during April and May 1933. He ordered the crew to fly into Saudi Arabia, and the pilot then landed at Jubail on the coast of Hasa, where the company had laid down an airstrip. But in so doing the pilot overflew an encampment of Bedouin, the nomadic people of the Arabian desert, and they reported this to the amir at Hofuf, Jiluwi, who was greatly disturbed by the news. He had learned that the aircraft was on its way, but he had received no orders about it from his government. Jiluwi knew that, since the people believed the airplane to be an instrument of Satan, trouble might ensue when it landed. He rushed a detachment of soldiers to the field at Jubail to protect the aircraft from the crowd. "The crowd surged forward, the soldiers laid into the crowd with canes and camel sticks, and there was a form of riot. When Jiluwi arrived, he ordered the arrest of the crew and the aircraft, which Jiluwi first had padlocked and then sent to Tarut Island where there was no airstrip."[16]

When the news of the airplane's arrival reached Riyadh, the king and Abdullah Suleiman were both extremely angry. The official reason for the anger was that the king was having trouble with the imam of Yemen, trouble that broke into war the following May of 1934, and he had no time to deal with the issues raised by the use of aircraft.

This event could have caused two potential problems for Ibn Saud. First, he was afraid that if an aircraft happened to fly too low or too far in toward Riyadh, the Bedouin might fire their rifles at the craft. These tribes viewed the airplane as they viewed the automobile — an abomination to be destroyed. The second problem concerned the religious authorities. Any strange occurrence in the Arabian skies could draw the ulema, the religious council, into urgent debate with the king, whom they would accuse of offending Allah, as they had done when he introduced the automobile, the telephone, and the radio into Arabia. The mullahs, or priests, were superstitious about a man-made machine flying in the heavens. They feared that the camera, while taking photographs for mapmaking purposes, might gaze upon the face of God and that the craft might fly into the holy airspace of Mecca and Medina, thereby provoking the divinity's displeasure.

The administration also saw potential political dangers in allowing these craft to be flown at will in Saudi airspace. One such incident had strained the relationship with Great Britain, which Ibn Saud still maintained as a counterbalance to U.S. power in the region. The British air force, which did much flying in the Hadramut fringe land between the southern edge of Arabia and the Indian Ocean, had recently lost at least one crew that had crash-landed in the desert not far from Aden. The survivors had been mutilated and murdered by fearful and angry Bedouin. As a reprisal, the British had bombed the tribe's dwellings.

At length, an agreement was reached by which Standard Oil was allowed to operate its aircraft, but only if they flew high, kept out of the skies over Mecca and Medina, and refrained from the use of radios, which was found to be the main concern of the ulema. But in the end, the company found air operations to be more trouble than they were worth. When the king was upbraided by some Bedouin at a *majlis,* a public meeting between the sovereign and his subjects held each day, that he was forsaking the teachings of the Koran, the king responded by restricting flights to the outer fringes of the concession area. This restriction, which went into effect in 1937, proved to be no great loss, for by that time the company's land vehicles had been equipped with large low-pressure balloon tires that enabled them to traverse the desert effectively.

The first employees of Standard Oil of California to move into Arabia did so the moment Ibn Saud ratified the concession agreement. Standard Oil sent telegrams to its geologists, instructing them to report to its headquarters at 220 Bush Street, San Francisco. Among these men was J. W. "Soak" Hoover, who was surveying in the Staked Plains region of Duval County in West Texas, when he received his telegram. It was August 22, 1933, a Tuesday. He remembered the occasion well. A graduate of the University of Texas, and a rough diamond in his early thirties, he celebrated his good fortune that evening. Hoover decided to keep a diary, and in it he would record everything that befell him during his long journey to Arabia and in the first phase of the attack on the Dammam dome, that strange shape looming out of the landscape like a container ship on a calm sea. It was not until morning that he began to pack his gear — watches, compasses, boiling-point thermometers, camera, field glasses, mapping case, and so on.[17]

Because the Depression had struck the oil industry, Hoover had expected his telegram to tell him that he had been sacked, not commissioned to go to Arabia, then a mysterious place on the far side of the world about which most Americans, including Hoover, knew little. Twenty-four hours later he had left by the *Overlander,* the train for New York City. By October 10, a Tuesday, the ship *Baroda,* on which he traveled, had arrived at Bahrein. He saw nine British destroyers at anchor. The British India Steam Navigation Company sent a truck to transport him and his equipment to the Standard Oil camp. Within a short time Hoover was joined by a number of men who were to become important in this saga of American capitalism. They then sailed the twenty-two miles of the Persian Gulf between Bahrein and the little pearling port of Uqair on the Arabian coast, a place of palm gardens and dead heat.

There he was met by Fred Davies, the camp boss. Moving as usual with his deliberate high speed, Davies told Hoover, who was employed as an oil prospector, to get moving as soon as possible on the Dammam dome. Within the week he had pitched his tent, assembled his burros and pack camels, and moved out with his bodyguard of Saudi soldiers — Ibn Saud might have pacified the Ikhwan through his defeat of Sheikh Dawish in 1929, but no one knew whether unreconstructed Ikhwan still lived in the desert fastness. Until that was known, Ibn Saud had refused to allow any company workers to go unescorted into the desert.

Hoover's team expanded with the arrival of an interpreter, a cook, an undercook learning his trade, a mechanic to attend to the trucks and cars, a mechanic's assistant, a driver, and four cameleers. For motor vehicles, Hoover had a Ford touring car and a half-ton pickup. Animals included twenty riding camels and a dozen baggage-carrying beasts, loaded with the party's goat-hair tents, grass mats for the floors of the tents, a silk tent, collapsible tables, chairs, cots, food, cooking utensils, kerosene stoves and lamps, and kerosene and gasoline in five-gallon drums. The animals also transported his chronometer, his transit, three compasses, drafting equipment, four one-gallon water cans, six water skins holding from six to ten gallons each, four oversized water bags, and an assortment of tools and spare motor parts, tires, and front springs. From 1934 onward, when other prospectors came on the scene, each field party took with it one radio to enable the party to keep contact with the base camp.

Each field party remained in the desert for as long as two months. The weather during the cool, or winter, season was typically as hot, but not as humid, as other times of year. Severe sandstorms could blot out the camp for days on end. In December and January the wind was often raw and icy. During that period, therefore, Hoover passed the time in his tent, inking in his observations on the maps. These were very primitive, for the interior of Arabia was largely terra incognita.

Only Saudi Arabs knew these regions of vast desert, but they were familiar only with their own local areas. Philby had passed through the regions where Hoover and his colleagues worked, and he made his notes and recollections available to them. On occasion, he would appear out of the desert at the head of a camel train, leading an archaeological expedition or collecting plants, insects, and animals. He said that he made these trips under the auspices of the British Museum in London, but the Americans generally believed that he was a British spy.

At an early date, the company retained Khamis, a Bedouin who spoke good English, as a guide, and in due course he became its chief guide. He briefed all parties going into the desert on the manner of the tribes. A copy of such a briefing has survived:

> "Do not ask the Bedouin a direct question when you first meet him," Khamis warned. "Do not ask immediately for directions, such as, what is the name of the *jabal* [hill] over there? You will get the wrong answer or no answer at all, for you are a stranger, and he does not trust you.
>
> "If you seek directions, greet the Bedouin as a friend, saying 'Peace be on you.'

"To this he will reply, 'And to you, God's peace.'

"'How are you?' you ask.

"You say, 'I am well, praise God,' and you add 'God give you health.'

"'God give you eyes,' you say.

"'God give *you* eyes,' he answers.

"'God give you strength,' you say.

"'God give *you* strength,' he answers.

"'God give you life,' you say.

"'God give *you* life,' he answers.

"Perhaps now, you should speak with more fervor. You repeat with much force, 'How *are* you?'

"He says, 'I'm all right. How are *you?*'

"'Praise God,' you say. 'Has it rained here?'

"'Yes, a little,' he says, and asks, 'Where are you going?'

"You tell him, 'We go hunting — up there toward the *jabal*. That is the *jabal* Abriq, is it not?'

"He says, 'No. That is the *jabal* Bijda.'

"Now he has given you information; but he may be lying because he does not trust you. So you must be sure.

"You say, 'Well, if that is the *jabal* Bijda, what is that *jabal* over there?'

"'Oh, *that* is *jabal* Abriq,' he says.

"'How is that?' you say. 'I know a man who lived there who said it was *jabal* Dhuma.'

"'No, no,' says the Bedouin. 'That is *jabal* Abriq.'

"So you say, 'How can you tell us where to go if you do not even know your own country?'

"'I do too know my own country,' he says. 'I can prove that is *jabal* Abriq by Said Ali, who has lived by this water hole for ten years.'

"And the Bedouin goes over to Said Ali and cries, 'Is it not so?'

"By this time, the Bedouin is angry and very argumentative; so you are pretty sure that he is telling the truth."[18]

Soak Hoover grew a biblical-style beard and learned to speak pidgin Arabic. A decent and mild-mannered man, he handled the Arab workers well. Above all he learned that first essential of life in the camps — to keep his nose clean and not to lose his temper with any Arab. To strike an Arab for any reason — irritating conduct, disobedience, carelessness with the equipment, stupidity, sleeping on the job — was the worst offense in the field. Also he learned another essential: that he must allow his Arabs to stop work and bow and pray in the direction of Mecca five times each day. The times at which these prayers were made varied from day to day in accordance not with a watch or whistle, but with the times of the rising and setting of the sun and the moon. The Arabs would suddenly stop all activity to lay out their prayer mats, kneel toward Mecca, and prostrate themselves in the fervor of their prayers.

Such a routine could unnerve and irritate even the most even-tempered of the American work bosses, especially when the workers were raising a rig or laying dynamite charge. During Ramadan, the Muslim month of prayer and fasting, the Bedouin took off half the day each day, whatever the blue-eyed infidel on the rig was doing. During that month, between daybreak and sundown, Muslims were not permitted to eat or drink. The law allowed them to rinse their mouths with water, but not to swallow it. Any Muslim breaking the fast could find himself in jail if caught by the prowling Committees of Public Morality. Such offenders might receive a public beating with the stem of a palm frond.

The workweek also differed from the typical Western pattern. The Saudi calendar allotted twenty-nine and one-half days to each month. This required that all documents bear two dates: the one in Arabic was meaningless to the U.S. staff, and the date according to the Gregorian calendar was meaningless to the Bedouin. Nor was the question of time any simpler. In Saudi Arabia, there were five and sometimes six different ways of measuring time. Many other factors made communication difficult. The language of the Bedouin contained no words for the tools they would have to use on the job. They did not understand industrial discipline and the need to accept that sleep, rest, and play would take place only at times laid down by the company.

The Bedouin understood little if anything of what the infidels said, and accordingly, a new dialect developed. It was known in the oil fields as "Aramco-Arabic." As the Arab struggled to learn what to do in return for one silver and sixteen qursh each day (about sixty cents), he had to take orders from a loud, crude, tough foreigner, the infidel of whom he was so suspicious. The manager of labor relations, B. C. Nelson, remembered that

> the most amazing thing about these times . . . was not that when [workers] were handed their bag of money they returned to the tribe with the glad tidings — but rather — that they ever came back to work! Industrial discipline was practically unknown, so the amazing thing was that there was only a 75% turnover in the first few years.
>
> Until this time the Saudi Arab had made little distinction between work and leisure time. They blended the two in the timeless way of an undeveloped rural society. Days and nights flowed together with leisure and work. . . . The impact of the modern age, accelerated by our Company, served to . . . present new definitions of work and leisure time.
>
> Now, for instance, sleep was for the first time divided into two sections — the permissible and that *not* permitted. Worse still, [the Arab] was forced to [differentiate between] what was personal business and what was Company business. The wider the modern age split these two basic activities, the more numerous on-the-job conflicts became.

Supervisors, American and foreign, had never encountered this basic misunderstanding. They could not understand how a workman
could go off and sleep during work time or why he disappeared for
varying periods of time to conduct some private business and then
reappeared with no apologies or feelings of guilt.[19]

And an incident during March 1934 showed how tolerant Hoover
and other U.S. workers had to be. After weeks of insolence from a
Saudi laborer, one of the drillers, Walt Haenggi, cuffed the Arab and
thereby provoked a vigorous complaint. The amir's representative at
the base camp complained over his radio to Abdullah Jiluwi, and Jiluwi
complained to the king. The king personally ordered Haenggi's immediate deportation; then the Americans at the base camp rallied behind
Haenggi. The Saudi political officer ordered all Arabs to strike until
Haenggi was sent back to the United States. For a time it seemed that
even those of the crew who defended Haenngi would be deported as
well. But the camp boss, Davies, reminded the political agent that the
king wanted oil. And there would be no oil if the Americans struck,
which they said they would do if Haenggi was punished in any way. The
antagonisms had cooled by the end of the day. The king withdrew his
deportation order, and, as the camp historian remembered, the camp
went back to work "the better, perhaps, for a clearing of the air and a
venting of the irritations — and also for the warning of how broad the
tolerance had to be on both sides."[20]

Despite the settlement of the Haenggi incident, the problem remained. "Touchy Arab pride often aggravated the natural misunder-
standings" between Arab and American "got hundreds of Americans
into very hot water through no real fault of their own." It was

> very difficult to predict just what might strike the Saudi as an insult.
> To actually swear at him was a criminal offense, for which many Ameri-
> cans were jailed, hauled into court and then deported, after paying
> fines. . . . In cases of open disagreement, the only sensible course for an
> American was to keep his mouth shut and his hands down and to walk
> away. To strike a Saudi, even in self-defense, was a sure ticket to the
> calaboose. Once in jail on such a charge, usually the best a foreigner
> could hope for was deportation. The testimony of Christian witnesses
> was not valid in Saudi courts. That of Moslems, on the other hand, is
> good as gold, and readily negotiable among them.[21]

Hoover arrived on the long, low hills of Dammam dome and recorded
in his diary for June 5, 1934, that his team had found sharktooth shale
and nummulites (a type of marine fossil) in a long hill with a large
depression in its middle. These indicators held out the strong possibil-

ity of a major oil find. The crew built a cairn of stones to mark the spot. Hoover wrote a report on the discovery for Fred Davies. On its basis and others like it, the company would decide in San Francisco whether it would be worthwhile to begin the second phase of the operation, drilling. Hoover recommended that drilling begin, a weighty commendation given the capital that would be required.

But drilling would have to wait, as the hot season arrived and work "in the field" — in the desert — was stopped. The field parties went on their holidays in places such as Lebanon. But soon the star Canopus appeared in the sky, heralding autumn and the start of the cool season.

The second season at Dammam dome began for Soak Hoover at the point where he had stopped work, the site now known as Dammam 1. The company had agreed that drilling should begin, and Walt Haenggi, the rig builder and roughneck, began setting up a rig.

The original team of ten Americans grew to thirteen, and one of them was a geologist of importance in the early history of Standard Oil, Max Steinecke. As a historian wrote of his arrival,

> It is conceded by those who worked with him that Steinecke was the man who first came to understand the stratigraphy and the structure underlying eastern Arabia's nearly featureless surface. As a field geologist he rated with the best anywhere and as a man, a companion, a colleague, he could not have been better adapted to the pioneering conditions he now encountered. Burly, big-jawed, hearty, enthusiastic, profane, indefatigable, careless of irrelevant details and implacable in tracking down a line of scientific inquiry, he made men like him, and won their confidence.[22]

The company built a rock pier, put up a security fence around the camp and the stores dumps, and constructed a quay. A road was built out to Dammam 1, along with eleven miles of pipes to draw fresh water from the springs that, oddly, welled up from the seabed. The rig was up and ready by April 30, 1935.

Progress was soon made in the essential business of finding a way to talk with the Saudi workers. The crews developed a Texas pidgin English with which to communicate, along with gestures, grunts, and shouts. A report on the experience related something of the early difficulties of even talking with the Saudi workmen on the rig:

> On a typical drilling rig, the foreman is an American and the crew is all Saudi. The boss driller is very often a Good Old Boy from Texas, and it was hoped that his brief exposure to the course in work Arabic would permit him to supervise his Arab crew, who had not had the opportunity to learn English, with reasonable efficiency. In practise it worked quite well, but . . . whenever a new Saudi employee was assigned to a rig, he had extreme difficulty communicating, not only with the Ameri-

can, but with other Saudis on the crew. It took a man several weeks before he fit into the team.[23]

On Haenngi's rig at Dammam, Haenngi wished to convey the idea of the word *down*, which was where the drill must go in order to tap the oil. Haenngi knew only the Arabic word for *up*, which was *fok*. When he saw the drill going in the wrong direction, Haenngi raised his voice three times its usual volume and shouted, "No God damn it!" Thus the term *Fok! No God damn it!* entered the language on that rig as the word for *down* — a truly choice morsel of "Aramco-Arabic."[24]

The earliest telegrams on progress at Dammam showed that, for the most part, the bit was descending into gray limestone. There were encouraging signs of tar and water. On August 15, the drill threw up slight showings of oil and gas at 1,774 feet. As Haenngi reported to Davies, and Davies reported to Bush Street, the results were "not important but encouraging." *Something* was down there. Five days later Davies was able to wire a report that they had reached a region that was giving them 50 barrels a day of oil. There was no reason for excitement; 50 barrels represented about half of what the average well in the United States gave off at this stage of drilling. But then, on September 12, Davies reported that for the past twenty-one hours they had had a flow rate of 98 barrels. That was more encouraging. Then came the telegram of September 21: Dammam 1 had produced 6,537 barrels that day. Dammam 1 had become a major find, if the figures were not a telegraphic error. San Francisco cabled almost frantically for confirmation.

The ensuing cables steadied the head office. The flow of 6,537 barrels might have been an aberration that occurred from time to time. Ten days later the flow decreased to a mere 100 barrels; and by November 27 the flow had ceased except for a strong showing of gas. They were, Davies reported, killing the well with mud while they began drilling at Dammam 2, close by. By June 20, 1936, Dammam 2 was producing 335 barrels a day. Good, but not good enough for San Francisco. A week later it produced at the rate of 3,840 barrels a day. Excellent. Then the crew had to shut Dammam 2 down — the storage tanks were full. But the effect on San Francisco was important; it loosened San Francisco's purse strings. They authorized drillings to begin at Dammam 3, 4, 5, and 6 in order to test a much larger area on the dome. But then the summer arrived, and it became too hot to continue work. It was a

> bleak and unlovely place for a man to live — bald, treeless desert blinding with sun and heat. There was not a glass of beer nearer than

Bahrein, to which they were seldom able to go, and not a woman in all
Arabia at whom they would have dared to look. The temperature when
one arose of a summer morning around 5:00 would be perhaps 92
degrees, with a humidity so thick that the mere movement of dressing
soaked a man in sweat. After breakfast, as the sun climbed and the
thermometer rose upward towards its top limit of 125 — once an engineer near the Iraq Neutral Zone read 132 degrees on the thermometer at noon — the humidity fell a little, and at 110 or 115 one often felt
cooler than in the early morning. But still it was no Sunday school
picnic to work a full shift with our clothes soaking wet, your whole body
itching and burning with prickly heat, your skin chafed raw under the
belt, and your head aching with the clang of the fierce sun.[25]

Whereas the bits at Dammam 1 had gone down to 3,200 feet without
real result, the flow at Dammam 2, which had produced so encouragingly, suddenly "went wet" — 225 barrels of oil each day and 1,965
barrels of water. No. 3 produced no more than 100 barrels a day, and
the crude was unfit for any use other than as road oil. No. 4 produced
nothing at 2,138 feet. It was, they feared, a dry hole. At 2,067 feet, No.
5, too, was a dry hole. No. 6 produced only more disappointment: tar,
some gas, a little oil. Dammam 7 was spudded in on December 7:

> What it would find was, by then, anyone's guess, but they all knew it had
> better show something. Time was running out at San Francisco, where
> the chiefs had only lately been so bullish. But confidence never really
> completely expired. There had to be hydrocarbons in the Dome. That
> had been shown by the performances of 1 and 2.[26]

Purchased by the company when No. 2 blew in and San Francisco's
confidence rose, the first air-conditioned, two-bedroom mobile cottages arrived, as did the first wives: Annette Henry from Syria and
Nellie Carpenter from Bahrein. Landing at Hasa, they were taken out
to the new cottages, which were squatting "baldly on the stone and
sand, without a bush, a spear of grass, a weed even. Their view was of a
lone derrick among the bare jabals, a fence enclosing an acreage of
scorched earth, a cluster of gaunt power poles. Never were two women
more appreciated, respected and revered."[27] Others arrived in September. Edna Brown, Erma Witherspoon, Patsy Jones, and Florence Steinecke arrived on the British-India steamer from Bombay. The camp
cooks, Chow Lee and Frank Dang, brought them their first dinner in
Arabia, chow mein and bread. There were anxious meetings about
whether they should wear veils when they left camp. Nobody knew what
the law was, so the answer was yes.

Operations on Dammam 7 began anew on July 6, 1936 — it seems
there was no summer leave that year. Nor was the company cheered by

Davies's cable stating that five Saudi workers were injured in a dynamite explosion in November 1936. And there was labor trouble at the company's operation in Bahrein, which might have repercussions at Dhahran. There, the police, angered at allegations that they had been stealing company property, began to show "a considerable truculence on occasion, and a willingness to manhandle Americans they caught in some misdemeanor or other. Violence was their heritage, a camel stick their natural form of argument. The camp was on edge . . . for fear some flare-up like the Haenggi incident of 1935 might bring the whole structure of compromise and mutual forbearance down around their ears."[28]

As the crews labored, Fred Davies was recalled to San Francisco where he remained for much of the spring and summer. Max Steinecke followed. There was to be a conference: should they keep operations going, or should they pull out? Texas Oil joined Standard Oil of California in a consortium to keep operations going in Arabia. At 222 Bush Street, Davies met with the board to decide whether to abandon operations in Arabia. The company was rumored to have spent some $15 million by now, and all they had to show for it was the promise of Dammam 2 and 7. (In fact, the company would spend $1.75 million on drilling before paying oil was discovered, and in all, by September 30, 1938, they would spend a total of $8.5 million on the entire enterprise.)[29]

When Davies and Steinecke appeared before the board in San Francisco, company executives spoke of the difficulties and high costs of operations at Dammam dome. The company had pulled out of foreign wildcats before; it could pull out of this one, too, and perhaps should before more millions went down the hole to join those already poured in. "The expense of Arabia had already run to a good many million dollars, and in late 1937 and early 1938 dollars did not grow on trees. The stock market was nearly as low as it had been at the bottom of the Depression. . . . They pinned Steinecke down. What did he honestly think of prospects?"[30]

Steinecke, of course, "did not like to recommend drilling until he had convinced himself that the gamble was justified. But once he was convinced, he never took refuge in scientific caution. . . . He was never embarrassed or hesitant about changing his opinion if new data proved him to be wrong."[31] But during his explorations Steinecke had encountered three strong prospects: Dammam, Abqaiq, and Abu Hadriya. He briefed the board on these prospects. They listened respectfully, for the "terrible tycoons" did respect Steinecke's scientific opinion. Having briefed them, they decided that a further meeting should be held on March 4, 1938, to decide whether the Arabian operation should or should not proceed. On that very day something remarkable occurred.

Floyd Ohliger, the camp boss in Arabia in Fred Davies's absence, sent a cable with mesmerizing news. Dammam 7 had blown back in and was producing oil at the rate of 1,585 barrels a day. Three days later, Ohliger reported that Dammam 7 was still producing, and at the rate of 3,690 barrels a day. That was the sort of music the Standard Oil board wanted to hear; the March 4 meeting proved to be not a wake, as Steinecke and perhaps also Fred Davies, had feared. Everyone began to congratulate everyone else on the courage they had shown in backing Arabia in the first place. Davies and Steinecke, too, were congratulated for their work and judgment. A tremendous moment in modern commercial history had occurred in Arabia. Dammam oil field had gone commercial, big time. Dammam 7's performance would be, in the long term, remarkable. Termed Aramco's discovery well, it would continue to flow for the next forty-four years until, in October 1982, it was shut down after producing 32.5 million barrels or, at 42 gallons a barrel, a total of 259 million gallons. Dammam 7 established the oil industry in Saudi Arabia.

The company began to pour personnel and equipment into Dhahran, changing the face of the desert. More buildings were constructed, including a headquarters, residences for families (designed for comfort in hot weather and furnished with a special cupboard to hold the alcohol-brewing equipment), improved bunkhouses for single men, shops, and storehouses. At Ras Tanura, about twenty-five air miles from Dhahran, the company began the construction of a large port, complete with a trellis quay that carried a railway line three thousand feet out into the deep-water area of the Gulf. On the quay was a ten-inch pipeline to carry oil directly from the Dammam field to a tanker tied up alongside the trellis.

Just as important was the encouragement this success gave to the crews on the Dammam dome and to the newcomers from the United States. Phillip C. McConnell, an early member of the enterprise, remembered that to the newcomers

> the desert of Saudi Arabia was a place of uncertainty, a place that presented, even threatened, entirely new experiences. The vastness of the open unending land produced a touch of awe, even fear. . . . Would it become a boundless prison, an unending monotony? To some the answer was "yes." But to the others the desert was a challenge and a

delight. In time, . . . the neophyte . . . would begin to see something in the great sweeps of rocky soil, in the majestic flow of the dunes, in the marvel of the night when the stars floated just beyond reach, and the moon turned the Gulf into a plate of burnished silver.[32]

Standard Oil's political agent at Jidda, William F. Lenahan, formally went to Riyadh to tell Ibn Saud that Dammam 7 had become commercial on October 16, 1938. He presented the king with the figures to enable the finance minister, Abdullah Suleiman, to calculate how much royalty Ibn Saud could expect to get in that year:

March 16	2,130 barrels
March 17	2,209
March 18	2,128
March 19	2,117
March 20	2,149
March 21	3,732
March 22	3,810
March 23	3,420
March 24	3,275
March 25	3,308

The list continued through April 22, when San Francisco cabled to shut the test down because headquarters was persuaded that the well was indeed commercial. By then total production was 100,000 barrels, and Ohliger advised in his monthly report that Dammam 7 could produce 2,000 barrels per day more or less indefinitely — and 100 barrels a day would have been excellent production in Oklahoma. At twenty-one cents a barrel in royalties, Ibn Saud's first check amounted to $1,523,648.[33]

The implications of this oil discovery were immediately apparent to the British, the German, the Italian, and the Japanese governments, the principal powers to be involved in the looming war. As a chief executive officer of Standard Oil of California, Otto Miller, told the U.S. Committee on Foreign Relations in later years, "When company officials first recognized the significance of the . . . oil finds it was immediately appreciated that its significance went beyond mere commercial implications. The finds were recognized as being of tremendous national importance to our country."[34]

There, on the Arabian shore of the Persian Gulf, were vast fields of oil. They were of special importance to the world's navies. Soon the European powers were vying for the wealth of oil discovered in Hasa. First, the Italians arrived. They had recently established a new domin-

ion in the Horn of Africa, just across the Red Sea from the Hejazi coast,
and Mussolini's agents were already seeking to expand Italian influence into Ibn Saud's territories. An Italian ship landed in May 1939
with a cargo of mule-pack artillery along with the ammunition the
gun would require for a sizable campaign. Whitehall sent members
of the British royal family, the earl and countess of Athlone, on a
state visit to Saudi Arabia, and they thereby became the first British
royalty to recognize Ibn Saud's dynasty. The Athlones were followed
by Standard Oil's main rival in the region, the Iraq Petroleum Company, then the largest oil producer in the world and a subsidiary of
that other giant in the Gulf, Anglo-Persian. They offered Ibn Saud a
good deal more than their 1933 bid — £100,000 gold and a rental of
£15,000 for exploration rights in parts of Arabia not yet spoken for.
Finance Minister Abdullah Suleiman did not bother to transmit the
offer to the king.

Japan also entered the oil sweepstakes. The Japanese minister at
Cairo, together with a geologist from the Imperial Geological Survey of
Japan and a secretary, were received by the finance minister, Suleiman,
in May 1939. The Japanese minister left almost immediately for an
audience with the king at Riyadh, to attempt to make a trade pact with
Ibn Saud.

> He left the geologist in Jidda to pump Lenahan [the Standard Oil
> representative in Jidda] with detailed and extensive questions on the
> oil operations [of Standard] and the stratigraphy of Arabia. Lenahan
> gave him freely whatever information was public knowledge, and none
> that was not. But he took no chances that the Japanese, hungry ... for
> oil, might buy something with a fabulous offer in Riyadh. He tele-
> phoned Floyd Ohliger, who was in Riyadh, to keep his eyes and ears
> open.[35]

As the British oil companies jostled with the Japanese and the Italians to gain the favor of Ibn Saud, the Germans arrived in the person of
Dr. Fritz Grobba, the German ambassador to Baghdad, rightly suspected of being the chief of the German intelligence service in the
Middle East. He was well received by Ibn Saud's private secretary Yassin
and adviser Gargani, and they had long talks on the question of Arab-
German unity and British iniquities in Palestine in supporting the
Zionists. Gargani made a special visit to Hitler just before World War II
broke out in September 1939.

The potential for German-Arabian cooperation was enhanced by
radio programs featuring Yunus al Bhari, an Iraqi journalist-adven-
turer who broadcasted from distant Berlin. Dan van der Meulen, the

Dutch consul, spoke of Yunus's "immense success" on Berlin Radio's broadcasts to the Arab world:

> His mordant tones were perfectly attuned to Arab ears and he quickly became the darling of coffee-shops throughout the Middle East. His heroes were the conquering Nazis and his butts the weakling English and their feeble allies. Germany was the real friend of the Arabs. In the Jews, did she not share the same enemy?[36]

In May 1938 the king, attended by a caravan of some twenty-seven hundred persons, arrived at Dhahran for a ceremony — the turning of the valves that were to pump the first oil into the first tanker. The president of Standard Oil of California, Bill Berg, and Torkild Rieber, chairman of the board of Texaco, received the king and presented him with a new Packard, bright red and completely equipped for desert travel. All the American women and children were presented to the king, Crown Prince Saud, and the viceroy of the Hejaz, Prince Faisal. All then went aboard the tanker, the SS *Schofield,* to be saluted by the ship's company, who were dressed in immaculate whites. In a tent city under the Dammam dome, Standard Oil of California and Texaco gave a banquet, and after much banging of tambourines and ululation by the Arab women, the king and Suleiman invited Lenahan to discuss a supplementary concession agreement.

What the Saudi government proposed, and what Lenahan accepted, was that for its excellent work on Dammam dome, the company would get a sixty-year concession to an area of Arabia of about fifty thousand square miles on the frontiers of Jordan and Iraq. Also, they would get a further sixty-seven thousand square miles in the south, backing up against the Saudi province of Asir, Yemen, and the British sheikhdoms in the Hadramut (a tract of land along the Arabian coast on the Indian Ocean). Further, the company would be granted two thousand square miles of the Saudi Neutral Zone, which was to prove as rich in oil as the wells of Hasa. The Saudis also reaffirmed the company's preferential rights in the central Nejd for sixty years. And so a total of about four hundred thousand square miles of territory was added to the company's original acquisitions — lands about the same size as California and Texas together. The company would pay the government £140,00 gold ($700,000), a rental of £20,000 ($100,000), and the sum of £100,000 ($500,000) when commercial oil was discovered in these additional lands.

The company built a small refinery at Ras Tanura to provide the Saudi government, free of charge, with the gasoline and kerosene it needed — kerosene, the Saudis' main fuel for cooking, was then worth its weight in rubies. The agreement was signed at Riyadh by Lenahan on May 23, 1939, and all agreed that the affair was a triumph for both the company and the kingdom.

Disaster struck on July 8, 1939, when the drill bit was down to 4,725 feet into what was reckoned to be the fourth-largest producing well on the dome, Dammam 12, a "gusher." The well had been "bottled up" from the moment of discovery, curbed "like a dangerous horse."[37] Dammam 12 was exceptionally dangerous, the more so because the hot season had come on. Davies and Ohliger were away on long leave, and so was the head driller, when Dammam 12 exploded in flames.

The three-man crew on Dammam 12 had no warning of what was to befall them. They were working on the derrick, inserting the perforating gun into the lubricator, when a sharp hiss sounded as gas under high pressure escaped. There was "a dull mushy Boom and a deafening roar like a waterfall or a hurricane."[38] Then came the explosion. Black smoke, shot with red and yellow flames, boiled up from about a mile beneath the surface as oil burned at the rate of, it was estimated later, ten thousand barrels a day for the next ten days. The flames blossomed upward until the derrick, 135 feet high, was engulfed and simply melted. The fire was under such pressure that it began to howl and scream. The two men handling the perforating gun, one American, one Saudi, suffered severe burns and died later that day. The third man, a Saudi, escaped without any burns.

The acting camp boss and chief driller, Harry Rector, had had no experience in fighting gusher fires, and neither had anyone else in the camp. Firefighting equipment, such as gas masks and asbestos suits, was scarce. The outbreak of the war crisis, between Britain and France on the one side and Germany, Italy, and Japan on the other, complicated the attempts to rush equipment to the scene. "For the 200 American men of Dhahran, isolated, remote from the equipment and expertise of experience professionals, the fire at Dammam 12 was a staggering challenge. It was one of the world's most spectacular oil-well fires. . . . Harry Rector, facing the worst emergency in the company's history, had not a single professional to call on."[39]

The summer heat in Hasa added a hellacious dimension to the disaster:

> On a mid-afternoon in July in the Eastern Province the heat does not beat down as it does in drier climates. It pours in a great engulfing tide, down from the brassy sky and up from the blinding rock and sand, and breathes like a steam boiler through every wind that moves. Even

with dark glasses, the eyes have trouble taking in all the light, and photographers, in the beginning, all think their light meters have gone crazy. The attention is inclined to wander, the body and brain to focus on minimum survival, on the mere exhalation and inhalation of hot wet air.[40]

The exact cause of the explosion was never determined. Somehow the perforator gun had gone off in the lubricator. The challenge of fighting the fire was heightened by the fact that, should the flames continue unchecked, the heat could fracture the master valve and the connections on the main casing. Then the well, which had cost a king's ransom to find and drill, would probably be destroyed. Other dangers threatened those at the site: Standard Oil's camp could be sprayed by burning oil, or toxic gas — hydrogen sulfide produced over the centuries in its caverns deep underground — could escape, and claim lives. Only recently in Iraq, a well had given off a large quantity of the gas, which then settled in a gulley. When some workers walked through the gulley, they were asphyxiated. Because of concern that such an episode might occur at the camp, the women were evacuated.

At daybreak, asbestos screens arrived from Standard's installation at Bahrein. The crew then attempted to get close to the fire, to locate its point of origin. They made a sort of Roman phalanx sheltered by asbestos shields, and then they advanced into the flames as their colleagues sprayed them with water from hoses, which kept the group wet and steaming. They saw the fire coming from a broken line below the master gate. But to get close enough to really fight the fire, they would need asbestos suits, more asbestos screens, extra fire hoses, fog nozzles, gas masks, and Bullard fresh-air masks. There was a good deal of this equipment at Abadan refinery just across the Persian Gulf and at Mosul and Kirkuk in northern Iraq. But this equipment belonged to the British firms, Iraq Petroleum Company and the Anglo-Persian Oil Company.

Rector wired San Francisco to get the head office started on plans to counter the fire by sending out the necessary equipment by air charter — a tremendously expensive operation. At the same time, Rector instructed an assistant to call the Standard Oil liaison in London, Roy Lebkicher, asking him to contact the head offices of the British companies at Abadan and the Iraqi oil fields and to order them to send the equipment. Also, Lebkicher was to charter an aircraft to transport whatever equipment the British could supply.

Lebkicher ran into difficulties, for in midsummer of 1939 London was in the midst of war jitters and was desperately preparing for anything. He couldn't get any equipment released in London, but by hunting all

over the United Kingdom, he and others in the London office managed to collect gas masks, asbestos suits and other gear and to put it
aboard a plane at Croydon within about 48 hours. . . . [The aircraft]
could only go as far as Rome, but Floyd Ohliger [he had arrived there
by air on his way back to Dhahran] there arranged a transfer to an
Italian plane; the Italians were remarkably eager to cooperate. The
British, harassed and in trouble, but not likely to permit Italians to fly
over and among their oil strongholds of the Middle East, intercepted
the Italian plane at Basra and took the equipment on from there. That
was July 13. Meantime, some asbestos suits, together with additional
fresh air masks, had been sent from [the Bahrein American Oil Com-
pany] and by Anglo [-Persian] from Abadan.[41]

Despite the influx of equipment, the crews fighting the fire suffered from heat exhaustion, which none at Dhahran knew how to treat
except by administering salt tablets. Standard Oil's plant in Bahrein
therefore sent Mollie Brogan, a registered nurse, with special medicines and supplies.

Having located the site of the fire and obtained adequate supplies of
firefighting equipment, three men dressed in the asbestos suits, linked
themselves together by steel cable, and shielded themselves with asbestos screens. Then they advanced into the flames and approached the
site of the fire:

> Before they were driven back, writhing and almost insane with the
> heat, they closed one wheel two turns; there it stuck. The control rod of
> the other was bent, and would have to be straightened out before the
> gate could be closed off. But the stuck one might yet be broken loose;
> they tried it again next day, four of them on a four-foot wrench, work-
> ing behind a bigger movable shield that the shop had built overnight.
>   With the hoses and fog nozzles spraying over their laboring bodies,
> and soaking the ground and the hissing, steaming shield, it was like
> working in the throat of a volcano during a cloudburst. But heaving
> together on the wrench, they broke the wheel loose and started it
> around, staying in the furnace blaze until it could not be borne an-
> other second. Then the control rod broke clean off, and they were
> dragged back to safety. But when they could look again they were
> cheered; the flame was definitely lower. They could not tell whether
> the roar was less or not; they had a feeling they would never hear
> properly again.[42]

As crews continued to fight the fire, that night San Francisco came
through with a plan that involved installing a "hot tap" on the well pipe.
After the hot tap was attached, mud could be pumped into the well to
seal off the oil shooting up from below. An engineer at the site was
assigned the task of designing the tap.

Meanwhile, news of the fire had spread, and certain experts were eager to get involved in this high-profile battle to subdue the flames. But the workers on site were proud of their risk-taking efforts and determined to complete the job themselves:

> The word had got around that not only was Anglo-Iranian coming in with men and equipment, but that Charley Potter, the drilling superintendant on leave in the States, had started by plane from Los Angeles to New York to meet Myron McKinley, the most famous oil-fighter in the world, [who] was on his way with a crew from Texas, and had announced that he was prepared to fly the Atlantic in a chartered airplane to kill the fire. This was not something many people had done in 1939, but the tired boys in Dhahran were not impressed. "Nuts!" Ed Braun is supposed to have said. "This is our fire." So while they owned it, they made the most of it.[43]

By July 15, a week after it broke out, the fire had been reduced to a quarter of its original size. Ohliger, by now at Dhahran, advised San Francisco that only one thousand barrels a day were now fueling the fire. McKinley never chartered his aircraft. On July 18, ten days after the first explosion, the crew put "the fire out like a turned-out light." They "sprang up from the ground, they turned to pound one another on the back; the shouting that for 10 days had gone unheard in the roar of the fire burst hoarsely into an abrupt stillness." Ohliger sent a cable to San Francisco: "Fire extinguished. Hole full of mud. Professional fire fighters not needed."[44]

Now came the reckoning. Two lives had been lost, about $500,000 of rig and equipment had gone up in smoke, the fire had cost the Saudi government some $2.2 million in royalties, and the company had lost earnings of some $10.5 million on the oil that had been consumed by the fire. Suleiman's only reaction was, however, to rebuke Ohliger with a warning: "Don't let it happen again!" The king was more appreciative of the firefighting effort. McConnell related that if he "had been seeking to determine whether the Americans could use alcohol without passing the practice to the Saudis, the Dammam No. 12 fire gave his government an opportunity to experiment. . . . Some special act of commendation was justified. Why not permit the Americans to import beer from Bahrain, *but for this victory celebration* only, and observe the results?"[45]

Ibn Saud met with the camp boss, Floyd Ohliger, and the king "emphasized to Floyd that this privilege was granted with the understanding that no Saudi would be permitted to touch even the containers of the offending liquid."[46]

The beer party was a great success, and the Americans took care that

no Saudis had any part in transporting or serving — to say nothing of
drinking — the beverage. Bolstered by his staff's responsible behavior,
"Floyd continued, at suitable intervals, to emphasize the American
desire for highly stimulating beverages, with the result that in March of
1940, a permit was granted for the continued use of beer by Americans
only."[47] But it was not long before reports leaked out that Saudi servants were sampling beer, as well as Scotch and bourbon. Soon the
Muslim divines forced the king to withdraw the permit.

Thus oildom went dry and the world went to war. Ibn Saud did so in
a significantly ambiguous manner. Australia and New Zealand declared
war on Germany immediately, and, although the South African cabinet
at first split, it did declare for war against Germany soon afterward. The
Dominion of Canada took a week to make up its mind to enter the war
on Britain's side. As for the British colonies, the Colonial Office announced with pride that all colonial territories had pledged their support, thus prompting the government to assume, across the board, that
all colonial peoples were content under British rule.

In the Middle East, Egypt and Iraq severed relations with Germany,
but, although Saudi Arabia had long been within the British sphere
of influence and had been pressed to declare for England, and it was
in Ibn Saud's financial interest to do so, the Saudi government made
it known only that relations between it and Germany had "lapsed."[48]
After September 1939, when he found himself in severe financial
trouble, Ibn Saud did conduct his affairs in a pro-British fashion, but
only when he began to receive important financial assistance from the
British. But even then, Ibn Saud did not declare war against Germany
until close to the end of the war, after he had begun to receive lend-
lease assistance from the United States and Great Britain, and then
only when the United States informed him that he should do so if he
wished to gain a place in the new United Nations.

Ibn Saud's ambivalence toward cutting off Germany may be explained by the fact that, just before the outbreak of the war, the king
sent an emissary, Gargani, Twitchell's former assistant, to see Hitler in
an attempt to obtain military and financial assistance from the Third
Reich.

[4]

PLAN ORIENT

ON JUNE 17, 1939, less than ninety days before the beginning of World War II, a Saudi Arab claiming to be an emissary of King Ibn Saud presented himself at the Berghof, Hitler's residence in the Bavarian mountains. The man was described as "the royal counsellor Khalid al Hud al-Gargani, special envoy of King Abdul Aziz Ibn Saud." According to the U.S. political agent in Jidda, Gargani was the "principal advisor to the King."[1]

Gargani was received by Hitler, the meeting having been arranged by Admiral Wilhelm Canaris, chief of the German secret service. His escort at the Berghof was a German secret agent, Werner-Otto George von Hentig, who had recently operated in the Persian Gulf states. A year earlier Hentig had met with Ibn Saud and had then gone on to Damascus to meet Gargani, the Arab of Tripoli who had escorted Karl Twitchell during his survey mission of Arabia of 1933–34. At Damascus, Hentig invited Gargani's views about a German plan to establish an Arab empire in the Middle East. He had also sought Gargani's views about the interest Arab leaders might have in an Islamic congress on this subject. Hentig had then toured Syria and distributed propaganda concerning German plans to settle the Arab-Jewish problem in Palestine — the burning issue of all Arab states, then as later.

At this same time another German secret agent in the Middle East, Fritz Grobba, the German ambassador to both Riyadh and Baghdad, offered German arms to Ibn Saud. Both Hentig and Grobba endeavored to form connections that would eventually raise the Arab world against the British and French empires, thereby depriving them of their oil supplies in the Gulf. Thus Gargani had arrived at the Berghof to talk politics and money with Hitler.[2]

Hentig recorded that Hitler received Gargani at 3:15 P.M. Gargani addressed Hitler in Arabic concerning the substance of a letter he had brought from Ibn Saud. After the address Gargani handed the letter to Hitler. During their conversation, Hitler stated that "he entertained warm sympathies for the Arabs for two reasons: (1) because we had no territorial aspirations in Arabia, and (2) because we had the same enemies." The two points referred to Britain's control of the Middle East in general and to France's control of Syria. Hitler elaborated on the second point by saying that "we are jointly fighting the Jews" and that he would "not rest until the last Jew had left Germany." Gargani responded by observing that "the Prophet Mohammed, who apart from having been a religious leader, had also been a great statesman, had acted in the same way. He had driven all the Jews out of Arabia."[3]

According to Hentig's account, Hitler repeatedly assured the envoy of his sympathies for the king and stated that he was prepared to give "active assistance" to Ibn Saud. At tea, Hitler referred to "the strong predilection which he had always had for the Arab world, gathered from his reading, since his childhood." Gargani continued in this rapport-building vein by raising the rather obscure question of what would "have become of Europe if Charles Martel had not beaten back the Saracens" and if the Saracens, "imbued with the Germanic spirit and borne along by Germanic dynamism, had transformed Islam in their own fashion." Hitler replied that "this line of thought" was "very remarkable," and on that note Gargani took his leave of Hitler just after 4:00 P.M.[4]

Hentig recorded that Gargani then met with Canaris and General Wilhelm Keitel, chief of the German supreme command. He stated that Ibn Saud considered the negotiations very important and wished to prevent the press from publicizing them. Hentig reassured Gargani on that score and then stated that Canaris and Keitel had agreed that Ibn Saud should be granted a credit of six million Reichsmarks to enable him to make an immediate purchase of four thousand rifles and eight million rounds of ammunition. Also, that sum would enable him to install a small munitions factory in the Arabian interior. Some light antiaircraft guns and armored cars would also be provided. The credit would bear an interest rate of 6 percent, which Gargani claimed to have accepted, the Koran's proscription against usury notwithstanding. The weapons and ammunition would be delivered as soon as possible and in a manner that would not conflict with a similar program that Italy, Germany's ally, had begun.

There seems no doubt that, for about eighteen months during the emergency just before the outbreak of World War II, Ibn Saud had dickered with the Germans and the Italians for a number of reasons: Hitler and Mussolini were known for their pro-Arab attitudes, Ibn Saud wished to secure German and Italian friends in the event that Britain lost the war, and Ibn Saud was desperately in need of money. His treasury was running dry through a sharp fall in the number of pilgrims who visited Mecca in the 1939–40 season. The head tax on the pilgrims was Ibn Saud's main source of revenue, and only thirty-seven thousand had visited the holy places during the season just passed, down from nearly sixty thousand during 1938–39.

Also he was seriously in debt. He owed some $200,000 to Philby's trading company in Jidda for Ford cars and Singer sewing machines delivered but not paid for, some $100,000 to Britain for arms purchases, $100,000 to Russia for a shipment of petroleum products in 1932, and about $120,000 to a Polish company from which he bought machine guns in 1930. He could not pay wages to his administration or army. But obtaining help from Hitler would have costs as well as benefits. There were signs that $750,000 held in his name by the Bank Misr at Cairo would be frozen, should he enter into a pact with Hitler through Fritz Grobba, who was at this time resident in Tehran, the main center for German secret works in the Middle East. Furthermore, a subsidy paid to him by a political party in Cairo, described as "substantial," would also be frozen. This subsidy went to Ibn Saud to help pay the capital costs of maintaining the pilgrimage.

Whether Hitler's government paid Ibn Saud the six million Reichsmarks is not known. But in August 1939, ten German five-ton trucks arrived at Jidda. Nothing arrived afterward, probably owing to the Anglo-French naval blockade instituted just after the outbreak of the war. Nor is there evidence of any further contact between Ibn Saud or Gargani with the Germans or the Italians.[5] But there is some evidence that, just before and immediately after the outbreak of the war, Philby made an attempt to enable Ibn Saud to insure himself against the consequences of a complete collapse of the pilgrimage once hostilities began.

In 1939, Philby went to London as Ibn Saud's "observer" at the British government's round-table conference on Palestine, called in a vain attempt to produce a settlement in the interminable Arab-Jewish quarrel over Britain's desire to establish a Jewish national home in Palestine. When the conference ended, Philby remained in London to attend the cricket season that had opened at Lord's. During that period

Philby met secretly with Dr. Chaim Weizmann, the Zionist leader, and proposed that if world Jewry paid Ibn Saud £20 million (about $100 million), then an important segment of Palestine could be partitioned so that the Zionists could establish a homeland there. The £20 million would be required to compensate and resettle the dispossessed Palestinians. Weizmann became interested in this proposal although he doubted that the Jews would be able to find such a large sum of money. But, he said, he was shortly to see President Roosevelt in Washington, and he would discuss the project with him. Philby undertook to discuss the project with Ibn Saud when he returned to Arabia.

The "Philby Plan," as the scheme came to be called, had far-reaching consequences involving Franklin Roosevelt, Winston Churchill, Ibn Saud, and Philby. Philby returned to Riyadh in January 1940 and resumed his place at court. He spoke to Ibn Saud about the plan, and the king's reaction was encouragingly ambivalent. Philby reported to his wife, Dora, who was acting as St. John's intermediary with Weizmann, that the king would "give me a definite answer at the appropriate time."[6] In the meantime, Ibn Saud directed, Philby should not mention the plan to anyone else. But when four months passed, Philby, believing that Ibn Saud was not interested, disobeyed his master's order and mentioned the project to the head of Ibn Saud's political office, Sheikh Yusuf Yassin. When the king learned this, he rebuked Philby most sharply. Philby heard nothing more about his plan, he assumed that Ibn Saud had rejected it, and he prepared to leave Saudi Arabia for the United States where, as the guest of Standard Oil, he was to speak in support of the America First organization, which was opposed to any American involvement in the war.

At the same time, with the fall of France in June 1940, he became dangerously outspoken when he appeared before the privy council to present his views on the likely outcome of the war. He announced that Germany and Italy would win, and quite shortly. So insistent did he become on this defeatist theme that Ibn Saud warned the British minister in Jidda. He also noted that Philby was headed for the United States, where he intended to spread his beliefs. The king had betrayed his faithful servant, and Philby's fat was in the fire. The British government was informed, and when Philby reached Bombay, he was arrested by the British security authorities and placed under close arrest aboard a British steamer bound for Liverpool, England. When the ship arrived he was transferred to Liverpool Prison, "the foullest jail in all England" by Philby's own account. On his release six months later, he was, as he complained, "exiled" in England until the end of the war.[7]

Following Philby's departure, Ibn Saud entered into negotiations with the British minister in Jidda, F. H. Stonehewer-Bird, to secure a substantial loan from the British government, which, together with income from oil, would enable his regime to survive. Since the British Empire contained a Muslim population larger than that of any other political entity, its tranquillity was essential to Britain's prosecution of the war. Ibn Saud was the leading political figure in all Islam, and therefore the British government responded favorably, if cautiously, to Ibn Saud's requests. Ships arrived in Arabian ports laden with Canadian flour, Egyptian wheat, and Indian rice, and in 1940 Britain sent a first tranche of financial aid, £100,000 gold, or about $500,000. In return the king professed himself to be neutral in the war, a profession that counted for much in the political warfare directed at Islam that broke out between Britain and Germany. In May 1941, Ibn Saud issued a royal decree to his subjects, forbidding them to become involved in any aspect of the war.

The king then made a request for an advance against royalties to Standard Oil. By mid-1941 the company had lent him over $5.5 million. But this was not sufficient, the king claimed, to maintain his economy. He advised William F. Lenahan, the company's political agent at Jidda, that he needed help large enough to substantially supplement British aid. If Britain would loan him $4 million each year, and the company $6 million, Ibn Saud would then be able to meet his budget of $10 million. Standard Oil replied that it would loan Ibn Saud $3 million with an immediate payment of $1.3 million, all sums to be repaid against his royalties from Hasa oil. Ibn Saud accepted this offer.

But at the end of 1941, Ibn Saud's plight worsened, or so he claimed, and it resulted in a serious situation, first involving Ibn Saud and Lenahan, and then the British and American governments. Standard Oil's management began to suspect that by helping Ibn Saud, the British intended to "diddle" Standard Oil out of its concession at Dhahran, an allegation that caused protracted trouble, eventually involving Roosevelt and Churchill. Next, trouble developed when Standard Oil declined to pay the balance of the $3 million loan. It had, it claimed, invested $30 million in the Arabian project with little to show for the investment, and its management decided that it could not, and should not, make any further loans.

Ibn Saud's attitude toward the company then became "strained and discordant," the U.S. government was advised, whereas his relations with Britain became markedly closer as the British poured gold and food into Jidda. Again Standard Oil concluded that the British had begun a campaign to corner Hasa Oil. At great risk, the company sent a representative from New York to Jidda to advise the king that it could not pay the $1.7 million due on the $3 million loan and that it was endeavoring to obtain the support of the U.S. government for Saudi Arabia. This, the king was assured, was being done "with all earnestness and diligence," and if the company was successful it would be possible "to increase the said loan to $6 million."[8] To that end, James A. Moffett, chairman of the board of Aramco, would go to see his "great and good friend" President Roosevelt.

Thus began a tangled affair involving Jewish causes in Palestine and American interests in Saudi Arabia. Officials of Aramco became ever more concerned as a German threat to the Persian Gulf developed.

As Winston Churchill recorded in his history of World War II, in July 1941, soon after the German invasion of Russia, the German army planning staff laid out future operations in the Middle East. It was called Plan Orient, and its intention was to overthrow the British there. As Churchill observed,

> Their major assumption was that the Russian war would come to a successful end in the autumn. If so — a big "If" — a Panzer Corps from the Caucasus of [Soviet southeastern Russia] would drive southwards through Persia in the winter of 1941–42. From Bulgaria, if Turkey were acquiescent, a force of ten divisions, half of them armoured and motorised, would traverse [Turkey] into Syria and Iraq. If Turkey resisted, double that strength would be needed and in consequence the plan would have to wait until 1942. . . . When the assault was made on Persia and Iraq, the Axis army in Libya would advance on Cairo.[9]

Churchill directed the British chiefs of staff to write their plans, taking into account Hitler's Achilles' heel — his oil supply. They were particularly vigilant, accordingly, about German clandestine activity in the Middle East, especially as it bore upon the Gulf's oil fields. The British army in the Middle East began a series of small but important military operations to neutralize the German and Italian secret services and to frustrate enemy preparations for military expeditions in several Middle Eastern countries. These operations included expeditions to the Italian colonies on the Horn of Africa and the Red Sea (January 1941), to Iraq (May 1941), to Syria (June–July 1941) and Iran (August 1941), and to Libya (May 1942). Though protracted, difficult, and costly in blood and treasure, these operations were successful. Thus, for the moment, Plan Orient had been contained. But Hitler had not abandoned it.

Thus, Aramco and its employees in Saudi Arabia were safe, for the time being. At Dhahran at that time, there were 371 Americans, 38 American wives, and 16 children. Arab and non-American employees numbered about 3,300. The most important ongoing operation was the production of twelve thousand to fifteen thousand barrels of oil daily, which was then shipped to Standard Oil's refinery in Bahrein. A small three-thousand-barrel refinery was built at Ras Tanura in 1940, together with a few family cottages on the sand spit. But although the refinery was started up in January 1941, it was shut down in June 1941.

Though the threat of German attack was minimal, by 1940 the Standard Oil enclave in the Gulf was still dangerously isolated. Wireless communications with San Francisco became difficult, and for a time impossible, when the British subjected Aramco to a special wireless discipline to avoid giving aid and comfort to the enemy. This proved most irksome to Aramco. But Ohliger overcame the problem by installing a wireless set in an Aramco boat, which was sailed into the Gulf beyond the three-mile limit when it had signals to send to San Francisco. This led to severe disputes with the British security authorities:

> For generations the British had thought of the Gulf as their private lake; they considered a monopoly of certain of their activities to be their right. The entrance of [the company] into the communications field, in order to protect the confidentiality of its private business, created waves that spread beyond the Gulf and into the higher levels of [the British government]. From there, the British concern was conveyed to the State Department, and from the State Department to [the company].[10]

Neither Ohliger nor the company had been surprised by the outbreak of war. Knowing that a world war might be beginning, the company had stockpiled much equipment at Dhahran. And as Wallace Stegner, in writing the semiofficial history of the war years at Dhahran, remembered: "It seemed plausible that the Axis, fully aware of the importance of Gulf oil to the British fleet, might have planted troublemakers, saboteurs, and possibly even armed groups in the area."[11] At the outbreak of war Ohliger pulled in all the geophysical and geological parties from the desert and put the exploration crews, with their cars and trucks, on patrol twenty-four hours a day around Dhahran and between Dhahran and the other wells, camps, and installations. Though they watched for such German operatives, the patrols never found any. Even if Axis clandestines had been installed in Saudi Arabia, it was unlikely that their presence would have gone undetected for long. For local political reasons, Ibn Saud had his "street eyes" posted everywhere, and the Bedouin desert telegraph was well known as one of the most efficient of all Saudi institutions. Even Arabs engaged in any suspicious-looking activities were reported to Riyadh by word of mouth or by the wireless stations that linked all the provincial capitals to Ibn Saud, wherever he was. He never moved unless he was accompanied by efficient mobile wireless equipment. Thus most of Saudi Arabia was under constant surveillance.

The British, too, operated an effective security system that prevented entry to the entire Middle East except through a few ports and airfields. Persons wishing to enter and leave the Arabian Peninsula, for instance, could do so only if they had papers issued exclusively at British consulates, and then only through two points, Jidda and Bahrein. If enemy agents were to land by parachute or small boats, they could not survive unless supported by preexisting cadres in Arabia, and, Ibn Saud always claimed, sooner or later he would discover their existence. Thus it was the daily challenges of working in Saudi Arabia, rather than war-related concerns, that occupied the minds of Aramco workers:

> Actually, after the first scare, the war did not affect them much except by the gradual choking off of their supply lines, and in the beginning that result was not too apparent. Other difficulties crept back to absorb them more — the routine problems of reconciling their heavily mechanized industry with local habits and with the local Arab representatives and police. Compromise and agreement were easier at the policy level . . . than between men in the field and the Saudi local officials. Here in the Eastern Province the contact was man to man, and since each man was the product of a culture profoundly different from that which had formed the other, there were inevitable incidents of misunderstanding, prejudice, conflicting notions of law and justice.[12]

Ohliger thus settled into a wartime routine in that small American enclave on the shores of the Gulf. For reasons related to the propagation of radio waves, war news became scarce. Therefore Ohliger was compelled to visit the British political agent in Bahrein, and he, at least, collaborated by sending a daily bulletin in the lighters that plied between Dhahran and Bahrein Island. The local Saudi officials, however, proved to be as difficult as ever. They still tended toward officiousness, exemplified in a serious matter that arose on December 19, 1939, involving a Standard Oil employee, John Ames.

Driving through the Dhahran camp at about sixteen miles an hour, Ames hit an Arab boy who darted onto the road from behind a parked tractor. Ames stopped within eighteen feet. Immediately it was evident that he was in big trouble. Ames took the boy to the camp hospital, where it was found that his condition was not serious; he had a broken leg and facial lacerations. But as Ames waited while the boy was treated, the Saudi police intervened and took him to jail. None of the Saudi officials involved had had any experience in dealing with such matters. While they consulted, across a thousand miles, with the authorities in Jidda, Ames remained in jail — a very unpleasant place. Eventually the case was settled, but it had another dimension that concerned Ohliger. As Stegner wrote,

> The possibility that an American might be subject to Shariah law was enough to make a man thoughtful. The Americans may have been largely ignorant of Shariah law but they did know there were some disturbing possibilities. . . . A small case . . . was not small in Saudi Arabia, where everything from food and housing to the most basic law of the land was under pressure along the frontiers of cultures.[13]

The Ames case also concerned Ohliger because it highlighted a trend in Aramco's dealings with the Saudis. They had begun to make difficulties for Aramco workers like Ames simply because he was American. Punishments meted out to American workers for offenses large and small seemed to get tougher during the winter of 1939–40.

To further complicate matters, a wave of pilfering began to irritate and worry Ohliger. Ordinarily, perhaps, petty theft would be considered a minor problem. A stolen chisel and the like could be easily replaced. But with the war, everything in the camp had become irreplaceable. As early as 1937, Ohliger reported to the Saudi government that "the heretofore innocent, aimless pilferage of company materials had reached such proportions that the company wanted the government police withdrawn." Ohliger knew, of course, that the pilferage was not "deliberate stealing but the simple assumptions of simple workers that a company as large as Standard Oil certainly wouldn't grudge a little item here and there."[14] Abdullah Suleiman, the finance minister, relieved the chief of police and replaced him with a much more cooperative one, thus easing the situation considerably. Yet pilfering continued to grow in prevalence until it could not be ignored, and in 1941 Ohliger complained directly to Ibn Saud. The effect was immediate. Punishment for theft was the severance of a hand; and by 1941 withered thieves' hands were hanging from the wire fences of the Dhahran compound.

In October 1940, the war reached Aramco's gates. To demonstrate Italian prowess to the Arab states, the Italian Commando Supremo undertook a small air operation during the night of October 18–19,

1940. A flight of four Italian Savoia Marchetti S82 long-range bombers took off from an airfield at Rhodes in the eastern Mediterranean. The flight was led by Ettore Muti, a major in the Italian air force and a leading figure in the Italian Fascist movement — he was the secretary of the party and also a general in the Fascist militia. Each aircraft carried sixty-six fifteen-kilogram high-explosive bombs, and the object of the operation was to destroy the oil installations on Bahrein Island, the British protectorate near Dhahran. They thought, it seems, that the oil company was British and therefore a legitimate target. In fact, the Bahrein Oil Company was owned by Standard Oil of California.[15]

Major Muti led his flight team in diamond formation over Damascus, the capital of French Syria. When they located the coast of the Persian Gulf, they descended to about four thousand feet in preparation for the attack.

As they did so, one of Muti's aircraft became lost in some clouds so that only three aircraft attacked Bahrein. When they began their bombing run, the British airfield control on Bahrein heard the engines of the approaching aircraft and, in the belief that the planes were friendly, lit the runway lights to guide them in. The Italians dropped their bombs at 2:20 A.M. and believed that they had started large destructive fires. They were wrong. The fires they saw were in fact burning hydrogen sulfide gas flares, which characterized all oil fields in those days. After the attack, the aircraft crossed the coast of Saudi Arabia and flew over the Arabian desert to Italian East Africa.

Not until later did the fourth Italian aircraft reappear and locate the Arabian coastline in the area of Aramco's installation at Dhahran. Observing flaring gas, and believing the flares to be fires created by the leading airplanes' bombs, the fourth aircraft bombed them. The plane then caught up with the other aircraft and landed in Italian East Africa at 8:40 A.M. on October 19.

On their safe return to Italy, the crews were received by Mussolini, who awarded them medals. A motion picture was made of their exploit, and much was made of the great fires, which, they claimed, their bombs had started. The reality was different. They had started no fires, inflicted no damage, and injured nobody at Bahrein, except for minor damage to a coke storage area. At the Aramco installation, bomb fragments from the fourth aircraft punctured a flowline, causing crude oil to run downhill at al-Salamah. But the damage was slight and caused no fire. When the Italians' celebrations had died down, the Italian foreign ministry sent apologies to both Saudi Arabia and the United States.

The raid's real achievement was psychological. That the Italians were able to fly such a long distance — they claimed that their flight was in excess of forty-six hundred kilometers — without interception caused alarm among the Americans at Dhahran. Moreover, Italian operations in Greece and Egypt seemed to presage an effort to establish forces in Syria, Iraq, and perhaps Iran. The Italians seemed also to be considering operations from Libya to close the Suez Canal. Therefore Standard Oil evacuated the women and children living at Dhahran. Many men followed, and the workforce dribbled away until only about eighty men were left.

Concern for the safety of Aramco personnel intensified when, in 1941, German general Erwin Rommel arrived in Cyreneica with the German Afrika Korps; his mission was to seize Egypt and then advance to the Gulf. German intentions became clearer when a special instruction from Hitler to German political and secret agents in the Middle East was captured:

> The Arab Freedom Movement is, in the Middle East, our natural ally against England. In this connection, the raising of rebellion in Iraq is of special importance. Such rebellion will extend across the Iraq frontiers to strengthen the forces which are hostile to England in the Middle East, interrupt the British lines of communication, and tie down both English troops and English shipping space at the expense of other theatres of war. For these reasons I have decided to push the development of operations in the Middle East through the medium of going to the support of Iraq.[16]

He concluded his statement: "Whether and in what way it may later be possible to wreck finally the English position between the Mediterranean and the Persian Gulf, in conjunction with an offensive against the Suez Canal, is still in the lap of the gods. . . ." As to Iraq, Hitler ordered his staff to "see how and with what he could 'give rapid support by all possible means to Iraq's struggle against the British.'"[17]

The attack by the Italians and knowledge of Hitler's goals in the Middl e East prompted Ohliger to develop an escape plan and a means of denying the Arabian oil fields to the Germans in case they reached the head of the Persian Gulf. Ohliger and his eighty or so colleagues, plus two female nurses, decided that the best escape route lay across Arabia into the British crown colony of Aden, in the southwestern corner of Arabia. Aden was well defended by the British. It had a major port and an airfield from which the crew could be evacuated to Kenya. There the British trans-African air route still operated to Accra on the Atlantic coast of Africa and thence to the Americas. How to get to Aden presented the main difficulty.

Ohliger developed a scheme in which he and his party would march the five or six hundred miles of unmapped, roadless Arabian territory between Dhahran and the British province of the Hadramut on the south Arabian coast. But getting to Aden from Dhahran required a march through Layla and thence across the Empty Quarter into the Hadramut.

Layla was the capital and main market town of the Aflaj, a most forbidding region on the edge of the Empty Quarter and the seat of Ibn Saud's regional governor. As Philby had reported after his exploration of the area in 1933, it was a place of dour and unreconstructed Ikhwan and had been the scene, in 1918, of the last serious revolt against Ibn Saud — by Ibn Saud's brother-in-law, Saud ibn Abdul-Aziz ibn Saud, husband of his beloved sister, Nura. A reactionary xenophobe and a religious fanatic, he had accused Ibn Saud of permitting foreign infiltration (Philby) of the stronghold of Islamic culture. Ibn Saud mounted a military expedition to put his redoubtable relative in his place. On entering Layla, Ibn Saud's troops beheaded a number of his brother-in-law's followers, but not Saud ibn Abdul-Aziz ibn Saud. He received a free pardon. The remainder of his supporters fled to Mecca and to the court of Ibn Saud's greatest enemy, King Hussein, the Hashemite overlord. Ibn Saud then returned to Riyadh with his brother-in-law.

But the people of Layla and the surrounding area never really accepted Ibn Saud. The region remained hostile to foreigners and to any strangers — even other Arabs and Muslims. Ibn Saud considered the area so dangerous that he allowed no American to travel there without his express permission.[18] Philby, while still in Saudi Arabia, advised Ohliger that the tribesfolk had not changed at all since he had visited them, and he stressed that the Americans should not go there unless accompanied by troops and a personal agent of the king.

Ohliger made sure that his staff would be well equipped for a possible desert trek. In the transportation yard, large tank trucks were kept ready, loaded with gasoline and water. Each American reported to a designated leader and was assigned to a given house, where victuals sufficient for one group were stored. Each group was assigned to certain trucks and other vehicles. Each truck was supplied with tools and spare parts such as fuel pumps and rear axles and the mechanical and carpentry supplies required for a terrible journey in a terrible climate. Personal luggage was limited to a single piece per person. Radio trucks would be included in each caravan; and the Aramco medical department furnished suitable medical supplies. The medical services had a truck in each convoy; and each truck and its gear were regularly inspected. Although all Americans must have been aware that plans for escape were being made, "the details of the plan were very secret, with possibly seven or eight persons familiar with all phases. . . . rumors [were] thick as sand in a windstorm."[19] But Ohliger was ready, should the need for escape become real.

Ohliger knew only too well the potential problems that the people of Layla could present, based on the experience of a team of Aramco workers who in 1939–40 had mapped 175,000 square miles of the concession area, principally in the remote northern edge of the Empty Quarter. In addition to their study of the region's geology and the locations of towns and villages, they soon also discovered the "reactionary xenophobic and religious fanaticism of remote tribal leaders in Saudi Arabia."[20]

This team had set out from Dhahran in April 1939, and it remained in the desert until the end of the Saudi Arabian cool season in May 1940. It was sanctioned by the Saudi government and led by a young geologist, Thomas C. Barger, a golden lad of Standard Oil. Born in 1909, the son of a small-town banker in North Dakota, he had graduated with a bachelor's degree in mining and metallurgy at the University of North Dakota and had come within twelve credits of another in chemical engineering. One of the original geologists who worked with Max Steinecke in Arabia from 1937 onward (the years of Steinecke's tremendous oil finds), Ohliger decided to pass Barger through Layla, about three hundred miles south and west of Riyadh and located under a ridge of hills known as the Aflaj.

Barger found the tribesfolk in that area to be much as Philby had described them: "It should be realized that the vast majority of the people spend half their day in prayer and other religious exercise, and should not be dealt with as fully reasonable beings. Their vision is hopelessly limited and their souls sour with fanaticism." He was well aware that he was headed into a hostile region of Arabia and advised the U.S. diplomatic mission in Jidda that "this district has been and still is extremely hostile to all strangers."[21]

By the end of April, Barger had set up his base camp at Jabrin, close to the Empty Quarter. With Barger were five other Standard Oil geologists. On the personal order of the king, the expedition's escort consisted of fifteen soldiers, not the normal six, and the king's agent was Muhammad bin Mansur, chief tax collector of Hasa, where Aramco was located. Jabrin was a large oasis under the Taufiq mountains between the long ridge of the Aflaj and the Empty Quarter. Barger was well received by the tribes wherever he went, except in Layla.

On March 26, 1940, Barger received permission from the Saudi government to enter Layla. In a letter to his wife, Kathleen, he related how

> coming from the east across a very flat plain the palms of Laila showed up first as dark blobs dancing in the mirage. These gradually settled down to dark masses of trees as we approached closer. . . . The two main towns, Laila and Saih, are about three or four miles apart, separated by a belt of dunes. We crossed them and made camp on a sandy plain about a quarter of a mile from Laila. . . . Laila is the seat of the governor and the only town with a market place.[22]

They camped outside the town walls and its date gardens. In his official report to Aramco and to the U.S. diplomatic mission in Jidda, Barger related how their arrival was "watched by a curious crowd on the outskirts of the town, but thereafter during our three-day stay no one [from Layla] approached our camp except some Bedu from the desert." That was unusual, and later their Arab escort suspected that they had been told to ignore the Americans by "a venerable and unreconstructed Wahhabi leader and fanatic, Sheikh Abd al-Aziz ibn Baz, who preached openly that the King had betrayed his trust by selling the land to the *Aganabi* [foreigners]." Abu Baz knew this because "he had seen Americans take over and cultivate land at El Kharj," not far from Layla. There, the Americans "employ and discharge Saudi Arabian workmen at will, build canals and use the precious water as they please." Was it right, Baz was asking rhetorically, "for the King to sell our land and our birthright to the Unbeliever?"[23]

Barger sent the captain of his escort, Abdul Aziz, a son or a nephew of Ibn Saud's brother-in-law, into the town to make Barger's salaams to the governor. When he returned an hour before sunset prayers, Abdul Aziz told the party that they had been invited to dine with Layla's governor. So they changed to Arab clothes and made their way through the unlit, narrow, empty, and silent alleys of the town, escorted by the Saudi troops. But to their surprise they found that the governor, their host, had "gone to Riyadh on business." They were met instead by his son.

> We arranged ourselves along the wall of a large courtyard covered with carpets and lighted by a few kerosene lanterns. As headman of our party, I sat beside the [governor's] son . . . whom we addressed in the third person as "O Emir."[24]

But they soon discovered that the governor had not been called to Riyadh and was still in the town. Barger assumed that he did not wish to meet them and was surprised by this seemingly unusual discourtesy, the more so since Barger was accompanied by the king's agent, the tax inspector of Hasa, and a man of royal blood, Abdul Aziz. In another potentially significant breach of typical practice, the governor's son did not join in eating with his guests. So they ate alone from "the broken-up carcasses of a whole sheep and numerous chickens. . . . When we finished we wished the blessings of God on our host who replied in kind, washed up and left."[25]

On the next day they visited ruins of castles in which a legendary Arabian king had, according to Philby when he visited the ruins in 1936, "stabled his horses and kept his women and eunuchs in a paradise of orgies."[26] Tribesfolk at Saih, more courteous than the people of Layla, told Barger that the castles had been destroyed by fire from heaven as punishment for the sins of its king — a fate, Barger learned from them, that was recorded in the Koran. It was also the site of "black pearls" that had once belonged to the legendary king. Barger examined some and concluded that they had resulted from a heavy shower of meteoric iron that, on falling, had created craters in which kinetic energy had generated heat and violent explosions. The "pearls" were grains of silica, coated black in the process. (A large, handsome piece of the iron mass decorated the forecourt of Riyadh University.)

That evening the team returned to Layla and ate supper with the chief of their escort, Abdul Aziz. Again they dined alone in circumstances that were

> chiefly noteworthy for the display of the sheep on our platter. The sheep's head was placed upside down so the jaws were flopped wide open. Johnny Thomas was particularly taken with the one-handed wrestling with the intestines which showed remarkable toughness and elasticity. Then [an Arab in Barger's expedition] had quite a struggle popping out one of the sheep's eyes. . . . It was just as well that the light was dim.[27]

For the first time, Barger felt uncomfortable in Arabia. As he wrote, "One might have thought that the town was deserted. We later found that the people had been ordered to stay away from us." Though it was said that the townsfolk of Layla declined to extend salaams to all strangers, the troops of the escort "considered this to be an affront not only to themselves but also to Ibn Saud, as they were his representatives."[28]

(There were a number of sequels to Barger's account of the xenophobia of the tribesfolk. In about November 1943, an American military aircraft crash-landed somewhere in the southeastern corner of the Arabian Peninsula — precisely where was never revealed — and those aboard were mutilated and left to die. Another incident concerned complaints from Sheikh Abu Baz at Layla, stating that the king was selling lands to the infidels. The king summoned him to Riyadh and, plying him with well-attested cases of the Prophet's employment of Christians and other non-Muslims, at least temporarily placated the desert zealot concerning the presence of Americans in Saudi Arabia.)

In May 1940, having spent seven months in central Arabia, Barger returned to Dhahran and concerns about the world war. With all his reports and findings in, Barger prepared to leave Oildom for the United States to report and to take his long leave. He was booked to sail for the United States from Bombay on July 10, although the actions of Italy in the war might make his passage uncertain. On June 10 Italy had declared itself to be at war with Britain and France, increasing the possibility that Italian forces in East Africa might invade Saudi Arabia from across the Red Sea.

On June 29, 1940, the British government announced that it reserved the right to take action if a hostile power occupied Syria; then the French government in Vichy, controlled by an agent of Hitler's government, broke diplomatic relations with Britain. Soon the British closed the Atlantic route. The Atlantic and the Pacific were now both closed to all but the most essential air and sea journeys.

On July 15, 1940, the British occupied Syria and Lebanon, thus bringing the war closer to Standard Oil's fields along the Arabian coast of the Gulf. On that day Barger left Bahrein in a British Imperial Airways flying boat bound for Calcutta. From Calcutta he flew to China, then to Hanoi, to Hong Kong, to Guam, Wake Island, Midway, Honolulu, and, finally, to San Francisco and his wife, Kathleen. Barger was fortunate; he had flown across half the world without hindrance during wartime.

At headquarters in San Francisco, there was debate about where Barger would be sent next. Kathleen made difficulties over his returning to Arabia, at least until the war was over. But, convinced by the pleas of Max Steinecke, she gave in, and Barger returned to Saudi Arabia.

He arrived in Dhahran in autumn 1941, where he was appointed chief of the government relations section of Aramco's management, the branch responsible for political work between the company and the Saudi government. He had developed a great sympathy for the average Arabs — their short life span, the diseases that afflicted most of them, their poverty. Barger was both an exemplary Standard Oil employee and a visionary. But for the moment, he found himself immersed in the problems of the king's finances, which had been only temporarily abated, not resolved, by British subsidies. He also became involved in Standard Oil's attempts to stave off the British government's apparent bid to please the Saudis and thereby gain the oil concession. The king, the princes, and the finance minister showered him with requests that, given the wartime shipping situation, he could not meet — water tanks for the roof of a palace at Riyadh, electrical refrigerators, air conditioners, truck axles, electrical light plants, door locks, talcum powder, facilities for a picnic that Ibn Saud wanted to give for the sheikh of Bahrein. Who else but the company could obtain these things? Barger soon learned the first law of diplomacy in Arabia — how to say no and yes without making an enemy in the house of Saud. He also had to deal with a severe problem that could spark royal anger — British plans to destroy the Persian Gulf oil industry should the Germans come any closer.

Perceiving a threat to the Middle East developing from two directions — Libya and the Soviet Caucasus — the British established a committee at Kuwait to coordinate the defenses of the Gulf. This included the involvement of the Americans (although they were still neutral) in Saudi Arabia and Bahrein. From the end of 1941 to the end of 1942, Ohliger devoted himself to planning the many tasks involved in (1) denying the Saudi oil fields to an enemy power and (2) so destroying the key points in Oildom that the fields would be useless to the Germans or the Italians, should they appear in the Gulf.

In September 1941, before the attack on Pearl Harbor, Ohliger attended the joint Anglo-American conversations to decide how and when the Anglo-American oil fields in the Middle East would be destroyed. But Ohliger declined to do more than prepare the Arabian fields for demolition. He was fearful that if Ibn Saud learned that the Arabian fields were to be destroyed, he would retire the concession agreement. But at some stage Ohliger changed his mind. During this period, Standard Oil concerned itself with the destruction of the very plant and wells that it had built at such high cost.

They determined that an air attack would do much of the job itself:

> The steel connections of the oil wells . . . controlled oil and gas under enormous pressures that reach several thousand pounds per square inch within the oil reservoir. An enemy attack by bombing would provide an excellent opportunity for destruction of these surface controls, resulting in wild wells hurling clouds of petroleum . . . that could be expected to erupt into billowing flame. Not only would enormous volumes of oil and gas be lost but the reservoir from which they were escaping would be seriously and permanently damaged.[29]

But, if possible, the company wished to save the oil and simply make it inaccessible to an invading force. Ten of the sixteen wells at Dhahran were shut down and plugged with cement (which could be unplugged when the emergency passed). Six were kept open on the grounds that the oil drawn from them was required by Ibn Saud. Nonetheless, the six wells were set with special equipment by a British engineer so they could be destroyed, should that become absolutely necessary. All wells were protected from air attack by several hundred bags of dry concrete and drilling mud.

Destroying oil pumps offered another potential means of withholding oil from the enemy. "Oil, being a rebellious liquid, rarely moves to where it is desired unless propelled by pumps. An oil field without pumps has little value, and pump replacement in wartime should have been difficult if not impossible."[30]

British military engineers from Egypt provided Aramco with "the advice of specialists in making equipment useless in a hurry,"[31] including a new weapon, the thermite bomb, which when detonated produced such ferocious heat that all metal around it simply melted. A British engineer with a supply of the bombs was stationed at Dhahran, ready to install them if the Germans landed. He stored them in his room at Dhahran — which he kept locked. He also received the supply center's intelligence about the whereabouts of the German armies, so that Dhahran might not be taken by surprise.

Aramco employee Les Snyder represented Dhahran and the Bahrein fields at the fortnightly meetings of the special committee formed by the British to coordinate the destruction of the oil fields in Arabia, Iraq, and Iran. This committee met in Baghdad. Preserving company records was an important consideration at these meetings. They would be "vital in reactivating oil operations," and Aramco's reports regarding drilling — considered most essential — were shipped to the States. Engineer and well records would follow if danger came close. And the object of all was to "scorch the earth" if the Germans appeared. When and how this ultimate decision might be made caused stress and uncertainty:

> At what point in the foreseeable crisis should the decision be made and action taken to perform the great destruction? On what day, at what hour should the manager and his close advisors decide to destroy what they and their comrades had labored to create over the years? . . . If they were destroyed, the enemy might be repulsed and the destruction become unnecessary, and enormous labor and many millions of dollars would be spent to rebuild and redrill. But if they waited too long, the enemy would arrive before the destruction was complete, and the denial attempt would have failed. When should the decision be made?[32]

Such were the preparations, therefore, when another crisis developed. Although the United States had not yet entered the war, in August 1941 a conference of the U.S. State Department and the War Department "agreed to face the possibility within three or four months, possibly less, that a large part of the Middle East, specifically Iran, Iraq, and Palestine, would be under [German] occupation." There was, therefore, "the possibility of German political agents taking over Iran without a battle." America's neutrality notwithstanding, the decision was taken to send a U.S. military mission to Iran, one of its purposes to "place us in a position to observe and control any movement within the Iranian Army tending towards its use as a fifth column in the event of a threatened Axis invasion."[33]

At this same time the British and the Americans entered into a period of close collaboration to restore British military and political security of the Middle East, particularly in the Gulf. Churchill told his generals that it was essential that the port of Basra in Iraq, with its large airfield, be secured for "the Americans are increasingly keen on a great air assembling base being formed there to which they could deliver [aircraft] direct [to the Russians]. This plan seems of high importance in view of the undoubted Eastern trend of the war."[34]

On August 25, 1941, British and Russian forces began to occupy Iran. This task took three days. The British and Russian armies had met in amity, Tehran was jointly occupied on September 17, 1941, and the pro-German shah, Reza Pahlavi, was compelled to abdicate in favor of his twenty-two-year-old son. Under British pressure, the new shah established a pro-Western government.

The eighteenth day of the eleventh month, Dhu al-Quadah, according to the Muslim calendar, and December 7, 1941, by the Gregorian calendar, was cloudless as work began at Dhahran. At the manager's house, Ohliger had just finished his breakfast when Bill Jones, the chief clerk, telephoned and announced:

> "Floyd! The messages are coming in all over the radio. The Japs struck Pearl Harbor in Honolulu and raised holy hell."
> "Japs! You sure?"
> "I couldn't believe it either. But I've been checking with George and Charlie at the radio shack. They say the air is full of it. It's no mistake. The news is all balled up, but they hit Honolulu out at the Navy base at Pearl Harbor."[35]

Only the day before, Ohliger's group "had been a small outpost of an American industrial organization, joined to the San Francisco parent by steamship and plane and radio. The day after the attack, . . . their home ties were severed . . . except by radio. Food, tools, other supplies might trickle in — or might not." The first radio communication received from San Francisco, to Ohliger at the radio shack, came two days after the Honolulu attack with "tolerant amusement, in code, and labeled 'strictly confidential.' It advised Ohliger of the attack on Pearl Harbor and that 'a state of war exists between the United States and Japan.' Inasmuch as the air had been full of nothing else for the previous two days, the need for secrecy seemed a bit superfluous."[36]

Radio became the lifeline of the Standard Oil installation in Saudi Arabia. In effect, mail communications ceased. "American ships and planes, no longer being neutral, were subject to attack and destruction. They were drawn from their commercial routes and used where they were most needed." Radio messages transmitted news of the war and industry-related information from San Francisco, but perhaps most important, they helped maintain morale:

> Uncertainties regarding a man's critical domestic problems might be adjusted or removed by a brief statement of assurance. Mother's appendix had been removed successfully and transferred to a pickle jar. The check for the mortgage money had been negotiated, and that nasty mortgage holder had been foiled.[37]

Although the British actions in Libya, Syria, Iraq, and Iran had temporarily nipped Plan Orient in the bud, Hitler lost none of his interest in the plan. He told the Japanese ambassador in Berlin — the British were reading the ambassador's Berlin–Tokyo signals — an object of the German campaign in South Russia in the spring of 1942 would be "to resume the offensive towards the Caucasus as soon as the weather allows. . . . We must reach the oil fields there and also in Iran and Iraq. Once we have got there we hope that we can assist the rise of the freedom movement in the Arab world."[38]

And in June 1942 it seemed that Plan Orient might be about to succeed, when Rommel demolished the British main force in the defense of Egypt, the Eighth Army. In the confusion of retreat back to the Egyptian frontier, the British lost their main fortress in Libya, Tobruk, which provided Rommel with a good port through which to support his advance into Egypt. Churchill was being entertained at the White House when news of the defeat came in. British casualties numbered some seventy-five thousand men, including the thirty-three thousand at Tobruk. The army lost great quantities of stores, and the remaining forces fell back to El Alamein, only seventy-five miles from Alexandria.

Doubting that the British command would be able to repulse Rommel at El Alamein, the British navy evacuated their fleet from Alexandria and retired to the Red Sea. The British authorities in Cairo began burning their archives on a day that history remembers as "Ash Wednesday"; it was believed in Washington that Rommel would take Cairo by June 30 and then gain the huge Middle East supply center in the Suez Canal zone near Ismailia a few days after that. General George V. Strong, chief of U.S. military intelligence, warned that it would be a matter of a week or less before the British experienced a huge catastrophe: the establishment of the Middle East as a German fiefdom. Strong recommended that the United States send no more supplies to Egypt "until the military situation becomes clarified."[39]

General George C. Marshall, Roosevelt's principal military adviser, predicted that, after doing his best to destroy the huge British military garrison in Egypt, Rommel would "move to take Cyprus, thence into Syria, and finally across Mesopotamia and down to the head of Persian Gulf." The "British Eighth Army (after blocking the Suez Canal) would probably have to retreat southward along the Nile into the Sudan." Marshall advised, too, against trying to hold the Middle East if Egypt was lost, declaring that a major American effort in that region would "bleed us white." Meanwhile, he was concerned with "evacuating American units and destroying American equipment left behind."[40]

The British were also predicting disaster. General Sir Alan Brooke, the chief of the Imperial General Staff, warned Churchill of a "serious threat" in the Persian Gulf. Egypt should be abandoned and American and British power should "concentrate on the defence of the Persian Gulf."[41]

Rommel's victory sent a violent shock wave through the Anglo-American leadership everywhere, even down to the level of Ohliger and Barger at Dhahran. To intensify the sense of menace in the Gulf, as Hitler opened his summer offensive in Russia in June 1942, powerful armored corps drove one thousand miles from Rostov into the foothills of the Caucasus. Hitler personally took command of this offensive, and advanced units reached the Caspian Sea and planted the German flag on the pinnacle of Mount Elbrus, the highest mountain in the Caucasus and the divide between Europe and Asia.

Mesmerized by Rommel's advance, Hitler wrote to Mussolini that if "Egypt could be wrested from England" as the German army seized Sebastopol in Crimean Russia, "the consequences of such a stroke would be of world-wide consequences." The "whole Eastern structure of the British Empire" would fall. Hitler wrote further to Mussolini on August 4, 1942, to ask him to deploy his three crack alpine divisions to

the Caucasus front to assist his Bavarian mountain troops. Hitler concluded, "I fervently hope that in a few weeks Russia will have lost her
most important source of petrol supplies, while in consequence our
own disastrous lack of these supplies will be definitely eliminated."[42]
Mussolini is said to have flown to Libya with a white horse, intending to
ride it at the head of his army when it entered Cairo. (He was, however,
denied that supreme moment.)

Miraculously, the German advances stopped in both Libya and the
Caucasus — both at the same time and both for the same reason, the
failure of oil supplies. In Libya, the British command had one advantage over Rommel: it was reading his wireless communications at will
between Rommel's headquarters, the Italian Commando Supremo in
Rome, and Hitler's headquarters in East Prussia. Thus aware of the
cargo contained in Rommel's seatrains, the British in Egypt began to
pick off tankers and ammunition ships. By October 1942 the British
had rebuilt the Eighth Army in readiness for a major counteroffensive,
while Rommel, still powerful but suffering from severe shortages of
motor fuel and ammunition, had become greatly disadvantaged.

On October 23, 1942, the British opened their counteroffensive
at El Alamein. Rommel's Afrika Korps was destroyed in what proved to
be one of the two decisive battles of World War II (the other was the
Soviet counteroffensive at Stalingrad), and Rommel began his long
retreat to Tunis. As he did so Anglo-American armies landed in the
French North African states of Algeria and Morocco to launch Operation Torch.

Roosevelt marked the occasion with a proclamation intended to
bring the Islamic states over to the side of the Allies. In the light of U.S.
involvement in Arab affairs for the rest of the twentieth century, it has
political significance and interest:

> Praise be unto the only God. In the name of God, the Compassion-
> ate, the Merciful. O ye Moslems. O ye beloved sons of the Maghreb.
> May the blessing of God be upon you.
> This is a great day for you and us, for all the sons of Adam who love
> freedom. Our numbers are as the leaves on the forest trees and as the
> grains of sand in the sea.
> Behold. We the American Holy Warriors have arrived. We have
> come here to fight the great Jihad of Freedom.
> We have come to set you free. We have sailed across the great sea in
> many ships, on many beaches we are landing, and our fighters swarm
> across the sands and into the city streets, and into the wide country
> sides, and along the highways.
> Light fires on the hilltops; shout from your housetops, and from the

high places, and say the sound of the drum be heard in the land, and the ululation of the women, and the voices even of small children.

Assemble along the highways to welcome your brothers.

We have come to set you free.

Speak with our fighting men and you will find them pleasing to the eye and gladdening to the heart. We are not as some other Christians whom ye have known, and who trample you under foot. Our soldiers consider you as their brothers, for we have been reared in the way of free men. Our soldiers have been told about your country and about their Moslem brothers and they will treat you with respect and with a friendly spirit in the eyes of God.

Look in their eyes and smiling faces, for they are Holy Warriors happy in their holy work. Greet us therefore as brothers as we will greet you, and help us.

If we are thirsty, show us the way to water. If we lose our way, lead us back to our camping places. Show us the paths over the mountains if need be, and if you see our enemies, the Germans or Italians, making trouble for us, kill them with knives or with stones or with any other weapon that you may have set your hands upon.

Help us as we have come to help you, and rich will be the reward unto us all who love justice and righteousness and freedom.

Pray for our success in battle, and help us, and God will help us both.

Lo, the day of freedom hath come.

May God grant his blessing upon you and upon us.

— Roosevelt[43]

There was jubilation among the company employees that Christmas of 1942. The siege in which they had been immured since September 1939 was being lifted as the German armies retreated from both the Caucasus and Libya, not to return. Plans for escape across the desert would not have to be implemented. Also, happily, wild duck migrating from Russia passed over the camp by the thousands. Some of them provided the excellent feast with which Ohliger, Barger, and their crews celebrated their deliverance from the German threat. Plan Orient had been defeated.

COLONEL EDDY

I N 1942, IBN SAUD began to warn Standard Oil of California that, through the collapse of the pilgrimage and the decline of royalty from the oil fields during wartime, his regime was at risk. The British were providing Saudi Arabia with perhaps $4 million a year, but he required $10 million each year to maintain his administration. Standard declined to help. Fearing that Britain's support for Ibn Saud revealed its intention to draw him into the sterling area (the financial instrumentality by which Whitehall ran its world empire) and that if this happened, the king would expropriate Aramco's concession and sell it to the giant Anglo-Persian Oil Company, James A. Moffett, chairman of the board of both the Arabian and the Bahreini operations, went to see his old friend President Roosevelt, on April 9, 1942.

Roosevelt warmed to Moffett's proposals. He asked for a memo, and on April 16 Moffett presented a paper asking the U.S. government to advance $6 million annually to Ibn Saud for the next five years. Standard Oil would deliver an equivalent amount of Saudi oil at "a special price" to the U.S. Navy. At the same time the State Department would ask the British government to increase its advances to Saudi Arabia. And as a sign of the company's anxieties about British intentions, Moffett asked Roosevelt to exact from the British government an assurance that it would not attempt to acquire any interest in the Hasa oil concession.

After much talk and many meetings, the secretary of commerce and federal loan administrator, Jesse H. Jones, who was hostile and suspicious of anything to do with oil companies, intervened. As he declared, "The national interest was not going to be served by extending financial assistance to a backward, corrupt and non-democratic society like

Saudi Arabia. Such aid amounted to paying homage to a self-styled monarch while at the same time using the government to support the interests of private enterprise." Jones insisted that Saudi Arabia was the political responsibility not of the United States, but of Great Britain. In Jones's view, and perhaps that of the secretary of state, Cordell Hull, it was evident that the Saudi government was attempting to "secure unreasonable advances of money from" the two U.S. oil companies by "persistent threats and pressures." The British, at the same time, were avoiding making any commitment about the amount of aid they would make until they were able "to determine how much the company would give." Aramco was therefore being subjected to a "squeeze play between the Saudi Government and the British," in which both were pressing the company to the limit.[1]

When Jones's point succeeded, Moffett formally asked Roosevelt and other officials to provide assistance to the king under the Lend-Lease Act. His proposal was rejected. The king, it was argued by Jones and others, was neither a democrat nor a combatant in the war with Germany and Japan and did not therefore qualify for such assistance. Then Jones, wearying of Moffett's persistence, told the president at a Cabinet meeting on June 18, 1942, that he "had no intention of making [Moffett] the loan." Roosevelt then gave Jones a note: "Jesse: Will you tell the British I hope they can take care of the King of Saudi Arabia. This is a little far afield for us. FDR."[2]

Thus the British government elected to make itself responsible for maintaining the economic stability of Saudi Arabia. During the next two years it advanced over $40 million to Saudi Arabia as grant-in-aid, containing no provision for repayment of either the interest or principle. Thus Britain became Ibn Saud's main benefactor. Ibn Saud thanked the British publicly and thus made it appear that Britain was the Arabs' best friend in the West — at a time when the Arabs had begun to believe that the United States was the Jews' best friend in Palestine. At a banquet at Mecca for leading Muslims making the hajj, Ibn Saud said,

> With gratitude we mention the cooperation and assistance rendered to this country by the British Government — for, were it not for God and the assistance of the British Government in arranging for supplies and foodstuffs and the necessary steamers for transportation of these, it would not have been possible for our Moslem brethren to find this abundance in this uncultivable valley.[3]

Suleiman, the second-ranking official in the kingdom, also remarked on British generosity during the hajj. Not often did Arab potentates praise Great Britain! Stung that Ibn Saud should publicly thank the British government while ignoring the part that Standard Oil had played in nourishing the king's fortunes, in mid-1943 the company resumed its lobbying campaign with the Roosevelt administration. Standard was assisted by several influential persons, including William Bullitt, undersecretary of the navy and no friend of England. He advised that

> the officials of [Standard Oil and Texaco] were much disturbed about the future security of their concession not only because of the normal insecurity in Arabia but also because they feel that the British may be able to lead either Ibn Saud or his successors to diddle them out of the concession and the British into it.
>
> American experts on Saudi Arabia are inclined to agree with this estimate of the situation. They point out that the Anglo-Iranian Oil Company had every opportunity to get this concession and, after examination, rejected it on the ground that there was no oil in Saudi Arabia — and have been regarding the concession with covetous eyes ever since the Americans struck oil.[4]

The Committee on Foreign Relations heard about the "adverse political and economic effects of our Government's policy of allowing the British to assume the position of chief financial backer and advisor of the Saudi Arabian Government. The consequences are becoming concretely manifest."[5] W. S. S. Rodgers, chairman of the board of Texas Oil Company, Standard's partner in the Arabian enterprise, and Fred A. Davies, president of Aramco, on February 8, 1943, sent a memo to the man chiefly responsible for oil in Roosevelt's Cabinet — Harold Ickes. It said in part:

> To further the cause of the United Nations in strategically located Saudi Arabia and in the Moslem world as a whole, the British government has in the past two or three years made substantial advances in cash and supplies. Such British assistance, made possible by the aid which the British government has been receiving from the United States Government, now totals in excess of twenty million dollars.
>
> In lieu of continuing these cash advances, the British government is now insisting that Saudi Arabian financial requirements be met by an internal note issue backed by the British Currency Control Board — the practice followed in British and British controlled territory.
>
> Concern is felt over the rapidly increasing British economic influence in Saudi Arabia because of the bearing it may have on the continuation of purely American enterprise there after the war.
>
> Direct aid from the United States government to the Saudi Arab government instead of indirect through the British as at present would check this tendency and give some assurance that the reserve of oil in Saudi Arabia will remain under the control of Americans; and conse-

quently remain available to American economy and to American naval and military forces of the future.[6]

At about this same time, mid-February 1943, the presidents of the two Aramco parent companies and Fred A. Davies came to Washington to appeal to the Department of State for direct aid to Ibn Saud. If Washington was willing to assist Ibn Saud, they would be willing, in exchange, to offer the U.S. government some kind of special access or option on Saudi oil. As that offer was making the rounds, Ickes lunched with President Roosevelt on February 16, 1943. He described the Saudi oil fields as "probably the greatest and richest oil field in the world" and that, knowing this, the British were trying "to edge their way into it." The British had never "overlooked the opportunity to get in where there was oil," and he reminded the president how "the air had been thick with the smell of oil" at the peace conference after World War I. Roosevelt had attended that conference as undersecretary of the navy and remembered well how the British had cornered Middle Eastern oil. There, for the moment, the question of Ibn Saud's finances rested.[7]

But in December 1942 in Jidda a meeting had taken place between Ibn Saud and the chargé d'affaires at the U.S. legation, Harry Shullaw, that was striking for its display of what tax inspectors call "conspicuous wealth." For two years Ibn Saud had been pleading poverty to all who would listen, yet he was still able to find the money for a display of power that surprised all who witnessed it. One such witness was a clerk at the legation, Clarence J. McIntosh, who wrote in a personal letter to his family a description of an audience with His Majesty at the Nuzla Palace:

> Amid flags raised above the Government houses and over Diplomatic establishments, and a 21-gun house-shaking and ear-splitting salute from the town's batteries, the King arrived in Jidda last Monday, December 7th, after a long trip from Riyadh via Mecca. His caravan consisted of some 5,000 cars, all American-made. His particular auto is a large red Packard equipped with all the latest innovations and handrails on the outside for his guards to hang on to. Others in his party were the 50 or so "sons," who are in reality Princes each having his share of cars and attendants. It takes 500 cars alone to move the Crown Prince. His wives and around 50 "daughters" also have a fleet of black, curtain-drawn limousines and hundreds of attendants.[8]

The American complaint about British activities did not go unnoticed at the highest levels in London and Cairo, the latter being the "second city of the Empire." It produced a major debate within the

British political and military leadership about Britain's role in the Middle East. The British minister resident, the highest British authority in the Middle East, wrote to his masters, the War Cabinet, a long paper showing that Britain had no interest in Hasa oil. He reinforced Britain's position in regard to the American entry into the Middle East, particularly on the rising question of their sending a U.S. military mission to Arabia:

> It is to the interest of the British Empire that America should have commitments in the Middle East. We cannot compete with her in financial largesse to Saudi Arabia, and there is no reason why we should object to her having a military mission there . . . so long as she consults frankly with us beforehand, does nothing which conflicts with our general defence scheme, acknowledges our primacy as representatives of the world security order in the Middle East, and gives us (on the ground of common interest in the peace and welfare of this region) her moral backing in the whole of that task. American goodwill and understanding will be important when we come to new settlements in Egypt, Palestine and Iraq, and we must try to eliminate the danger of rivalry with her in any field out here. . . . America is the only true partner which we shall find in building up a solid structure of social and military security in the Middle East. Her work in education and health has already been of great value to these countries. . . . Her major interests coincide with ours in that she needs security for the exploitation of mineral oil, aviation bases, and social contentment rather than unrest.[9]

According to this report, the only serious difference between England and America concerned Palestine. But, the ministry resident observed, there was much suspicion among the Americans that the British were trying to elbow in on the Hasa oil concession. This impression had to be corrected. As long as the Americans were willing to cede Britain's primacy in the region, their involvement in the Middle East ought to be encouraged.

As to the attitude of the British Empire toward Saudi Arabia, the minister wrote prophetically and shrewdly:

> The power and influence which Saudi Arabia can exert in Middle Eastern affairs depends on a single factor, the prestige and masterful personality of King Ibn Saud. This is now waning because of his great age, and it will vanish altogether when he dies. Saudi Arabia will then become another military vacuum. She seems likely to be rent by internal conflict, and a revival of Wahhabi fanaticism may cause some trouble on her frontiers.[10]

The foreign secretary, Anthony Eden, endorsed the minister resident's paper. "The American oil interests in Saudi," he wrote in a paper

intended to inform the British and American governments in July
1943, "are deeply concerned in the province of Nejd, which may well
become a separate and affluent state." Otherwise "so far as I can see,
the greater the American interest in any part of the Middle East, the
better for us."[11]

In April 1944, the British chiefs of staff also had something to say
about the American presence in the Middle East in regard to a possible
confrontation with the Soviet Union:

> Russia is a potential future danger to the Middle East area. Even if she
> could meet her total oil requirements from her own resources, she
> might still be tempted to look with envy upon the outlet to the Indian
> Ocean afforded by the warm-water ports of the Persian Gulf. To be able
> to count with justifiable confidence upon American assistance against
> this danger is an overriding advantage.[12]

Yet in spite of their desire for American support in the region, the
British had reservations as well:

> The British were fearful that the Americans would try to eject them
> from the Middle East and deny them even the oil reserves currently
> under their control. The region was considered central to imperial
> strategy and to the governance of India. Ibn Saud, as keeper of the holy
> places of Islam, was a person of very great importance to Britain,
> which, in India, ruled over the largest number of Moslems of any
> country in the world. He might also prove to be a most important
> factor in Britain's efforts to find a way out of the dilemma in Palestine,
> then a British mandate torn by mounting strife between Jews and
> Arabs.[13]

The deputy prime minister, Clement R. Attlee, a socialist who would
succeed Churchill as prime minister at the end of the war, felt that it
was essential that the Middle East question should be raised as soon as
possible and at the highest level. Rattled by what seemed to him to be a
diversion from the main issue of his ministry in Washington — winning the war with Germany, Italy, and Japan — on February 8, 1944,
the British ambassador in Washington, Lord Halifax, asked for and
obtained an immediate meeting with Roosevelt. Roosevelt saw Halifax
that same evening at the White House. Halifax voiced his irritation and
apprehension about U.S. oil ambitions in the Middle East; Roosevelt
responded by producing a map of the Middle East drawn by him in
pencil. Persian oil, he told the ambassador, is yours. We share the oil
of Iraq and Kuwait. Saudi Arabian oil is America's.[14] Halifax was not
satisfied. Given the American attitude toward the British in Persia at

present, there was no guarantee that they would not seek an oil interest there.

By spring 1944 the question of America's oil interests in the Middle East had become so muddled that the government decided to send an American oil expert to the Middle East and establish the facts of the situation. The expert was Everette Lee DeGolyer. A short, dumpy, and energetic man, at the time of Pearl Harbor he had become one of Ickes's chief deputies at the Petroleum Administration for War, helping organize oil production throughout the United States.

Arriving in Saudi Arabia, he inspected the Dammam and the Abqaiq fields. "We haven't seen anything but a pretty barren land on this whole trip," he wrote to his wife. "In fact Texas is a garden in comparison to some places we have seen."[15] The Aramco employees took him to three oil-bearing structures that had already been tapped in Saudi Arabia, with reserves estimated at 750 million barrels. But in visiting other such structures he formed the impression that the reserves would be far larger. The same applied to reserves in the other countries along the Gulf, especially those at Kuwait, Iraq, and Iran. On his return to Washington, as the great debate on oil proceeded vigorously, he made a report on the significance of the Persian Gulf oil fields:

> Given reasonable time and a very moderate amount of oil field mate-
> rial, any single one of these four groups [of Anglo-American compa-
> nies operating in the Middle East] can develop and maintain within its
> own properties sufficient production to supply world requirements.
> For the next 10 to 15 years at least, the Middle East is likely to develop
> and maintain a productive capacity of as much as four times its prob-
> able market outlet.[16]

DeGolyer reported further that the proven and probable reserves of the region — Saudi Arabia, Iran, Iraq, Kuwait, Bahrein, and Qatar — would amount to twenty-five billion barrels. Informally, he thought the reserves would be "much, much larger." He mentioned figures of one hundred billion barrels for Saudi Arabia and three hundred billion barrels for the entire region. He held the view that "the center of gravity of world oil production is shifting from the Gulf-Caribbean area to the Middle East — to the Persian Gulf area, and is likely to con-tinue to shift until it is firmly established in that area." And as oil historian Daniel Yergin wrote, "DeGolyer's words were more than just a eulogy. They were a prediction about a dramatic reorientation in the oil industry that would have a profound impact on the direction of world politics."[17]

Recognizing the importance of Middle Eastern oil, officials within the U.S. government sought ways to absolutely secure the Saudi oil concession and prevent the British from horning in on it. Reversing his earlier decision, Roosevelt determined in early 1943 that Ibn Saud would be eligible for lend-lease aid. This show of favor, it was hoped, would keep the Saudi king happy and the oil concession in American hands.

At that same moment, the State Department began to receive reports that seemed to contravene British assurances that it would respect American interests in Saudi Arabia and elsewhere. Secretary of State Hull decided to send a fresh and vigorous figure into the Jidda turmoil to reestablish American power and prestige in Saudi Arabia. The man concerned was Colonel Eddy.

Colonel Wilfred Alfred Eddy, lately of the U.S. Marine Corps and the Office of Strategic Services (OSS), was born in 1886 at Sidon, where his parents were missionaries. He grew up and learned Arabic there. His parents were not anti-British, as were so many American missionaries. Both were of British stock, and it is well remembered in the Eddy family that one of the fundamentals that Mrs. Eddy taught her children was that they "were hewn from the rock of England, never forget that." Late in 1943 Eddy resigned from the OSS to take up a State Department post as chief of mission in Saudi Arabia, to fully maintain America's prestige and influence in Saudi Arabia and ensure that British envoys were not attempting to subvert the American presence in Arabia. By the time Eddy was ready to begin his journey, the question of Anglo-American relations in the Middle East had assumed a serious aspect. Churchill felt compelled to write to Roosevelt that there was "apprehension in some quarters here that the United States has a desire to deprive us of our oil assets in the Middle East on which, among other things, the whole supply of our navy depends" — a question that, Churchill further advised the president, was likely to become "one of the first magnitude in Parliament."[18]

The president responded in unyielding and almost peremptory fashion. He agreed that "a wrangle on oil" between the two governments "must be avoided," but he was "disturbed about the rumor that the British wish to horn in on Saudi Arabian oil reserves."[19] The British were sure that the U.S. oil barons had begun to try to steal the Anglo-Persian Oil Company, just as those same oil barons believed the British in Saudi Arabia were trying to steal Aramco.

In December 1944, Colonel Eddy arrived in Jidda to take up his post. He was said to have "an enormous purse" — $70,000 — with which to establish himself. As he did so, serious allegations began to spread about the conduct in Jidda of the British minister, S. R. Jordan. Chief among the complaints about Jordan's conduct came from the U.S. Navy undersecretary, William Bullitt:

> The recent British move to set up a bank of issue for Ibn Saud, and the more recent act of the British Chargé d'Affaires in Jeddah — who just after our Minister, Mr. Kirk, had visited Ibn Saud, and promised him Lend-Lease aid, informed Ibn Saud that he could get further American Lend-Lease *only* by applying to the British authorities either in Jeddah or London — seem to indicate a desire to strengthen British influence over Ibn Saud at the expense of American influence, in a manner not quite healthy for the oil concession.[20]

Also, despite Foreign Office assurances that American interests in the Middle East would be respected, the American consul in Jidda informed the State Department that Jordan had persuaded Ibn Saud to dismiss various of his officials known to be pro-American.

Yet Jordan's own telegrams to London displayed little that could be interpreted as anti-American. To the contrary, Jordan himself reported that the Saudis were seeking to play the British against the Americans "in order to provoke an auction between rival benefactors." Jordan's advice was that Britain should get out of the bidding. "The Americans wish to sink millions of dollars in the sands of Saudi Arabia," he reported in September 1944, adding that "they will be taking billions out of the same sands in the form of oil. But I see no reason why we should be drawn into the vortex."[21]

But the allegations against Jordan persisted. The U.S. secretary of state Hull called the British ambassador, Lord Halifax, to Foggy Bottom and, Hull recorded in a memo on June 26, 1944:

> I said that our officials in the Middle East were convinced beyond peradventure of doubt that the British representative at Jidda in Saudi Arabia was doing his level best to injure the American Government's relations with the King and, in other ways, endeavoring to undermine the American situation, and that we just could not put up with this without constant and louder complaint.[22]

The ambassador requested that Hull's department heads "give his British associates the full facts on this point, and then he would be prepared to move in accordance therewith."[23] That ended Jordan's career at Jidda. He was relieved and transferred to a lesser job as a commercial consul at Jerusalem. Jordan's departure from Jidda, however, proved not to be the end of the troubles. Nor did it have much effect on Eddy's attitude toward the British legation. Jordan's succes-

sor, Laurence Grafftey-Smith, personified the corps d'élite who ran the
political affairs of the British Empire. Born in 1892, the son of a clergy-
man, Smith had had extensive political and linguistic training at Pem-
broke College, Cambridge, and, like Sir Andrew Ryan, he had joined
the Levant consular service, which maintained relations between Britain and the Turkish Ottoman Empire.

As Smith soon noted of the Anglo-American relationship in Arabia,
"In those closing months of the war America was becoming con-
vincedly aware of her imperial destiny" and had only to force Britain
and France out of the Middle East "for the desert to blossom like a
rose."[24] Whether Smith did or did not become infected with anti-
Americanism, he liked to point out the fact that his wife was an elev-
enth-generation American closely related to the former U.S. president
Calvin Coolidge. Yet despite his attempt to use this connection to prove
his solidarity with the Americans, by October 1945, official relations
between Eddy and Smith had become troubled. The situation had
become exacerbated when two members of the U.S. Congress, while
visiting Jidda, had asserted afresh the story that Britain had again been
trying to steal the Aramco oil contract. They also accused Smith of
using American trucks, jeeps, gold, foodstuffs, and other lend-lease
stores in this effort.

In response, Smith complained to the Foreign Office about the
many irritations he had suffered since Jordan's sudden departure:

> Mendacious allegation of British obstruction of American oil interests
> in Saudi Arabia especially needs full ventilation and denial. I believe
> that Americans used this bogey officially to obtain Congress approval
> for current lend-lease programme here. . . . American complaints
> about the lack of cooperation by British officials in Saudi Arabia are
> pathological in origin. Initiative in the aggregate has always come from
> them. They then consider our self-defence offensive and call for "door-
> mat co-operation."[25]

Smith's complaint did not go unnoticed at Foggy Bottom. A tentative
settlement was established in which American officials in Jidda became
responsible for economic relations with Ibn Saud while the British
remained responsible for political relations. There was confidence at
the Foreign Office that the Americans, for all their power and wealth,
would not be able to do without British wisdom and experience in
dealing with Arabs and, more particularly, Russians in the Middle East.
In the postwar world, Britain would be the Greeks, and the Americans,
the Romans. But this arrangement could not last. Neither did Smith's
appointment. It was terminated as ruthlessly as Jordan's when the State

Department also complained about him. As Smith wrote in a memoir, "Among American businessmen and in the Republican Party there are 'fairly clear ideas about a system of informal empire by which the United States would control economic resources without formal annexation.'"[26] This was his estimation of the diplomatic and financial moves that U.S. government and Aramco officials were making in regard to Saudi Arabia.

Smith was surprised to be recalled by the Foreign Office before his tour of duty was up. He had expected that, after Jidda, he would be sent to Baghdad as ambassador, a major post in the British system. Instead he found himself in the new state of Pakistan as high commissioner, a lesser assignment. This is how he came to explain his demotion: Years later, while he was "on an international commission in Khartoum," his wife was "informed by the U.S. representative of that time that I had a very good dossier at the State Department; but while in Jedda, I was more than once accused to London of being anti-American."[27]

Now, early in 1945, Roosevelt decided secretly to meet with Ibn Saud personally in Egypt after the Yalta Conference between the president, Churchill, and Stalin. Doubtless the king's recent anti-Zionist remarks about the Palestine situation played their part in the president's decision, and he did not wish by his statements and actions to jeopardize the U.S. oil concession. Ibn Saud agreed to the meeting, and this put pressure on Roosevelt to clearly express his attitudes toward Zionism and Pan-Arabism. Both the Jewish and Arab leaders felt they enjoyed the president's favor in their quarrel, but neither could be certain of him. He had given the Arabs assurances that he would do nothing about Palestine without first consulting them. But he had also reassured the Jews that he would not forget their aspirations for a Jewish homeland in Palestine. When the Jewish question was being discussed at Yalta, he declared himself a Zionist. But then he made an entirely different statement as he was making his farewells to Churchill and Stalin. The remark was so potentially volatile that a decision was taken at the highest level of the U.S. government to delete it from the official record of the conference. This statement did not enter the public domain for forty-five years:

> Marshal Stalin then said he thought more time was needed to consider and finish the business of the conference.
>
> The President answered that he had three Kings waiting for him in the Near East, Ibn Saud, Haile Selassie of Ethiopia and Farouk of Egypt.
>
> Marshal Stalin asked whether the President intended to make any concessions to Ibn Saud.

The President replied that there was only one concession he thought he might offer and that was to give him the six million Jews in the United States.[28]

At this time, when the Palestine issue was beginning to flare up as the world war drew to a close, publication of these words could have been disastrous for Roosevelt. Though seemingly he said them lightly, they would not have been taken lightly.

Churchill was thunderstruck that Roosevelt had made plans to enter a British sphere of influence without first having advised the British government, if only as a courtesy. In addition to his surprise, Churchill felt challenged personally by Roosevelt's statement to Stalin and, as Eddy claimed, he "burned up wires to all his diplomats"[29] to arrange a meeting of his own with Ibn Saud. He succeeded, but he could see Ibn Saud only *after* Roosevelt.

The Yalta Conference at an end, Roosevelt set out for Egypt and the Great Bitter Lake on the Suez Canal. He hoped to calm Ibn Saud's disquiet about American policy concerning the establishment of a Jewish national home in Palestine — a matter that, Ibn Saud had made clear to Eddy, might have consequences for the concession agreement with Aramco. The king left Jidda Harbor on the U.S. destroyer *Murphy* in the early evening of February 12, 1945. His retinue included his brother and two of his sons, Crown Prince Saud and Prince Faisal. Present also were the minister of finance, Abdullah Suleiman; the deputy minister for foreign affairs, Sheikh Yusuf Yassin; another Saudi foreign office official, Fuad Bey Hamza; courtiers such as the divine who conducted prayers and also served as the king's astrologer and fortuneteller; a number of aides-de-camp; the king's personal radio operator; hostages from the Mutair and the Beni Khalid tribes, held to ensure the good behavior of those tribes during the king's absence; the king's food taster, chamberlain, and chief valet; and the keeper of his privy purse, the chief server of his coffee, his deputy, and ten guards in full regalia with sabers and daggers. Ibn Saud's party numbered forty-eight.

The king's meeting with Roosevelt took place on the U.S. cruiser *Quincy* on the Great Bitter Lake of the Suez Canal zone. It was of high political importance. First there was the delicate matter of alliance in the war. Roosevelt clearly sought to defeat Nazi Germany as one of the Allies, but Ibn Saud was neutral, although friendly to the Allies. He did maintain contacts with the Germans, in the first year of the war at least. Thus it was unclear exactly where the king stood on this matter.

A second complicating factor in this meeting was the rivalry between Roosevelt and Churchill. Both leaders sought to make points with Ibn

Saud at the expense of the other; their diplomatic parties gave the impression that Ibn Saud was their special friend. For example, Eddy claimed that at the meeting with Roosevelt, he alone acted as the interpreter and that, later, Ibn Saud showed him all the paperwork relating to the meeting that was to take place between Churchill and Ibn Saud. These documents placed the British in an unflattering light. Commenting on an after-lunch conversation between Roosevelt and Ibn Saud, Eddy noted that they

> talked as friends of the responsibilities of governing, of the encouraging progress of the Allies in the war, of compassion for the multitudes rendered destitute through oppression or famine. The King smiled in knowing assent to the President's jovial confidence about the English: "We like the English, but we also know the English and the way they insist on doing good themselves. You and I want freedom and prosperity for our people and their neighbors after the war. How and by whose hand freedom and prosperity arrive concerns us little. The English also work and sacrifice to bring freedom and prosperity to the world, but on the condition that it be brought to them marked "Made In Britain."[30]

Eddy reported that Ibn Saud agreed with Roosevelt's estimation of the British and, further, spoke to Eddy of his thoughts comparing Roosevelt and Churchill:

> The contrast between the President and Mr. Churchill is very great. Mr. Churchill speaks deviously, evades understanding, changes the subject to avoid commitment, forcing me repeatedly to bring him back to the point. The President seeks understanding in conversation; to dispel darkness and shed light on the issue.[31]

Ibn Saud also directly questioned the president about seeds of doubt, sown by the British, regarding the reliability of American support for Saudi Arabia. The British had been trying to convince him that they were the only party concerned with the long-term welfare of the Saudis. During his meeting with Roosevelt, Ibn Saud inquired,

> "What am I to believe when the British tell me my future is with them and not with America? [Their representatives] constantly say, or imply, that America's political interest in Saudi Arabia is a transitory war interest; her aid as short-lived as Lend-Lease; that Saudi Arabia lies in a path bounded with sterling controls, connected by British communications, defended by the Royal Navy and Army; that my security and economic stability are bound up with British foreign policy; and that America, after the war, will return to her preoccupations in the Western Hemisphere."[32]

Roosevelt took this opportunity to assure Ibn Saud that the best postwar prospects for Saudi Arabia lay in opening the door of commerce and opportunity to the United States and other countries, rather than sanctioning a British monopoly. Ibn Saud temporized by stating his general agreement with this viewpoint, yet noting that no doubt the British would continue their attempts to keep Saudi Arabia within their sphere of influence.

Another subject of great concern to Ibn Saud regarded the conflict between Arabs and Zionists concerning a homeland for the Jews in Palestine. Again he baited Roosevelt with descriptions of Churchill's pushiness in dealing with the king, hoping the American president would offer him more support. Ibn Saud said that Churchill had emphasized how much the king owed to the British:

> "Great Britain had supported and subsidized me for twenty years, and had made possible the stability of my reign by fending off potential enemies on my frontiers. Since Britain had seen me through difficult days, she is entitled now to request my assistance in the problem of Palestine where a strong Arab leader can restrain fanatical Arab elements, insist on moderation in Arab councils, and effect a realistic compromise with Zionism. Both sides must be prepared to make concessions and he looks to me to help prepare the Arab concessions.
>
> "I replied that, as he well knows, I have made no secret of my friendship and gratitude to Great Britain . . . however, . . . what he proposes is not help to Britain or the Allies, but an act of treachery to the Prophet and all believing Muslims which would wipe out my honor and destroy my soul. I could not acquiesce in a compromise with Zionism. . . . Zionism from any quarter must indubitably bring bloodshed, widespread disorder in the Arab lands with certainly no benefit to Britain or anyone else. . . .
>
> "In turn I requested assurance that Jewish immigration to Palestine would be stopped. This Mr. Churchill refused to promise. . . . I reminded him that the British and their Allies would be making their choice between (1) a friendly and peaceful Arab world, and (2) a struggle to the death between Arab and Jew if unreasonable immigration of Jews to Palestine is renewed."[33]

Again, as he had done in letters concerning the problem there in 1939 and 1943, Roosevelt assured Ibn Saud that nothing would be done in Palestine without the Arabs being consulted. That was that; Ibn Saud claimed afterward that he regarded the president's statement as a matter of honor as well as politics.

Within a month of this conversation, a meeting was convened by Dean Acheson of the State Department, concerning U.S. assistance to Saudi Arabia. Because of loans already outstanding from the U.S. government and Aramco, it would be about five years before Ibn Saud would begin to receive royalties from the sale of oil. This lack of incoming funds could plunge Saudi Arabia into a deficit of about $50 million

over the next five years. Because of the desire to keep the Hasa concession in American hands and because Ibn Saud became anti-American
only when his treasury was empty, the State Department introduced a
very munificent plan to secure the king's loyalty. Beyond the oil royalties it would later receive from Aramco, Ibn Saud's government would
be financed over the next five years in the following manner: It would
receive a $10 million supply program and a $6 million supplemental
supply program for 1945. The Export-Import Bank would loan Ibn
Saud $5 million. Long-term financing of the Saudi Arabian govern-
ment would keep it solvent until oil revenues matured. A $5 million
loan would enable Ibn Saud to establish an office of MacKay Radio, the
U.S. world telecommunications corporation in Jidda, to be owned by
the Saudi government but run by Americans. The reason for this loan
is obscure, but doubtless it was a response to the trouble between
Aramco and the British Cable and Wireless Company over the security
of the oil company's radio traffic between Dhahran and San Francisco
during the war. The United States would pay the construction costs of a
large airfield at Dhahran, which would become Saudi property after
five years. The U.S. government would pay the sum of $300,000 into
Ibn Saud's private accounts at two U.S. banks in New York City. The
reason for this deposit is not known. The United States would enable
Ibn Saud to open a diplomatic mission in Washington. And, lastly,
would the king like to own a DC3 aircraft? The king accepted.

With so much U.S. money involved in Saudi Arabia, secret service
activities also went on just below the surface of Big Oil politics. In
1944–45, Eddy became involved in a pretty OSS operation to obtain
health intelligence about Ibn Saud. The need for such information was
obvious — the house of Saud might not survive the king's death. If the
dynasty did not survive, then neither would the kingdom. Who would
take control, and what would happen to the relatively new united kingdom of Saudi Arabia? Would it disintegrate into four sovereign states
— the Hejaz, the Nejd, Hasa, and Asir? And what would become of
Aramco, which had won the concession to "the richest commercial
prize in the history of the planet?" What would become of America's
large investment in Arabia? And who would gain possession of the
great airport, which was also a major bomber base?

Thus it became Eddy's mission, amid much else besides, to keep an
eye and an ear open in regard to the king's health. For the first time, it
seems, the high authorities of intelligence in Washington sanctioned
an operation to acquire that most intimate intelligence, the contents of

the toilet. As a retired American diplomat was to remark, "Only rarely could a foreign potentate's stool and urine have been of such interest to our intelligence people."[34] Plans for Project Switch reached the desk of William J. Donovan, head of the OSS, on March 16, 1945. The author was Colonel Harry S. Aldrich, chief of the OSS in Cairo.

Outlining Switch, Aldrich noted that Roosevelt had given Ibn Saud a C47 Dakota as his personal aircraft. The plane was to be flown by a more or less permanent American crew. Aldrich reported that he had asked General William L. Ritter, deputy chief and chief of staff of U.S. forces in Africa and Egypt, "if there would be any objection to putting one or two [OSS men] in the crew, if we could find qualified men, for intelligence purposes." Ritter had agreed, provided the approval of the commanding general, Benjamin F. Giles, was obtained. And as Aldrich continued, "I believe he warmed to the idea largely because of the fact that the British are definitely 'in' with Ibn Saud and the Americans definitely seem not to be."[35]

Ritter and Aldrich had also "discussed the difficulties of our getting one or two men in the crew without arousing suspicion." Colonel Eddy, who applauded the plan, had also suggested "a way to solve the difficulties of getting our people on the crew without arousing the suspicion of the regular crew members." The king, Eddy said, was "apprehensive of trusting the royal lives to native pilots and crew," and Eddy had suggested that OSS find Muslim Americans to serve as permanent crew paid by the king. If "we could get such men," Aldrich continued, "we would have no difficulty in rationalizing the bringing in of 'outsiders' for the crew." He added that it might be possible to "make the whole crew ours."[36]

General Giles did in fact approve the project, but there were substantial risks involved. According to Aldrich, both risks and opportunities characterized the project, but "without the President's specific approval, it could be a very dangerous game for our agency." Also the project would be "good red meat for our national enemies" and "ditto for our foreign enemies — especially the British."[37]

On April 2, 1945, plans for the project had reached the desk of the chief of the OSS secret intelligence service in Washington, Whitney H. Shepardson. What did he think of the idea? It was, Shepardson minuted, "a beautiful project" but by far "the most delicate one that we have yet entertained." The risks "are vast, with all kinds of repercussions unfortunate for OSS if the project is blown." Shepardson thought that "for a dozen reasons" there was "an 85% chance that the project *will be blown.*" Shepardson proposed, therefore, that Aldrich be commended "for a brilliant sortie of the imagination" but that Project Switch be dropped.[38]

Donovan did not, however, agree, and he made plans to push forward. But for once, Donovan's executives attempted to overrule him, trying to impress upon him the "extreme dangers" of the project — that "ten people already knew about it, some of whom were not in OSS." The Switch file seems to indicate that at length Donovan agreed, although reluctantly.[39] However, in the world of the secret service, where *no* does not always mean *no,* this communication may not mean that the plan was scrapped.

The aircraft duly arrived on April 14, 1945 — the day of official mourning for Roosevelt, who had died suddenly — and Eddy formally delivered it to one of Ibn Saud's sons, Prince Mansur, viceroy of the Hejaz. Eddy made a brief speech in which, on War Department orders, he was very careful not to link the name of President Roosevelt to the gift. (This may suggest that the aircraft could well have had a special purpose.) Eddy, with fulsome oratory, presented the aircraft to Prince Mansur:

> The United States Army Air Force have prepared for service in your great country, this American airplane, which it is now my honor to turn over to you as Viceroy of His Majesty.
>
> The plane is identical with those which during the past year have carried Saudi and American officials on business of our common interest; identical also with the many thousand planes which have transported American soldiers in their work of destroying the accursed enemy. Now that your great Kingdom is our ally, in name as it always has been in deed, it is a pleasure for us to anticipate this veteran type of plane serving you steadily on His Majesty's business.[40]

Prince Mansur replied,

> In the name of my father, His Majesty Abdul Aziz al Saud, I accept gratefully this most handsome airplane, a gift from his beloved friend, President Roosevelt. The Kingdom of Saudi Arabia will value this gift for many reasons in addition to its valuable and efficient service in transportation: it will always recall the giver, your late President, for whom His Majesty conceived unparalleled admiration; it will knit more firmly the strands of friendship between our nations as it weaves its way back and forth over our land, guided by American hands; it will recall to all Saudi Arabians the magic of American invention, and your humanitarian ideals, as it speeds on errands of justice and mercy, as American ideals have sped to the far corners of the earth.[41]

These speeches were followed by an inspection of the plane. "Emblazoned with the coat of arms of the Kingdom of Saudi Arabia, and tastefully furnished for the comfort of the King, it was greatly admired. The special fittings include a ramp to enable the King to board the plane, a bed, kitchenette and lavatory fittings." A U.S. crew, to be "rotated every month or two," would operate the aircraft.[42] The Briton Grafftey-Smith was a passenger on that first flight, together with St. John Philby.

Meanwhile, a number of British eminences visited Ibn Saud, thus giving the king further opportunities to play the United States and Great Britain off against each other. Anthony Eden, the wartime British foreign secretary and a future prime minister; Britain's first soldier, Field Marshal Lord Alanbrooke; the commander in chief of the British fleet in the Mediterranean, who arrived at Jidda in the heavy cruiser *Newcastle;* and St. John Philby's son, Kim, a high official of the British Secret Service in the Middle East — all these and others were feted by Ibn Saud. Eden considered friendly relations with Ibn Saud to be of the utmost importance to Great Britain. Concerning American involvement in the Middle East, he recognized the importance of the U.S. presence in helping to preserve Britain's primacy in the region:

> A potential aggressor [such as Russia] might hesitate to interfere where both American and British interests are involved. There will be no advantage therefore in challenging the American claim to strategic interest in the Middle East oil. Our own interests being wider, the ultimate object should be to conclude a world-wide agreement with the United States by which each Government would undertake to assist the other with oil supplies in time of emergency or war.[43]

The most interesting visitor was Kim Philby. Widely regarded as Britain's ablest intelligence officer during World War II, he was also an important Soviet secret agent, a fact that was just becoming clear in high British and American intelligence. He was now on his way to take up the post of chief of the British Secret Service station at Istanbul, Britain's main base for secret operations into South Russia. St. John was pride itself when Kim arrived. But young Philby found little that impressed him, although the king sent his DC3 aircraft to collect "Feelbee's" son. As Kim Philby wrote in a memoir:

> Neither then nor thereafter did I feel the slightest temptation to follow [his father's] example. The limitless space, the clear night skies and the rest of the gobbledygook are all right in small doses. But I would find a lifetime in a landscape with majesty but no charm, among a people with neither majesty nor charm, quite unacceptable. Ignorance and arrogance make a bad combination, and the Saudi Arabians have both in generous measure. When an outward show of austerity is thrown in as well, the mixture is intolerable.[44]

St. John, however, was beside himself with joy that at last he and his son were together in Saudi Arabia. As St. John wrote to his English wife (by this time he also had an Arab wife), he felt ecstatic at the courtesies extended to Kim by the crown and court. In all, Kim spent five nights and six days at Riyadh, sharing a room with his father in the palace guesthouse.

On the last but one night, the king gave a banquet in the palace for Kim and another visitor, the Egyptian minister, at which there was the "usual long row of whole sheep on platters." The amir Abdullah, the king's brother, placed Kim at his right hand, and after the banquet the amir gave Kim an elementary book on Arabic to study, "saying he really must learn the language now that he is to be so near and will have a chance of visiting the country again." At the end of the visit, the king presented Kim with a white headdress and gown woven with gold thread, and £30 in gold, which Kim, surprisingly, accepted.[45]

Meanwhile, Parker T. Hart, the first U.S. consul to be positioned at Dhahran and Bahrein, took up his post and thereby established himself inside one of the most prized and closely guarded of all British imperial possessions, the Persian Gulf. In this appointment, Philby had played a part, for he had been advising the OSS in London on British policy in the Gulf and Arabia.

St. John had been "spotted" as a potential adviser — a polite term for informant — by an American intelligence officer, Donald Downes, as he passed through Bahrein while recruiting spies for the U.S. naval intelligence service. As Downes wrote, he became interested in how this "thoroughly English scholar" had become "so estranged from his homeland that he had conspired against England in her extremity."[46] On his return to New York in 1942, Downes joined Donovan, a leading Wall Street lawyer then forming the OSS. Donovan had defended Standard Oil and other U.S. oil companies against massive cartel charges in a case heard at Madison, Wisconsin, in 1936. He was, therefore, interested in Big Oil and prominent personalities in the Middle East.

Donovan asked Downes to provide him with a list of names of dependable persons to work in the Middle East in the U.S. interest. Downes mentioned Philby. He wrote that Saudi Arabia and Ibn Saud were "the real key to influence in the Eastern Islamic world today." Ibn Saud "is an Americanophile" who "depends for his income to a very great extent on the Standard Oil Company of California." His political adviser, Philby, had turned "violently against his own country," England, while becoming "very pro-American." He was "trusted and even beloved to the tribes from the Oman to the Shammar in the North and from Alkoweit to the Yemen." Downes believed that the official tasked to recruit Philby should, "if he is at all careful," be able to enlist his cooperation and thereby "cast a great deal of light on this extraordinary and magnificent part of the world."[47]

Philby was released from detention in Britain in the spring of 1941 and was considered unemployable by the British government. Joseph Charles, of the British Empire section of the OSS in London, was introduced to Philby, and they lunched together about once a month from late 1943 onward. Charles's interest lay in Britain's treaty powers with the Persian Gulf sheikhdoms, a matter that deeply interested the Near East desk of the OSS in Washington. In February 1944, Washington asked all OSS outposts for information about Philby. Charles replied to the chief of the division that he knew Philby "fairly well" and that he thought him to be "one of the wisest men I have ever met." Charles then reported: "He is still very interested in Near East politics and is very highly regarded by the Near East people here, but I don't think he has any official work." He noted that Philby had encouraged Ibn Saud to favor the Americans over the British in granting the oil concession because he "thought [the Americans] wouldn't try to extend their influence in that part of the world by means of the concessions. The British Foreign Office learned about Philby's advice to Ibn Saud, and it is, I think, the main thing that they have against him, although his whole point of view would be disturbing to them."[48]

Yet another branch of the OSS had quite a different opinion of Philby. In June 1944, Major Carleton Coon, a Harvard anthropologist and an OSS secret agent, was working on a paper for Donovan called "Intelligence work in Arab Countries." Coon had served on Eddy's staff in the Mediterranean, and they were well known to each other. Philby was also known to Coon, who, in 1934, had entered Saudi Arabia without permission to make anthropological studies of the Wahhabs. Philby had set some of his thugs on Coon, and the fight had culminated in Coon's deportation, an indignity that the professor had not forgotten.

Coon's paper argued that the enhancement of American interests in the Muslim world depended upon the survival of the Ibn Saud dynasty. But first, Coon argued, if this was to be achieved, the OSS needed to erase St. John Philby's influence at the Saudi court. And as Coon advised Donovan, St. John was

> an extremely jealous man. He considers Arabia his private preserve as far as all scientific work is concerned, and in 1934 he influenced the king to prevent me from doing field work in physical anthropology

there. Any archeologist, anthropologist, geographer, geologist, etc., who comes to Saudi Arabia to work will have to reckon with Philby, and if Philby cannot wreck an expedition politically, he will do it by other and less agreeable means. It must be remembered that Philby can get any number of Arabs to do any dirty work he desires for him, and that he is an insanely jealous man. Only exceedingly well-trained men can hope to handle the Philby problem.[49]

Despite Coon's adverse opinion, Philby provided Charles with much important information about Britain's position in the Gulf states, where a number of important oil structures had been found by an Anglo-Persian subsidiary, Petroleum Development, Ltd. And it was that association, combined with Philby's services to Standard Oil of California before the war and his encyclopedic knowledge of Arabia, that helped him to regain acceptability in U.S. oil circles, despite rumors that he belonged to the British Secret Service.

In March 1944 the Foreign Office in London circulated a major paper regarding Britain's position in the Gulf, entitled "Memorandum on the Oil Concessions in the Arab Sheikhdoms of the Persian Gulf." It reflected the dictum of Queen Victoria in colonial matters: "What we have, we hold." The little states that Britain wished to keep within its sphere of influence included Qatar, a promontory of about twenty-five thousand people and three thousand square miles south of Bahrein, and the seven "petty sheikhdoms" of the Trucial Coast (named for the Maritime Truce imposed in 1820 by the East India Company). These included Abu Dhabi (10,000) souls, Dubai (20,000), Sharja (12,000), Ajaman (2,000), Kalba (2,000), and Muscat (16,000).

Each of the rulers of these states had undertaken, according to the British paper, "to have no negotiations with or receive representatives of any power other than the British Government," without whose consent "[the ruler] is precluded from alienating any part of his territory or from granting any concession for oil, pearl fishing, etc."[50] (Muscat was in a slightly different category.) The writer went on to show that all the treaties, some of which dated back to the late eighteenth century, derived from considerations of trade and the need to clear the Gulf of pirates, slavers, and, later, gun runners.

The paper claimed that the British government had respected the independence of the rulers in internal affairs and had intervened only in the case of a "serious mal-administration or of the threat of a breach of the peace likely to endanger our own or foreign interests." Under this system, the British government claimed, "the states have for long enjoyed a period of political tranquillity and relative posterity, while

Great Britain on her side has insured herself against the establishment of any hostile power in the Gulf to threaten our communications with India."[51]

In recent years, however, "the strategic importance of the Persian Gulf has greatly increased, for two reasons, firstly because of the development of air transport and, secondly, through the discovery of large and strategically placed oil reserves in the territories of the sheikhdoms." The oil was, of course, of the first importance for a sea power like Great Britain. The oil discovered in the sheikhdoms was "quite close to the sea" so that Britain was "no longer dependent upon the goodwill of countries [such as Persia, Iraq, and Saudi Arabia] anxious to assert their own national independence."[52]

Then the paper came to its main points. The political complexion of the region was indeed changing in ways that might threaten Britain's position as leading power there. Movements of "national self-consciousness" could begin to destabilize the area, in the way they had already affected Iraq and Egypt. Most especially, if Britain was to maintain in the Middle East the current "satisfactory state of affairs, we must avoid entering into any arrangement with the Americans which are likely to result in the introduction in the area of a foreign power to rival our political influence." The Americans, particularly Standard Oil of California, had already established themselves in Arabia, Bahrein, and Kuwait. In general, the United States had been taking "an increased interest in this area both from the point of view of oil development and with an eye to post-war civil aviation."[53]

Parker T. Hart represented, therefore, the American political foothold in the Gulf that the official who wrote that paper feared so greatly. As Hart advised the State Department, he had been well received by everyone everywhere — except the British political agent in Bahrein, who was responsible for overseeing Britain's interests throughout the Gulf. Hart reported that the agent received him with "official frostiness."[54]

Hart noticed that the king "made no secret of his preference for American, as against British, economic interest in the country, and stated to Floyd Ohliger in an interview three months ago at Riyadh: 'The British are my friends, the Americans are my partners.'"[55] The Americans simply had to live within the restrictions laid down by the Muslim government: advance permission was needed for Americans to visit towns, religious laws and the customs of the land were to be respected, liquor consumption was tightly controlled or ruled out altogether (the restrictions varied over time), and Arab workers were to be treated well. Following these guidelines — and replenishing the royal treasury on occasion — kept them firmly in the king's good graces.

Therefore Hart had cause to believe that Aramco stood on "the threshold of what is presumed to be a fabulous career." It was "uncorking" its wells as the threat of German invasion ended with Rommel's defeat in North Africa. Hart's statement to the State Department concluded with his assessment that

> full marks must be given to Aramco for a remarkable achievement in the development of a pro-American bias. Although there is hardly a man in the Government Relations Department of the company who speaks more than "pidgin Arabic," the local amirs, sheikhs and lesser lights of this coast appear to regard company men as their good and respected friends. There seems to be no antagonism based on religious and racial differences. . . . There is also a common denominator of humor and practicality which becomes apparent in friendly "leg-pulling" adored by Arabs and Americans alike.[56]

As World War II ended, British influence in the Middle East began to wane, although Britain remained the paramount political and military power. The abrupt cessation of lend-lease aid in August 1945 — a measure directed against the Soviet Union, although it provided cold comfort to Great Britain — was followed by Britain's acceptance of American primacy in Saudi Arabia. The United States was in "a harshly unsentimental mood"[57] in its relations with its ally, but on the other hand, Whitehall believed, the United States would not be able to run the region alone. Theirs would be, Whitehall intended, a relationship resembling that of the Greeks and the Romans in antiquity — the British would supply the wisdom and experience in governing the region, and the Americans would supply the military power to preserve the tranquillity so necessary to major oil operations.

But Whitehall was mistaken. The American oil industry was determined to take over the immense British oil industries in Iraq and Iran, as Persia had now become; and the moment peace arrived in the Gulf, American officials of the Truman and then the Eisenhower administrations began to conspire against the British hegemony in the belief that American republicanism would be more beneficial to the Muslim world than British imperialism. This stage of great power rivalry lasted for the next twenty-five years. So, as the British sahibs and memsahibs departed, they were replaced by American sahibs and memsahibs. The result was the same as that of Queen Victoria's expansion of British power into the Gulf — an unending series of conflicts, both bloody and political. Such was the power and wealth that Aramco had begun to acquire that, despite whatever policy might be advanced by the State Department, the policy that counted was Aramco's. In its independence of Washington during this postwar stage, Aramco's management came to resemble the potentates of an independent sovereign state, with its own intelligence and political branches. Aramco began to assist Arab revolutionary causes militarily, politically, and financially in order to eject the British oil companies from the fourth main source of oil in the Gulf, that of the small Gulf states along the rim of Arabia between Bahrein and Aden. And as William E. Mulligan, one of the policy and political officers at Aramco and a former corporal in the U.S. Air Force at Aden, stated: "APOC and IPC became our enemies, not anyone else."[58]

[6]

THE COMPANY TOWN

IN 1946, ARAMCO BEGAN to airlift Americans in Skymasters and Constellations to build the capital city of Oildom on the "Pirate Coast" of Arabia at Dhahran, just across the Persian Gulf from Bahrein Island. Some of the new throng enlisted for much the same reason that others joined the French Foreign Legion: there was something they wished to forget. One was Michael Sheldon Cheney, son of the New York drama critic, Sheldon Cheney. He had just been demobilized from the U.S. Army, and something, possibly his marriage, had gone wrong with his life in postwar San Francisco when he saw a want ad in a city newspaper. "The type of ad will be familiar to anyone who is, from necessity or morbid curiosity, a reader of the 'Help Wanted' columns," he wrote in a memoir. Such ads, usually the largest on the page, aimed to

> lure able-bodied men to such exotic foreign scenes as the Pacific Islands, Sumatra, Korea, Morocco, or, most regularly, Saudi Arabia. In 1948, such an ad persuaded me to exchange the life of a California suburb for that of an oil camp, set in the windswept wilderness of the Arabian desert. In that desolate world lit by a perpetual glare, of scorching sun by day, of gas flames by night, I joined several thousand voluntary exiles from the United States who have, as a body, spent the past quarter-century in a string of lonely camps, raising a monumental thirst while making a determined effort to disprove Kipling's thesis that the best is the same as the worst at any point east of de Lesseps' strategic ditch [the Suez Canal].[1]

His morale and finances at low ebb, Cheney met a school friend and fellow soldier in a San Francisco bar who was himself about to go out to Dhahran as a member of Aramco's government relations department, a private diplomatic and intelligence service whose wardrobe, his friend told him, "included a stock of black bow ties and cummer-bunds, evidently uniform wear for [meetings] with Arab potentates." He had been in Oildom just after the war, and he was eager to get back. The salary was tax-free; everything was paid for by the company, includ-ing vacations; the minimum tour of duty was two years, but Cheney's friend intended to spend fifteen years out there, with short leaves in the Greek Islands, perhaps, or Lebanon. Life was very good, he related, with "fine houses, green gardens, swimming pools, milk shakes, even women, with figures presumably as nicely rounded as those of the salaries." There would be, by contract, long leaves of three months or more every two years, back in the United States at company expense. He would, he claimed, save every cent he made and retire after fifteen years with a fat pension besides.[2]

Cheney signed on not with Aramco, as he at first believed he would, but with Bechtel International, the heavy construction firm. His first interview took place in a paneled suite, but his actual signing on for employment in Saudi Arabia took place in a much grittier setting, a room above a second-hand clothing store on Market Street in San Francisco:

> I presented myself before a natty gent with a pro footballer's build, a large cigar and a voice trained on straight bourbon. He peered dubi-ously at my application form.
> "You sure you want to go to Arabia?"
> I said I guessed I did.
> "Well, it's your funeral." And so I became a stiff.
> Technically, I was not a full stiff. Having signed on as a personnel clerk, I fell into the office-working sub-species known as Shiny Pants. Still I was a part of that sweaty body of American construction men who have hammered, shoveled, welded, blasted and bulldozed their way across the earth in the service of the big building companies. . . . [At New York, he] reported to the designated rendezvous, a dingy hostelry near Times Square, its sparsely furnished lobby gave the impression of having recently been under artillery fire. A dyspeptic clerk greeted me without enthusiasm: "You another of them Ay-rab stiffs?"[3]

A university graduate who had worked until recently for one of the head offices of a leading oil company, and a man of some social stand-ing, Cheney realized that there had been a mistake in his employment. But he was in no mood to straighten out the error in New York. Nor was there time. He described his first impression of the rest of the Arabia-bound crowd:

> I couldn't have missed them. The hotel seemed excessively populated by a race of red-faced, uninhibited Oklahomans in various stages of undress and insobriety. Apart from the noise they produced, they were

extremely visible. Living much of their lives in drab work clothing, construction men, like soldiers, show a marked preference for gaudy plumage off the job. I threaded my way down the corridor between reeling frames garbed in vibrant sports jackets, pastel slacks, padded gabardine suits, Hawaiian shirts, hand-painted neckties, tooled boots, snakeskin belts, and Stetsons of every size. At the end of the hall I was greeted by my roommate, a fashion plate in jockey shorts, high-heeled boots and a silk tie with a graphical anatomical study. He insisted I have a pull at his whiskey bottle. I needed it.[4]

Good-humored, literate, and an outstanding writer, Cheney recorded that most of the men around him "were in a state bordering rigor mortis by take-off time." Three days later they arrived over Arabia. Cheney recorded:

No raucous banter now enlivened the cabin. Its occupants struggled with cramped sleep or stared out morosely at the dreary landscape unrolling below, hour after hour. First there were the bare brown hills, then black and twisted lava, then strange dun cones with queer wind-tails sweeping away beyond them. Even these disappeared, and we flew on over barren desert and an occasional speckling of scrub or an eroded gully, bone-dry, twisting away over flat horizons.[5]

At last the engines were throttled back, the cabin temperature rose, and the Persian Gulf appeared, "flat, wave-less, throwing the sun back into our eyes like a sheet of tin." Heat "really closed in as the plane lurched down onto a long runway. Shirts clung to backs, seats grew damp and a fug of heat and sweat filled the cabin as we slowed, turned and taxied past corrugated iron hangers to the terminal."[6]

Cheney's arrival resembled that of the hundreds of Americans already working in Saudi Arabia and the many thousands who would arrive later. It was a sobering time:

We rose, surrendered our passports and filed out, each taking a quick, grim glance at this desolate world before stumbling to earth and across the windswept ramp to the terminal building. We were swallowed into a large, gloomy chamber packed with civilians, soldiers and airmen, Arab and American, jostling and gabbling at each other in a steamy atmosphere.[7]

It was dark by the time Cheney cleared the airport in Dhahran, a Strategic Air Command base near the Aramco compound. The car he was in passed the Saudi police post at the main gates of the camp. As they passed the guard shack, Cheney noted a "withered brown object" hanging from a wire. He was told it was a human hand — punishment for the second time a thief was caught stealing. This lesson in Koranic law continued:

Three-time losers were relieved of a foot as well. Murderers were beheaded. Punishments were administered publicly, as adult education. If the offender was an Aramco employee, the ceremony was held at the company's gate at quitting time.[8]

"Lovely country," Cheney's companion remarked to his escort. The escort replied: "You don't know the half of it."[9] The car headed into Whiskey Gulch, a line of small huts thatched with palm fronds. This was where the Saudi workers lived.

But there proved to be another world at the camp. It was called King's Road, where Aramco's senior staff lived. Cheney wrote:

> Ahead, a paved avenue curved away past neat blocks of houses set in lush gardens. Homes built of stone, mellow orange brick and white plaster, with broad windows and long verandas, rested in the shade of palm, acacia and feathery tamarisk. Smooth lawns lay between jasmine hedges and clumps of oleander heavy with bright pink blossoms.
>
> A block from King's Road, the greenery fell away and we debouched into a squalid open space in which lay several long, shabby buildings with rows of small windows set in cracked plaster walls.[10]

These proved to be "the sheepsheds," where Cheney was to reside. He was led into a building resembling the wartime temporary quarters of an army camp — and indeed Dhahran resembled just that, an army camp with the officers' quarters green and pleasant, the other ranks' a hellhole.

Cheney slept the sleep of the dead that first night. Then "the repeated blasts of the camp siren" shocked him "into awareness of my first Arabian dawn." The workday began at 7:30 A.M., "but the camp's fire whistles shrieked at intervals from 6:30 on to ensure the proper state of shattered alertness among employees." He struggled into his clothes and went for breakfast.

> We joined our fellow initiates at the mess hall, a cheerless institution despite the cloths on the trestle tables, the curtains at the windows. The steamy atmosphere of a mass feeding establishment remained, heavy with the memory of a million graceless meals. A scattering of morose late-comers dabbled with the food in the greasy gloom, a lone female stirred muddy coffee at a corner table.[11]

There were, it seems, many such women, a special breed, "tough broads" who drifted from one construction site or oil camp to another throughout the world. Secretaries and clerks by trade, they were eagerly sought after the world over. For them the wages were five times what they were "Stateside." They came from all quarters of American life and, because they were the only unattached American women, few remained single after their midtwenties. They were interesting and rare phenomena amid modern American frontier life. Where most came from, few ever discovered. Where most were headed remained for the most part a mystery.

The odyssey of Cheney's first morning in Arabia continued:

> We picked a clear space and sat down, peering at the mimeographed menus that promised more than could be produced. An Arab waiter in once-white jacket and trousers shuffled over, sandals slapping dully on the concrete floor.
>
> "What you want, sob?"
>
> It dawned on me that this "sob" was not an expression of commiseration, but the Indian title "sahib." The waiter leaned on my chair, scratching his genitals, while we ordered.
>
> "Okay, sob."
>
> He shuffled away, returning presently with rancid bacon and reconstituted eggs. We downed these in silence and trooped away to the camp theater in a mood well suited to our briefing in the nature and conditions of work and life in Saudi Arabia.[12]

The briefer began with some elementary niceties and then got down to the meat of his talk: the restrictions of living in Saudi Arabia.

> "Most of the privileges we have in camp — liquor, movies, dancing, gambling — are strictly forbidden outside. They're against the Saudi law and the Muslim religion, which are the same thing under this government. And, except for the special dispensations inside camp, we obey their laws and customs. That's the first principle of this operation — the Arab is always right."
>
> He rapped the desk for emphasis.
>
> "You'll find this a very strange country. But remember — we look just as strange to them. Until fifteen years ago this was a closed world. All foreigners were infidels and enemies. Some of them aren't used to having us around yet.
>
> "Always remember this: It's their country. It's up to us to make allowances, to give way, to adjust to them; not the other way round. You may find it quite an adjustment."[13]

The briefer proceeded to outline some of the adjustments in detail, eventually ending with a review of all the rules and restrictions. He ended with one important reminder:

> It was unwise to jump into a vehicle and drive away without checking first to see if [a Saudi] was sleeping in the shade underneath. We were discouraged, too, from giving Saudis lifts in our cars and trucks. Still unused to speed they might, on reaching their destination, simply step out while the vehicle was still traveling at forty miles an hour. The driver invariably then went to jail on a manslaughter charge.[14]

The instructor distributed forms "asking our preferences in methods of disposing of our bodies in case of death" — there were several
morticians and a mortuary at the camp — and then he ended his talk
by welcoming the group to Arabia.

Cheney went to work. At first he kept track of the passports of U.S.
workers and obtained exit visas for those who ran afoul of Saudi law or
who left for other reasons. Over half the men who came out with
Cheney could not stand life in Arabia. There were more of these than
the company ever let on, sons of Oklahoma caught looking for the
red-light district or stiffs who had forgotten the advice about Saudis
and wheeled vehicles.

Cheney's description of his first months of employment paints a vivid
picture:

> I normally conjure up a nocturnal scene suggestive of a medieval art-
> ist's conception of hell. Night after night, at midnight or one or two
> A.M., I started off work amid the raw outlines of an oil camp etched in
> reflected fire against a smoking crimson sky. In the lurid light of the
> flares, buildings, bodies and the desert itself sweated a lukewarm dew
> in the smothering night of the Persian Gulf's edge. For background
> music I had the distant rumble of aircraft engines and the fretful
> epithets of the bibulous stiffs I herded toward them.[15]

Immediately after the establishment of the Aramco consortium, the
first chairman and chief executive officer, Fred A. Davies, had arrived
in Dhahran from New York to take over the company's operations. The
tall, beefy Davies had been the first Standard Oil employee to take up
work in eastern Arabia after the signing of the concession in 1933. He
had since then grown greatly in stature in the company. Although he
was an oil engineer, he had developed a reputation as a superb oil
politicker in Washington. He was probably already a millionaire, and
his main deputies in the camp were Floyd Ohliger, James MacPherson
(a Scots-born American citizen in charge of oil field operations), and
Tom Barger, the "conscience of Aramco" and responsible for political
affairs as liaison with Ibn Saud, Abdullah Suleiman, and Sheikh Yusuf
Yassin, now the chief of Ibn Saud's political office. Whether Davies and
his team were equal to the political crises they would encounter is
questionable. They were first-rate oil company executives who had one
main political task: to keep the king sweet.

At the end of the war, Davies and his "cabinet" did not doubt that the
Arabian concession would be far more difficult to maintain than it had
been to acquire. The king had only one object in mind in his relations

with Aramco: to squeeze as much money, materials, and equipment out of the company as possible. When sometimes he failed, he was apt to suggest that the concession was at risk.

Aramco's relationship with Ibn Saud was further complicated by the Palestinian question. He threatened that if the United States supported the Zionists and enabled the formation of the state of Israel, then he would cancel the concession and offer it to the British. As W. F. Owen, Aramco's counsel, would remember, the Zionist question "almost spelled the end of all American enterprise out in the Middle East." Davies and his team therefore tried to persuade Ibn Saud and his advisers that "the Israeli problem [was] separate from their other relationships with the United States."[16]

Davies's second major challenge involved the mood of the camp. The workforce, and even the management, had divided into cliques, the Texans and the Californians (reflecting the partnership between Standard Oil of California and Texaco). In that isolated outpost, the Aramcons felt especially loyal to the particular company that had hired them — either Texaco or Standard Oil. This loyalty was the more pronounced because once employees had finished the contract with Aramco, they could return to their original company, pension rights and seniority intact. And as Cheney described the relationship between the two factions, "Aramco was, in effect, a neurotic child . . . subject to the whims, qualms and jealousies of each [faction]."[17] They dwelt, in short, in a house divided.

Late in 1948 the American vice consul at Dhahran, Francis E. Meloy, wrote to Washington that he had "the honor to report concerning a conflict which exists beneath the surface in the Aramco organization." This conflict, Meloy advised, was carried over to the management of Aramco's operation in the field. The community was "highly class-conscious and authority-fearing." California's ethos, that of San Francisco's airs and graces combined with the pioneering and mining-camp spirit of so many of Standard Oil's bright young workers, was responsible for some of this disorder. The rest were pure Texas. So antagonistic had the two sides become that the senior staff "came to blows and succeeded in demolishing the bar in the Dhahran Clubhouse in a near riot. At one point five different fights were going on in the same room."[18]

The strife culminated in the sacking of James MacPherson, who ran the camps and the oil fields under the title of vice president and resident administrative officer. The reasons were several. Scottish-born and a naturalized American, he had English friends at Bahrein and Kuwait, and that was enough to make his loyalties suspect. Also, he was far too friendly with the U.S. consulate in Dhahran, another suspect body that was always avid for news from the secret world of Aramco. As Parker T. Hart, the American consul at Dhahran, reported to the State Department, "To the Consulate, Mr. 'Mac's retirement is a distinct loss. Of all of Aramco's management, no one has been so consistently frank and cooperative as he has."[19]

Plainly, MacPherson had been Hart's best informant inside Aramco and, in an industry in which silence was golden, especially in relations with representatives of the U.S. government, that was a crime. But there was another reason why MacPherson was leaving Aramco, and that had to do with another schism that had developed in the board-room. One group favored a "smash and grab" in Arabia — they were playing for high, short-term profits and planning on Aramco's quit-tance when Ibn Saud and Abdullah Suleiman became impossible to deal with. MacPherson belonged to the other group (which included Barger), whose members hoped to stay in Saudi Arabia for the long term. Though this plan required continual compromise with the king and his government, they believed that in the end it would produce far larger profits than the smash and grab. Moreover, MacPherson had been most critical of Aramco's board of directors. As Hart reported to Washington, "Mr. Mac"

> remarked scornfully to me on several occasions that the attitude of the Board in general is characterized by primary attention to world-wide balance sheets and profit before all else, rather than the realities of the Near East and particularly the special factors existent in Arabia. He stated that Aramco had been a "gold mine" and that there was no reason to scrimp in what Aramco did for Arabs either in such benefits as health centers and education, or for that matter in royalty pay-ments.[20]

The loss of "Mr. Mac" removed from the scene an ambitious expert at a critical time. Oil production was expanding exponentially. Ras Tanura refinery, originally designed for a daily capacity of 50,000 bar-rels, was pushed and streamlined to give it a throughput of 127,000 barrels. Drilling at the great oil fields at Gawar and Abqaiq was re-sumed in 1944 when a stabilizer was set up to remove the poisonous and corrosive hydrogen sulfide gas. Oil was discovered at Qatif in June 1945, at Ain Dar in June 1948, and at Fadhil and Haradh in January 1950. These discoveries brought the total number of proven oil reser-voirs in Saudi Arabia to seven, any one of which could, it was estimated, supply all Europe with petroleum products for decades to come. Daily oil production from three of these reservoirs rose from 20,000 barrels a day in 1945 to over 246,000 in 1947. It passed the 300,000-barrel mark at the beginning of 1948, and as 1949 began it had passed 500,000.

MacPherson's efforts were reflected in the growth of Aramco from less than 2,900 employees at the end of 1943 to 18,637 five years on. In addition, 1,617 Americans and about 5,200 Saudi Arabs worked for contractors on Aramco expansion projects, mainly constructing buildings to transform Dhahran from a ramshackle oil town into the most modern commercial conurbation on the Gulf. He revitalized the government relations services that acted as a diplomatic link to the Saudi, the U.S., and the British governments. He installed his best and brightest officers in all locations important to Aramco throughout the world.

But the Aramco board members acknowledged none of MacPherson's accomplishments. They wanted a "real" American in his job. They alleged that he lacked the "degrees of good judgement and analytical ability required by the importance of his position."[21] When MacPherson departed to become a high executive of Getty's Gulf Oil in Kuwait, Parker T. Hart made this observation concerning the future leadership of Aramco:

> No doubt a good man can be found for the chair that Macpherson is giving up. Who he will be, no one here knows at the moment. MacPherson is convinced it will not be F. A. Davies or Ohliger. He will not be surprised if the choice is a "dark horse," new to Arabia but pliable to Board interests. Whoever he is, he will enter his position at a most delicate moment and will do well to proceed with great caution and tact vis-à-vis the Saudi Government.[22]

In the reshuffling that occurred after MacPherson's departure, the "terrible tycoon" W. F. Moore became president of the company in Arabia. He was a Texan and a bit of a ruffian. He focused on profits and production and countenanced no social contact with the "Ay-rabs." No chairman or chief executive was appointed, and Fred A. Davies took over MacPherson's responsibility as operations chief. Floyd Ohliger became chief of government relations. Under Moore, relations with the consul in Dhahran and the U.S. minister in Jidda, J. Rives Childs, a lordly character much concerned with American primacy, remained as formal and strained as ever. When the king made an official visit to Aramco in January 1947, Childs rebuked Moore about the dress of the Aramcons lining the route and advised the secretary of state,

> I regret to state that the appearance presented by some of the Americans did anything but add dignity to the occasion. . . . Most of the Americans present were in their shirt sleeves, without neckties, and some of them were wearing most unprepossessing looking shirts whose tails hung outside their trousers. . . . Arabs are very simple in their

social relations, but I have always found them to have a very high sense of dignity and propriety, and I cannot believe that the negligent appearance which these Americans presented could possibly have made a favorable impression.[23]

Childs also reported a certain arrogance in the attitude of Aramco's management. As Moore's management increasingly took on an atmosphere of company secrecy, Aramco's government relations officials began to assume some of the responsibilities normally handled by foreign service officers, diplomats of the State Department. As Childs wrote to the State Department,

> Unfortunately the Arabian American Oil Company was in Saudi Arabia before the legation at Jidda or the consulate at Dhahran. The King and his Ministers, few of whom are familiar with normal diplomatic procedure as practised by countries which have a settled tradition of diplomatic intercourse, became accustomed, in the absence of American official representation, to dealing with ARAMCO as they would with representatives of a foreign government. By the time that a Legation and Consulate had been established in Saudi Arabia, the affairs of ARAMCO and of Saudi Arabia had become so intermingled that it was natural that the Saudi Arabian Government should continue to deal with the Company on its old footing and, equally as natural, for reasons of prestige among others, that the Company should continue to perform diplomatic functions. . . . I have the highest regard [for the Company management officials who had so usurped the functions recently] but the Department will appreciate that, with the best will in the world, it is not easy for men voluntarily to relinquish privileges they have once enjoyed.[24]

By 1948 the State Department had become greatly concerned about Aramco's assumption of extraordinary powers. Department officials made it a top priority to "make King Ibn Saud and his Ministers know the United States Government and its representatives in Arabia as well as they know Aramco and to look to the government representatives in Saudi Arabia for any contacts that are not strictly the business of Aramco." Thus the king would gain "confidence in the United States Government and depend upon it for fair dealing." Moreover, the State Department should "indicate to Aramco officials that the Department might be able to help the company considerably in its diplomatic relations with the King."[25]

By 1950, Dhahran began to acquire the appearance and aura of an American company town. It was said to resemble Bakersfield on the edge of the Mojave Desert in California, as it was in the 1950s — a little world of split-level houses with outskirts of dreary tin-roofed shacks, cement-block bars, and filling stations. In Dhahran a hot wind blew often, and the vast emptiness of the surrounding desert created a sense of isolation and silence. Twenty years earlier, the places where the Aramco employees lived had been covered with sparse vegetation characteristic of the desert and utilized only by wandering Bedouin, with their flocks of sheep and goats and their herds of camels.

Barger called in experts to make a study of the town for the review of the senior staff. Solon T. Kimball of Columbia University wrote encouragingly of how he was impressed, "as all must be who see what has been accomplished, with the magnificence of American know-how." Yet he also voiced the difficulties he perceived in the community: "Although one may hear frequent praises for the things that Aramco does for its employees, . . . nevertheless, there are deep currents of disquiet and frustration, and perhaps even more serious personal consequences."[26]

Kimball found, too, that Dhahran, this outpost of American civilization, this state within a small state, consisted of nearly 10,000 people. The other two Aramco townships, Abqaiq and Ras Tanura, held about 5,000 each. Of the 20,400 people Aramco employed, 4,000 were Americans, 13,400 were Saudis, and 3,000 were of other nationalities. Counting the family members of American personnel, the Aramcons numbered about 6,400, or about one third of the company town population.

Each town, Kimball found, was divided into "five distinctive sections that correspond to internal social divisions or economic functions." In the "vibrant heart" of each town was located "the offices, warehouses, supply depots, equipment yards, repair shops, and the vast array of towers, tanks, and pipes that are necessary for the processing, refining, and transmission of oil." It was "within this area that one can also find the major retail and service centers, that are reserved for the use by the 'senior' staff, a group composed largely of Americans but with a scattering of other nationalities." Here, "one may buy stamps and post a letter, get a hair cut or a beauty treatment, buy groceries, household supplies, and essential personal items. All these activities are directly supervised by Aramco."[27]

The other four areas were "residential, each separated from the other. . . . The divisions correspond closely with the structure of the bureaucratic hierarchy and ethnic divisions among the employees, . . . which gives emphasis to the social divisions within the whole."[28]

The senior staff camp was easy to identify. In it, each house was

> surrounded by a small grassed yard usually enclosed by a hedge. There are other plantings including flowering shrubs, low desert trees and, in some instances flower gardens. . . . Streets are paved and frequently

curbed, and have night lighting. There are only slight variations between the recreational facilities of each senior staff camp. Each one possesses an auditorium that is also used as a movie house and for amateur productions; a luxurious club with snack bar, bowling alleys, library, dining room, lounge, and terrace for dancing and social gatherings. Two senior staff camps have swimming pools, while Ras Tanura residents use an immense beach on the Persian Gulf. In addition, one may find baseball diamonds, tennis courts, soccer and football fields, and desert-style golf links. Dhahran has a riding stable.[29]

Houses varied in size and construction. The "unclassified officials," those found in "the upper echelons of the bureaucracy," occupied the larger and more elaborate residences. Lesser employees lived in more modest quarters in the "intermediate" area. They were rated in the system as "semiskilled and nonsupervisory." Most were "other nationals" recruited from countries of the Middle East, and Africa and the Mediterranean. Their "barrack-like dwellings" consisted of concrete or cement-block structures. The third, or "general," camp was of similar construction and arrangement, offering "modest recreational facilities, a market for buying foodstuffs and other items, and one or more mosques."[30]

The fourth residential area, "neither planned nor welcomed," was "reminiscent of the Hoovervilles of depression days." Homes were made of "every conceivable kind of scrap material with a scattering of more traditional palm-leaf native *barastis* and an occasional substantial building of concrete block."[31] Here, as Kimball described it, the general laborers,

> mostly Saudis, may bring their families. One can see occasional sheep, goats, and burros, and the camels tethered nearby may belong to an employee or his visiting relatives. One also finds an incipient native *suk* or market, perhaps a garage and gasoline pump, and other evidences of an emerging indigenous community life. Both Aramco and the government are disturbed by these settlements, and efforts are under way to encourage their replacement by the development of planned Arab-type towns through subsidies and other devices.[32]

Kimball also commented on the sense of isolation experienced in the American enclave. The fact that the religious authorities of the land viewed the Aramcons as a threat heightened their sense of insecurity. Though the U.S. employees might try to live within the restrictions imposed on them, "new decrees are issued without previous warning and are thought to be unpredictable and capricious."[33] The employees looked "to the high officials of Aramco to provide them protection, although they are also aware that certain breaches of law mean immediate deportation, a fate viewed more favorably than languishing in an

Arab jail." The Muslim code regarding diet, dress, abstinence from alcohol, daily worship, and fasting continued to complicate the lives of Aramco employees. Bans on alcohol consumption disturbed the

> customary behavior of a great many people. American men who engage in hard outdoor labor are known to relish an evening's beer or more, and the oil field workers have always been respected for their capacities. I heard several lament the passing of beer in particular. These employees recounted the many pleasant evenings when large numbers would congregate at the clubs to visit, gamble, or dance. They complained that soft drinks never quite provided the same spirit of conviviality, and they regretted the passing of, to them, pleasanter days of good companionship.[34]

It was against that background that Peter and Ellen Speers, of higher management, came to town. To the company they were known as "unclassifieds," of the highest rank in the hierarchy; to the stiffs, "the shiny pants"; to the Saudis, "sobs" and "memsobs." The Speers joined the senior staff at the time that Cheney was writing his memoir about Aramco's social circumstances. Born in Lahore, capital of the Punjab in British India, and the son of missionaries, Speers had attended Princeton, had served in the U.S. Army during the war, and afterward had studied international affairs. His wife, the former Ellen Mac-Daniels, was a daughter of a Cornell University professor and had majored in political science at Oberlin College. After Oberlin, she went on to the Fletcher School of Law and Diplomacy. Next she worked at the State Department's Near Eastern desk in Washington and later met Speers in Greece, where both served with an official U.S. team observing the Greek elections after World War II. After returning to the United States, Speers learned Arabic in the Near Eastern program at Princeton, the best such program in the United States. They married, Speers joined Aramco, and the company sent him to the American University in Cairo for six months to continue his Arabic studies. Ellen taught the history of philosophy at the university.

When he returned to Dhahran, he joined the staff of George Rentz, the company's Arabist and chief of what would become the Arabian Affairs Division, Aramco's intelligence and analysis section in government relations. So that, if necessary, he could match wits with the British, the company sent him, at its expense, to the London School of Oriental and National African Studies to work on a thesis about the development of modern Arabic. Then he went to the government relations' policy and planning staff, where he dealt with important

policy issues affecting Aramco, including the rise of Arab nationalism, the growing Saudi desire to take over Aramco, the Arab oil boy-
cotts, the consequences of the Arab-Israeli wars, and pressures from
the Saudi government concerning price and production issues.

Looking back on his experience, Speers considered Aramco to be "a
unique company" because of its "informal and egalitarian organization." Nobody said, "'I'm a vice president. I don't want to talk to you.'"
In Saudi Arabia, "everybody had a lot in common . . . living in this
strange environment for a few years at a time. And we all had the same
shortages, the same needs. So people were more or less equal, and
everybody pitched in to set up things like nursery schools, or to organize a club. Most people were proud to be associated with Aramco. . . .
For the most part, the families came to like it too. . . . For the children
who grew up there it was home. And [after getting an education else-
where] many of them went back."[35]

Women had their own adjustments to make to life in Saudi Arabia.
As Ellen Speers remembered, the Saudi poet Rashid ibn Mubarak ibn
Hamad al-Ruzaiqui prepared an ode, entitled "A Greeting" and redo-
lent of Saudi conventions of addressing women, when a group of wives
arrived:

> Welcome and welcome and most welcome are you all; and most
> blessed and auspicious is this hour in which there have come to the
> Research Division in Damman, for the purpose of visiting, watch-
> ing, and seeing, the honorable ladies and the chaste women, mak-
> ing their most amiable, with eyes flirting with the eyes of gazelles,
> and with looks stirring in watchers the so-far still feeling of yearning,
> Madame Calli, Madame Hope, Madame Shirley, Madame Madge, and
> Madame Ellen, and met with their beloved friends and companions
> Miss Lois, Miss Grace, Miss Mary, Miss Frances, Madame Maybell, and
> Miss Elsie.
>
> Welcome to the Ladies; this is a blessing; My dear friends, the chaste
> women are coming to visit you; They have arrived most and most
> welcome; A thousand welcomes to them; Verily they are the wives of
> men who are lions of battles.[36]

The Speerses' first home in Saudi Arabia was a two-bedroom apart-
ment, with a living room–dining room combination, a long and narrow
kitchen, and the standard company-rented furniture — colonial re-
production suites for the living room and dining room, all-metal bedroom furniture, and "a couple of shag area rugs on the cement floor."
All the floors were plain cement, on which, later, the company laid
either blue or green linoleum. Later still, Aramco provided parquet
flooring, but only "if your linoleum had been down for x number of

years or if you had clout." Over the years the Speerses replaced Aramco's furniture with their own.[37]

Ellen Speers also commented on the housing situation and the hierarchy that determined a worker's chances of obtaining a comfortable living situation:

> I think that the limited housing probably caused more grief than practically anything else, particularly if you and somebody else were hoping for the same house. When a house became available, you could apply, "I'd like to have that house," and then you'd find that you didn't get it because so-and-so had more points.
>
> Most of the time we were there housing was in short supply and there was a great deal of difference in the quality and amenities — with cement block duplexes with small rooms being the least desirable; the more spacious two- to four-bedroom, two-bath homes of various vintages and floor plans, some more desirable than others.
>
> Housing was assigned according to an elaborate formula. The number, sexes and ages of your children determined how many bedrooms you were entitled to. Points allotted for grade level and years of service were combined to establish your place on the list of applicants.[38]

In her "orientation program" to prepare her for life in Arabia in the early 1950s, the company suggested that Ellen Speers bring with her "three evening gowns," as there was nothing, but nothing, to buy locally:

> Aramco came to what was essentially a desert. There was a small fishing village, called al-Khobar, which was ten miles away, maybe. But it was one, maybe two, blocks of dirt street. I think there was a mosque, and then these little stall shops, just a single room going back twenty feet. Each of these would have a very miscellaneous collection of a few canned goods, maybe flashlights or batteries, enamel bowls and enamel teapots, rubber sandals, and three-yard lengths of materials worn by the Yemenis and the coastal people wore as sarongs.[39]

The only commodities available locally were fish and pearls, though the company did have a system whereby goods could be purchased from companies such as J. C. Penney, Montgomery Ward, and Bloomingdale's; Aramco arranged for their shipment, which took about eight weeks. Also, furnishings in Danish teak or Hong Kong rosewood could be purchased by mail and were then shipped by the company.

In Oildom, every place was within walking distance or accessible by riding a company bus. It was just as easy to get around socially. Though rank within the company affected the amenities available to an Aramcon, the Speerses noted that camaraderie, rather than snobbery, characterized relationships among company employees.

Mrs. Speers may have been invited to bring three evening dresses with her, but she rarely wore them. Her husband never wore a tux and did not have one. She claimed that there was not a dress code, either for business or socializing. For the men it was "khakis and a short-sleeve shirt or just casual slacks." People "could be quite dressy for parties. You know, all of us had a cocktail-type dress wardrobe and some long dresses were worn. . . . Some people would have formal dinner parties just to use their formal attire." Most entertaining was done in the home, because there was no other place to do so.[40]

> When I first arrived in Saudi Arabia a feature of social life was a "Payday Thursday" brunch. . . . The libations [were] typically a pink gin (two jiggers of gin poured into an old-fashioned glass full of ice and a dash of angostura bitters). Someone would go to the Saudi town and purchase Arab bread. An array of cold meats, cheeses, and other fixings and snacks would be spread out on the table and people would help themselves.
>
> The banning of the sale of alcohol and the change to the five-day week doomed this informal entertainment.[41]

Much planning went into some of the parties: "You couldn't go out and hire entertainers. Pin ceremonies (the recognition of five, ten, etc., years of employment), departure on long leaves, retirements, etc., were occasions which called for something special. Movies, poems, skits, musical revues, elaborate constructions involving some inside joke . . ."[42]

Early on Aramco began to import servants. Women servants were forbidden by the Saudi government, but houseboys were brought in mainly from India, Yemen, and Aden. The company provided living quarters for them in the "sheepsheds," and Aramco "contracted with somebody in India to hire people. If you wanted a houseboy you'd go in and sign a contract and you were responsible for their wages and transportation."[43]

In the spheres of education, recreation, and culture, the company was, Ellen Speers recounted,

> terrific about providing facilities; but the running of the organization and the facilities was the responsibility of the employees and their families. The bowling association, for example, would decide the rules, but Aramco provided the pinboys, the upkeep of the lanes. So it was with the tennis association, the golf club, the hobby farm, the yacht club, the photography club, and so on. Professional entertainers were flown in from the States to teach amateur dramatics. The top-ranking Australian tennis players . . . were brought in to coach the Aramco Tennis Club players.[44]

The schools had American teachers, paid by the company, and an American curriculum. Hundreds of thousands of dollars were put into it. The school system ran on a "three months on, one month off" plan, so that children going on vacation wouldn't miss a whole term. Tutoring was arranged for a child who had been away. Since the schools did not go beyond the ninth grade, Aramco had an education assistance plan whereby the children of senior staff expatriate employees were sent to the best schools at company expense, less a modest deductible. An allowance was made for children's travel to and from offshore schools; children attending the American Community School in Beirut traveled home by company aircraft for both Christmas and spring vacations. Those attending school in the States received one trip a year at Aramco's expense. The company's munificence seemed endless.

Every detail in life received its attention — free medical care, retirement plans, savings plans, television, radio, the company newspaper. New houses were equipped with a small room for the brewing of alcoholic beverages. The parents arranged programs for youngsters, such as Little League baseball, swimming, crafts, archaeology clubs, Girl Scouts, Boy Scouts, and weekly sales of homemade baked goods — the proceeds became the children's spending money. One family bought a potato-chip maker at a time when potato chips were not available, and the boy salesman cleaned up. Women were helped to establish hairdressing businesses and beauty parlors; Aramco started a kindergarten, and preschools became a cottage industry; Aramco brought in male beauticians from Beirut; an executive's wife, Maya Marinovic, started a Montessori kindergarten. At the beginning there was one swimming pool; over time the company built two more — then it designated one for men, one for women, and one for children. The company provided the equipment and the quarters for every conceivable hobby. The facilities were free, except for a nominal fee deducted from each member's paycheck.

The company's benevolence knew few bounds, except in one direction: all women had to conform to the Saudis' code of female behavior. Women were allowed to drive inside the camp, but not outside it and never alone — the Saudi Committees of Public Morality feared that if Occidental women were allowed to do so, they would offend against the moral statutes of the Koran. The company, always sensitive to local customs, requested that women never venture abroad unless their arms were covered down to their elbows and the legs down to the knees. The uncovered legs of women and girls were sometimes sprayed with black paint by disapproving Saudis. Each summer the company would issue a directive: "Please get your teenage daughter, when she goes to Khobar, to wear something besides a mini-skirt and a tank top." Someone who dressed in this manner, Ellen Speers remembered, was regarded by the Saudis as a whore.[45]

The Saudi religious police were never far away, especially at Christmastime. A high point of each year for many years, the senior staff put on a Christmas pageant "with real camels and Mary on a real donkey and so on." Santa Claus arrived by helicopter and was driven down Main Street in an open car. As Speers noted, "That got to be very popular with the local people. The Saudis from outside the compound started coming to watch the thing." But it "got to be too popular." Saudi officials came to suspect that the pageant "was missionary work, which it wasn't." The people "would come out to cheer Santa Claus. Most of them didn't know who Santa Claus was." Nonetheless, the Saudi government ordered that the pageant be stopped. Although Aramco provided the Saudi workers with mosques, the Saudis did not reciprocate in the category of religious tolerance. No churches were built, and no priests or clerics were allowed at the camp, except occasionals who slipped in disguised as schoolteachers. In the end, senior staff camp became "a killjoy world. The lights went out and so did the fun."[46]

The Saudi Arab workers lived in a completely different world. The Arabs were most often fresh from the tiny villages in the deserts. Their habits were governed by rigid tribal and traditional precepts and Mother Nature. Their lives were shaped around the call to prayer five times a day. They typically lived a nomadic life, moving about to find grazing and water for their camels and sheep. Their code of behavior and laws were based on those of the Prophet. They rendered obedience only to their sheikh. They had little understanding of money; they mostly obtained necessary goods by a barter system. Dates growing in the oases formed a staple of their diet. Their world was little changed since the days of the Book of Genesis.

These Arabs were lured to work for Aramco not through any desire to improve their destinies. They believed their lot in life was already determined by Allah. They came to work for Aramco for one particular reason:

> Word spread to the desert and townspeople that in exchange for some physical effort the blue eyed foreigners would give a man a handful of silver! And so they flocked to Aramco's budding oil centers to find their "pot of silver" — and also to satisfy their great curiosity about what was taking place.[47]

Soon these Bedouin workers grew to understand more about the world beyond the desert and learned ways to improve their lot in life. This involved the discovery that Aramco was not particularly benevolent to its Arab laborers. Their earliest tutors were bitter, unhappy Italian ex–prisoners of war who had been captured by the British during the 1940–41 campaign in Italian East Africa. They had been provided to Aramco, which at the time was desperately in need of workers with modern labor skills; a thousand had volunteered for the work as a way to earn good money and thus get one step closer to home. Aramco later regretted employing them; some were heavily Marxist and sowed dissatisfaction among their colleagues at Aramco. Others successfully opened shops and a restaurant near Aramco. But they were far too successful, and the Saudi government ordered them to close their businesses.

They were replaced as supervisors by Palestinians dispossessed by the conflict in Palestine. The best-educated of the Arabs, they quickly established themselves as valued workers. The Palestinians also raised the awareness of the Saudi Arabs, relating their "bitterness and suffering to their brother Arabs." The Bedouin "became aware of the severe social and political problems outside their own sphere." Also, they "heard of many wonderful things that were commonplace in the lives of his brother Arabs but which had not yet come to him." Thus they spread a sense of dissatisfaction among the Saudi Bedouin. Several of these Palestinians later became political activists.[48]

One such case involved Nasser Said, a former Aramco employee of Syrian origins and a member of the Federation of Arab Trades Unions. After he left Aramco in 1957, he publicly claimed that he represented the Saudi oil workers in Aramco. Aramco inquiries showed that Said had visited the Soviet Union in 1957 and "circumstantial evidence gives ground to suspect the existence of some clandestine organization among Aramco's workers which maintains liaison with the outside world."[49]

But indeed, there was ample reason for the Arab workers to be dissatisfied with their treatment by Aramco. The company's management of this workforce came to be seen as an example of "capitalist exploitation" in the Middle East. The "blue-eyed infidels" were in many ways treating the Bedouin as third-class citizens. Their pay was low, their housing was poor, medical assistance was expensive, and racial discrimination was in evidence everywhere. Americans lived in air-conditioned houses and enjoyed movies, private clubs, lounges, swimming pools, and tennis courts. The Muslim peoples at the camp, on the other hand, lived in palm-leaf huts and received only emergency medical aid. An Afghan diplomat visiting Dhahran recounted how he saw a drinking fountain of ice water posted with a sign that said FOR AMERICANS ONLY. Conditions at the Dhahran Arab Hospital, in the opinion of the U.S. consul, were "a disgrace to the Company and indirectly to Americans." Until "two months ago beds were lined up in the narrow corridors; flies infested the place; patients with infectious diseases were not properly segregated."[50]

In the mid '40's, the Saudis' representatives presented the company with four demands: higher wages, permanent housing, an end to discrimination in favor of foreign laborers over Saudi workers, and an improvement in conditions at the Arab hospital. And when their demands were not met immediately, their demonstrations turned ugly. Then the government's troops arrived with "gun butts swinging and quickly took the starch out of unprepared Saudi workmen." The American consul advised the State Department, more in hope and sorrow than in anger, that "the officials of this Company are optimistic that their recent labor troubles are but a passing phase in the gigantic development of what is probably the largest oil field in the world — America's new frontier."[51]

Living standards at the Arab camp improved a little after this confrontation, but significant changes would not arrive until almost a decade later. When the Palestinians moved away to more lucrative work, American "personnel specialists" were recruited in the United States from "the low end of the labor market"[52] and sent to Aramco in a liberty ship. They lived in the bachelor quarters of Bunkhouse 25, two men to a room with old Aramco steel furniture that was painted a uniform gunmetal gray. The specialists both lived and worked there:

> Bunkhouse 25, known as al-Barsamah to the Arabs, became an administrative center responsible for Wages and Salaries, Sanitation, Vacation Schedules, Discipline, Transportation and Chits, Arab Housing, Recruiting, Cost of Living Indexes, Fingerprints and Photographing, Personnel Statistics, Firewood Distribution, Transfers, Cooperative Messes, Personnel Files, and the Donkey Farm.[53]

The specialists became responsible for prodding the Saudis into work at the donkey farm, which lay near the west sewer pumping station. The work entailed

> tossing vagrants (human and goats) out of the Saudi Camp; supervising the collection of garbage; photographing braided Bedouins for personnel records; pricing vegetables in Qatif; helping to remove bot-

tles and tin cans from clogged "Eastern Style" w.c. drain pipes; and [serving] as midwives to she-asses in labor at the Donkey Farm.[54]

Nelson found himself in charge in "the back room" of Bunkhouse 25, where the Arab "disciplinees" gathered to hear the complaints against them by their supervisors. Usually the offense was sleeping on the job. The atmosphere of "the back room" reminded Nelson of "the Pit in Chicago or the Night Court in lower Manhattan." The disciplinees clustered around the desk of the personnel specialist. Impatient to have his case heard after waiting his turn for one or two days, each Arab would wave his chit, the document laying out the charge against him, in an attempt to catch the attention of the American:

> "*Aish faik?* What's up with you?" the Arab interpreter sitting alongside the American would ask the nearest Saudi disciplinee.
> "I don't quite know," the Saudi would say. "My *Sahib* in Ras Tanura is no good with me any more and sent me here with this chit":

> Ras Tanura
(No Date)

> Arab Personnel,
> Dhahran.
>   This here Abdullah, No. 1312, won't work no more. Give him three days off without pay [as punishment]

> Thanx,
John Riley
Longshoreman

Telephoning was an unpredictable affair, and with three score other disciplinees impatiently awaiting judgement, a half hour could not be wasted in attempting to get through to Ras Tanura to ascertain the details.

"Tell him: 'Three days without pay,'" the Personnel Specialist would instruct the interpreter.

After several minutes of two-sided volatile Arabic, the interpreter would say: "He doesn't want to work for Sahib Riley any more."

"All right. Tell him after he has had his three days off, we will transfer him somewhere else. Next case."[55]

Aramco Muslims referred to the pre-Muhammadan, unenlightened centuries as Asr al-Jaahiliya, the Age of Ignorance. Saudi employees referred to the company's Bunkhouse 25 period of industrial relations as Aramco's Asr al-Jaahiliya.

Under this regime, which lasted from 1945 to 1960, the turnover in Arab employees reached 75 percent and stayed at that level for years until Bunkhouse 25 was pulled down and new facilities for Arab personnel were built elsewhere. A form of "penal reform" was introduced with the object of "helping the employee improve his performance, correct his attitudes, or change his habits to conform to more acceptable standards."[56] After the improvements, the turnover came down to 10.8 percent.

Yet as conditions for Saudis improved, as they eventually did, an unexpected factor accompanied their increase in pay and prosperity. They were running into debt because Aramco had failed to advise Arab employees in the management of money. As their earning power increased, many of the workmen stood "fact to face with the dilemma of how to keep the creditors from their door." This state of affairs had arisen through the "strong dependence on paternalism and a feeling that any difficulty they are in is not a personal difficulty but a jointly shared problem with the Company." The supervisors now found themselves "deeply involved in the personal lives of the Saudi workmen." They complained that most Saudi workers would not realize that "a major part of their financial dilemma could be solved by reducing expenditures rather than increasing wages." Like their government, they all wanted more money, and, as Nelson warned:

> This feeling has generated a curious rationale on the part of our Saudi workmen. They agree that the lot of the employee is better in Aramco than almost anywhere else in the Kingdom but that somehow the Company has not done enough and has let the employee down. This has led to demands for more money, improved benefits and a lot of talk about how "things would be resolved for the better if unions were allowed."[57]

In these circumstances, Abdullah Tariki, son of a Bedouin who ran camel trains, emerged from obscurity to force the reforms that would improve the situation of Arab workers at the Donkey Farm and elsewhere at Aramco. Educated in Kuwait, sharp-witted, slight and boyish in appearance, he proudly wore the red-and-white-checked headdress of the Saudi Arab — well aware that to the Aramco rednecks he was just a "raghead," a term as insulting to a Saudi Arab as *nigger* is to blacks. Somehow he came to the attention of Abdullah Suleiman and, having learned to speak English well, from time to time acted as Ibn Saud's interpreter during his meetings with Aramco officials. Suleiman looked after Tariki and provided him with a grant to study in Cairo and then at the University of Texas, where he took a degree in petroleum engineering.

Tariki had married an American girl from Poughkeepsie, north of New York City. Tariki was very proud of his bride. Again through Abdullah Suleiman's patronage, in the early 1950s Tariki became director of

Aramco's petroleum and minerals resources, the Saudi government's first native representative in Aramco management. One of the articles of the 1933 concession agreement had in fact obliged Aramco to train Saudis to hold increasingly higher positions in the company. But little such training had occurred.

A bright, able, and proud young man, Tariki expected that the company would have a house ready for him when he arrived. But this proved not to be the case:

> The mentality of some Aramco management at that time was pretty much "We're in charge here, this is our company" and . . . instead of anyone helping him, taking him over to where the housing was controlled, introducing him and so on, they turned him loose and said, "Go get yourself a house." I think he may have had a bit of a chip on his shoulder when he arrived, but that certainly added to it and caused some of the troubles that came later. . . . In comparison with most Saudi officials in those days, he was well educated and had had a lot of practical experience [in the oil industry]. . . . He had some pretty advanced ideas . . . about how Saudi Arabia ought to have more of a say in its own oil at that time. You'd have to say that it was a pretty controlled situation; the oil companies set the price.[58]

Even then, in the 1950s, the company did not admit Tariki to the senior staff camp, as his rank entitled him — he was the most important Saudi official responsible for oil. For a time he was relegated with his bride to a lesser camp. Although Aramco made him a member of its board of directors, Tariki was disliked and even feared by Aramco management.

The consequences of Tariki's poor treatment were serious for Aramco and for the entire Anglo-American oil industry in the Middle East. For when Tariki returned to Riyadh, he began to advocate the expropriation of Aramco, an idea that found much favor within the Saudi government. Also, imbued with much anti-Aramco fervor, he attended the first Arab Petroleum Congress as a delegate of Saudi Arabia, and he would eventually be largely responsible for forming the cartel of oil-producing countries known as the Organization of Petroleum Exporting Countries (OPEC). This cartel would become as powerful an entity as the oil companies themselves.

Just after Tariki arrived in Dhahran, a riot involving Saudi workers at last spurred the revolution in company thinking that was so desired by the Saudis. A group of twelve young Saudis educated in the United States decided to demonstrate against conditions in the "general camp" where the Saudis lived. The demonstration began at the Saudi

police station, a U.S. Air Force bus was stoned in the ensuing disturbance, and people were injured.

> On the following morning, start of a new work week . . . the entire
> Saudi labor force stayed out. Americans went to work as usual . . . but
> there was a strange absence of the usual shuffle and slap of Arab
> sandals. . . . Then, finally, [the group of twelve] openly came forward
> with a petition, actually a long list of demands ranging from pay in-
> creases to ice water. This they presented to the company, with a copy to
> the government, representing themselves as spokesmen for the bulk of
> Saudi employees.[59]

The Saudi government did not support the demonstraters. Instead,
Crown Prince Saud accused them of subversion, and the government
uttered a decree:

> God has decided that this house (the Holy Land) ought to be a place of
> resort and security for mankind. . . .
> It does not permit the Shrine to be the field for political action,
> propaganda, etc. It repeats and renews the warning and announces to
> all people, those who are residing, travelling, immigrating, and in the
> neighborhood, that every action which is not consonant with the wor-
> ship of God is absolutely forbidden. It notifies, again, that political
> propaganda, no matter of what kind it may be, is prohibited.
> The Government will take vigorously the necessary procedure to-
> wards every one who will not obey these orders.[60]

But despite this clear warning from the government, none of the
strikers returned to work. "More back-to-work orders came through.
The strikers made no move. . . . At the end of the second week, a payday
came along," and most of the strikers returned to work. "The rest came
back during the third week, thus evading the rule that anyone absent
without leave for three consecutive weeks was automatically dropped
from the pay roll."[61]

Thus the Arabs made a united stand to better their situation in
Aramco. The repercussions were significant:

> There was a certain amount of weak chortling that they had given in
> without gaining their demands; but that was obviously a false interpre-
> tation. The strikers had neither given in nor abandoned their demands.
> They had returned to work when it suited them to do so. They had de-
> fied the government, and the government had avoided the challenge.
> Believe in the King's despotic power was seriously weakened. As for the
> company, it had lost most of its control over its own labor affairs.[62]

The strike had a profound effect on management. Newly a public
relations officer of the company, Cheney recorded that Aramco, fearing that next time it might lose the concession, began to run

a corporate welfare state that might startle many a feather-bedded American or British industry. Set against the harsh background of poverty, hunger and disease that Arabia has always known, the wages and guarantees of well-fed longevity that the oil industry [began to offer] its Saudi employees [verged] on the fantastic.[63]

Aramco's basic wage scale more than doubled, and by 1957 the average annual income among all Saudi employees had risen to $1,300 — astronomical for Arabia. The marginal living quarters and working conditions that had characterized the Arab worker's life in the 1930s and 1940s were indeed transformed. Cheney noted that the Saudi

is given free lodging in company quarters with all facilities attached, plus recreation halls, swimming pools, sports grounds and libraries. He is given free transportation to and from work, and to his country home on weekends. He is paid overtime for any work exceeding the standard forty-five hour week. He is given four weeks' vacation a year on full pay. He is given free medical care for himself and his family. . . .

He is offered cash rewards for overcoming illiteracy in classes given free by the company. If he wishes to pursue further learning, he is offered free technical training which he can parlay into a liberal education, much of it on company time and while drawing full pay. At the end of his training he may win a company scholarship to a foreign university.

He is enticed to stay with Aramco by cash rewards. . . . He is entitled when necessary to extended sick-leave on full pay, and his family to munificent death benefits if he dies. If he is laid off, he receives a full year's pay. As for the risk of being discharged, it practically takes a royal decree to fire a Saudi these days.[64]

Still, despite the fact that the lot of the average Saudi employee had improved to a dramatic degree, the Aramco compound had hardly become thoroughly egalitarian concerning the Arabs. Only a small handful would rise to the level of management and the privilege of living in the senior staff camp during the 1950s and even the 1960s. Aramco would long consist of a predominantly Saudi workforce managed almost entirely by foreigners.

ALMIGHTY EXCOM

T HE ARABIAN AMERICAN Oil Company opened the postwar era in a confusion of sharp crises and noisy controversy. The most important problem involved the relationship between the company and Ibn Saud, especially the contretemps known as "the gold pound controversy." This had ricocheted about in Saudi-American oil politics since 1940. In 1946, it came to a head because resolving it was essential to Aramco's most salient goal: entering into partnership with Exxon, the largest oil company in the world, and Mobil. It would thereby establish the largest and the richest consortium in the history of commerce.

Under the concession agreement of 1933, the company was required to pay Ibn Saud his royalties in gold. But during the war, the price of gold had become distorted and inflated, and therefore the company sought to pay Ibn Saud at the official rate of gold posted in New York City. The government countered with the claim that it must be paid at the exchange rate in Jidda, where the price was double the official rate in New York City. Always a controversial issue, the dispute finally blew up. The Saudis refused to accept their royalties for 1947 and imposed demands that would have multiplied their payments fantastically. A U.S. legation money wizard asserted that, if Aramco had complied, the Saudi government would have been in a position to

> buy gold in the United States at $35 per ounce, and ship this gold to Jidda. If, as the Government contends (and its contention can mean nothing else), this gold, after it gets to Jidda, can be sold for more than $70 per ounce in dollars, the Government could more than double its money in dollars with each gold purchase. Starting with $1,000,000 and doubling its money on each transaction, [it] would

have $1,024,000,000 in ten transactions. In the 14th transaction it would be able to buy most of the gold reserve of the United States Government, and in the 15th would own the entire stock of monetary gold in the world with millions of dollars to spare.[1]

The king would not abandon a favorable position handed to him through the fortunes of war. Yet in order to negotiate with Exxon and Mobil to establish a consortium, to market Aramco's oil, Aramco had to settle the gold controversy without bowing to impossible demands made by Ibn Saud. But even with diplomatic intervention, the controversy was not settled. Accordingly, W. F. Moore went to Riyadh to negotiate with the king and his finance minister. Moore was not at his most tactful when, in June 1947, he met the king and Abdullah Suleiman at the palace. As Crown Prince Saud said to the American minister, who reported this to the U.S. secretary of state, "There had been very heated and acrimonious discussions and Mr. Moore had on two occasions broken off the discussions."[2] But after hundreds of hours of negotiation, the king intervened and ordered Suleiman to settle. His precise motivation is far from clear, but it was absolutely certain that Aramco could never have found the money to settle the controversy to his liking.

Also, the king may have softened because at this time Aramco had agreed to provide him with his heart's desire — a passenger and freight railroad across 357 miles of desert to link Riyadh with a new deep-water port at Dammam, near Dhahran on the Persian Gulf. The cost of construction, including port facilities, would be about $70 million. Moreover, the king had demanded that Aramco build a waterworks at Jidda for him in time for the next pilgrimage. Aramco management had declined, but was "very much afraid that it may be compelled to do so in order not to incur the King's displeasure."[3] And the king had in fact continued to insist that Aramco undertake the work because he did not want to ask the British to build the waterworks. He was worried that if he did so, and if they accepted, it would lead to yet more British commercial penetration of Arabia, and he wished to avoid that. (Still, Aramco never actually built the plant.)

Aramco's position was not invincible enough for its executives to be able to say a firm no to Ibn Saud in anything. And the king had his reasons for wringing every possible drop of support from the company: "He sees American troops being rapidly withdrawn from abroad, leaving him increasingly dependent upon the British for protection. Lendlease is ended, and there are to be no more gratuitous handouts."[4] Thus he relied heavily on Aramco to fill the ever-dwindling royal coffers and to add certain modern conveniences to his kingdom.

To resolve the gold controversy, Moore had no choice but to accept the king's somewhat reduced, but still exorbitant terms. His letter of acceptance models the humility of the language that Aramco used when addressing the sovereign in intricate matters:

> Your Majesty:
> I and my colleagues are most grateful to your Majesty for your friendly and gracious reception this morning.
> I am most happy to confirm my acceptance during the meeting of your offer to settle the gold pound controversy. . . . Promptly upon my return to Dhahran, I shall issue appropriate instructions implementing our agreement. . . . I understand that Your Majesty's Government prefers to have payments made monthly.
> We shall be glad to abide by the instructions of Your Majesty's Government in this respect.
> The settlement of this controversy, I am sure, removes a great weight from Your Majesty's shoulders.
> It certainly does from mine. The Company will do all that it can to make Your Majesty proud of the Company's continued performance.
> Those of us who have come to your beloved country to settle this matter extend our heartiest thanks for your friendship and hospitality.
> Please accept my most sincere respect.[5]

The settlement was this: the company would pay what was owed to the government at the rate of $12 per gold pound, not the $8.2397 at the present New York rate of exchange.

Moore's lack of graciousness during the deliberations was not casually brushed aside by the Saudis. Crown Prince Saud reproached Moore, declaring that loss of temper was never a proper way of solving difficulties.

With the gold controversy settled, the Aramco merger entered the second stage of negotiations. A partnership with Aramco was of tremendous importance to Exxon and Mobil. By 1947, Texaco had tripled its market share both east and west of Suez. At thirty-three cents a barrel in production costs, the Aramco consortium could market Arabian crude for as little as ninety cents and still turn an excellent profit. The other American majors felt distinctly threatened: they could not sell for less than $1.30 and up. It was reported officially that Aramco could "alter fundamentally the market positions of the established international companies"[6] led by almighty Exxon and its smaller but vigorous partner, Mobil. With its immense production and its huge reserves, Aramco threatened the entire world pricing and marketing structure, American as well as British.

Exxon peered into the future and concluded that at present it had sufficient crude in the United States and Venezuela to supply most of its markets in both the Eastern and the Western Hemispheres. But demand would increase, and the company would have to acquire a larger stake in Middle Eastern production to keep its European markets. That meant obtaining an interest in Aramco: "Exxon and Mobil rightly concluded that their long-term market prospects in Europe were unfavorable if they failed to get a share of the vast low-cost reserves of the Arabian American Oil Company."[7]

Furthermore, "Saudi Arabia's petroleum could be produced so cheaply that if California Standard and Texaco could not be persuaded to use Exxon's and Mobil's outlets, it would be able to use Aramco to build up a marketing organization no other firm could compete against." And as a Standard Oil of California executive told a trade publication, "What each large oil group fears more than anything else is the entry of a powerful newcomer in the established order of world oil markets." Therefore Exxon and Mobil decided early in 1946 to offer their markets and their capital to Aramco in return for a piece of the Arabian venture. Aramco's owners were approached in May 1946, and they offered a receptive ear. Aramco's board found that access to the additional markets provided by Exxon and Mobil would "guarantee a more rapid expansion of Aramco's production," and, just as important, stepped-up production would enable Aramco to meet King Ibn Saud's constant demand for oil royalties. Moreover, Aramco was aware, too, that both Standard Oil of California and Texaco had worries in the midst of their newly found wealth. They needed more capital to reassure Ibn Saud that the oil fields were being exploited on a scale that would bring him increasing revenue.[8]

A study by Standard Oil had earlier concluded that "Aramco's market outlets for crude would be 9.2 billion barrels over the 53-year life of the concession." But if Exxon was to merge with the company, Aramco could even double its market outlets to 18.8 billion barrels and thereby double Aramco's net worth from $1.1 billion to $2.2 billion. In the late 1940s and early 1950s, such figures were breathtaking. A billion dollars was a sum quite beyond the comprehension of most folk. In corporate life during 1945–50, millionaires were still an object of awe. All in all, Aramco saw much that was attractive in uniting with Exxon and Mobil.

Still, there were objections to the proposed union. One smacked of romance. Exxon was buying, rather than exploring, its way into Aramco. A member of the Aramco board argued that, without a merger, Aramco was competitively "very strong" against Exxon. Why should Aramco therefore enter into a union with Exxon to obtain absolute primacy in the fields of both production and sales? But this was a lone voice.

By the end of October 1946, the Aramco merger plans had begun to take shape. The corporations involved took time to study the antitrust risks in what they proposed to do. They were, their lawyers warned, asking that the U.S. government permit them virtual control of a major segment of the world's oil reserves. As the Mobil general counsel observed,

> I cannot believe that a comparatively few companies for any length of time are going to be permitted to control world oil resources without some sort of regulation. This is a political question. What restraints will be imposed and by what authority falls within the realm of conjecture. Our job seems to be to play the game as best we can under the rules now in force.[9]

On December 4, 1946, the general counsels of Texaco, Mobil, and Exxon went to discuss the Aramco negotiations with the U.S. attorney general, Tom Clark. He expressed no objection to the continuation of the negotiations but asked that the drafts of the contracts be sent to him when they were ready. This was neither a green nor a red light, but an amber one. The drafts were duly sent to Clark, and he, again, raised no objections, although he did say that if the Department of Justice had any comments to make on the drafts, then the general counsels would be informed. This rather casual attitude was indeed curious, for the proposed union did represent, in real dollar terms, the most important merger ever to have taken place in the United States. Surely the corporate lawyers expected a bit of controversy or at least curiosity from government officials. But nothing further was heard from the attorney general or anyone else at the Justice Department, and the merger contracts were signed on March 12, 1947.

There was, accordingly, great rejoicing at Dhahran and at the headquarters of the now four members of the consortium. Exxon had put up $76.5 million for a 30 percent share in Aramco's stock; Mobil had paid $25.5 million for a 10 percent equity. Thus the combined assets of Aramco's four parent companies in 1948 amounted to $6.247 billion. All four members ranked among the top twelve U.S. corporations in total assets; and Exxon then ranked above all other American corporations with assets of $2.996 billion.[10] The Californians owned 30 percent of Aramco; the Texans, 30 percent; Exxon of New Jersey, 30 percent; and Mobil, 10 percent. As of the end of 1949, these four companies were owned by more than 1.1 million shareholders. The parent companies received 50 percent of Aramco's profits. The combine established a board of directors that determined the price to be paid Aramco for crude; and the crude price, in turn, fixed the prices to be paid for refined products.

The agreement to merge represented the end of the second stage of negotiations. But since nothing is simply or quickly done in the world of gigantic combines, there had to be a third agreement — how much each of the Aramco partners would take in crude out of Saudi Arabia — and how Aramco would be controlled. These issues were so tangled that, as one Aramco employee observed, "Only a theologian would have been able to interpret the documents accurately."[11] As a result, company relationships within the combine were rarely amicable or simple. Even so, it made huge profits, as will be seen; and this factor led to unending and imperious demands by Ibn Saud and his government for more money, and yet more money.

To meet the requirements of the law of tiny Delaware, where Aramco was incorporated, and to control the enterprise, Aramco created a special committee known as the Executive Committee, or Excom. Excom developed a reputation, especially among the Saudis, for secrecy, lust for power, and greed. Little was known publicly about its members or how it worked, except that the members of the entity were drawn from the boards of the four owner companies. The Saudis distrusted Excom because it controlled the price of oil and the Saudis' royalties, yet allowed the Saudis no representation on the committee. This aspect of Aramco's relationship with the Saudi government eventually became so strained that, in 1950, fearing as always a rupture in the concession agreement, Excom agreed to bring two Saudis onto the board. This, however, brought new problems to the surface.

As one of Aramco's career lawyers explained, Saudis "couldn't be expected to act impartially on company matters, and in the company interest if it had to do with negotiations and deals with the Saudi Government, because they were officials of the Saudi Government."[12] In 1959, therefore, the Aramco board established another committee on which Saudis did not and could not sit; it seems they also knew nothing about it. It was called Ancom, short for the Committee on Agreements and Negotiations.

The question of Ancom's legality did arise. The company's legal expert in Delaware advised, according to W. F. Owen, an Aramco senior lawyer,

> "Well, the Delaware law doesn't say you can do it. On the other hand, it doesn't say you can't do it. Well, let's do it. See where it is." Well, it was accepted by Delaware. . . . Ancom was the same as Excom except that it

didn't have any Saudi representative on it. . . . We never had a bit of bad feedback from the Saudi Government.[13]

Even when they were represented on the committee, Excom remained bewildering to Saudi executives. With tens and then hundreds of millions of dollars in royalty being passed through the complex machinery of Aramco, with fine points of abstruse law being expounded by a platoon of clever, collegiate lawyers from the United States, the Saudis' bewilderment is completely understandable. (But eventually the Saudi government would catch up by appointing some clever lawyers of its own and asking pertinent questions about Aramco's complex executive arrangement.)

Company finances also were a source of misunderstanding and disagreement. Baldo Marinovic, who fought against the German army in Yugoslavia in World War II, joined Aramco as a financial officer in 1955. He proved to be one of the cleverest of them all. Born in 1925 in Yugoslavia, he joined a Wall Street firm of investment bankers, then attended Yale and received a master's degree in international finance, and finally spent time at the Carnegie Endowment for International Peace as a research associate before he was recruited into Aramco's New York office. In 1959 he was sent to Dhahran as finance administrator, second in command in the handling of cash, bank accounts, and insurance matters in Hasa.

Marinovic recalled the primitive and rather casual means of financial management used in the early days of his employment there. Hasa was isolated by the desert from the capital, Riyadh. "The government itself wasn't very well organized. There was no central bank" but rather "something resembling [one,] called the Saudi Arabian Monetary Agency." Because of the Koran's strictures regarding usury profit was permitted, but interest was not. A peculiar blend of innocent trust and informality attended financial transactions, such as the disbursing of the payroll. Marinovic's cash vault accumulated "millions and millions" of riyals, the Saud silver coinage exchangeable at the rate of about four riyals to one dollar. The only way to distribute the payroll was by hauling the money, several million dollars in riyals, in an old Volkswagen van from Dhahran to the three outlying Aramco sites. The driver drove the forty miles out to each district. He had no guards, no protection. Everyone in the desert knew when it was payday, but there was never any problem with theft or ambushes. The sacks of riyals were dumped outside the cashiers' offices in the three producing districts, Dammam, Ras Tanura, and Abqaiq. Marinovic's other main responsibility in those early days was his work with the Local Industrial Development Department, which helped local Saudi entrepreneurs start and run businesses. It was Marinovic's job "to scratch up the money," to get the banks to make loans quite often with Aramco's guarantees. Thus Marinovic came to meet the merchants and shopkeepers, some of whom in a few short years became "millionaires and even billionaires."[14]

Of all the events that occurred during his first stay in Arabia, one brought home to him powerfully the odd attitude of the Saudi dynasty to the company's money. They considered his shack to be their bank:

> One day I received a call from a vice-president of finance, and he said "The governor of the Eastern Province, Amir bin Jiluwi, is going for medical treatment in Europe. He wants a $200,000 loan and is sending somebody to pick up the money within the hour."
>
> Now you have to know that bin Jiluwi was the son of the old bin Jiluwi, who was the right hand man to [Ibn Saud] in the conquest of Riyadh and the establishment of the House of Saud on the throne of Saudi Arabia. This Amir bin Jiluwi was an absolute terror. . . . He had no hesitation in having people beheaded or hands chopped off. But at the same time, he was very fair and highly respected [along the Gulf coast]. . . .
>
> Anyway, I rushed down to the cash office and I said, "Do we have any greenbacks?" We scurried through our reserves, and we managed to accumulate $200,000. We were still counting when this old Bedouin . . . showed up with his camel stick, and he had a boy driving a pickup. He asked for the money.
>
> After the usual exchange of pleasantries, I said, "Well, fine, would you like to come in, so we can count the money?" He gave me a withering glance and he said, "We trust Aramco." And he just had the boy pick up this crate of money and take it in the pickup, and off they went.
>
> Two months later, I had a call . . . saying that "Amir bin Jiluwi is sending back the money, the loan. Somebody's coming up to Dhahran." I said, "Fine." So I thought I would see this old gentleman again, and went down to the cash office. In fact a few minutes later he arrived.
>
> He had riyals; he didn't have dollars. So there were a couple of bags of riyals. He had this boy take the riyals out of the truck, dump them in front of the cash office. I said to myself, "I don't know what's in these bags. What do I do now?" And then I decided that there was no way I could ask him to wait while the money was counted. I just had to trust him.
>
> After the old man left I had my cashiers count the money, and it was actually five riyals over.[15]

Marinovic's next appointment was as treasurer to the head office of the Aramco overseas subsidiary, an agency located at The Hague, where food, equipment, and motor vehicles were purchased not with "the almighty dollar" but with the millions of pounds sterling and other "soft currencies" that the company and the owner companies acquired by selling oil in the U.S.-backed operation to revive the European economy after World War II. He kept an eye on the head offices of Aramco's "enemies," the Anglo-Persian Oil Company and the Iraq Oil Company, and their subsidiaries' activities in the British-protected "petty sheikhdoms" scattered throughout Arabia. His work was not espionage, but a "keeping track of what was going on, keeping in touch and trading information, basically, on shortages, problems, labor problems, and so on."[16] But naturally he gathered bits of information that benefited Aramco as much as intelligence gathered in more official efforts.

Later, Marinovic became Aramco's treasurer in New York City. He was thirty-eight years old, and he was plainly being groomed for a position at the highest levels of financial operations in New York and Dhahran. Excom was located in New York, and Marinovic became an Aramco representative on the committee. He called certain other members "the offtakers," the people who bought oil from Aramco and then sold it to their customers. Thus Marinovic illuminated a very obscure corner of the Aramco consortium:

> The offtakers were the affiliates of the four owner companies who were actually lifting Aramco's oil and oil products. . . . They kept changing names all the time, but for example, for Standard Oil of New Jersey, now Exxon, it was Esso International. These subsidiaries were actually buying the oil from Aramco and then reselling it.[17]

The payments to the Saudi government were

> due on the same day. . . . Each month we would determine how much money Aramco needed for the following thirty days, and whatever was left over was paid out to the shareholding companies as dividends. This all occurred on that single day. . . . [This] involved a tremendous amount of coordination. There were huge amounts of money involved also. So mistakes were simply not acceptable. Every fifteenth of the month, believe me, was always an exercise in tension.[18]

Marinovic became one of the most powerful of all Aramco's financial wizards. He clearly felt uncomfortable describing the intricacies of his work.

> I was [Aramco's] senior finance representative in New York, I was the one that had to go in and explain to them, "All right, this is our cash situation, this is what we have, this is what we expect to get from our sales, this is how much we have to pay to the Saudi government in taxes

and royalties, this is how much we need to retain for our own operations, this is how much is available for dividends."[19]

In this important role, Marinovic naturally met with numerous high-ranking executives of Aramco's member companies on a regular basis. One of his most critical responsibilities was financial forecasting. This was complicated by the fact that he received conflicting reports from Aramco's various locations throughout the world:

> From the Beirut office, from The Hague, from the Tokyo office — each of them would come in and forecast how much they thought they would need the following month. . . . Then we would exercise judgment, because we didn't believe some of these forecasts. We had to exercise judgment, when we felt they were either exaggerating or not forecasting enough; so we would have to come up with some kind of reasonable number. It was an art more than a science.
>
> If you underforecasted your requirements, then you would run out of money before you received new money the following month. If you underforecasted your requirements, the owner companies would get mad because you didn't pay out enough in dividends. So it was a balancing act.[20]

For the Aramco consortium, much, perhaps everything, hung on Ibn Saud's health, both physical and mental. In his sudden terrible rages he might overreact and commit any excess — such as expropriating Aramco. If he died in the near future, he might be replaced by a regime that was unfavorably inclined toward the company — at least the Aramcons feared this. Regarding information about the king, Philby was an excellent source — anyone who took the trouble to intercept his extensive correspondence with his English family would have learned much about Ibn Saud's health and his state of mind. Whatever the case, Aramco and its partners were gambling a king's ransom on maintaining the status quo in Arabia. While the king lived, the company believed (probably wrongly), the concession agreement was safe.

Born in 1888 or thereabouts — Ibn Saud himself did not know the year in which he was born — he was therefore approaching his sixtieth year when the Aramco merger took place. This was an advanced age for a Saudi of his generation. How much longer would he survive? How much longer could he rule?

A frugal man in his personal life, Ibn Saud rarely indulged himself at the great banquets that he gave frequently. Rather, according to Philby, he ate only bread and meat gravy, with fruit as a dessert. He neither drank alcohol nor smoked tobacco, and his main form of exercise was a daily walk or an occasional hunting expedition. When he felt unwell, he submitted to cupping, a process in which skin was scraped from behind his head and from one of his heels and the blood was sucked out. He claimed great results from this procedure, which he usually underwent in Sheikh Yusuf Yassin's office on the twenty-fifth, twenty-seventh, or twenty-ninth day of the lunar month. As Philby related, Ibn Saud believed the phases of the moon influenced "his bloodstream in much the same way as they controlled the tides of the sea."[21] He commonly underwent mild electrical shock treatment, and he would drink water from only two wells: the Jarana well at Mecca and the Hassi well near Riyadh. When he traveled, his private tanker of water accompanied his retinue. He was still potent, so he claimed. He had four wives, innumerable concubines, and he related with gusto his conquest of virgins — in all, by Philby's count, he had "known" 145 virgins in his mature years.

A panel of four doctors attended to Ibn Saud's medical needs. They were, it seems, practitioners of the Yunani medical lore, which he held to be the equal of European medicine. It designated four types of persons: plethoric, phlegmatic, melancholic, and bilious. Ibn Saud believed himself to be in the fourth category. He used a tree-bark extract that he considered "a sovereign remedy for all internal troubles, and equally effective for external application to dirty or festering wounds." When he was really ill, which was rare, special passages from the Koran were read to him, and, Philby remembered, he had often heard him "express his conviction that it is an effective method of treatment." Otherwise, "the royal palace has proved a veritable goldmine for medicos and dispensers in the methods of the modern West" — the annual budget of the Saudi government's medical department was £24,000 gold, around $100,000. In the department there were no less than twenty doctors, fifteen of whom were employed in Riyadh and five in Mecca. A "qualified woman assistant" worked at the king's harem.[22]

Under this system, veiled in secrecy, Aramco could obtain little information about the king's health. But in 1947, the U.S. minister at Jidda managed to persuade the king to submit to an examination by the legation doctor, E. A. White. He provided what is thought to have been the king's first Western-style physical examination; and the results were encouraging, if overly optimistic. White saw the king four times in 1947. At his first meeting with the monarch he found

> a powerfully built, striking figure, six foot tall, weighing over 200 lbs., with a bearded and lined majestic countenance, deep set searching eyes, and a deep powerful commanding voice, but withal a ready merry

twinkle of the eye with which one is completely at ease. The reception was most cordial and pleasant.

. . . Allowing for difficulties in language translation, as complete a history and medical examination as possible was done. His Majesty's *Chief Complaint* is pain in the legs and knees, the left leg particularly over a period of 30 years, increasing in severity during the past 4 years. He gives a *Family History* of arthritis of old age in his father during the latter's declining years. *His Past History* includes a gunshot injury in the region of his left hip 30 years ago, a fall without fracture on the left leg 30 years ago, and a sabre injury to the right foot 25 years ago. He has had no diseases other than malaria and trachoma in his youth. Venereal disease is denied. The *Present Illness* consists essentially of intermittent pain in the knees, particularly the left, without swelling, increasing in severity in recent years, together with some pain and soreness in both feet.[23]

The doctor found evidence of arthritis and that the king was blind in one eye. But his overall impression confirmed Ibn Saud's health and vitality:

His mind is fertile and agile and he has control over himself as well as his entire kingdom. His prognosis for life expectancy, all things considered, is, I should judge, at least 10 to 15 years.[24]

Doctor White's findings doubtless encouraged Aramco and the U.S. government to believe that Ibn Saud was a good bet and would remain so for some years to come, barring assassination. But White's report appears contrary to the opinion of Philby, who saw the king more or less daily between 1945 and 1953 and who had been an intimate of the king since 1917. Between 1947 and 1949 Philby, a shrewd and observant man, became ever more pessimistic about his old friend. In a letter in 1948, Philby depicted the king as a sick man no longer in full control of his regime: "Life is astonishingly dull here nowadays, with the King always somnolent and all the high-ups concerned only with feathering their own nests. No wonder that Palestine has gone west with all the incompetence and graft that is ruining the Arab countries!" And writing to his English wife, Dora — he also had a Saudi wife — on December 16, 1948, Philby indicated that Ibn Saud the statesman was no longer as stately as he once was: "The Saudi Arabian Government is in a bad way with corruption widespread in the highest circles and inefficiency evident at every turn. . . . Ibn Saud has seen his best days and lost the power of initiative which once made him great."[25]

Philby also noted how palace life was affected by the king's dwindling powers:

The scale of corruption here is something unbelievable, running into millions [of pounds]; and the poor old king just doesn't know (and doesn't seem to care) what is going on. Of course finance and economics have never been his forte, but one has to come to the conclusion, however regretfully, that he is too old and tired for his job, and has completely lost grip.[26]

The royal family had lost count of the royalties that flooded in as the demand for Saudi oil increased sharply. There was endless expenditure on glitter and luxury, for Ibn Saud was an indulgent father. As Philby wrote to Dora: "It is sad to see such widespread decadence in a country that had a greatness of its own when it was poor." By 1951, Ibn Saud's life had begun to ebb. When in September he tried to make the pilgrimage, he collapsed on the first day. He remained alert, but Philby was aware he could not last much longer. He remained at Ibn Saud's side, and the king, too, remained loyal to his old friend, proclaiming on one occasion when prescribed a blood transfusion: "Give me some of Feelbee's. He's never ill."[27]

As Aramco became established as an organization, the San Franciscan style of management, gentlemanly probity in business matters combined with conservative dress and manners, dominated the executive level of the company's corporate culture. Young Ivy Leaguers were much sought after as recruits, particularly those who had seen military service and possessed personal discipline. New recruits were sent to a mansion owned by Aramco in Rhode Island for special training in the company's affairs and then transported to Dhahran. The company's finest did not travel by Aramco's shuttle service, which carried rough, tough working men. Instead, they flew first class on Trans World Airlines.

The company's preference for conservatism and circumspection was greatly shaken by certain postwar investigations into its ways of doing business. Aramco's maneuvers to keep Britain from gaining the oil concession and its supplying of oil to the U.S. Navy came into question and generated uncomfortable publicity and a challenge to Aramco's lawyers.

In January 1947, James A. Moffett, the wartime chairman of the board of Aramco, filed suit against Aramco for $6 million. Moffett claimed that he had, under contract, rendered services to Aramco from April 1, 1941, to January 1, 1942. He was now seeking payment because he had successfully fulfilled his assignment. According to his statements, his

> services resulted in the Government of the United States requiring the Government of the United Kingdom, as a part of certain financial negotiations between the United States and Great Britain, "To assume

the budget requirements of the Kingdom of Saudi Arabia for the duration of the war with the resulted saving to Aramco of at least $30 million and the salvation of its oil and mineral concessions, the value of which have been variously estimated from two to ten billion dollars."[28]

Moffett claimed that he had, under Aramco's direction, approached his friend, President Roosevelt, to see whether Ibn Saud's financial requirements could not be made a lend-lease matter. It was a fact of the historical record that Moffett had sought Roosevelt's support. But whether he did so under an influence-peddling contract with Aramco was the question at hand. As Moffett related in the legal documents of his suit, Aramco had employed him under a contract in which, he claimed, he "was to use his influence with the President of the United States and other Government officials to effect a financial relationship between the Lend Lease organization and the Saudi Arabian Government."[29]

That such a senior figure in the oil industry should sue the company whose board he had chaired was, to say the least, disquieting. As Aramco announced in its employee journal:

> This was a serious claim, fantastic as it seems to be. Aramco, through its lawyers, instigated a comprehensive investigation in order to determine how best to handle the matter. It was realized that important policy decisions were involved.
>
> As the Aramco lawyers delved deeper and deeper into the facts, it became more and more apparent that Mr. Moffett's belated claim — it was not brought to the Company's attention for several years after the alleged rendering of the alleged services — was utterly without merit. . . . When Mr. Moffett's lawyers proposed settlement, they were advised that Aramco valued the claim at less than nothing and intended to fight it as long as Mr. Moffett proceeded to present it.[30]

In February 1949, this case was submitted to a jury in New York. They rendered a verdict favoring Moffett for $1,150,000. The lawyers of Aramco, and the judge, too, were amazed by the verdict. In April 1949, the judge "set the verdict aside on the grounds that (1) Mr. Moffett had not proved his case, and (2) that if there was the kind of contract that Mr. Moffett claimed existed, the contract was void as contrary to public policy."[31]

Aramco's company bulletin commented on the judge's decision as follows:

> One of the reasons Aramco decided to resist the claim was Aramco's knowledge that Aramco would never make a contract with anyone to influence the President and other Government officials. The judge, in effect, ruled Mr. Moffett had not proved this fantastic "influence"

employment and asserted further that influence was something that could not be sold in any event.[32]

Moffett appealed the judge's decision. The case was argued before the Circuit Court of Appeals on October 9 and 10, 1950, and this court also decided in favor of Aramco. But "Mr. Moffett, not satisfied to let the matter rest, requested the U.S. Supreme Court to review the findings of the Circuit of Appeals. . . . The Supreme Court in March refused to consider the matter further."[33]

Thus, in this moment of victory, Aramco was able to assure its employees of its principled resistance to false accusers in search of a piece of the company's financial pie:

> The decision was additional proof, if any was needed, that Aramco's policy of resisting unjust claims is an undeniably correct business principle. A company of Aramco's prominence in the business world is often made the target for unjust claims by persons who believe that Aramco will prefer to pay something in settlement rather than to be subjected to unfavorable publicity and expenditure of large sums in defense. Such persons in every instance will be disappointed because Aramco is convinced that good stewardship demands refusal to pay one cent of its stockholders' money as tribute to injustice.[34]

Moffett's case was, therefore, at an end in the courts. But it was not at an end elsewhere, especially in Congress. About a month after Moffett's complaint was officially registered, on February 27, 1947, C. W. Barthelmes, of Arlington, Virginia, a man with connections with the U.S. Navy, asserted in a letter to President Truman that he had "several matters in connection with the Arabian American Oil Company's dealings with the United States Government which I believe to be of sufficient national importance to bring the matter to the attention of both your office and Congress."[35]

First, the oil supplied by Aramco to the U.S. Navy was officially declared to be inferior and, worse, liable to damage the engines of all warships that used it. According to Barthelmes's accusation, the same quality of oil was still being supplied to the U.S. Navy; the U.S. Navy had been overcharged by Aramco; "in the period November 1, 1945–January 1, 1947, the U.S. Navy took delivery of some [22.5 million] barrels of products for which the Government paid in excess of [$33 million] resulting in an estimated profit to [Aramco] over and above production, royalty, and manufacturing costs of approximately [$15.5 million]." The oil involved constituted "practically the entire output of Arabian American's refinery; that the refinery would be inoperative but for Aramco's contract with the Navy; and it also constituted "nearly one half the entire U.S. Navy's fuel requirements."[36] The third and doubtless the most important point concerned the nature of the business that led to the establishment of Aramco in 1944.

The allegations of Barthelmes and Moffett, as well as other matters, led to an official investigation of the association between Aramco and the U.S. Navy and between Aramco and the Saudi government. This was undertaken by the Special Committee Investigating the National Defense Program, under Chairman Senator Owen Brewster, a Republican of Maine. On the morning of April 4, 1947, a Cabinet meeting decided that the Departments of State, War, Navy, and Justice and the Reconstruction Finance Corporation should prepare a case regarding the charges against Aramco. James Terry Duce, a vice president of Aramco, was "required and requested" to provide all Aramco documents concerning these transactions. Detailed information regarding monies paid to Saudi Arabia was gathered by the designated parties and forwarded to the Department of Justice, where the assistant attorney general, John F. Sonnet, was preparing the government's case. The acting secretary of state made it known that he wanted all phases of the State Department's involvement reviewed.

After much inquiry, Brewster's committee attacked Aramco's parent companies in April 1948:

> The oil companies have shown a singular lack of good faith, an avaricious desire for enormous profits, while at the same time they constantly sought the cloak of United States protection and financial assistance to preserve their vast concessions. . . . The United States Government extended direct and indirect lendlease and other assistance to the Saudi Arabian Government in excess of [$99 million] of which only approximately [$27 million] is likely to be recovered.[37]

These advances had been secured through the efforts of Aramco, which had two reasons to solicit U.S. financial support: "First, in 1941, to relieve themselves of the onerous burden of supplying large funds to meet the budgetary requirements of Saudi Arabia; and second, in 1943 direct U.S. lend-lease was requested by the company to eliminate the danger of its concessions and earnings falling under the control of [Britain]."[38]

As incentive to the United States to grant aid to Saudi Arabia, Aramco had offered to sell oil to the United States under a proposal to the president, dated April 16, 1941, at forty cents per barrel. Under another proposal made on February 8, 1943, as a further inducement, the company offered to set aside reserves and to sell its petroleum products at "prices well under the world prices" or at "cost plus a nominal profit."[39] But Aramco allegedly charged $1.05 a barrel and thereby overcharged the U.S. government some $30 million to $38 million between January 1, 1942, and June 30, 1947.

After noting these findings, the committee turned over its records regarding minerals, fuel, and strategic and critical minerals and materials to the National Resources Economic Committee, a subcommittee of the Senate Committee on Interior and Insular Affairs that was investigating national petroleum affairs. Certain records obtained from Brewster's committee were indeed pertinent to those investigations. The first concerned section 11 of the committee's report:

> Our Government during the last war . . . greatly benefited by the service of the ablest men in industry. Many such men served this country with distinction, and at great personal sacrifice to their fortune and health. However, . . . in rare cases there have been a few who designedly sought key positions in Government service so that they could control situations for selfish interests.[40]

Such allegations were serious, the more so against a background of world war. Perhaps in a different era, they would have led to a large-scale investigation. But in the political climate of the 1950s, the impetus to explore possible wrongdoing by Aramco was stilled by the fresh emergency of the times: the Soviet Union was on the march into the Middle East and by the continuing conflict between the Arab states and Israel. Perhaps most important, any overt criticism of Aramco became unthinkable as, slowly but surely, its empire in Saudi Arabia became a showpiece of the superiority of U.S. capitalism in comparison with Soviet Communism.

Thus Aramco slipped through the net of federal investigation. President Truman emphasized, however, that he wished the case to be pursued vigorously in the civil courts. And so it was for a time. But when Eisenhower became president and Dulles the secretary of state, they considered political expediency and national security to be best served by discontinuing any such investigations.

In defense of Aramco's actions during World War II, Charles E. Hughes, Jr., counsel for the Arabian American Oil Company, the Bahrein Petroleum Company Limited, and the California Texas Oil Company, Limited, had on February 16, 1948, submitted a memorandum to a Senate committee investigating petroleum arrangements with Saudi Arabia. Hughes referred to James A. Moffett's charge that Aramco and its parent companies had "deliberately defrauded" the United States Government in regard to oil prices charged to the U.S. Navy.[41] As Hughes stated in his memorandum,

The chairman made plain from the beginning of the October hearings, by his comments and questions, that he thought Aramco's . . . prices to the United States Navy had been unfair, upon the theory that Aramco had been an especially favored recipient of Government aid and . . . should, on that account, have given the Navy drastically lower prices than they did.[42]

Hughes dismissed this charge based on the testimony of a secretary of the navy, James V. Forrestal, who stated that the oil purchased from Aramco "was the cheapest oil that we [the Navy] ever bought." And "for oil destined to [navy] forces west of Pearl Harbor," the next-lowest-priced source of American oil would have been "42% greater than the price it paid Aramco; . . . in addition the transportation cost would have been greater." The evidence indicated that "the prices of Aramco were as low or lower than any prices available to the Navy from other sources, and that buying at those prices the Navy saved many millions of dollars."[43]

In addition to defending pricing and quality in Aramco's sale of oil to the navy, Hughes made the point that Aramco had served the national interest during World War II by helping to stabilize Saudi Arabia through its relationship with Ibn Saud (and its financial support of the Saudi government) and through encouraging the U.S. government to supply lend-lease funds to a strategically important country.

Then, with skill, Hughes turned the attention of his readers from Moffett's allegations to another matter, the British involvement in Aramco's affairs. Even if Hughes's charges were spurious, they nevertheless deflected attention from the accusations of fraud. The uproar was, Hughes alleged, the work of America's first ally, Great Britain:

> One important purpose of [Aramco's lend-lease] proposal was to guard against political and economic consequences which might result if Britain were the source of assistance to that nation. . . . Britain could not afford in her own national interests to allow the stability of Saudi Arabia to be jeopardized; and also she could well afford to give even the total amount of financial assistance requested by the King because of the resources she would be receiving through loans and lend-lease. But, if this were allowed to happen, Britain's prestige and influence would be so enhanced that Saudi Arabia might well be drawn into the so-called sterling area. That . . . might well result in the necessity of making Aramco a British corporation, instead of an American, or a division of Aramco's concession, limiting the American participation to that relatively small area which had already been developed.[44]

As Charles Rayner, petroleum adviser to the State Department, had said in evidence:

This sort of British aid was exactly what the companies did not want, and what it was the purpose of their proposal to avoid. . . . Sensing the imminent danger that such steps would draw Saudi Arabia into the sterling area, the companies approached officials of the United States Government with representations of the alarming consequences of its policy and a proposal designed to remedy them before it was too late.[45]

Thus, the prodigious efforts of Aramco's lawyers resulted in eventual dismissal of the question of possible wrongdoing. The all-important maintaining of the oil concession had once again determined the priorities of company and government officials.

From the start of the Aramco consortium's operations, Excom and Ancom were never far from the lurid, complex, expensive, and prodigious difficulties of doing business in the Middle East. An early major challenge to Aramco's primacy as the world's largest oil exporter arose in the early 1940s. It involved Aramco's desire to export oil from Arabia through a pipeline to Sidon, one of the great seaports of the Phoenicians and of every great power in the Levant.

The transportation of large quantities of oil from the Persian Gulf to the Mediterranean and then to the European markets, where it was a vital factor in implementing the Marshall Plan for the postwar recovery of Europe, had proved to be "a major problem even in this day of massive undertakings."[46] The distance a tanker had to travel between Ras Tanura, Aramco's main refinery and ocean terminal in Saudi Arabia, and the Mediterranean Sea via the Suez Canal, was about thirty-six hundred statute miles, and the voyage took an average of nine days. A delicate political situation also threatened to block the route whereby the oil reached Europe. With eighty thousand troops, dumps of matériel, airfields, and many square miles of military installations, the British army was firmly in control of the Suez Canal zone. The Anglo-Egyptian treaty giving the British base rights in the zone still had ten years to run. But the reign of the Egyptian king Farouk had become increasingly uncertain, and if he was overthrown, the British might be forced out of Egypt (this in fact would occur) and the canal might be blocked. Who then would operate the canal? How would the oil reach Europe? And what would be the consequences if it did not?

Therefore, in 1945, Aramco embarked on an important program, the building of the Trans-Arabian Pipeline (Tapline) from the Abqaiq oil field across 1,068 miles to the Mediterranean coast — about the distance between New York City and Miami. The original intention was to build the terminal at Haifa, in British-mandated Palestine. But that plan was shelved when Palestine erupted into warfare between the Jews and the Arabs. Instead, the plan as adopted would build a pipeline beginning at the mammoth Abqaiq oil field, extending across the Saudi desert along the Iraqi frontier and across parts of Jordan, reaching down to the Lebanese coast, and ending at the port of Sidon. The plan became much celebrated as a tribute to Yankee industry, vision, and resourcefulness. It would be the longest crude-oil pipeline in the world, most of it would cross desert previously inhabited only by Bedouin, the workers who would lay the pipeline would be the first Westerners to set foot in much of the desert, and "the shipment of pipe and materials and the movement of men were larger in volume and involved longer overseas voyages than any single project previously undertaken in peacetime."[47]

The project was truly prodigious. Special mammoth trucks were designed and built to haul the pipe across the desert. Four pumping stations were to be built, each the size of a large village and complete with schools, clinics, water wells, stores, and airstrips. The capacity of the line would be 470,000 barrels of oil daily. Plans were completed in record time in December 1946, and the line was also to be built in record time. Aramco created the Trans-Arabian Pipeline Company as a separate, nonprofit entity so that the politics of Aramco and Tapline might not become intertwined in dealings with Arab governments. That hope was misplaced; the pipeline proved to be an unending problem in company-government relations.

The Palestinian troubles aside, the agreements with the countries involved — Saudi Arabia, Jordan, Lebanon, and Syria — were made quickly. Jordan and Lebanon signed in August 1946, Saudi Arabia in July 1947, and Syria in September 1947. But difficulties soon surfaced in Saudi Arabia. There, as J. Rives Childs, the U.S. consul at Jidda, reported to the State Department, he discovered the existence of cliques known as "the Syrians" in the Saudi foreign ministry at Mecca. These were the protégés and compatriots of Syrian-born Sheikh Yusuf Yassin. Yassin now held five posts in the government: minister of state, secretary to the king, director of the diplomatic branch of the privy council, deputy minister of foreign affairs, and representative of Saudi Arabia to the Arab League. Sheikh Yassin received five salaries for these appointments, plus an annual bonus, plus living expenses, plus what Childs termed

> occasional spontaneous gifts of a thousand or two gold sovereigns from the King. These emoluments are all paid regularly while all other employees of the Saudi Government, including even the lowest meni-

als and private soldiers, are now going into their fourth month without remuneration.[48]

The second clique was that of Fuad Bey Hamza, who was nominally minister of state for development projects. He therefore administered the extensive aid pouring in from the United States and also those portions of the Aramco royalty allocated to development by Abdullah Suleiman. He was an influential adviser to Ibn Saud. His clique was not as large as Yassin's, and Childs warned Washington that although Sheikh Yusuf and Fuad Bey "wasted no love upon each other, it is felt that they might combine forces should a growing opposition to them demand it."[49]

They both enjoyed great favor with the king:

> Sheikh Yusuf and Fuad Bey are, after Sheikh Abdullah al Sulaiman, Minister of Finance, the most powerful nonroyal personalities in Saudi Arabia. . . . The King has great affection for them because they joined his service in the days of hardship and struggle, at the time when the King was slowly and painfully unifying and expanding his domain to its present frontiers. . . . They are loyal servants of the King and bring to their positions no mean ability. . . . It would also appear that the King . . . feels that by retaining these two persons in his service he is cementing his good relations with Syria and The Lebanon. . . . Both Fuad Bey and Shaikh Yusuf have kept fences mended in their countries of origin and have gone out of their way to ingratiate themselves with Syrian and Lebanese diplomats in Saudi Arabia.[50]

Childs also noted that the Syrians at court evinced "an insatiable desire for money" and carried out "unblushing attempts to arrange matters so that their efforts on behalf of the King do not go unrewarded." But this greed hardly caused a stir at the palace because "most Saudi Arabs, from the King on down, expect some measure of greediness on the part of public officials and view it philosophically."[51] High-placed members of the privy council, such as Abdullah Suleiman, were known to receive large salaries and were shrewdly investing their savings outside of Saudi Arabia in case they should fall from favor at court.

The first trouble with the signatories to the Tapline convention (the agreement among the parties involved) had little to do with money, but with Palestine. Barely three months after the signing of the convention, the United Nations, on November 29, 1947, adopted a resolution to partition Palestine into an Arab state and a Jewish state. All over the Arab East, voices demanded the use of the "oil weapon" as a means to pressure the West to favor the Palestinian Arabs, rather than the Jews. Refusal to permit the transit of oil across Arab territory through the pipeline would certainly be an effective means of political pressure. But the Arab countries reacted differently to this proposal, each having its own self-interest to guard:

> Of the three transit countries, it was natural that Syria — a veritable heartland of Arabism — should feel and act more strongly than the other two. Jordan, as a Hashimite kingdom in alliance with Britain, was certain to behave with moderation. Lebanon's old Phoenician traditions precluded an extremist policy likely to result in serious economic losses.[52]

Sensitive to "a highly emotional public opinion," the Syrian government and parliament delayed ratification of the pipeline agreement, despite their desire to benefit "from such pipelines as might be constructed through their territory." And the Syrians "proved very tough to deal with." After seemingly successful negotiations, they would stall and say, "'Everything is settled — except there is one small point. . . .'"[53]

The Syrians did weaken considerably when a rumor floated throughout the Middle East that Aramco intended to carry out a miniature Marshall Plan in the Middle East by spending $2 billion on the expansion of industry. Then another rumor circulated that if Syria remained obdurate, Aramco would abandon the Levant project and divert the placement of an oil terminus to Egypt. But the Syrians in the court at Mecca knew the truth of Aramco's intentions and, it seems, kept their compatriots informed in Damascus. The company's need for land rights in Syria also delayed the convention's ratification: the Syrians in Mecca knew which land Aramco desired and informed their friends in Damascus, so land prices soared. Nor did Aramco's attempts to end this racket achieve very much. Sheikh Yusuf and his Syrian clique in the administration had made themselves indispensable to the king and could not be ousted, although Prince Faisal, the foreign minister and viceroy of the Hejaz, knew very well what was going on.

But then came a breakthrough of sorts. Although Syrian university students demonstrated against the Tapline convention in Damascus on February 26, 1948, and called for a general strike, toward the end of March, parliament was reportedly ready to consider ratification and expected that a majority would vote in favor. But on the night it was to be ratified, there was a coup d'état and Colonel Husni as-Zaim overthrew the government in a bloodless coup. This caused new doubts as to the fate of the convention. On the day after the coup, Owen and William A. "Sandy" Campbell, the head of Aramco's government relations in Beirut — a sort of company diplomatic service — asked for an audience with the new president. To their surprise, Zaim greeted them warmly with these words:

"I imagine you are somewhat disheartened because you had very high hopes of your convention being ratified. I want a couple of days to study this. I know a lot about it right now. But I'd like you to come back in two or three days, and we can talk."[54]

When they returned in hopes of moving forward with this badly stalled $750 million project, Zaim told them,

"Well, I've looked at it, and I think it's going to be good for Syria. It's going to give us employment . . . and it's going to renew our contacts with people from other countries. We've been very much isolated, and too much so, in the past. So I am prepared to sign the convention today and have it ratified by my Council of Ministers tonight."[55]

But by 1949, three years after the Syrians had signed the convention, they had not yet ratified it. Progress was occurring in other places. In Saudi Arabia, Bechtel, the San Francisco engineering and construction firm, had begun building the pipeline at Abqaiq, while Williams Brothers of Tulsa, Oklahoma, had begun to build the terminal at Sidon.

But, of course, as with most business deals in Syria, there was a snag. In New York, the Aramco lawyers, examining the credentials of the Syrian government, asked whether Zaim had had the authority to sign the convention and whether the agreement would hold if he was overthrown. Was the Syrian government a de jure or de facto government? Was the deal binding? A leading lawyer, Manley Hudson, determined that "this was definitely a de jure government by all the standards of international law, and that this was a binding agreement and would be so recognised by the family of nations."[56] In fact, the U.S. government had just recognized Zaim's government. The Aramco board thus wished to move forward with the ratification.

Owen and Campbell returned to Beirut, where Zaim was sponsoring the annual Red Crescent Ball at a mountain resort just east of the Bekaa. Owen and Campbell were the guests of honor of President Zaim and his wife. All seemed well that heavenly night under the stars. But all was not well. Owen had noticed that when he arrived with his party, "there was a great shuffling of military personnel. They looked confused and scurrying hither and yon. The presence of four Americans wrecked their plans."[57]

The intention of the Syrian military that night was to assassinate President Zaim. The presence of four Americans had forced them to abandon the attempt. As Owen remembered,

We had to drive back from Bludan from the party. We'd said good night to Zaim and his wife. We'd gotten to bed and about five o'clock we were both awakened by our communications people who said they'd just heard on the Syrian radio that Zaim had been assassinated. . . . About

seven o'clock we got another call, people who'd been monitoring the
Syrian radio, that Henawi had declared a Law of Nullities [canceling]
everything Zaim had done, every law he had passed, every ratification
he had made, everything he had done.[58]

Owen and Campbell got their plane and flew to Damascus to see
Colonel Henawi, who had taken control of the government. He turned
out to be, Owen remembered, "not a benevolent dictator" but "a pretty
rough character." They made no comment "despite their revulsion" at
Zaim's murder as "it was a political act," but they did protest the law of
nullities as "it applied to the Tapline Convention." Owen announced
that he had "right here in my hand an opinion from the former chief
judge of the World Court, one of the most respected and influential
lawyers in the world, saying that it was a valid act and it couldn't be
undone by any subsequent government."[59]

Colonel Henawi summoned his legal adviser, who basically told
Henawi that, as the new president of Syria, he could do anything he
liked. This did not sit well with Owen and Campbell, and they expressed their dissatisfaction. At about 11:00 A.M., Henawi, having
thought about Owen's statement briefly,

> asked us to wait [in Damascus and] come back at four [that] after-
> noon. Apparently by four they had reviewed the whole thing, [for]
> Henawi said to me, "Whatever report you've got of my remarks, my
> announcement over the Syrian radio this morning, I was mis-
> quoted. . . . What I did is I announced a Law of Nullities on everything
> except the one international commitment that my predecessor had
> made, and that was the Tapline Convention. It remains valid."[60]

Henawi gave Aramco permission to begin work immediately in Syria.
Later Owen noted how important the timeliness of his office's intervention was in securing the new president's cooperation: "[The legal
opinion we had on hand] just turned the tide, because otherwise, if we
hadn't had it then, he'd have [confirmed] the Law of Nullities, and
then he'd have been so deeply in that he couldn't have said 'I was
misquoted.'"[61]

It proved to be an expensive venture from the start. It was difficult to
find a Syrian lawyer to help acquire the rights of way needed for the
passage of the pipeline across Syria. This important task was also an
odd one. "Because of a curious Syrian law," the details relating to the
right of way had to be "all on one piece of paper." So "we had to cut and
paste and hook paper together until we had a twenty-nine-foot-long
document rolled up in a scroll."[62]

The first oil went through the pipeline and was loaded into the first

tanker at Sidon on December 2, 1950. It had taken four years' negotiation with the various Arab governments involved to get them all to
grant the rights of way. Aramco claimed that the new pipeline "enabled
Aramco to enjoy in 1951 the largest rise in production of any year of its
history [before 1960]. The increase was about 215,000 barrels per
calendar day, from an annual average of 546,703 barrels per day to
716,541 per day."[63]

Great prosperity was at hand. But so were great problems and large
unexpected costs. As Owen recalled, when oil started to flow from
Abqaiq to Sidon, the Saudi government felt that Aramco owed them
money on the oil when it arrived at Sidon for loading into the tankers.
The government had already been paid royalty upon extraction, but as
Owen remembered, the king decided that he wanted to "double dip."
This was the start of an epic in Aramco legal history known as "the
Sidon price claim." It began in 1950 or thereabouts and it lasted into
the 1960s. And as Owen remembered it, "We finally settled. They were
claiming $283 million and we settled for $180 million on it."[64]

[8]

THE PALESTINE CRISIS

I N 1947, THE CONFLICT in Palestine between the Jews and the
Arabs threatened the Middle East with a regional war in which Ibn
Saud, Aramco feared greatly, would take part on the side of the
Arabs. The United Nations resolution calling for a partition of
Palestine provided the spark that would ignite the conflict. In the
background, however, a curious incident had occurred a number of
years before that involved Philby. It appeared to reflect an ambivalent
attitude to the age-old conflict on the part of Ibn Saud. Now that his oil
riches were beginning to replenish his treasury, he seemed reluctant to
take a political or military position that would place this wealth in
jeopardy.

In the last days of peace and the beginning of World War II, Ohliger
lost the services of his main political adviser at Ibn Saud's court. Philby,
a vigorous right-winger, had gone to London as Ibn Saud's "observer"
at the British government's round-table conference on Palestine; all
parties interested in the Palestine question were invited to attend. Britain's original intention was to partition Palestine and thereby create a
national home for the Jews. A British proposal to transfer Arabs, forc-
ibly if necessary, from land intended for the Jews had proved unwork-
able. The Arabs vigorously protested against the proposal that they be
sent to other Arab lands.

The British abandoned the plan and announced instead a new policy in 1939. Fifteen thousand Jews would be admitted to Palestine
during the next five years, after which Jewish immigration would be
subject to Arab agreement. Jewish land purchases would be restricted,
and within ten years an independent binational state would be established.

This policy was rejected by both Arabs and Jews, the latter because, they protested, it was a repudiation of the Balfour Declaration of 1917, which pledged British support for the establishment of a Jewish nation in Palestine, provided that the rights of non-Jewish populations were respected. The former demanded the establishment of an Arab Palestine and the prohibition of further immigration, as well as a review of all Jewish immigration since 1918. The British chiefs of staff, who regarded the Middle East as second in importance only to the British Isles as a base for military operations, refused also to back the second plan because it promised only disaster for British arms throughout the Middle East. More important, perhaps, was the possibility that the Arab leaders would deny Arab oil to Britain and France, the two main Western powers with interests in the Arab East. At that point, Philby, still in London, presented a secret proposal of his own to the Zionist leader, Chaim Weizmann.

In 1939, at a small luncheon at his home in Hampstead, attended by Weizmann, Moshe Shertok, political secretary of the Jewish Agency, and Fuad Bey Hamza, deputy foreign minister of Saudi Arabia, Philby proposed that if the Jews paid Ibn Saud £20 million ($100 million), they could have western Palestine as a national home, the existing Arab population there would be transferred elsewhere, and the Jews would try "to secure for the Arabs national unity and independence, which would be achieved 'under Ibn Saud alone.'" And if at the time Weizmann received the proposal cautiously, declaring that the Jews did not then have "the power to deliver the goods," he did agree to "explore the issues further" when he went to the United States shortly, where he expected to see President Roosevelt.[1] Philby agreed to do the same with King Ibn Saud when he returned to Mecca as, he said, he would also be doing soon.

Whether the king had authorized the scheme is nowhere clear, but there is evidence that he knew nothing of it when Philby presented it to him on his return to Mecca in January 1940. The king's reaction was encouragingly ambivalent. He would, Philby reported to his wife, Dora, who was acting as St. John's intermediary with Weizmann, "give me a definite answer at the appropriate time."[2]

In the meantime, Ibn Saud directed, Philby should not mention the plan to anyone else. Four months later, Philby disobeyed his master's order when he mentioned the project to the head of Ibn Saud's political office, Sheikh Yusuf Yassin. When the king learned that Philby had mentioned the plan, he rebuked him most sharply.[3]

Philby heard nothing more about the plan, he assumed that Ibn

Saud had rejected it, and he prepared to leave Saudi Arabia for the United States where, as the guest of Standard Oil of California, he was to speak to the America First organization, which opposed American involvement in the war. At the same time, with the fall of France in June 1940, he was dangerously outspoken in presenting his views to the privy council on the likely outcome of the war. He announced that Germany and Italy would win the war and quite soon. He was so insistently defeatist that Ibn Saud warned the British minister in Jidda of Philby's views and his plan to spread them in the United States. Philby's fat was now in the fire. The British government was informed, and when Philby reached Bombay he was arrested by the British security authorities. He was then placed under close arrest aboard a British steamer bound for Liverpool in England; and when the ship arrived he was transferred to Liverpool Prison without trial on charges that he had contravened the Defense of the Realm Act. On his release six months later he was, as he complained, "exiled" until the end of the war. His passport was withdrawn and not returned to him until 1945.

Thus Philby was immured at a time when, unexpectedly, his Palestine scheme had begun to flower. Weizmann had mentioned it to President Roosevelt in the hope that he might be able to offer security for the £20 million; Roosevelt had mentioned it to Churchill; Churchill saw some merit in it; and in 1943 Roosevelt sent an agent, Colonel H. B. Hoskins, lately of the State Department and now attached to the new American intelligence organization, the Office of Strategic Services, to Riyadh to discuss the plan with Ibn Saud. But Hoskins complicated Philby's original plan by recommending a meeting between the king and Weizmann. In an aide-mémoire to Roosevelt, Ibn Saud explained that his position on Palestine and the Jews had not changed, and that all the king desired was that "the obvious rights of the Arabs, which are clear as the sun, may not be dimmed by historic fallacies or social and economic theories of the Zionists, which theories God has not ordained."[4]

Regarding the president's proposal that Ibn Saud meet with Dr. Weizmann, Ibn Saud declared,

> I wish the President to know that we meet anyone who comes to us, whatever his religion. . . . But the Jews are a peculiar case and the President must know about the enmity which is between us in earlier and in recent times. This enmity is well known and mentioned in our holy books. . . . From this it is clear that we cannot . . . discuss anything with them nor trust in their promises. . . . There is a great personal enmity between [Weizmann] and me owing to the criminal affront

which this person has committed against me by choosing me from among all Arabs and Moslems to charge me with a dastardly thing — that is that I should become a traitor against my religion and my country. . . . He sent me a well-known European person [Philby] who asked me to abandon the question of Palestine and the support of Arab and Moslem rights in connection therewith against a payment to me of £20 million, which amount would be guaranteed by His Excellency President Roosevelt himself. . . . Is there any affront or baseness greater than this? . . . I have no doubt that His Excellency the President would not accept that this should be attributed to me or to him.[5]

Perhaps if the negotiations had been arranged to take place behind the scenes, the various parties might have come to an agreement. But suggesting a meeting with Weizmann had poisoned Philby's subtle plan. In fact, this aide-mémoire seemed at the time to have put paid to Philby's career at Riyadh, for plainly the king had disavowed him — as all confidential agents may be rejected when their schemes become an embarrassment. And as Weizmann noted to Roosevelt, the king had declared that he "would never again permit Mr. Philby to cross the frontiers of his kingdom."[6]

But had Philby in fact acted with the king's knowledge and consent, as was suggested by the presence of Fuad Bey Hamza at the first meeting with Chaim Weizmann? Perhaps he had floated the idea of the £20 million plan as a means to provide Ibn Saud with the funds he needed to keep the kingdom financially viable when the pilgrimage to Mecca, hitherto his main source of revenue, began to collapse at the outbreak of the war.

Probably by 1943 the king, surrounded as he was by advisers hostile to any contact between the king and the Zionists, disavowed the Philby plan as an acute embarrassment. After their meetings, Colonel Hoskins of OSS prepared a memorandum for Roosevelt and placed it in the president's hands when he returned to Washington in September 1943. As Hoskins reported, "If, as a result of my mission, the false impression that has for some time existed in certain high British quarters that there was even the slightest possibility that Ibn Saud could be bribed to be of assistance to the Zionists can be completely dissipated, my trip will certainly have been useful."[7]

Hoskins also noted Ibn Saud's

very sincere resentment at even the implication, which of course he did not believe, that you [Roosevelt] had any part in the attempted bribe. . . . The King was entirely sincere in his reason for remaining silent regarding the effort of the Zionists to bribe him for his support and that this silence in no way whatsoever implied any willingness on his part to consider acceptance of the offer. The fact that the King's silence in this regard was misinterpreted by Dr. Weizmann as well as by various important British officials is one of the strangest developments in the whole case. . . . I was impressed by his wisdom in the clear recognition of the limitations of his power in regard to matters extending beyond Saudi Arabia. While admitting his ability to influence millions of Moslems in various parts of the world, he fully realized that he had no mandate to speak for them on Palestine or any other subject outside of his own Kingdom.[8]

Hoskins concluded his memo with a word about Arab political attitudes after the British victory in the battle of El Alamein. Based on past experience,

they are suspicious of Anglo-American policies and more than anything else fear being faced with a *fait accompli* by some new Balfour declaration that would deprive them of Palestine and give it to the Jews as a Jewish State. This the one million Arabs of Palestine will not willingly accept and in this refusal the Arabs of Palestine have the support of the remaining 49 million Arabs of the Middle East.[9]

Hoskins warned that force would be required if a Jewish state in Palestine was to be established.

This paper was not quite the end of the £20 million "bribe." On March 8, 1944, S. I. Rosenman, one of Roosevelt's aides, minuted that he had just seen the secretary of the U.S. Treasury, Henry Morgenthau, and discussed the purported bribe. In 1942 Weizmann had sent a letter to Sumner Welles, the undersecretary of state, giving his explanation of the attempted bribe. Weizmann mentioned that Philby had been the catalyst of the proposal and had presented an outline to him and his colleagues. According to Weizmann,

we replied that Jewry, though impoverished, will be able to meet the financial burden, of which part would have to take the form of Palestinian goods, or work on land to be developed for resettlement of Arabs. But the political part of the programme could only be implemented by Great Britain and the United States.[10]

Philby discussed this matter with Hoskins:

[Hoskins's] account of his conversations with King Ibn Saud had not in the least shaken my conviction — a conviction on which I was prepared to stake my whole reputation, which was all I had to stake since I had already sacrificed my career by my fight for Arab independence — that, had he gone out to Arabia with President Roosevelt's firm offer, made on behalf of the American and the British Governments, on the lines of "the plan," that offer would have been accepted. I could only draw the rather disappointing conclusion that the British and Ameri-

can Governments are not prepared to make the relatively light sac-
rifice involved in "the plan" even to save the Jews from persecution,
torture and death.[11]

Philby advised Weizmann that he was convinced that the king might
yet accept an offer along the lines of their original plan. But

> it must be a firm offer . . . to be accepted or rejected as it stands without
> modification or bargaining. . . . No harm can come of putting the
> matter to the test. Either "the plan" is accepted, or the *status quo* re-
> mains intact without prejudice to anybody. For my part, I guarantee
> (for what my guarantee is worth) that the suggested firm offer will be
> accepted if made by any reasonably intelligent person of indisputable
> goodwill on behalf of the two Governments concerned.[12]

However, this plan would never come to fruition.

But was Philby now permanently out of favor with the king, after the
embarrassment Philby's plan had caused him? Not likely. When the
British historian and Zionist intermediary Louis Namier, who was involved in "the plan," discussed this with Philby and Weizmann, Philby
had stated that

> so far from being a *persona non grata* to the King owing to my connec-
> tion with this business, I remained in Arabia until July 21st of that year
> (1940) — six and a half months after the fatal communication, and
> practically all the time as the King's guest at Riyadh or in his desert
> camp. Indeed, on June 1st His Majesty made me a gift of a newly-built
> house on the assumption that I should live permanently in Arabia.[13]

Concerning his future relationship with the king, Philby had taken it
into his hands to confirm his conviction that he would continue to be
welcome in Saudi Arabia:

> The suggestion of my return to Arabia being unwelcome to the King
> was obviously susceptible of a very simple test. The very same sugges-
> tion had been officially made once before (in February 1941) and I
> had applied the test with the result that I had been categorically as-
> sured by the Arabian Minister in London not only that I would be
> welcome back in Arabia, but that he was ready at any time to give me
> the necessary visa for the purpose of returning thither.[14]

When Philby arrived in Cairo on his way from London to Saudi
Arabia in 1945, the king sent his DC3 aircraft to bring St. John on to
Jidda. Arriving at the Green Palace, his home in Jidda, everything had
been kept just as it was when he left. Next morning came Ibn Saud's
telegram ordering St. John at once to Riyadh, where he found "all the
same people and the same doings." Nothing had changed except the
cost of living and the princes' new habit of traveling not by camel or

car, but by plane. He dropped into the routine of saying his prayers five times a day, attending three court sessions daily, arguing with the king, and listening to the evening readings from the Koran. In November 1945 the king paid all his remaining prewar debts to Sharquieh, Philby's trading company in Jidda before the war, using as coinage some four hundred four-pound gold pieces minted in the United States and worth £8,000. Ibn Saud also sent Philby two personal presents. The first was four thousand riyals, about $1,000. The second was a new consort so slim, pretty, and lively that Philby called her "an eight cylinder girl." Rozy provided Philby with four sons, two of whom survived and were educated at the Princes' School in Riyadh. Also, the king gave St. John a "palatial" residence at Riyadh, worth a princely £15,000, as a present for life and stated that he wanted "Hajji Abdullah," as he always called Philby, to spend the rest of his life in Saudi Arabia. That was, Philby wrote to his English wife, "more or less my idea too."[15] Certainly it was the twists and turns of diplomacy that had forced the king to feign disfavor with Philby after the bribe plan turned sour. Philby's welcome back into the fold could hardly have expressed more favor and downright affection.

The Palestine crisis finally burst around Aramco with the 1947 United Nations vote to partition the country between the Jews and the Arabs. Ibn Saud, claiming that he had been betrayed by both the Roosevelt and the Truman administrations, broke down and cried when the news of the UN vote reached him. W. F. Owen, an Aramco lawyer well and favorably known to President Truman, reflected something of the attitude of the Aramcons:

> As great a president as he was, [Truman] knew nothing about international affairs, and did the U.S. and the world a massive disservice in pressuring the Philippines to vote for partition and thus created the greatest cancer of the last fifty years.[16]

Owen's reaction was mild compared to the reaction of an oil executive in the United States. Because the crisis occurred as Aramco sought to run Tapline from Dhahran to Sidon on the Mediterranean, across the very Arab countries that now seemed about to go to war over Palestine, Max W. Thornburg, vice president of Texaco, one of Aramco's parent companies, expressed dismay that the Truman administration should have prevailed on the UN "to declare racial and religious criteria the basis of political statehood." In one step, said Thornburg, the Truman administration had extinguished "the moral prestige of America" in the Arab states and that the "Arab faith in her ideals" had also been destroyed.[17]

Within the U.S. government, opinions diverged on the merits and dangers of supporting the partition of Palestine. Kenneth W. Condit, the Pentagon's official historian, stated that the "elected officials of the government tended to support partition, while the bureaucracy, military and diplomatic alike, were nearly unanimous in opposing it." Expecting that the United States would have to enforce partition and thereby might face Arab-allied Soviet Russia in battle, the Joint Chiefs of Staff recognized the threat not only of "grave danger of serious disturbances throughout the Near and Middle East," but also that "access to vital supplies of oil in Iran, Iraq and Saudi Arabia would be prejudiced." The United States might have to fight an "oil-starved war."[18]

On December 1, 1947, the American minister, J. Rives Childs, received a telephone call from Ibn Saud's palace in Riyadh. He was to come immediately to an audience with the king. When could he be there? Childs left right away. First he met Sheikh Yusuf Yassin. Of that meeting Childs reported ominously that "the feelings of the Arabs in Saudi Arabia are more embittered than they have ever been toward the United States, by reason of our Palestine policy." Yet, as Childs reported to the State Department of his first meeting with Ibn Saud, "fortunately for us, the King is a realist and recognizes that his immediate economic interests are bound up with the United States. He himself has repeatedly stated that he will not permit anything, even our Palestine policy, to bring about a breach of relations with us."[19]

Doubtless, Child's report brought a measure of relief to the Truman administration, struggling as it was with a dilemma that seemed to have no solution — sustaining U.S. oil interests through Aramco by promoting a pro-Arab policy and maintaining a positive relationship with Ibn Saud, while at the same time appearing to assist the king's mortal enemies, the Jews in Palestine.

As the crisis deepened, Childs was shown to be correct in his judgment. Ibn Saud would not fight over Palestine and Aramco, and his oil was safe. But at times it seemed sure that Ibn Saud would break his compact with the United States, but for financial rather than political reasons — perhaps he would force the company to pay him greater royalties. Further, Ibn Saud was coming under ever greater pressure from Syria and Iraq to break off relations with the United States and at least to suspend the concession agreement. But the king was aware of the cauldron of internal dynamics — shifting alliances, national interests, ancient conflicts — governing the maneuvers of the Arab countries during the Palestine crisis. He held to his own interests while proclaiming his loyalty to his "Arab brothers." At an audience with Childs, Ibn Saud declared that at the forthcoming meeting of the Arab League, he would be

> entirely at one with the Arab states so far as our dispute with Zionism is concerned. There is no difference of opinion among us on that score. I do desire, however, to make a distinction between such an attitude and the attempts being made by my antagonists in the Arab world to draw me into direct conflict politically or economically with the United States. I shall henceforth be subject to even greater pressure in this respect extending to demands that I cancel the oil concessions. The crucial question for me is to know whether and to what extent I may count upon United States aid in enabling me to resist any incursion from Iraq or Trans-Jordan which might be the consequence of my failure to yield to the pressure being put upon me to come into open economic conflict with the United States by the cancellation of the oil concessions.[20]

Childs was at first enormously relieved to hear the king's words. But as the king continued, it became increasingly clear that, though he would not be drawn into military conflict with the Jews in Palestine, the king might need U.S. assistance to defend his kingdom against his old enemies, the Hashemite kings of Jordan and Iraq. When the audience ended, Childs withdrew from the council chamber into an anteroom to prepare for his return to Jidda. There he encountered two of the king's counselors, Fuad Bey Hamza and Khalid Gargani, who advocated war against the Jews. They wished to talk to him. Childs assented. Their object was to ensure that Child understood fully what the king had been driving at:

> Their conversation indicated Arabs were extremely perplexed as to the course of action to follow with respect to the Arab state to be established in Palestine. . . . The danger was that Abdullah [the Hashemite leader of Jordan, Ibn Saud's oldest enemy] might be tempted to absorb this part of Palestine.[21]

For the moment Arab honor was acquitted. Then, even as Childs left Riyadh in his motorcar down the track back to Jidda, he was stopped again. Fuad Bey Hamza had a message for him: "He had been commanded by the King to inform me that we would hear probably many alarming things but that we were not to interpret these rumors and reports as indicating any change in His Majesty's attitude or policy toward the U.S. For example His Majesty has ordered a partial mobilisation of the Saudi Army." Amir bin Jiluwi, governor of Hasa, where Aramco was located, had been instructed to send "sufficient troops into the Dhahran area to be capable of coping with any disturbances." Then Fuad Bey Hamza made a specific request for the aid that Ibn Saud had alluded to during the audience: "equipment for two motorized Saudi divisions" and "some fifty military planes." He added that "of course, His Majesty would give the most binding assurances that these would not be used under any circumstances against US but would be employed only for the defense of Saudi Arabia."[22] Clearly the king felt threatened by Jordan and Iraq. Yet Childs had to reply that, under the current circumstances in Palestine, it might be difficult to procure the requested equipment.

The next morning, December 8, 1947, Childs was approached by Crown Prince Saud, who hastened from Mecca to Jidda to reassure Childs that the arms and equipment would never be used against the United States nor "to conflict in any way with [U.S.] interests." They would mainly be used to protect Dhahran and the oil pipeline. Turning to the arms embargo in Washington, Saud wished to know whether it extended equally to Jews and Arabs. Childs assured him that it extended "to shipments to anyone, whether Jew or Arab, in the countries concerned." Childs also assured Saud that "if the military aid His Majesty was seeking was not extended this should not be taken as any indication of any lessening of friendship on our part towards Saudi Arabia." He observed further that, with an eye to the security of the Aramco contract, "I personally felt confident that our vital interests in Saudi Arabia were so great that we would take practical measures to prevent anything against the interests of His Majesty."[23]

Crown Prince Saud was eager to emphasize the ties that bound Saudi Arabia and the United States, including the fact that the Saudis were not demonstrating against the United States, as were activists in other Arab countries. Though grieved by U.S. support of the UN decision to partition Palestine, Saudi Arabia still considered the United States a friend.

Eventually, feeling an extreme need for the arms, Ibn Saud would issue veiled threats to be fulfilled if the United States would not provide military assistance. For example, he would continue to grant the U.S. long-term renewal rights at Dhahran air base but he would *not* grant those rights unless the United States met his requests in a timely manner. If not, he would renew the lease for one year — and then only if the United States met Ibn Saud's informal requests for certain types of military assistance.

On December 11 further news was received from Dhahran, seeming to show that the view of the king, the crown prince, and their advisers

might be changing, and that Aramco might be forced into becoming a
co-belligerent with Saudi Arabia. The son of the governor of Hasa had
revealed that he had been charged by the king to organize four armies
to assist Palestine. Arabs employed at Aramco were already working for
three-day periods from which the resulting pay was donated to a Palestine fund. According to official reports, there was "no tension" among
the Arab workers on the oil fields, and the king had given "strict orders
that all meetings be orderly, explaining that the Americans here are
friendly and helpful to Arabia and must, therefore, not be molested in
any way. Aramco is getting full reports on developments through loyal
Arabs in strategic spots."[24]

Meanwhile, the Washington agent of Aramco reported to the State
Department that he had received a long telegram from the president
of Aramco, W. F. Moore, who was in Dhahran. A very tough Texan, he
and the camp boss at Dhahran, Floyd Ohliger, who was also very tough,
had confronted the king's agent in the province, Amir bin Jiluwi, in
regard to the kingdom's mobilization plans. Jiluwi had advised them
that he had received a "royal decision" to conscript males between
ages twenty and fifty to fight the Jews, but only those who were not
in essential work at the Arabian American Oil Company. They were
being grouped into "armies." But where would they get arms? "We
will get them," Moore was told. And how would they get to Palestine?
On foot? By aircraft? By camel? There was only "ominous silence."
Moore wondered whether the Saudis planned to "commandeer
Aramco's large fleet of balloon-tire trucks capable of traversing the
desert between Dhahran and Palestine." But Jiluwi had avoided discussing this point.[25]

Childs stayed in contact with Crown Prince Saud, now the commander in chief of the Saudi armies, during his attendance at the Arab
League conference in Cairo. The foreign ministers of Jordan and Iraq
had "requested Saudi Arabia to break relations with U.S. and cancel
the oil concession." The Saudi delegate had replied, just as Ibn Saud
had said, that

> Saudi Arabia was at one with the other Arab states in opposition to the
> establishment of a Jewish state but saw no reason to run counter to
> Saudi Arabia's own interests by severing relations with U.S. if Iraq and
> Jordan insisted Saudi Arabia would break relations not with the U.S.
> but with Iraq and Jordan.[26]

Thus far, therefore, it seemed to Childs that Ibn Saud had been as
good as his word. But new and ominous undertones were emerging. As

with all business in Saudi Arabia, official assurances were liable to change, suddenly, without warning, and sometimes capriciously, especially when the topic at hand concerned arms and munitions. In such transactions the Arabs typically demanded much more than they could expect to get, in order to get something. So it was during these critical days. By December 16, 1947, there were signs that distrust was creeping into the relationship between Childs and the king and his emissaries — based on fear that the United States might break the UN arms embargo and supply the Jews with arms, while not doing so for the Arabs.

Then Aramco received an unexpected visitor with business from the Oval Office of the White House. E. A. Locke and an associate, Julio Herrera, arrived in Dhahran on February 3, 1948, bearing a secret message from President Truman to Ibn Saud, which concerned the partition of Palestine. Locke was received by the vice president of Aramco in charge of government relations, Ohliger, who, as a result of what his visitor had to say, called George Rentz, Aramco's principal Arabist, to his office. Rentz was to contact the king's secretariat at the palace in Riyadh and arrange for Locke to have a private meeting with the king as soon as possible. That Aramco government relations should have been entrusted with the handling of Locke, a presidential envoy, reflected Aramco's growing tendency not to use U.S. government agents, but to do its political and diplomatic business itself — a course that J. Rives Childs resented and about which he protested on occasions to the State Department in Washington.

Ohliger arranged an audience for that same day at 11:00 A.M. in Riyadh. The interpreter was George Rentz. Locke was received in the audience room of the residence of the crown prince, Saud, where Ibn Saud was present that day. Saud was in the room and, to Rentz's surprise, so was the court doctor, Midhat Shaikh al Ardh (he had understood that Midhat was in jail, on the charge, Rentz wrote in his report, "of having been involved in a plot to poison the King").[27]

The king received them. There was some small talk about the difference between the wintry weather of Washington and the cool season in Arabia at that time, and then the king got down to business: "Locke emphasized that he was not speaking in an official capacity, since he was now only a private citizen, but he felt that his experience in government work . . . qualified him as an interpreter of trends in Washington."[28] After noting how much the president valued Ibn Saud's friendship, he mentioned Truman's interest in various farming and railroad-building projects currently underway in Saudi Arabia. Since

U.S. funds had paid for these projects, their mention served as a reminder that Saudi Arabia had benefited greatly in its association with the United States. Thus Truman encouraged Ibn Saud to refrain from any action that would require the president to criticize him.

In explaining Truman's view of the Palestine question, Locke pointed out that, whereas the king and other leaders in the Middle East had had many years of experience in dealing with the problem of Palestine, the president had come face to face with it only during the past two years. Having much to learn, the president had depended on his advisers. Locke felt sure that the president had been wrongly advised. However, the Americans were striving to become better acquainted with the Middle East. Locke told Ibn Saud further that he would be returning to the United States quite shortly. Had His Majesty "any message or words of advice on the subject that he wished to transmit to the President?"[29]

The king cut to the chase regarding the president's supposed lack of knowledge about the conflict. He

> began by saying that he had no new advice or recommendations to send to the President. All that he wished the President to do was to reread the various letters that he had written to him on the subject, letters in which the facts of the situation had been set forth. If the President had heeded what the King had told him in these letters, he would not have been misled by unsound advice.[30]

The king then went on to explain to Locke his view that Communism would infiltrate the Middle East by way of the Jewish state in Palestine. He believed that the USSR favored partition for exactly this reason. This was the only insight that he wished to pass along to Truman.

Thus the meeting ended. It seemed that its purpose was to give Truman a chance to play for time and to angle for information about the mood of Ibn Saud at this eleventh hour in the Palestine drama. Truman wished to know whether, if he continued his support for the Zionists and if war came, Ibn Saud might yet cancel the concession agreement. The Saudis, however, were not much impressed by Locke's statements. As one of the king's advisers stated tellingly as the party made its way to luncheon, "We are pleased to know that the American people are learning, but the price of their education is the blood of the Arabs."[31]

On Rentz's return to Aramco headquarters, he received somber news: the president of Mobil, one of the Aramco partners, had met with the secretary of defense, James Forrestal, and the oil executive had declared that, as a result of the Palestine unrest, his company and its associates were suspending work on Tapline from Dhahran to Sidon. The Syrian government had turned down Aramco's request to establish the pipeline terminus at Sidon until the United States altered its policy on Palestine's partition. Would it do so? The answer could not be long delayed.

On May 14, 1948, the British army lowered its flag in Jerusalem. The British withdrawal from Palestine was now complete, and the League of Nations mandate to the British government to rule Palestine was at an end. By midafternoon of that day, full-scale fighting broke out throughout Palestine. At 4:00 P.M. David Ben-Gurion read the declaration of independence of the State of Israel. It contained this statement to the Arab world: "We extend our hand in peace and neighborliness to all the neighboring states and their peoples and invite them to cooperate with the independent Jewish nation for the common good of all. The State of Israel is prepared to make its contribution to the progress of the Middle East."[32]

President Truman extended de facto recognition to Israel at 6:10 P.M. that same day. A historian of these events, Howard M. Sachar, observed one reason why Truman accorded that high privilege to Israel: "There was a national election approaching, and the votes of the major urban communities could be decisive." Senior British diplomat at Jidda, Grafftey-Smith, noted that Truman remarked to four American envoys from Arab states who made pro-Arab representations to him about his Palestine policy: "I am sorry, gentlemen, but I have to answer to hundreds of thousands who are anxious for the success of Zionism; I do not have hundreds of thousands of Arabs among my constituents."[33]

Twelve days after the birth of Israel, rumors abounded that Truman was about to lift the arms embargo to enable the United States to ship arms to the new state. The United States agreed to provide immediate financial aid, totaling $53 million, to Israel. Then Loy Henderson, chief of the Near East and Africa division at the State Department, advised Secretary of State George C. Marshall that a vice president of Aramco, James Terry Duce, had just received a telegram from Fred A. Davies, the manager of Aramco in Arabia. The king had stated "for the first time that he may be compelled, in certain circumstances, to apply sanctions against the American oil concessions" because "the pressure upon him of Arab public opinion was so great that he could no longer resist it." And under what circumstances would Ibn Saud lower the boom on Aramco? Duce reported that "the making of changes in our arms policy, so as to permit the shipment of arms to the Jewish state, would create such circumstances."[34]

Soon Childs warned the State Department that Ibn Saud had made a threat concerning the oil concession. He would come

> for the last time to ask our help, adequate armaments, and our advice. He did not want the U.S. to treat this approach casually. . . . He was very seriously concerned. He could send Crown Prince or Prince Feisal to U.S. to make known his views but their visit would advertise unduly his concern and he wished to avoid the disastrous consequences of failure of their mission.[35]

The history of U.S. arms provision to Israel would be long and tangled. The first formal Israeli approach had come in March 1949, when the Israeli foreign minister apprised the undersecretary of state that "Israel wanted to hire a limited number of US Army reserve or retired regular officers as advisers in military organization to the Israeli Army." This was regarded at the Pentagon as the thin edge of a wedge intended to produce, at a later date, more considerable assistance. Israel was told therefore that "the Israeli proposal was contrary to US law, and that any military assistance to Israel should be provided by a military mission consisting of regular officers on active duty."[36] Nothing more was heard of the Israeli request.

At that same time, the official U.S. position would not "allow the export of arms which would permit a competitive arms race in the area [the Middle East]" and would therefore limit arms exports to those needed for "legitimate security requirements." This was further defined by the National Security Council, which allowed export of "reasonable amounts of military material to Israel and the Arab states" within the scope of "legitimate security requirements" in order to promote "internal security as a basis for general security in the Near Eastern Area." The State Department permitted "a few export licenses for arms and equipment to both Israel and the Arab states" at a "low level." But gradually Israel began to increase its orders and request advanced weapons, including tanks, armored cars, howitzers, antitank guns, antiaircraft guns, and jet aircraft. This latter application was refused.[37]

Such was the situation governing the supply of arms to the Middle East during 1947–50. But there was another, broader issue at stake in the question of supplying arms to Saudi Arabia in particular — U.S. interest in the country.

For some time past, a joint Pentagon–State Department committee had examined the importance of Saudi Arabia to the United States. Concluding that its security was vital to the national security of the

United States, it next addressed the possibility of supplying military advice and arms to Saudi Arabia. This led to a discussion of the "special problems of internal security" in Saudi Arabia. These were "unusual" because

> it is a country of 729,000 square miles — $\frac{1}{4}$ as large as the United States. Saudi Arabia is principally inhabited by nomadic tribes, whose life is ordered by ancient tribal laws.
>
> Internal security is presently maintained primarily by the character of the House of Saud and Saudi Arabian forces of approximately 10,000 poorly equipped and trained men. Increasing development of political and economic conditions in Saudi Arabia should assist in the maintenance of internal security.
>
> Meanwhile, it is believed that a military solution to Saudi Arabia's special problems of internal security is of first importance. It is thought that King Ibn Saud's internal security forces should be increased, trained and equipped along western lines for the purpose of preserving order under the peculiar desert and oasis conditions existing in Saudi Arabia, and for the purpose of lending effective assistance in time of world hostilities. There is no doubt that Saudi Arabia would be willing and able to use such forces in an appropriate manner in Saudi Arabia.[38]

The problem of external security also had to be reckoned with. Ibn Saud had consolidated his control of Saudi Arabia in 1925 by ejecting the Hashemites from control of Mecca and the Hejaz. They now ruled in Iraq and Jordan, and the king was on the alert lest the Hashemites attempt to regain control of western Saudi Arabia. According to Ibn Saud, the Hashemite kings were also flirting with Yemen, thus encircling Saudi Arabia. He also believed that the king of Jordan was offering concessions to the Jews if they would agree to help him retake the Hejaz. The king's "frequent requests for military assistance from the United States over the past few years have undoubtedly been partially motivated by this apprehension."[39]

Furthermore, the committee reported,

> Saudi Arabia is apprehensive of the intentions of the USSR. Only a military solution could remove these apprehensions. Saudi Arabia would be willing and able to use such forces to resist aggression including the protection of the United States oil installations. It may be said also that Saudi Arabia would undoubtedly provide the United States with an assurance that it would not use its security forces for external purposes unless attacked.[40]

With that in mind, they also noted that the Saudi government might "assist other countries in the Near East which are friendly to U.S. to maintain security" — namely, Egypt, Lebanon, and Syria. And in the event of world war, the committee believed that "Saudi Arabia would concert with the other Arab states to assist the United States and would in fact play a role in leading the Near East on this course."[41]

Thus, in addition to continued political and economic support, the Pentagon–State Department committee recommended military aid to Saudi Arabia, specifically to develop internal security forces. No doubt this assistance would contribute to the stability of the region:

> There is no doubt that assurances could be obtained that military aid could be used to achieve the aforementioned United States objectives. There is no doubt likewise that a military solution will contribute political and economic solutions because it will remove King Ibn Saud's fears of aggression by a Near Eastern state, will further stabilize his control and will, most importantly, increase its ability to resist exploitation and infiltration by the USSR. Saudi Arabia is more able to undertake a program of improving its military strength than any other Near Eastern state without injury to its economy because its national income has increased in recent years from approximately 20 to 80 million dollars through oil revenues.[42]

Yet Ibn Saud failed to obtain an arrangement with the Truman administration by which he would get American arms in return for his complaisance in the matter of Palestine. This was a great blow. As Philby, now restored fully to his position as Ibn Saud's only trusted Anglo-Saxon adviser, wrote at the time, he was sure that "the Jews have not a shadow of legal or historical right to go to Palestine" and he counseled therefore that the question be taken out of the hands of the American and British governments by taking it to the International Court of Justice for a ruling. He advised, too, that "Britain and America have from the beginning been firmly minded to ride roughshod over all considerations of right and justice in favour of Zionism, and they could at all times bring irresistible force against the Arabs on that issue." In that advocacy, Ibn Saud and Philby received some support from George Keller, vice chairman of Standard Oil of California, who testified before a Senate committee on U.S. policy in the Arab-Israeli conflict as a whole: "We were in a situation where our government's policy in this area was causing almost intolerable aggravation from day to day in our relations with the Saudi Government."[43]

Such statements did little good for the king, Philby, or Aramco. Philby found that he "fell from grace" in taking the "practical view that the Arabs could only save themselves from ultimate disaster by compromising with the hostile elements whose conscience did occasionally prick them to set limits to the Zionist dream."[44] He could do no more himself.

Still, the king had much to be glad about — if not in politics, then in wealth. Before oil was discovered, he was lucky to raise $500,000 in tax monies with which to run the kingdom. Now, as the decade was ending, his revenues were rising toward $100 million (£25 million) by 1950. Only yesterday, Philby remembered, "Old Cyclops" — Ibn Saud — had been hard-put to pay the kingdom's bills. Now he was in a position to rival Hatshepsut and Solomon in wealth.

But Ibn Saud's sun was setting. He began to ramble or doze at the meetings of the Supreme Council. Philby thought he would do well to leave the politics of the Levant to the Jews and the Arabs who lived there. He mumbled in council at times that Gog and Magog — as he often referred to the North Koreans — were emerging from their cave to challenge God himself. And as Philby remarked as 1949 passed into 1950: "Ibn Saud is by no means unique among men in desiring to be an eyewitness to doomsday. Long live the king! And may his works live long after him!"[45]

They did. The revenues from Aramco for 1950 proved not to be £25 million gold, but £50 million. But Ibn Saud never lived to see the day when he could have claimed to be the richest man in Arabia.

[9]

THE KING DIES

IBN SAUD'S LIFE BEGAN to ebb in 1950. President Truman's physician, General Wallace H. Graham, began a series of secret journeys from Washington to Riyadh in an effort to keep alive the man who was, according to U.S. interests, the most important figure in the Middle East. But Graham could do little for a man crippled by deepening senility, arthritis, general enfeeblement, and gathering blindness in his remaining eye. The king, Philby wrote to his English wife, was

> a sad sight now, silent and lifeless and rather morose. I attend his sittings [of the *diwan,* the council of ministers and advisers of which Philby was a member], but now he only sits in the afternoons with nothing to say to anyone: and I rather doubt if he has actually seen me, though I have shaken hands with him and saluted him several times at his sessions. He just seems to look into space or downwards to the ground, without any sign of recognition of anyone.[1]

That was St. John's last letter about Ibn Saud. The king's last coherent words were, according to St. John, "A man's possessions and his children are his enemies."[2] Before he passed he did formally delegate some of his powers to Crown Prince Saud. But, although the crown prince represented the embodiment of much that was regrettable about the royal princes, Ibn Saud did nothing to prevent Saud from succeeding him. And so it was.

During the long period of Ibn Saud's decline, the American minister to the Saudi court, J. Rives Childs, made inquiries about the abilities of the crown prince, Saud, and of Prince Faisal, who, it was assumed rightly, would become crown prince when Saud acceded. Both Saud and Faisal had visited the United States, but it did seem that Faisal held the stronger views on the relationship between the two countries. In 1948, Faisal delivered a long harangue

> against American support of Jews in [the] Palestine struggle. After setting forth [a] bitter catalogue of events at [the United Nations] at Lake Success climaxed by American recognition of Israel almost before Israel was proclaimed, Feisal stated this was proof of American lack of political wisdom or morality. Feisal said Americans are pure materialists, they are not interested in moral considerations, and consequently lack the wisdom in human affairs which can only flow from virtue. . . . It was up to the British to teach the Americans political wisdom.[3]

That was not all Faisal was heard to say that afternoon at Taif. He asserted that "most American diplomats in the Middle East were aware of the justice of the Arab cause but he was shocked to find how little weight their judgment carried in the United States." His fears concerning the spread of Communism led him to conclude "that it would be to the advantage of the anti-communist powers to undertake the war [against the USSR] before it became too late."[4]

Faisal visited the United States in 1946 for meetings with President Truman and with Secretary of State Dean Acheson, who wrote a memorable word portrait of Faisal:

> The Amir, striking in a white burnous [robes worn by the Arabs] and golden circlet, which heightened his swarthy complexion, with black, pointed beard and mustache topped by a thin hooked nose and piercing dark eyes, gave a sinister impression, relieved from time to time by a shy smile. . . . As he talked with President Truman, it seemed to me that their minds crossed but did not meet. The Amir was concerned with conditions in the Near East, the President with the conditions of displaced Jews in Europe. . . . The Amir impressed me as a man who could be an implacable enemy and who should be taken very seriously.[5]

No such opinion was rendered of Saud. He was as tall as his father, with similar features. He had a considerable presence, but his features were marred by spectacles that resembled the goggles of a diver or a welder. These gave him a shifty appearance. Much was expected of him: was he not the eldest son of the much admired Ibn Saud? He had contributed mightily to the strength of the Saud dynasty by the same process used by his father — copulation on the grand scale. He claimed to have thirty-six sons, some said forty-eight, all born of the daughters of ruling families and of the tribal sheikhs. In this way he had bound the tribes in loyalty to him. The sheikhs called him "Saud, the white-hearted," an admiration buttressed by the system of tribal subsidies that had succeeded so well for his father — silver riyals and Maria Theresa dollars scattered by the fistful by an enormous black slave.

Ibn Saud had spent much time in preparing Saud for the succession. As Philby wrote, when Saud was appointed crown prince, Ibn Saud had seen to it that his heir was "closely associated with the king himself in the governance of the country."[6] Ibn Saud had sent Saud on extensive trips abroad, where he imbibed ideas from Europe and America intended to "stand their country in good stead" as Saudi Arabia took "its place ever more effectively in the comity of modern nations." Ibn Saud never permitted Saud or his brothers to forget "their duty to their country which bred them; and to the faith and race of which they are the purest representatives."[7]

Saud, together with his thirty-five brothers and innumerable grandsons, great-grandsons, and other relatives, composed

> a royal family of truly prodigious proportions. The survival of the Saud dynasty into distant centuries seems assured beyond a peradventure. . . . All its members have been brought up, under [Ibn Saud's] own guidance to regard themselves as a band of brothers: united for the common weal, and taking precedence at court in the order in which they came into the world, without regard for their individual provenance, or the social status of their mothers. Not least among the achievements of the king must be reckoned this knitting together of such a cosmopolitan group of relations, among whom, in spite of long and careful study of their mutual reactions, I have never been able to detect any trace of the animosities and dissensions which so nearly wrecked the dynasty in the generation of [Ibn Saud's] uncles.[8]

In addition to his remarkable success in establishing a dynasty, Ibn Saud also brought under control the Bedouin of the desert in a feat of tribal administration. They

> were not long in recognizing their master in the young man who ruled Riyadh at the beginning of the century. And they were soon harnessed to a machine destined to crush their own independence out of being: though used at first with consummate skill and discretion to destroy, with their aid, all the rivals who might claim their allegiance in future struggles for hegemony in Arabia. All these tribes are now, without exception, law-abiding pastoral communities; prosperous enough in the new general prosperity of the desert, or partly settled in agricultural groups, tilling the lands which they formerly ravaged in search of loot.[9]

For the moment the reins of the realm were in the hands of Saud, with Faisal assisting in his position as viceroy of the Hejaz and foreign minister. The relationship seemed to work, but as the king drifted between life and death, Philby felt the need to utter this warning: Ibn Saud had allowed no delegation of his powers, except to the finance minister, Abdullah Suleiman. Both Ibn Saud's heirs, the crown prince and the viceroy of the Hejaz, "exercise the king's functions in his absence from their spheres; but they do so on his behalf and subject to reference to him of all matters of moment, which in effect means everything but the details of pure routine."[10] Similarly all ministers and advisers could exercise no personal initiative in any situation without reference to Ibn Saud. Thus the members of the royal family and the court did not tend to develop true leadership skills and instead they became expert in currying favor with the monarch.

Philby did not highly regard the ministers and officials of Ibn Saud's court (with the exception of Abdullah Suleiman):

> Not one of them has proved able to . . . give the country the lead of which it is desperately in need. And, considering that they were all poor men twenty-five years ago with no assets but their brains, and are all rich men now after years of basking in the king's bounty, their performance can only be regarded as disappointing. It is perhaps significant that in all this period there has not been a single case of resignation of office as a mark of disapproval of any particular policy or action.[11]

But even Suleiman would be implicated in the scandalous financial problems that were surfacing in Saudi Arabia because of the royal family's almost unimaginable spending habits. True, Suleiman had introduced a new Saudi currency throughout the kingdom, and he established everywhere offices for the collection of taxes and other dues — improvements, to be sure. But he was ever "content to write off as a lump sum the financial provision required by the king and the various provincial governors, mostly members of the royal family, for use at their unfettered discretion and without any obligation to account for such funds." Suleiman had so constructed the affairs of the Hejaz and the oil fields of Hasa that the country qualified for loans and other financial support from the Western countries: "during the lean years of the war, his skill in extracting doles from Britain and America in support of his efforts to keep the country content met with well merited commendation." In the wake of such successes, he "soon established virtually undisputed sway over all branches of the government."[12]

This aid, together with the wealth from the oil fields, offered the country a tremendous opportunity to improve the well-being of all its people, to develop industry and educational programs, and thereby to grow more independent of the Western powers that assisted Saudi

Arabia in order to protect their interests there. Therefore — and this is the rub — it "needed a little restraint and judicious administration to place the country beyond the reach of want forever, and to raise it to a high level of permanent prosperity. But riches begat extravagance on a scale never before experienced in Arabia."[13]

At a dinner at Crown Prince Saud's garden estate at Riyadh, Philby noted that "every item on the menu had come from America in refrigerator planes." Similarly, at Suleiman's palace he discovered a replica of "a submarine nightclub with walls of glass, through which the circumambient fish could watch the dancing!" It had been discovered by Suleiman on one of his visits to the United States. He had it copied and then reconstructed in the Arabian desert.[14]

Many believed that the kingdom would not survive Ibn Saud's passing, that it would disintegrate into the sovereign states of Nejd, Hejaz, Asir, Hasa, and perhaps others, like the Gulf sheikhdoms. What then? Would an Arabian emerge to seize Aramco as, in May 1950, Prime Minister Mohammed Mossadek of Iran had overthrown and exiled the shah of Iran and then, under the influence of the U.S. ambassador in Tehran, nationalized the Anglo-Iranian Oil Company? This action had come close to provoking a war between Great Britain and Iran.[15] Everyone questioned how long Ibn Saud would last — vast budgets and large capital investments depended on the answer. But, like all potentates, Ibn Saud was particularly secretive about his health, and details were hard to come by.

There was equal concern about Ibn Saud's successor, Crown Prince Saud, and his fitness as a ruler. On this point, the U.S. minister Childs questioned Philby, and then gave this estimation to the State Department:

> Amir Saud has nothing of the electric magnetism of his father and is likely to give Saudi Arabia a rather dull reign so far as the impact of his own personality on events is concerned. It is recognized that Amir Feisal, the second son who is Viceroy of the Hedjaz and Minister for Foreign Affairs, is not only a more colorful but an abler person. Mr. Philby feels that there has been sufficient time for King [Ibn Saud] to consolidate the power and influence of his dynasty upon Saudi Arabia. Mr. Philby also believes that while Amir Saud as ruler would not afford anything spectacular in the way of administering the country, the modernization of the country would inevitably be speeded up.[16]

Ibn Saud died at Taif, the hill resort outside Jidda, at 10:30 A.M. on November 9, 1953. As the king's body was flown to Riyadh for burial, the Saudi foreign ministry formally announced his death to the diplomatic corps. First came a brief Wahhabi prayer uttered by the grand mufti of Riyadh, which was followed by the formal announcement.

Ibn Saud was buried in the desert outside Riyadh at sunset that same day, his feet pointing to Mecca and his body wrapped only in a winding sheet and attended only by his faithful black bodyguard. There was no headstone, for to have erected one would have been, according to Wahhabi law, blasphemous, and so the ever-moving deserts claimed him.

Immediately after Ibn Saud's death, the royal family met and accepted the crown prince, Saud, as King Saud. His brother Faisal, viceroy of the Hejaz and foreign minister of the kingdom, became crown prince, as Ibn Saud had directed. The green flag of the Wahhabs was not lowered, for it was inscribed with the word of God, and the ulema, the religious council, would not permit the flag to be flown at half-mast for the passing of anyone, even a ruler like Ibn Saud, who had done so much to honor his Creator.

The executives of Aramco were much relieved to learn that the succession appeared to be going as Ibn Saud had hoped, without interruption in the affairs of the state. The company published a tribute to him in its newspaper, *Sun & Flare*, noting a number of the king's (often U.S.-supported) accomplishments:

> All members of the Company joined mourning the death of King Abd al-Aziz ibn Abd al-Rahman Al Faisal al-Saud on November 9, 1953.
>
> The world at large appreciates the heroic accomplishments of His Majesty in the first quarter of this century, thanks to which Saudi Arabia became a sovereign and independent state. Once unity had been achieved, His Majesty devoted tireless efforts to the social and economic improvement of his country. Wells were drilled in many parts of the country and projects for the development of water supplies undertaken. . . . Arrangements were made for the importation of increased quantities of food and clothing. His Majesty had modern airports built at the larger cities. . . . A wireless communications network spread across the country, and telephone systems were installed. . . . Projects were inaugurated for bringing electricity to a number of cities of Saudi Arabia. Roads were built, and the harbors . . . were transformed into deep-water ports. . . . In June 1952 His Majesty was able to fulfill a long-held wish by canceling the pilgrimage fees, thus making it easier for Muslims throughout the world to realize their ambition of performing the pilgrimage to Mecca. His Majesty had historic mosques strengthened and repaired, and new mosques were built. Hospitals and other public health facilities were provided for the pilgrims and the citizens of the Kingdom. Many schools were opened for the education of the Saudi youth.[17]

And that was that. The new king began a new reign. In his last months Ibn Saud had shown that, as he said after the United States recognized Israel, the Americans in his country were no longer brothers but business partners. Following in this vein, in a message to the Aramco president, W. F. Moore, the Aramco management learned that the new king had "demanded" that he send a representative to Riyadh within ten days with full powers to settle the differences between the company and the Saudi Arabian government. It was an ultimatum. He wanted Aramco's agreement on a number of issues, including Saudi membership on the company's board of directors (a question that Moore had been evading for months) and the establishment of Aramco's main headquarters in Saudi Arabia, so that government representatives could check the company's bookkeeping records and confirm the correctness of royalty payments.

A member of the National Security Council made these observations concerning Saud's message:

> The King's message climaxes a series of demands which discussion between the Minister of Finance and Aramco representatives in Jidda has failed to resolve. These difficulties have been exaggerated by Sheikh Abdullah [Suleiman] to support a charge of Aramco non-cooperation. . . . The real issue may be a deliberately adopted policy in order to soften up the company either for the purpose of making the company more pliable to his demands, or to build up a case against Aramco preparatory to an attack on the concession.[18]

Restored to the comforts of Nasiriyah Palace and his harem after long travels in the kingdom at the start of his reign, King Saud began to follow the foreign policy that the times dictated to him — disastrously so. Under the revolutionary guidance of Egyptian president Nasser, the Middle East potentates had found it convenient and advisable to sack their British advisers, who had, in the main, helped stabilize the region since the end of World War I. Recently, King Hussein of Jordan had sacked Glubb Pasha, founder of the Arab Legion, the best army in the Middle East. Now Saud found a reason to sack Philby, the longest-serving of his father's courtiers and possessing a remarkable list of accomplishments: he had helped Ibn Saud found his dynasty and his kingdom, located American capital to give the country the wealth it now enjoyed, had done more than any Saudi to promote sane foreign policy, and had devoted his entire career to the establishment of a monarchy and an administration that the great powers could take seriously. There were too many kings in the world who were jokes, but Ibn Saud was never one of them — Philby had seen to that.

Philby had displayed no sign of sadness at the king's death, although their friendship had lasted for thirty-five years, fifteen of them with Philby sitting with the court. In fact, despite his long-standing loyalty to the king, Philby's overall opinion of the reign of Ibn Saud was highly critical, and he made no attempt to conceal his opinions. Through his failure to understand the importance of budgets and bookkeepers in state affairs, Ibn Saud had left the country in debt and in danger of bankruptcy, despite the country's oil riches. "I don't think I shall ever forgive my old friend for letting corruption rip to this extent," Philby wrote to his English wife on November 17, 1953. "For the moment obviously there is loud praise all round for the great things he did; but sooner or later he will have to stand at the bar of history for an investigation of his failure to control things when the country began to be rich."[19]

In fact, Philby may even have mentioned his concerns to the new king. Certainly the record shows that Saud was disconcerted by something that Philby had to say. Having lunched with King Saud, St. John recorded that he had found little inclination in the new king to produce an administration that would cleanse the severe corruption, especially the lavish spending of the princes. Ibn Saud's practices would be continued by King Saud. At court, the same cast of characters held sway — the finance minister, Suleiman, the first deputy foreign minister, Yusuf Yassin, and "the Syrians" — all still vying for power and wealth.

Soon Philby began to find court life irksome, and since Ibn Saud's death he had "felt quite rebellious against the whole comedy." He intended, he said, to expose it in a chapter of a book he was writing on modern Saudi Arabia. Though he tried to withhold his true feelings during the official period of mourning, these intentions did not outlast the obsequies. St. John began to lecture against corruption and extravagance in high places. He denounced the young princes for picking up their morals "in the gutters of the west." He denounced them for drinking alcohol. The deserts were littered with broken-down Cadillacs, which the princes were unable to repair and for which they had not paid. And in February 1955 he lectured the staff of Aramco at Dhahran on the extravagant habits the princes had brought back with them from their sojourns in the United States. He was booed and shunned by the Aramcons for that. He complained that the treasury had established no reserves, that the "brine of corruption" lay heavily upon the entire administration.[20]

Persuaded that the substance of these speeches derived from "external influences" — Communism or imperialism — early in March

1955, a delegation from Saud came to call on Philby. Philby, they announced, must leave Saudi Arabia. His Aramco lectures had exhausted the royal patience. Later in the month, he was told by the same delegation that he might stay if he wrote a letter of contrition to the king and if he agreed to submit all his future writings to a censor. But that he refused to do. St. John did call upon King Saud to speak quietly with him about internal and external enemies, but, so it is said, King Saud spat upon his father's old friend, as did the rest of the court.[21]

So Philby had to go, and he went. He was stripped of the £180 (about $450) yearly allowance that Ibn Saud had given him for life. The Saudi crown seems also to have regained title to the houses that Ibn Saud had given to Philby, for life, at Riyadh, Jidda, Taif, and Mecca. When he asked permission to go to Mecca to pack up his possessions and to gather his Arab wife, Rozy (who may have been one of Ibn Saud's daughters from the harem), and his two sons for the trip through Medina into Jordan, he was refused. He must leave Saudi Arabia immediately and by the shortest route, along the road beside Tapline. Rozy and the children were to go to Mecca and pack, and then follow when granted exit permits — which, it can be presumed, were contingent upon Philby's silence and discretion concerning Saudi affairs of state when he reached his place of exile, Beirut, that babbling brook of Near Eastern politics.

Philby left Riyadh on April 15, 1955, traveling across the desert by Land Rover. Along the way, he made his usual observant notes, commenting on the terrain, the birds, the state of the pipeline, and the number of lengths of pipe per mile. By conventional standards he was not penniless, only poor and without prospects of employment except in the pitiless world of penny-a-line journalism. Although fit, he was far too much of an independent spirit to be employable. And as he wrote to a friend in London, he would make his home in Lebanon, but how he would manage, he did not know: "I think I must be quite the only person who has ever left [Saudi Arabia] with no share of the spoil."[22]

At an early date, King Saud established a relationship with the new Arab messiah, President Gamal Abdel Nasser of Egypt; and in September 1955 Nasser visited Saudi Arabia as Saud's guest. The Egyptian leader was so deliriously received by the Saudi population that, it is said, Saud became anxious for his throne. However, an alliance grew up between the two states when the Western powers, especially the British and to a lesser extent the Americans, began to regard Nasser as a major enemy. When Nasser nationalized the Suez Canal, a world crisis broke out. All the great Western corporations, Aramco included, began to see that if Nasser was allowed to keep the canal, they, too, might find their interests imperiled. The British prime minister, Anthony Eden, recorded in his diary that he foresaw a possible domino effect if Nasser continued to gain power:

> [Nationalizing the Suez Canal is] the opening gambit in a planned campaign designed by Nasser to expel all Western influence and interests from Arab countries. He believes that he can get away with this, and if he can successfully defy eighteen nations, his prestige in Arabia will be so great that he will be able to mount revolutions of young officers in Saudi Arabia, Jordan, Syria and Iraq. We know from our joint sources that he is already preparing a revolution in Iraq, which is the most stable and progressive [country] in the Middle East. These new governments will in effect be Egyptian satellites if not Russian ones. They will have to place their united oil resources under the control of a united Arabia led by Egypt and under Russian influence. When that moment comes Nasser can deny oil to Western Europe and we here shall all be at his mercy. . . . We have many times led Europe in the fight for freedom. It would be an ignoble end to our long history if we tamely accepted to perish by degrees.[23]

Great fears developed in Britain and Europe that their oil might be at risk, as it proved to be. The British foreign secretary, Harold Macmillan, told a messenger from President Eisenhower that if Britain lost its position of influence in the Middle East, not only would its oil be lost, but also it would be reduced from being a world power to a status approximating that of the Netherlands. Eisenhower, sensing a major danger to American interests, urged restraint on the British leaders. This fell on deaf ears. Eden prepared with the French and, it emerged later, in secret with Israel, to undertake a major military operation to overthrow Nasser. Eden also ordered his secret service to arrange Nasser's assassination.

As war seemed inevitable and imminent, Aramco sought to protect its oil resources by giving aid and comfort to the Saudi foreign and defense ministers, *and* to Egyptian secret agents in Jidda. Together, these Saudis and Egyptians intended to undertake secret operations to raise a revolt against the British in British-protected South Arabian fringe lands between Oman and the British military base in the crown colony of Aden. And Aramco undertook to assist them. Thus it embarked on secret operations against the United States' main ally, Britain.[24]

Rights to these fringe lands had been contested for many years. In August 1952, in one of his last major decisions before his death,

Ibn Saud had ordered an invasion of British-protected South Arabia. Prince Turki ibn Abdullah ibn Ataishan led forty men in Aramco vehicles to seize the Buraimi oasis. He proclaimed himself governor, although Ibn Saud was well aware that Buraimi was in the territory of the sultan of Muscat and Oman. Aramco knew also that near Buraimi, at the village of Fuhud, there was "a billion dollar" oil prospect owned by what William E. Mulligan called "the old enemy, the Anglo-Persian Oil Company." Thus Aramco supported the Saudis in their attempt to gain control of the region.

The Buraimi oasis was located in one of the most remote parts of southeastern Arabia, and it consisted of nine villages of about ten thousand souls, about ninety miles east of Abu Dhabi on the Trucial Coast. Ibn Saud recognized no claim but his own to the oasis and the villages; he held that the population there was independent but under Saudi protection. Had the people there not paid *zakat*, the religious tithe, to his divines for generations?[25]

On establishing himself as the governor of the new Saudi province of Buraimi, Prince Turki proclaimed that the day of liberation from the feudal overlord had arrived. He alluded to the "imperialistic foreigners" — the British — and he announced that fifty-nine tribal chiefs had affirmed their allegiance to Ibn Saud. But the British believed the inhabitants owed allegiance to the sultan of Muscat under British protection. They accordingly reacted vigorously to Prince Turki's arrival in the oasis. They sent detachments of Trucial Scouts, native levies led by British officers, to the oasis. The British air force, which had a base at Sharja on the Gulf, flew frequent flights over Buraimi, dropping anti-Saudi messages; it looked as if an armed clash was imminent and inevitable.

But first the Saudis in Jidda sought the good offices of the United States, and on October 26, 1952, a standstill agreement proposed by the U.S. ambassador was signed by British and Saudi representatives. The Saudis proposed a plebiscite in the disputed area; the British proposed arbitration. The negotiations, as usual, took forever. Not until July 1954 did both parties agree that all forces should be withdrawn from Buraimi, leaving only small detachments at the oasis until arbitration. British oil operations begun at Fuhud — where they claimed to have a "billion barrel" structure — could continue, and Aramco could prospect in the south and the west up to the line informally agreed upon by Britain and Saudi Arabia in 1935.

Throughout this time, between 1947 and 1955, George Rentz, Aramco's leading Arabist and chief of the Arabian Affairs Division,

placed his considerable resources in the service of the Saudi government. The company provided, free of charge, "historical, geographical, and ethnographical material about the Arabian Peninsula for use
by the Government in its boundary disputes with neighboring countries."[26] It composed and published the major research papers *The
Eastern Reaches of al-Hasa Province and Oman* and *The Southern Shore of the
Persian Gulf,* both important to Saudi Arabia in proving its claim to
certain territory in the regions. Aramco also provided extensive mapmaking services to the government.

This assistance culminated in the research, writing, and printing by
Aramco of Saudi Arabia's memorial to the Buraimi Arbitration Tribunal proceedings, which began in Nice on January 22, 1955, and continued in Geneva. The tribunal consisted of Dr. Charles De Visscher of
Belgium, Dr. Ernesto Digigo of Cuba, Dr. Mahmoud Hasan of Pakistan,
Sir Reader Bullard of Great Britain (an old Jidda hand), and Sheikh
Yusuf Yassin of Saudi Arabia. Rentz and Mulligan of Aramco supported
the Saudis. The representatives of Britain and Saudi Arabia presented
their memorials, and the proceedings were well underway when, at
their meeting in September, Bullard announced that Britain had evidence that the Saudi government had offered a bribe of £30 million
($85 million) in one cash payment to the brother of the ruler of
Abu Dhabi if he would defect to Saudi Arabia. According to another
version of the story, a senior CIA official, Kermit Roosevelt, had "offered 400 million rupees" ($90 million) if Sheikh Zaid, brother of
Sheikh Shakhbut, ruler of Abu Dhabi, would "repudiate" his brother
and "cede the [Buraimi] oasis to King Saud, thus "preventing the Iraq
Petroleum Company from operating in the disputed territories and
leaving the field open to Aramco." Sheikh Zaid then told the British
authorities of the bribe, and Reader Bullard acted to terminate the
tribunal hearings. The veracity of this story is not known.[27]

The size of the bribe surprised the tribunal, but, as the British
pointed out, the sum involved would seem no more than "chump
change" if the Saudis gained sovereignty over the Fuhud oil field. Bullard further claimed that Sheikh Yassin had attempted to bribe the
Pakistani delegate on the tribunal. On September 16, Bullard resigned
and walked out. Rentz and Mulligan of Aramco took the view that
Bullard's indignation had much to do with Britain's weak claim in the
matter; they believed that if the proceedings had continued, the tribunal would have found in favor of Saudi Arabia's claims to Buraimi. That
decision, in legal terms at least, would have ended British protection in
the area. The British concession agreement with the sultan of Muscat

and Oman for the Fuhud oil field could then have been declared invalid.

On October 26, British-officered forces of the sheikh of Abu Dhabi entered Buraimi, overpowered and ejected the Saudi police contingent, and occupied the oasis. In a note presented to the Saudi government, Britain claimed that the boundary established in 1935 was now valid, and a diplomatic note warned the Saudis not to violate the new frontier. Saudi protests, followed by condemnation of the British action and a call by the Arab League's political committee on November 14, 1955, for neutral supervision of the disputed area, were of no avail. The troops remained in occupation, and in a general movement strengthening Britain's position in South Arabia, the forces of the sultan of Muscat in December seized the town of Nizwa, seat of the imam of Oman, the religious and secular leader of Muscat-Oman's hinterland. The imam, a Nasserite, fled, and Prince Turki was unceremoniously deported, flown in a British aircraft to Dhahran.

In due course the British foreign secretary, Harold Macmillan, in a diary note, related that he had repudiated the arbitration agreement because the Saudi representative had resorted to bribery; and in any case, the Saudis "had no real claim" to Buraimi. According to Major W. O. Little, the British intelligence officer in the Gulf, Aramco was deeply involved in the intrigues and had offered the sheikh $60 million if he would abandon his ties to the British and convey the rights to his oil to Aramco. The sheikh declined the bribe. The oasis was vital to British oil interests. He acknowledged that the legal position was "rather tricky" but "the political situation is urgent. We must act, firmly and quickly, if we are to retain our prestige and hopes of more oil in this area." He had "thought it wiser not to consult the United States" and therefore the "State Department had been upset because they had had no prior warning" of the British occupation of Buraimi.[28]

But with the Middle East inflamed by Nasser's fiery anti-Western oratory, the Buraimi incident began to assume a growing significance. A revolt broke out in Oman under the leadership of Talib, the brother of the imam, with the goal of overthrowing the sultan of Muscat and Oman, Said bin Taimur, who, Macmillan recorded, Britain was morally bound to protect. "British friendship and support had been afforded to the Sultan for more than a century, to have withheld our assistance at this critical moment would have involved a grave loss of confidence among all friendly Sheikhs and Rulers throughout the Gulf."[29]

Meanwhile Talib had visited Saudi Arabia and Egypt, and he had obtained what Macmillan called "a substantial supply of arms and money."[30] Britain responded by sending the sultan arms and stores by air, as well as authorizing the sultan to employ "the Trucial Oman Scouts under British officers." British frigates were patrolling the coasts of Muscat and Oman to prevent the infiltration of arms; and British air force aircraft were sent to blast Talib's positions in the mountains.

Macmillan sent a message to President Eisenhower, bringing to his attention rumors that the revolt and the Saudi occupation of Buraimi had been "fomented by some of the American oil companies in order to damage their British rival who had obtained concessions in that region."[31]

In his reply to Macmillan's message, the president denied the rumors, and Macmillan "naturally accepted" the disclaimer. But Macmillan's confidence was misplaced. At that moment U.S. secretary of state John Foster Dulles decided to make a trip to London to see Macmillan, who had become prime minister. Though he knew that the topic of discussion would be Muscat, Macmillan palmed off the meeting to the public as a discussion of disarmament, a much less volatile subject.

Dulles liked Britain and its gentlemanly institutions, but he was an enemy of the British Empire and believed that its long-shining sun was finally setting. Regarding the contention between Britain and the United States over control of South Arabia, Dulles intended to double-cross Macmillan, who had been Eisenhower's political agent and friend in the Mediterranean during the war.

After Dulles's visit to London, Macmillan duly made a statement in the House of Commons to clarify the reasons for Britain's actions in South Arabia. It neatly substituted "friendship" for clear treaty obligations as reason for its defense of British support of the sultan:

> The difference between a formal obligation and the obligations of a longstanding relationship of friendship is not readily apparent to the local Rulers and people. If we were to fail in one area it would begin to be assumed elsewhere that perhaps the anti-British propaganda of our enemies had some basis to it and that Her Majesty's Government were no longer willing or able to help their friends.[32]

The House accepted the government's view, much to Macmillan's surprise.

Three hundred and sixty troops of the Cameron Highlanders, a Scots regiment, were sent to Oman, and by mid-August 1957 Macmillan felt able to note that the trouble there seemed to be over. But a fortnight later he recorded that the affair was dragging on, as in fact it did, until about 1961 — in a sporadic and not very dangerous form of guerrilla warfare.

Aramco's direct involvement in Saudi operations to gain control of South Arabia was suspected by the British government, but it could not be proved until the emergence of Mulligan's papers in 1993. In those five hundred files was one detailing the Buraimi case. It showed that in 1955, angry that the British had roughly treated Prince Turki, Sheikh Yusuf Yassin had approached Aramco in Jidda and presented it with a plan hatched jointly by the Saudi army and a major of the Egyptian intelligence service in Jidda. The plan involved raising the Omani tribes against the British-protected sultan of Muscat and Oman and, with Aramco assistance, driving the British out of South Arabia.

According to a memorandum dated February 7, 1956, "the year of Suez," some of Aramco's senior political staff met with Sheikh Yassin and some Egyptian officials in Jidda. At that time, Aramco was fearful that, through the precedent created by Nasser's seizure of the Suez Canal, the Saudi government might nationalize Aramco. But if Aramco was to collaborate with the Saudis in ejecting the British from Buraimi, Aramco stood to gain leverage with the Saudis, as well as invaluable fresh oil deposits to add to its holdings. After meeting with the Saudis and Egyptians, Homer C. Mueller, a high-ranking member of Aramco's political staff, agreed to present to management the possibility of Aramco's involvement in this adventure. Mueller had promised Yassin complete secrecy except within the highest circle of Aramco management; he did not wish the Saudi plans and the collaboration with the Egyptian government to become known to the British embassy or to the press. Mueller realized that meeting with the Saudis and Egyptians had been tantamount to attending a war council. Mueller's report shows that Yassin had practically said as much:

> With regard to the extent of the Company's participation in such an effort, I pointed out to Sheikh Yusuf that I was not in a position to make any commitment beyond the furnishing of information. He replied that he would depend upon our Division for research, upon Messrs. Davies and Ohliger for equipment and authority, and upon Mr. Duce [the Aramco political agent in Washington] for bombs. On more than one occasion Sheikh Yusuf was belligerent in speech.[33]

After that meeting, Mueller returned to Dhahran on December 9, 1955, accompanied by a Saudi army lieutenant colonel. Aramco management agreed to support reconnaissance efforts in South Arabia, and to that end approximately twenty-five Aramco vehicles were readied for the trek. The Aramco company logo was painted on all equipment, to disguise the true nature of the mission. This twenty-day operation (December 16, 1955–January 5, 1956) involved both land and air reconnaissance.

Why so many vehicles were required, and why the mission took so long, was not explained by Mueller in his aide-mémoire. It seems possible that Aramco vehicles transporting the Egyptians also carried war stores into Oman (they did arrive there, one way or another). In George Lenczowski's authoritative work, *Oil and State in the Middle East,* he noted that "British sources maintain that an Omani force numbering some 500 men underwent training" at Dammam, and that their instructors were Saudis and Egyptians. Also, "the Omanis had obtained some military equipment from outside, including land mines, but the immediate origin of these weapons has not been disclosed."[34]

There is no lack of evidence that Aramco allied itself with Saudi and Egyptian officials to make mischief for Britain during a major international crisis. Nor was this the end of Aramco's meddling in British affairs in South Arabia. There is equally good evidence that Aramco's Arabian Affairs Division, headed by Rentz and Mulligan, directed an extensive political warfare campaign to condemn Britain in the United Nations. It appears that this division also had connections to the CIA and the FBI.

The Buraimi conflict evidently made for lively times. Mulligan called it "an interesting little war between us and the limies." His quarterly report to management showed that he had become not only an intelligence officer, but also a propagandist:

> The members of the Division gathered and transmitted large quantities of data regarding the Buraimi dispute to New York. The work entailed translating and editing documents, interviewing important persons, and arranging for still and motion pictures for public relations use. This data was forwarded to Dr. George Rentz, who had been in the States during the greater part of the quarter rendering assistance to the Saudi Arabian Permanent Delegation to the United Nations.[35]

With the failure of the Buraimi Arbitration Tribunal and a general lack of interest at the United Nations, Rentz turned the memorial into a glossily covered indictment of British activities in South Arabia, for presentation to the General Assembly. Its title page, clearly summarizing the Saudi Arabian position, read:

The Buraimi Dispute

A Summary of Facts Regarding
British seizure of territory in
southeastern Saudi Arabia after
terminating arbitration proceedings
for a peaceful settlement.[36]

The recast memorial was only one effort among many, on Aramco's part, to win support for the Saudis' attempt to gain control of Buraimi.

The Buraimi dispute, later known as the Omani War of National

Liberation among Omanis, lasted from 1954 until 1961. The action and the cost in human life were almost negligible: British military casualties in Oman over the seven years of guerrilla war totaled eight dead and two wounded; a handful of Arab levies were killed or wounded in the sultan's forces. The political result of the conflict was this: The UN representative sent to Oman reported that there was no war and no military occupation.

The meeting of the UN Security Council on Oman took place on August 20, 1957, and as Macmillan recorded:

> The most I had been able to persuade the American Administration to do was to "abstain." The President argued that this would probably be as useful as a negative vote. He proved right, for the Arab request failed to obtain the necessary seven votes, in spite of Russian support. The question therefore fell to the ground and was not discussed.[37]

Aramco and the Iraq Petroleum Company reached an informal understanding that their survey and drilling teams would not approach within five miles of the borderline between South Arabia and Saudi Arabia first established by the Anglo-Saudi 1935 agreement and reestablished by the British unilaterally in September 1955. This agreement left a ten-mile strip of no-man's-land to minimize the possibility of a clash between the two companies.

Despite Aramco's efforts, most of the South Arabian peoples involved in the dispute preferred retaining their historical connections with the British to the prospect of accepting the Wahhabi embrace. The South Arabian oil remained British, much to the profit of the Omani and Qatarian populations who, according to the CIA, in 1989 found themselves in the enviable position of being among the most prosperous in the world.

The UN settlement was never accepted by the Saudis. In fact, in the spring of 1996, with considerable secrecy and at large cost, the Saudi government retained a firm of Washington lawyers to sift Mulligan's papers for fresh evidence concerning the boundaries and the legality of tenure of the new generation of South Arabian rulers.

As victor, Macmillan had the satisfaction of summarizing the entire affair:

> The successful operation in Oman helped to restore confidence in that part of the Arab world, especially throughout the Gulf. For it proved that the British Government remained unshaken by the misrepresentations of its policies, at home and abroad, or alarmed by the parrot-like accusations of "colonialism" and "imperialism." As a result we were able in subsequent years to operate in Jordan and Kuwait both to protect our friends and to defend our own national interests.[38]

[10]

DOUBLE-CROSS

THE BURAIMI INCIDENT TOOK place more or less contemporaneously with the Suez War and its aftermath, and so we must return briefly to that war. By the end of that short conflict, the Suez Canal was badly blocked by sunken ships, making it impossible for tankers to make the transit from the Red Sea to the Mediterranean to what was then the main market for Aramco's oil — Europe. There were only two ways to get the oil to Europe: around Africa (a costly and slow option) or by way of the Trans-Arabian Pipeline (Tapline). But even as the Suez crisis subsided, America and Britain became alarmed by the Soviet penetration of Syria, through which Tapline crossed on its way to the great oil terminal at Sidon.

Linked as the Syrian government was to Egypt by close ideological ties and special military agreements, in November 1956, just after the Suez invasion, all three pumping stations of the Iraq Petroleum Company were blown up by Syrian saboteurs, acting with official Syrian connivance and, perhaps, Soviet support. The action stopped the flow of oil from Iraq to its Mediterranean terminals in Banias, Syria, and Tripoli, Lebanon, close to the Syrian frontier. The flow of 25 million tons a year of Iraqi oil to Britain and Europe caused much damage to the Anglo-European economies and had forced them to turn to the Americas, thereby creating a severe balance of payments problem when they were compelled to pay for the oil in dollars. The Syrians permitted no repairs before March 1957, thereby intensifying the damage. Aramco capitalized on this state of affairs by adopting a separate diplomacy:

> It was not appropriate for Aramco, as a private company, to take any public stand on the international political crisis. Consequently it withheld official comment. But working as it did in the Saudi Arabian

environment, the company could and did express understanding of,
and sympathy with, the [Saudi] public reaction to Egyptian events.
When a Red Crescent drive was initiated among its Arab and Moslem
employees for the victims of warfare in Egypt, the company's facilities
were made available to the voluntary collectors, and its public relations office served as a channel of information. . . . Furthermore, F. A.
Davies, chairman of the Board of Directors, declared that the company
itself would contribute an amount equal to that collected by the employees. The co-operative spirit displayed by the company on this occasion did a good deal to relieve the tenseness evident among Arab and
Moslem employees when the news of the invasion of Egypt reached the
Eastern Province. Aramco's willingness to subject its shipping operations to inspection by Saudi officials — the latter were unusually sensitive to the attributes of national sovereignty — paid a dividend in the
maintenance of mutual confidence.[1]

Aramco also benefited from the fact that it was strictly an American
company, separate from the French and British, the parties that had
declared war on Egypt. "As a result, neither the principal producing
operations nor the pipeline transit of Aramco's oil to the Mediterranean were interrupted."[2]

Elsewhere in the Gulf, however, severe damage was done to the oil
fields. There were riots in Bahrein and in the British-protected sheikhdoms in South Arabia, and the Kuwaiti oil fields were damaged. In
August 1957, the Levant became sown with Soviet intrigues. With the
Soviet penetration of Syria, a highly secret correspondence began between Prime Minister Macmillan and the U.S. administration. Macmillan expressed the view in a letter to Dulles that "this Syrian venture is
only one step in the Russian game and that their aim is to extend
Communist control bit by bit throughout the Middle East." He continued: "When we built up NATO together, there was no great economic
injury which the Russians could inflict on us. But the Syrian pipelines
are at present most important to the economy of Britain and Europe."[3]

Therefore, Macmillan proposed a clandestine plan to drive Communist influence out of Syria. If successful, "it would be an open defeat for
Communist expansion" and would encourage all the friends of the
West in the Middle East. On the other hand, if unsuccessful, "it would
be the greatest possible disaster. The neighbouring countries who are
wavering would go over to Russians, and Iraq would collapse." Such an
operation ought to be undertaken by Syria's Arab neighbors, led if
possible by Iraq, still a reliable British friend.[4]

John Foster Dulles accepted the British proposal and asked Allen
Dulles, his brother and the director of the CIA, to reexamine the

possibilities of "internal action in Syria." As a British liaison officer in the American capital reported to Macmillan on September 7, 1957,

> the United States judges that Syria has become, or is about to become, a base for military and subversive activities in the Near East designed to destroy the independence of those countries and to subject them to Soviet Communist domination. . . . This same view is taken by the governments of all five nations bordering on Syria, as well as by the United Kingdom. . . . If any of Syria's Arab neighbors were physically attacked by the Sino-Soviet *bloc,* the United States, upon request, would be prepared to use its own armed forces to assist any such nation or nations against such armed aggression.[5]

This pledge to assist any Middle Eastern nation facing the threat of Communist aggression became known as the Eisenhower Doctrine. Having been elected to a second term and having recovered fully from a heart attack that had laid him low in 1956, Eisenhower further addressed the Russian menace in Syria by inviting Prince Abd Allilah, crown prince of Iraq, to meet his administration in Washington in January 1957. Also, at the same time, King Saud arrived in Washington because, as Eisenhower also related, "We wanted to explore the possibilities of building [him] up as a counterweight to Nasser. The King was a logical choice in this regard; he at least professed anti-Communism and he enjoyed on religious grounds a high standing among all Arab nations."[6]

Wilbur Crane Eveland, a CIA officer posted to Beirut, was also in Washington at this time and described how King Saud was introduced to a CIA operation to remove Nasser from power. His visit to the United States a success, Saud endorsed the Eisenhower Doctrine through which the Eisenhower administration hoped to bring stability to the Middle East. In return, and at long last, the United States undertook to strengthen the Saudi armed forces with equipment and munitions valued at $300 million, including a number of F86 Sabre jet fighters. The United States further agreed to set aside $50 million to train Saudis in the use of these weapons and equipment. And so Saud returned to the Middle East, where he terminated the assistance he had earlier agreed to give to Nasser.

Fully established by his political victory over the British, the French, and the Israelis, on February 1, 1958, Nasser established the United Arab Republic, a union of Egypt and Syria, by a vote of 99.9 percent. This development caused disquiet at both the Nasiriyah Palace and at Aramco's headquarters. The Soviet-backed Egyptian and Syrian regimes were now on their doorstep. Tapline was plainly menaced, as were the tanker terminals at Sidon.

Fourteen days later the Saudi regime and the Aramco management found that they had reason for concern. At a press conference in Damascus on March 5, 1958, Lieutenant Colonel Abdul Hamid Serraj, the Syrian army's chief of intelligence, claimed that King Saud had, through a father-in-law, Assas Ibrahim, offered him a bribe of £1.9 million to arrange the assassination of Nasser by placing a bomb in his aircraft when next he visited Damascus. Serraj also noted that Saud hoped that the alliance between Egypt and Syria would collapse, putting an end to Russian influence in Damascus. The bribe had been delivered in three checks, for £1 million, £600,000, and £300,000. Serraj said that he had cashed them at the Damascus branch of the Arab Bank. For good measure, Serraj gave out photostats of the checks. He was quoted as saying that the United States was aware of the plot.

In Riyadh there was only stunned silence, which in itself seemed an implicit admission of guilt. The main reaction otherwise was a statement on Mecca Radio, saying that Saud had ordered a strong guard to be placed around the Egyptian embassy in Jidda to protect it from "the anger of the people." Later a story emerged that the Saudi security authorities had discovered that the Egyptian military attaché in Jidda, Major Ali Khashabi, the man with whom the Saudi government and Aramco had recently collaborated to overthrow the British in South Arabia, had planned to assassinate King Saud. King Saud had therefore decided to retaliate by arranging the death of Nasser when next he visited Damascus.

The logic behind this plot was well expressed, in the form of a fable, by Denis Healey, the British defense minister, somewhat later:

> A frog was sunning himself on the banks of the Nile when a scorpion walked up and asked for a lift across the river.
>
> "No fear," said the frog, "if you get on my back you'll sting me and I'll die."
>
> "Nonsense," replied the scorpion, "if you die, I'll drown."
>
> The frog thought it over, and agreed. When they were exactly half way across, the frog felt an agonising pain between his shoulder-blades and realised he had been stung.
>
> "Why did you do it?" he asked, as his limbs began to stiffen. "You know you'll drown."
>
> "Yes, I know," replied the scorpion. "But after all, this is the Middle East."[7]

The CIA attempt to subvert the Syrian government now collapsed. So did a British plot to kill Nasser — the weapon to be a Remington electric razor filled with *plastique* explosive. With the collapse of the

Anglo-American secret operations in Syria and against Nasser, the disaster visualized by Macmillan now occurred.

On July 14, 1958, a regiment of the Iraq army on the move through Baghdad suddenly revolted. The young king, the regent, and Prince Abd Alillah were murdered, and so was Britain's great friend in the Middle East, Prime Minister Nuri es-Said. The Baghdad Pact (a mutual security agency to counter Soviet expansion in the Middle East, made up of Turkey, Iran, Pakistan, and Great Britain, with the tacit assistance of the United States) collapsed, and both King Hussein of Jordan and King Saud felt threatened. This was, Macmillan recorded, "devastating news, destroying at a blow a whole system of security which successive British Governments had built up, greatly to the interests of the Iraqi people and supported with generous aid in money, skill and experience."[8]

The president of Lebanon, Camille Chamoun, felt that the sovereignty of his country was under severe threat, and he invoked the Eisenhower Doctrine. Within hours, the U.S. Sixth Fleet — whose commander during the Anglo-French invasion of Egypt had driven his fleet through the convoys to disrupt them — approached Beirut. Eisenhower elected for what he called "drastic intervention," and major units of the U.S. Marines and the U.S. Army were soon landing on the Beirut beaches. Simultaneously, the British landed a light brigade of paratroopers at Amman to maintain the regime of King Hussein. And in Cairo, Nasser aimed his sights at Aramco, the jewel in the American crown in the Middle East. Nasser's radio service, the Voice of the Arabs, made clear his intentions toward King Saud and Aramco — with a poem:

> O, Slave of Aramco, stooge of imperialism,
> You built Nasiriyah on sweat (and moving sand).
> Ah, slave of Aramco, stooge of imperialism.
> You did this with the sweat of the free in your land.
> People shall have a hand in exploiting their land
> And the day is at hand when they will have revenge.
> They live in your prisons, tortured and behind bars.
> Now you no longer pray, but kneel to the dollar;
> America will not from the free protect you,
> Nor will Dhahran Airbase when they rise against you,
> When the free do revolt and the oppressed avenge;
> O, Saud (brace yourself) for they shall have revenge,
> Yes, the people and the free shall soon have their revenge.
> You have nightly soiled the land of the Prophet
> O, Symbol of debauch, baseness, and treachery;
> You are true corruption, disgrace, and lechery.
> But the chains shall fall off, oppression be no more,

And the free shall tear down your palace of horror
And put up for themselves a castle of honor.
Tomorrow's at hand when we shall have revenge
For we shall, O Saud, certainly take revenge.[9]

During the 1950s it became evident to Aramco management and to
Excom that Rentz's and Mulligan's Arabian Affairs Division, the intelligence collection, research, and analysis branch, knew all too little
about the personalities and policies of the Saud dynasty. Aramco was ill
equipped to establish what was happening in the struggle for primacy
between King Saud and his brother, Crown Prince Faisal — a conflict
that could threaten the concession agreement.

To address this problem, Norman Hardy, then Aramco's chief executive officer, formed a special committee of top management. The minutes were kept by the acting chief of Arabian Affairs, J. W. Pendleton,
who recorded Hardy's opening statement:

> It is becoming more and more apparent that very little is known about
> how the Saudi Arabian Government operates and, consequently, about
> how the Company should conduct its business with the Government
> for the greatest benefit of both. The Government has grown tremen-
> dously in size and complexity. The King has become increasingly inter-
> ested in foreign affairs; and just who or what is responsible for domes-
> tic affairs is not clear. No longer can Company officials, as in the past,
> go direct to the King with their problems, or obtain a definitive deci-
> sion on important matters from the Minister of Finance. We do not
> know what channels to follow to try and get our business done.[10]

The committee consisted of four of the best and brightest in the
Aramco management, H. B. Beckley, R. M. Henry, G. E. Mandis, and
Pendleton. The group met for about two weeks, and its task was, as
defined in a memo by Pendleton,

> to *think*, to generate ideas, not to rush at the problem, take voluminous
> notes, or write a book. It should proceed at its own pace and not as
> though it had been saddled with the task of devising a crash program.
> On the other hand, it is expected to come up with some practical ideas
> within a reasonable period of time — several months, say. The group
> should feel free to invite anyone from within or without the Company
> to meet with it but should avoid having so many people that the meet-
> ings will develop into town hall conventions. It seems likely that the
> regular members of the group will generate their ideas while they are
> doing their regular jobs and then discuss them at group meetings.
> While the group should not be regarded as secret, undue publicity
> should not be given to it and its activities.[11]

But great care was needed to ensure that the new committee did not make its predicament worse by offending the Saudi government. Article 36 of the concession agreement provided "that the Company or anyone connected with it shall have no right to interfere with the administrative, political or religious affairs within Saudi Arabia."[12]

The company's ignorance concerning affairs of the Saudi court (the criticism against Rentz was that he was too much concerned with his own pet scholarly projects and too little interested in intelligence) became apparent when, in 1954, Aramco's chief executive, Fred A. Davies, hurtled into the office of Bill Owen, Aramco's counsel, and slammed a letter down on Owen's desk: "The letter was in Arabic with its English translation on top. 'What do you think of this, Bill?' It was a one-sentence letter from SAG saying that 'as of this day Aristotle Socrates Onassis has the exclusive rights to ship all Aramco oil that is extracted by Aramco or any other company from Saudi Arabia to any place in the world.'"[13]

The rich tanker operator and Owen's "beady-eyed Greek," Aristotle Socrates Onassis, had recently visited Jidda, and there had been much speculation among the Jiddawi merchants about what he might be up to. He was in fact launching the first major challenge to Aramco's concession agreement, with the knowledge and encouragement of King Saud, his finance minister, Abdullah Suleiman, and his deputy, Sheikh Yusuf Yassin. Owen saw immediately that the letter challenged article 22 of the concession agreement of May 29, 1933. The government had thereby granted to the company

> the exclusive right for a period of sixty years with respect to a described area to explore, prospect, drill for, extract, treat, manufacture, transport, deal with, carry away and export petroleum and other hydrocarbons, and to use all means and facilities Aramco should deem necessary or advisable in order to carry out the purposes of the enterprise.[14]

The letter further "requested and required" Aramco to deal with Onassis. Owen saw immediately that it would cost millions of dollars in legal fees to defeat that challenge. When Davies asked Owen whether the Saudi government could legally make such a change, Owen replied that the concession agreement specifically granted Aramco the right to ship oil — and that this right was implied in all the stipulations of the concession. So Davies decided to take a direct but diplomatic approach with the Saudis:

> Fred said, "Well, we've got to answer this right away and say that we're not complying with it. You can write the letter." So I wrote a letter, a polite letter, telling them we just received this, there must be some

misunderstanding because they did not have this right to give to Mr. Onassis. And therefore it was in violation of our Concession, and therefore we would continue to operate as we had in the past.[15]

The company's complaint — which led to one of the most expensive legal suits ever — contested the government's granting of permission to Onassis to establish a private company at Jidda, to be called the Saudi Arabian Tankers Company, Limited (Satco). Onassis had promised much in return for the right to ship Saudi oil, including educational and employment opportunities for Saudi workers and financial emoluments to the Saudi government. But perhaps most important, Onassis had offered to "provide a minimum of 500,000 deadweight tons of tankships under the Saudi Arab flag and to maintain this minimum during the thirty-year term of the Onassis agreement."[16]

As Aramco judged, King Saud had had a fit of *folie de grandeur.* He wanted a Saudi mercantile marine to fly the Saudi flag over the seven seas. Onassis had offered this, and Saud had accepted without giving much thought to the implications of the deal. Davies suspected that the Onassis deal was at least in part an expression of the displeasure of Sheikh Abdullah Tariki, the government's director of petroleum and mineral resources and the man whom Aramco had treated so badly when he arrived at Dhahran in 1954.

Davies, who had recently replaced Moore as chief executive officer at Dhahran, objected on a number of grounds. The first was that Aramco had been unaware of the transactions between Onassis and Saud until the moment the letter reached him. That suggested that the government had behaved surreptitiously and therefore not in the spirit of the 1933 agreement, in which both parties had undertaken to keep each other informed of all developments relating to Saudi oil. Davies made the following specific complaints:

> Such implementation would (a) be contrary to and violate both the letter and spirit of the existing agreements between the Saudi Arab Government and The Company; (b) be contrary to long-established business and arrangements and procedures developed in reliance on these agreements; (c) be contrary to world-wide custom and practice in the international oil business; (d) have a disastrous effect upon the presently established sales outlets for Saudi oil and the possible future development thereof; and (e) be wholly impractical.[17]

Consequently, Davies advised the government, "a dispute has arisen between the Government and Aramco . . . as to the true interpretation of the Aramco Concession Agreement."[18]

The character and personality of Aristotle Socrates Onassis gave the case a certain glitter. Born in 1906 in the Greek quarter of Smyrna on the west coast of Turkey, Onassis had begun to make his fortune dealing in tobacco and, later, in whaling. He arrived in Jidda as a sharp-witted shipowner with an extraordinary reputation. He had taken Maria Callas, the leading opera diva of her time, as his mistress. He became the most famous Greek of his time, she the most famous Greek woman of her time; he the richest Greek entrepreneur, she the queen of La Scala. They lived in great style on the shores of Lake Garda. They sailed the world in Onassis's yacht, a former destroyer that Onassis had bought for $50,000 and converted into an oceangoing showcase of luxury, at a cost of $4 million. He was an agreeable shark, a man grown rich by operating his fleet of small and grimy tankers wherever they could turn him a drachma, a pound, a mark, or a dollar.

Later, it became clear that Onassis's intermediary had been one of the wealthiest families in Arabia, the Alirezas, at a meeting in the Cannes Yacht Club. The Alireza brothers stood to gain a down payment of $1 million and then seven cents for each ton shipped, with a guaranteed payment of not less than $168,000 a year. The Alirezas had arranged for Onassis to meet with Sheikh Suleiman at the finance minister's villa. There he signed a secret document and then went on to an audience with King Saud, who presented him with the traditional gifts, two gold-sheathed daggers and two Arab ponies, a stallion and a mare. Onassis then departed to advise Aramco's liaison officer with King Saud of the contents of the secret document that he had just signed. As soon as its terms became known, Onassis began to encounter the full but silent wrath of not only Aramco, but also the U.S. government. And as Onassis would lament later, "Never before in the history of business was so much power combined to fight and destroy an individual."[19]

The letter dispatched, Owen began to assemble a phalanx of top lawyers to meet this challenge. Aramco's chief lawyer, George W. Ray, Jr., was on a world cruise with his wife, having left a message that he was not to be disturbed except in emergency. Davies decided that this was indeed an emergency. Within fourteen days Ray was in Jidda, and, Owen recorded, "In the meantime, we hadn't heard from the Saudi Government, or we'd have had to act, after our stern letter that we were not paying any attention to [the Saudi government's] order."[20]

Ray anticipated that this crisis would require both strong counsel and a lot of time. In fact, Aramco was three years at it, and the lawyers' bills "ionosphericated," a term coined by Davies. The legal team's knowledge and experience were prodigious. Lowell Wadmond, one of the foremost trial lawyers in the United States, became chief counsel.

Oliver Marsden would be a future president of the American Bar Association; Hal Fales, a future head of White & Case; Steven Schwabel, a future legal adviser to the State Department and a future judge at the International Court of Justice at The Hague; Lord McNair was a leading expert in Big Oil disputes with the Gulf rulers. Most of these eminences set up shop, with Owen and Ray of Aramco, in Geneva, beside the lake and the mountains. "We had all kinds of power," Owen recalled. They employed a Belgian legal expert and some of the leading Arabists of the time, for the case would be heard in Arabic, French, and English. Other specialist lawyers drifted in and out as the need arose. "It was a big production." said Owen. "I can't begin to tell you how many millions of dollars it cost."[21] The object of the first phase was to ensure that the case was heard by an arbitration tribunal, as the concession agreement conceded, and not in a civil court.

The new American ambassador, George Wadsworth, presented Saud with a written communication showing the immensity of the threat to American interests in Saudi Arabia. Would the king ratify the agreement with Onassis, as was required before it became law? Requiring revenue desperately as usual, Saud ratified the deal on May 14, 1954. Then Aramco put the case directly to Onassis:

> The next day Onassis met with the Aramco brass and was told what they must already have guessed. The American oil companies refused to recognize the validity of his contract on the grounds that it violated their own contract. They were not prepared to negotiate, even though they realized that such a move might jeopardize their position in Saudi Arabia. Onassis was told that when his ships arrived at the Aramco terminal at Ras Tanura to take on their first loads of Saudi oil they would be turned away.[22]

Onassis reacted to the Aramco threat cleverly; he named his newest tanker after King Saud. A delegation arrived at the yards in Hamburg with holy water from the sacred well at Mecca, which the Prophet had used. The ship was blessed, and the *Al Malik Saud al-Awal* slid into the Baltic to begin its career.

At the State Department, meantime, the staff concluded that, if for some reason the case did not go to arbitration, then the U.S. government should undertake a campaign to force Onassis to relinquish his contract. If the case went to arbitration, additional legal work would be needed to ensure that the proceedings accorded with Saudi and Muslim law — a complex and expensive matter indeed. Numerous legal opinions would have to be obtained from leading experts. After many months of soliciting these opinions, Aramco was delighted to find that all the authorities were unanimous — Aramco alone had the right to transport the oil, and Onassis did not. To summarize their findings,

> under Hanbali law . . . the exclusive and absolute right of ownership is Aramco's to dispose of the oil as it wishes, there being no limitation found in the Agreement. They say, too, that even though Aramco had not been given such an exclusive right, by the clear intendment of the Concession Agreement, it would nevertheless possess it; and that the Government is under an obligation to observe the rights of Aramco and to place no restriction or limitation upon them.[23]

This conclusion was important politically: it legitimized Aramco's operations in Saudi Arabia and condemned King Saud's and Onassis's attempts to steal Aramco's rights. Such findings doubtless gratified the Excom and Aramco lawyers, for they expected that at least some of their advisers would take the view that the law of sovereignty appeared to favor the government — that a sovereign state had the right, if the authority of the state required, to change the interpretation of a contract. A case in point would be Egypt's nationalization of the Suez Canal in 1956 and the seizure of the Anglo-Iranian Oil Company in 1951–53, when the Iranian government invoked force majeure as its argument. Aramco was decidedly lucky that its case was heard previous to these precedent-setting actions.

Although the CIA in Jidda arrived at the opinion that the deal was a case of "a smart Greek" selling the Saudi government a bill of goods and prestige-hungry Arabs jumping at the deal, the State Department took a grave view of Onassis's intervention. Secretary of State John Foster Dulles thought he detected hints of a scheme culminating in eventual nationalization of Aramco. Dulles agreed that the U.S. government must back Aramco for, as Dulles's brother, Allen, director of the CIA, is said to have declared in reference to Aramco, "what is good for American trade is good for the American government."[24]

Therefore, Dulles instructed the U.S. ambassador to Arabia, Wadsworth, to remind Saud of the "catastrophe" that had befallen Iran when, through the Anglo-American boycott of Iranian oil in 1951–53, that country had "barely survived" the three years in which it was deprived of oil royalty. Saudi Arabia depended entirely on oil for its foreign exchange and, Dulles wrote, "the King and his advisors should ask themselves where they would stand after three years or even one year without the oil revenues."[25] Wadsworth needed to be careful, however, not to overtly threaten or humiliate the king. He should offer King Saud a satisfactory, face-saving pretext for breaking the Onassis agreement.

Meanwhile, the company and the State Department decided upon a two-track approach to undermine Onassis. Aramco would assemble the legal opinions necessary to its case and refer its complaint to arbitration; the U.S. government would look for ways to force Onassis to abandon the agreement.

Aramco used its beneficence toward the Saudis as further ballast in its case. Had not Aramco developed the entire lucrative oil operation that had so increased Saudi wealth? The company was now mining oil at the rate of more than 900,000 barrels of crude oil per day. It currently employed

> some 4,000 Americans, some 21,000 Saudi Arabs, and some 5,000 other nationalities. [Aramco's investment in Saudi Arabia] is reflected in 250 wells drilled, some 700 miles of pipe line, loading facilities at Ras Tanura capable of handling six to seven tankships per day, housing, a training program available to all Saudi employees, medical facilities which provided, in 1954, for some 5,500 hospital cases and some 450,000 outpatient calls, a capital investment of approximately $524,250,000, a current operating budget of $133,765,000 per year, and a current inventory of some $62,000,000. It is reflected also in a capital investment of some $158,900,000 by Trans-Arabian Pipeline Company in the pipeline from Qaisumah to Sidon, Lebanon.[26]

Therefore the company had come to friendly arbitration to protect the "basic concept of the Concession Agreement which has been the prime force in all the efforts to date, that is, freedom to export and prosper; to protect its right and privilege to realize for itself and for Saudi Arabia maximum returns for the great natural resources which have been entrusted to Aramco for development."[27]

But Aramco's case was no mere matter of figures. Floyd Ohliger, now a member of the board of directors and a vice president of Aramco, added emotional thrust as he described how he had been hurt by Saud's betrayal:

> I have enjoyed the confidence of ranking Ministers of His Majesty's Government, and of Representatives of the United States Government, including those of Cabinet level and Special Envoys of American Presidents. The personal friendship of the late great King and me was especially close for an occidental. His son, now His Majesty Saud ibn Abdul Aziz, has been an intimate friend as a young man, Crown Prince and King.
>
> My vocation and avocation have been the industrial and social advancement of Saudi Arabia through the oil development. Toward this end I have devoted much time in study and discussion with members of the Saudi Arab Government and in acquainting nonSaudis, such as

industrialists, officials and representatives of the United States Government, with the needs, potentialities and aspirations of the Saudi Arab Government, in the interest of gaining political and financial support for the Saudi Arab Government.[28]

Ohliger was a man with a cause.

While Aramco lawyers collected their depositions, the government machine had been working against Onassis. The services of Robert Maheu, an ex–FBI officer skilled in industrial matters, had been retained "to scuttle the contract." An able man, he became famous, or infamous, at a later date as the chief of Howard Hughes's gambling casinos. As a first measure he made contact with some of his CIA associates. They "bugged Onassis's offices for a week with disappointing results."[29] Later, a more shadowy operation was staged in Beirut. Colonel Eddy, of Aramco's government relations in Beirut, met with a young CIA official at the Grotto aux Pigeons restaurant in Beirut and during the meal, he remembered, Eddy passed him a check for $2 million dollars, with instructions to deliver it to Maheu. The officer never knew why he was assigned this task, but he followed through.

Maheu met with Karl Twitchell, who had retired recently from mining the gold tailings at King Solomon's gold mines near Jidda, having made a profit of $2 million over the years. Maheu persuaded Twitchell to return to Saudi Arabia "to undertake a private mission to the Saudi court to convince the king that it would not be in his interest to implement the agreement with Onassis."[30] Twitchell may have had some success, for Saud seemed to have a change of heart about the deal at that time. Twitchell's intercession did not stop the process by which Aramco took the dispute to arbitration.

Maheu then developed a contact with Stavros Niarchos, another shipowner and a brother-in-law of Onassis. Niarchos was favorably known to Allen Dulles, who had vacationed aboard Niarchos's yacht. Niarchos opposed the Onassis deal with King Saud. He believed that it would have a "dire effect" on the balance of power in the Middle East because Onassis would next "take his profits, estimated to be $17 million in the first full year, and increase his tonnage, thus enabling him to repeat the scheme in other oil producing countries." Then there would be "no way to stop him from extending himself indefinitely." Niarchos stated that Onassis's principle weakness "was his current cash position, which Niarchos estimated to be a mere $5 million." If the deal was blocked, Niarchos concluded, "Onassis would be in considerable trouble, with excessive tonnage, high debt repayments and the implacable hostility of his clients, the oil companies."[31]

Niarchos led Maheu to a certain Spyridon Catapodis, a former close friend and business associate of Onassis. Their friendship had soured, and it was not difficult to induce Catapodis to make sworn testimony to the British consul at Nice on September 24, 1954, which was, if true, "highly damaging to Onassis's cause." It portrayed "Onassis as a compulsive schemer," it contained "revelations" that were likely to cause dissension within the king's privy council, and asserted "that Onassis had set up a deal and obtained exemption from Saudi Arabian income tax by a system of payoffs." It "purported to show that $1.25 million had been paid in bribes to various Saudi ministers and palace officials." It mentioned why Onassis had wished to keep the agreement secret *after* Saud had signed the document: "he said he expected to enter into an agreement with Aramco, whereby he would get either a large amount of money or some other valuable concessions in return for canceling his agreement with the Saudi Arabian government."[32]

As if this was not enough, Catapodis also declared that

> Onassis repeatedly boasted to me that . . . he was going to break up the influence which Aramco has been exercising in Saudi Arabia for many years. I . . . advised him not to antagonise Aramco. Onassis told me that he knew exactly what he was doing, and he felt confident that, in the end, he would play an important part in the development of the natural resources in Saudi Arabia, which ultimately would make him the richest and most powerful man in the world.[33]

When the deposition came to Maheu, he realized that "he was about to earn his money." His job was "to acquaint King Saud with the allegations it contained." And to that end he traveled to Jidda to seek an audience with the king through Twitchell. Twitchell took the documents to Saud, and within a day, one of the king's advisers met with Maheu in the lobby of his hotel. The king, Maheu's visitor announced, was personally grateful for the information and had decided to "have done with Onassis." However, he had signed the contract and so there were "delicate questions of personal pride." That would be satisfied if Maheu leaked his document to the press. Maheu agreed to this, and it soon appeared in various newspapers in Europe.[34]

The king now had grounds to cancel the contract. This was exactly what Aramco wanted to hear. Over tea in Jidda, Fred A. Davies met with Onassis. The talk was full of complex issues relating to the rates that Onassis would charge to remain competitive with other tankship owners; everything Onassis said showed that he intended to impose a monopoly. This was duly reported to Saud, who agreed that the dispute must therefore go to arbitration. Wadsworth reported this to the State Department:

Aramco has yielded nothing in substance or in principle and has gained valuable Royal assurance that, whatever be the result of arbitration, Saudi-Aramco relations will continue on a basis of full cooperation; and Onassis, when finally pinned down on the rates issue, has weaseled and outsmarted himself.[35]

The case now went to Geneva. When the tribunal rendered its finding, as it did in 1958, the jurists found in favor of the company. The Muslim member even felt it necessary to censure the Saudi Arabian government for its conduct, which did not accord with Muslim law. Thus Aramco slipped from the trap that Onassis had attempted to set. The World Court found in Aramco's favor in 1958.

As the relationship between King Saud and Crown Prince Faisal went from bad to worse during the Onassis affair, William Mulligan of The Arabian Affairs Division of Aramco found an interesting source of information close to Saud. An Aramco employee named Jose Arnold, a Swiss-American dining hall superintendent, was on hand when Saud and a party of twenty-four guests in three beautifully appointed air-conditioned buses arrived unexpectedly at an Aramco camp in the deep desert one day in 1954. They asked for luncheon. Arnold made a quick dish of chicken cacciatore that Saud found so delicious that, through Aramco, he asked if Arnold could be appointed to him as chief steward at all of Saud's ten palaces. At first Arnold declined; he was not, he said, a chef. He accepted only when Saud asked Aramco if Arnold could be sent to him to supervise the culinary arrangements and to train Saudis to take over from him. Saud also wished to appoint a Swiss-American to his kitchens because of a recent scare — the cooks at Nasiriyah Palace had attempted to poison him.

For the next five years Arnold, a middle-aged man given to temperamental outbursts but capable at his work, was at the king's side. Saud called Arnold "Yusuf," and Arnold came to like the king. He was, Arnold wrote in a memoir, "a kind, gentle, simple man of the desert." But Saud made the mistake of trusting his advisers completely. He was "totally unaware of the deceit with which they pursue their selfish aims." He was "at the mercy of" some of his aides who were involved in a "sinister conspiracy" to keep him as "a kind of prisoner in his own domain. As I watched the process feed upon itself, I developed a deep sympathy for this ruler rendered helpless by the perfidy of those he trusted." The object of the manipulation was, Arnold wrote, gold. The aides had "million dollar jobs," provided they survived the intrigues that went on every day of the five years that Arnold was in Saud's service.[36]

Arnold accompanied the king on all his travels in the kingdom. Saud usually spent the hot season at his summer palace in Taif, a small village in the mountains about fifty miles northeast of Mecca. There, constituting another astounding charge against the king's privy purse, a new palace, the al-Hawiya, had been made ready for occupancy by 1958. Like all the king's palaces, al-Hawiya had an "upstairs" regime for the king, the princes, and his harem, and a "downstairs" where the servants lived and worked. In Arnold's words,

> the living quarters for the kitchen staff at Taif had all the comforts of a foxhole with cement walls. They consisted of a barracks-like row of small units. The only windows were unscreened openings near the top of the wall, and through these portals passed some of Saudi Arabia's most challenging vermin. Bugs, beetles, bats, flies, mosquitoes, and lizards made each night an exciting experience in living terror. Scorpions snuggled into cracks in the walls and floors by day and into shoes by night.[37]

Arnold was a shrewd observer of life in Saud's personal life, his private entourage, and the court. Though not politically minded, he knew a good story when he heard one. At Taif Arnold had access to that most secret corner of the kingdom, one that few if any Occidentals had penetrated other than Philby — the king's harem. Aramco was interested in that realm — petticoat politics was often important:

> In separate but equal spreads, the ladies of the harem and King Saud with his entourage enjoyed frequent excursions. We served picnics in the palace gardens. We also served them in the orchard groves, in the vineyards, and in the mountains. A truckload of Persian rugs, dispatched in advance, was spread in casual opulence on the ground. Sofas and chairs were also provided. Each party was driven to its open-air caravansary, there to lounge in shaded luxury under a pale-blue cloudless sky, and await the trucks carrying food.[38]

Arnold met Saud's favorite wife, Umm Mansur, "who had become wealthy through her service to King Saud." Mother of five of the king's sons, she was "a surprisingly unattractive woman physically, fat and with ugly features that she coquettishly revealed occasionally by letting her veil slip." She was also "an extraordinarily kind and pleasant person, and she had earned the confidence of the other ladies of the harem."[39]

It was said that King Saud

> had given her a million dollars on the birth of her last son, and her jewels revealed her wealth. She habitually wore three rings, each set with large diamonds, a tiny diamond-studded watch, and a pair of spectacular diamond earrings. . . . Moreover, Umm Mansur, like the other members of the harem, wore elegant original gowns from the

leading fashion designers in Paris, hidden under the black purdah robe that completely covers all Saudi Arabian women.[40]

The second most influential woman in the harem was a concubine, an attractive woman from Lebanon given to the king by one of his visiting doctors. Among the forty to fifty women typically in the harem, there seemed to be little trouble with jealousy. But they did face one major problem —

> monotony. Religious restrictions kept them from having any part in public or social life, and they were confined to the harem . . . except for a rare trip to the Riyadh zoo or a rare ride outside . . . in limousines equipped with one-way glass that prevented them from being seen. Most were illiterate, of course. . . . They vented their frustration on their servants by demanding constant attention.[41]

In 1957, Saud moved to what became his principal residence, the Nasiriyah Palace in Riyadh. Arnold described it as "the ultimate in majestic grandeur." Financed entirely from the king's cut of Aramco's oil royalties, it had cost $25 million to build and furnish:

> Its surrounding wall of orange-pink cement, seven miles in circumference, twenty feet high and three feet thick, enclosed a large and independently functioning community. [There was a] reception palace made of the same orange-pink cement as the wall, a magnificent white marble residence palace, an opulent harem palace surrounded by exotic gardens, a two-hundred-bed hospital, the King Saud University for the sons of the royal families and their slaves, large and comfortable homes for the families of the members of the court and the harem, a military barracks, the royal garages, and acres of landscaped gardens. The storerooms in the basement of the reception palace would hold sufficient food to sustain the community for two years.[42]

Yet despite the opulence, the palace had been poorly planned and constructed. The inattention to important details made Arnold wonder where the $25 million had gone. The contractors had given little thought to basics such as electrical equipment, a sewer system, and the kitchen. The kitchen equipment was partly from England and partly from the United States, which had different electrical voltages; this led to endless complications. The pilferage and fraud were enormous. When Arnold took an inventory, he found that of a $500,000 order for porcelain, kitchenware, glassware, cutlery, and so forth, only $200,000 in merchandise had been delivered. Someone had double-ordered barrels of Limoges china; therefore one consignment went to the king, the other to his finance minister, Suleiman, although the payment for both came from the king's privy purse. Such scenarios seemed to be repeated in each room of each of Saud's palaces.

The palace's opening proved to be

a spectacle that would have stirred the imagination of the late Cecil B. deMille. The entire facade of the reception palace, the center of the festivities, was aglow with light from tremendous flower-shaped lamps thirty feet high ranged along the front terrace of the vast structure. The main entrance — the beautiful triple arch of traditional Middle Eastern architecture, with its openings framed in delicate latticework wrought in cement — was even more brilliantly lit by floodlights. . . . Cadillac, Chrysler, Lincoln, and Mercedes limousines roared up to the palace entrance in fender-crunching disorganization. . . . Wealthy Riyadh merchants, members of the royal family, and King Saud's advisory staff emerged from the cars and moved quickly and gracefully up the steps.[43]

After coffee in the *majlis,* the white-marble meeting hall, the guests followed King Saud into the banquet hall, which was lit by huge chandeliers. There they joined him in an orange-juice toast to the completion of the palace. The banquet lasted not more than fifteen minutes when the king, having had a sufficiency, rose and so terminated the meal.

Three nights later King Saud took his party into the desert in a long mechanized caravan — more than fifty vehicles with soft wide-track tires. The bodyguard rode out in front, followed "by storage vans, trucks, portable kitchens, tank cars full of water, a large air-conditioned dining room, air-conditioned cars for sleeping, and an air-conditioned eighteen-wheel trailer that served as King Saud's mobile palace." This had been built for him in Tulsa, Oklahoma, and "it came equipped with an outsize bed, to accommodate the tall monarch, a royal bathroom with an extra large tub with gold fixtures, and an elegantly appointed sitting room decorated in green silk damask threaded with an intricate pattern in gold."[44]

The king's entertainment was always on a huge scale. His budget for operating the kitchens in his ten palaces was $5 million a year. Each month Arnold reported to Aramco on the amounts of food used: typically this included 6,200 pounds of beef, 1,850 pounds of lamb, 1,250 pounds of veal, 3,150 pounds of chicken, 2,700 pounds of turkey, 650 pounds of squab, 430 pounds of duck, 380 pounds of brains, sweetbreads, and liver, 900 pounds of sole, 600 pounds of shrimp, and 170 pounds of scallops. These groceries Arnold's cooks transmuted into daily meals for an average of 850 persons. Their cost per day was about $3,200. The wages of Arnold, the Italian cooks, the Arab cooks, the kitchen boys, the drivers, the laundry workers, the assistant steward, the waiters, the clerks, the guards, and the storeroom workers totaled about $4,200 each day.

Arnold sent daily reports to Aramco when the need arose, monthly reports on his culinary operations with special reference to King Saud and his dietary problems, and annual reports when requested. The reports, copies of which went to the chief Aramco political agent in Riyadh, R. I. Metz, gave details of whom the king had entertained and what purchases the king and his household were making — significant and helpful information as Aramco tried to keep its finger on the pulse of the Saudi royal family.

Overall, Arnold's reports documented the essence of Saud's lifestyle: self-indulgence on the grand scale. This propensity to spend extended to the royal princes. In 1959, Saud's twelve-year-old son, Prince Mubarak, received a $1 million palace as a wedding gift. The walls of the audience chamber, the *majlis*, were covered with tapestries — Gobelins, according to Arnold. From the ceilings in the hallways, the banqueting chamber, and the glass-enclosed terrace hung chandeliers. At the far end of the large reception room, two full-size playground swings hung from the high ceiling to provide diversion for the youthful occupants of the palace. Wrought-iron flower baskets lined both sides of the reception room, each filled with fresh flowers flown in each day from Beirut.

Arnold related with relish how, on the eve of the prince's wedding, his palace caught fire. Faulty wiring in the neon lights over the bed canopy in the master bedroom shorted out and set the palace ablaze. Firefighters, electricians, and laborers worked all night to extinguish the fire, repair the wiring, and clear away the mess. New rugs and furniture were taken from the harem palace to replace what had been ruined by fire and water. But everything was ready in the morning, including a $10,000 display of fireworks, which were officially banned in the country.

Arnold also shared insights into a dimension of royal life typically denied to Aramco — how the king and the crown prince were preparing their sons for public life. Such information was extraordinarily sensitive; when, in 1953, an opportunity arose to obtain information about the Princes' School, where Saud's, Faisal's, and the other princes' sons were educated, Aramco decided the document had to be destroyed as information too dangerous to preserve in the files. But a copy found its way to the U.S. consulate at Dhahran. Its contents were not encouraging. During a visit, an Aramco official, presumably a member of the staff of Arabian Affairs, had talked at length with the royal family's twelve teachers, mainly Egyptians and a few Saudis. The school's buildings, located on the grounds of Saud's palace in Riyadh, were grouped around a lawn and were air-conditioned. Sixty-five to seventy princes attended. Classes began at 8:00 A.M., when the princes arrived in their chauffeur-driven automobiles. Each prince was attended by fifteen to twenty personal servants, bodyguards, and attendants, and some six or seven accompanied each student to the classroom and remained with the prince as long as he remained there, which was not always very long.

The curriculum included geography, English, history, physical education, general science, mathematics, Arabic, and religion. The princes' attendance was "fairly regular" but "classes have to be cut short because of the gradual loss of interest of the students as time wears on and the difficulties of imposing school discipline on the young princes." A prince's attendant was

> supposed to go fetch a glass of water, sharpen pencils for the prince, and do similar chores. . . . If the royal pupil felt he had had enough for the day, he just ordered the *khawi* [bodyguard] to gather his things and left the school. It was the *khawi*'s duty to see to it that the pupil was not imposed upon by the teacher and made to stay until the end of class.[45]

Although the teachers had been able to effect some changes in this routine, their litany of complaints continued:

> All of the work must be done in school, since the teachers have not yet succeeded in getting homework done or even assigned. This is said to be one of the greatest difficulties met by the teachers in their job. Furthermore the Crown Prince often takes extended trips with all his younger sons, and without the teachers, so that classes are interrupted for considerable periods of time. It also happens that the princes want to go hunting and prevail upon their father to organize a hunting trip of two or three weeks, which also means discontinuing classes.[46]

No teacher was permitted to punish the royal pupils except the director or headmaster himself, and this only in the presence of the crown prince. By and large,

> the outstanding problem for the teachers appears to be the competition afforded by the *khawis*. A fight seems to be going on between the two groups, the goal of which is the princes' favor. . . . It is said that the *khawis* are undoing in the afternoon and evening what the teachers are trying to build up during school hours. The *khawis* are said to supply alcohol to the youngsters, and in some cases homosexual relations between the princes and their escorts are strongly suspected.[47]

As to recreation, though movies were forbidden to the rest of the Saudi population, the royal princes had access to them. Egyptian cabaret films were an especial favorite.

Reports on any aspect of the royal family's life were valuable to Aramco. And as luck would have it, one of Mulligan's brightest sparks in Arabian Affairs, Miss Phebe Ann Marr, found a way into the harem at Nasiriyah Palace, thereby affording Aramco another view of harem life in the capital. The sister-in-law of Adlai Stevenson, the Democratic presidential candidate in the campaign against Eisenhower in 1956, she had come to visit Saudi Arabia, and protocol accepted that she might, if she wished, be entertained by Saud's women. A former president of Oberlin College, Mrs. Stevenson was also accompanied by Helen Metz, the wife of Aramco's political agent at Riyadh, and Marr. Marr reported that

> the meeting took place in His Majesty's private quarters adjoining the dining hall. The King was surrounded by about twenty of his favorite wives, sisters, and daughters, to whom we were introduced after several minutes of pleasant conversation between His Majesty and Mrs. Stevenson.
>
> I had the impression that the King met with the women of his family in this manner almost every evening and that all were expected to be on hand to attend him if requested. Among those present with the King was Princess Maudhi, who had reported to him on her recent trip to the Eastern Province. A great deal of importance is attached to this gathering, and presence at it is a mark of prestige.
>
> Later in the evening, we had dinner with one of His Majesty's wives, Umm Talal, a woman in her early forties. . . . She was cordial and said she was accustomed to receiving foreign visitors. . . .
>
> We were taken on an extensive tour of the inner palace grounds by an Egyptian girl, Suzie Ansari, who has been tutoring the daughters of Umm Talal for the past two years. The harim quarters resemble a city within a city and are separated by an iron fence from that part of the Nasiriyah complex devoted to the conduct of the King's official business. . . .
>
> The size of a woman's house depends upon her status, and all women of the same status have houses of equal size. The chief position in the harim is occupied by the King's mother, who has a separate residence next to a building used for entertainment on such special occasions as weddings. Also adjacent to this palace are three adjoining apartments occupied, we gathered, by the three favorite wives of the monarch. . . . The King's own private quarters are in a building near to, but not adjoining these three apartments. . . .
>
> No men were in evidence inside the women's quarters; all of the servants we saw were women. Since men have . . . been . . . manifestly in control of the women of the royal household during their visits to the

Eastern Province, it may be assumed that men perform certain of the administrative duties connected with the harim. The women's quarters were surrounded by gardens, fountains, and a lagoon complete with small boats. . . .

The princesses said they seldom left the inner palace grounds while they were in Riyadh. . . . They wore dresses with fitted bodices, long sleeves, and floor length bouffant skirts of the richest materials. On their heads they wore the *milfa* (a long, black scarf) which they wrapped around their hair and which covered their shoulders. Umm Talal, in addition, wore the traditional *thaub* (a voluminous, diaphanous overdress).

Their dresses are designed in Paris, they informed us, by Christian Dior and others, and the material is selected by agents in Paris and Rome. The material and design is then brought to the harim by an agent, but the garments are actually sewn in Beirut. The princesses wore little or no jewellery.[48]

Although good manners required that the visitors ask only the minimum questions about the harem and its place in the social and political life of the dynasty and the kingdom, Marr's brief portrait does suggest that, in addition to procreation and dalliance, the harem had an important political function. King Saud spent much time each afternoon and evening in the company of his wives, or at least his favorites, and these women were well informed about court life and its politics. Marr concluded her report with an understatement: "Mrs. Stevenson seemed very pleased with her visit to Saudi Arabia," but "she was somehow left with the impression that this is still a man's country."[49]

But it seems evident that more happened in the harem than Marr reported. The stakes in the rivalry between Saud and Faisal were large; whoever succeeded would rule the kingdom, and that meant, for the harem, an assurance of the wealth and power that usually accrues to the womenfolk whose mate succeeds. Loss in such stakes meant, on the other hand, a reduction in social standing and material comforts. Also, loss in the power stakes sometimes meant a reduction in the number of wives and concubines that the loser could afford to keep. What happened to such abandoned women? Certainly the threat of such a fate ensured that the harem women took a strong interest in following, and perhaps influencing, the political developments in Saudi Arabia.

[11]

ABDICATION

ENTZ AND MULLIGAN OF the Arabian Affairs Division felt the loss of Philby as an adviser ever more keenly as King Saud's turbulent government grew harder to understand in the years 1953–56, the period in which Nasser became president of Egypt, nationalized the Suez Canal, and made an arms deal with the Soviet Union that seemed to push the Middle East inexorably toward regional war. Philby now lived the life of a retired English gentleman in the mountains behind Beirut at the village of Ajaltun. There he had rented a small but pretty white-painted villa with a red tiled roof and surrounded by apple and peach orchards. The air was crisp and clear, and the villa afforded a grand view of the narrow coastal strip and the sparkling blue sea far below. It seemed that he might have reached a peaceful haven. He was joined by his Arab wife, Rozy, the little Baluch girl given to him by Ibn Saud, and his Arab sons, Khalid and Faris. Dressed in a white linen dinner jacket and black tie, on occasions he went to the Beirut Casino to emcee social occasions and the annual beauty queen contest. He wrote a series of articles for the London *Sunday Times* on Saudi government corruption, and he was the toast of the city's unending cocktail parties.

As Aramco went about its business of discovering all it could about Saudi government affairs, Philby saw much of the richest man in Beirut, Husain al-Uwaini, a politician and merchant much involved in Saudi commercial affairs and Aramco's expansion along the Gulf coast of Hasa. Through al-Uwaini, Philby was invited to return to Riyadh early in 1956. The invitation was not from King Saud, but from the crown prince, Faisal, who was the Saudi foreign minister at that time. Faisal was very well disposed toward Philby, for they had known each other ever since Philby had squired Faisal around England and Ireland in 1920, while Faisal was on a state visit as the guest of King George V. Faisal had given Philby's son Kim a thirty-carat diamond as a keepsake of the visit.

In March 1956, al-Uwaini visited King Saud in Riyadh. There Saud produced a draft letter for Philby's signature. It expressed contrition and asked leave to return to Riyadh. When al-Uwaini gave the letter to Philby, he refused to sign it until the Saudi government paid its debts to him, which included a claim for $1 million (£400,000) on a major contract to build a palace for the amir Abdullah, one of the late Ibn Saud's brothers. This debt had not been settled.

In May 1956 he received word that his conditions would be met. Accordingly, Philby arranged to return to Riyadh. But in the interim his articles had appeared in the *Times,* and in one of them he had taken the British position in regard to the Buraimi dispute. He had asserted that Sheikh Yusuf Yassin had indeed attempted to bribe local witnesses and some neutral arbitrators and that Yassin had "bungled" the Saudi case. His statements brought him "a spate of criticism, even vilification," and Arab newspapers pronounced that "he had accumulated a fabulous fortune, that he had abandoned Islam, that he had been paid a huge salary as adviser to Ibn Saud, or that he was a friend of the Jews."[1] These accusations led to a warning that he would be murdered if he went back.

In the end, trusting in al-Uwaini's word that his conditions would be met and that he would be received as a friend, Philby returned to Riyadh, so he was assured, for an audience with Saud. But when he arrived he found the king had gone fishing in the Gulf. He cooled his heels for a week or so and was about to return to Beirut when he was summoned by Faisal. He arranged for Philby to see the king at Dhahran. He attended upon Saud and Faisal at a banquet given by Aramco and returned to Riyadh afterward in the royal train — Aramco's railway line across the desert between Riyadh and Dhahran had by now been completed — and then resumed his place at court in the belief that his demands concerning debts were being met. But they were not met. The king did present him with about $4,000, and when Philby protested, unsuccessfully, about the rest of the debt, he immediately returned to Beirut. There he resumed taking his independent line on Arab and Western politics: "The East does not trust the West, and there is no means of inducing it to do so until every vestige of the old Western imperialism is removed from its lands."[2]

He was still there when his son Kim arrived in Beirut to take up his position as Middle Eastern correspondent for *The Observer* and *The*

Economist, and as spy for the British Secret Service. Kim had been cleared in Parliament of the accusations that he was a Soviet spy. He arrived in September, just before the Suez invasion by the British, the French, and the Israelis.

Old man Philby introduced Kim to his huge range of friends and political associates; Kim moved in with his father just as St. John was confronted by al-Uwaini with yet another request from Saud to return to Riyadh. It was arranged that Kim would accompany his father and his Arab family on an overland car journey. But this part of the plan fell through when Israel attacked Egypt on October 29, 1956. Since military operations by Britain and France against Egypt were now inevitable, a cable from London to Kim Philby ordered him to remain in Beirut even as he was leaving the city. But St. John went on to Riyadh.

There his allowance of £180 was restored, his sons were entered for their education at the Princes' School at Nasiriyah Palace, and, St. John wrote to a friend in England, "I have dropped into my old life as a common courtier as if there had never been any interruption of it."[3]

He spent most of his time in Riyadh, living in an old-style house made of red mud and rejecting suggestions that he move to one of the modern concrete houses. He spent his days hammering away on his old typewriter in a room lit by a naked bulb, writing a long book on his experiences as the British political agent to the court of the amir Abdullah in Jordan in 1924 (it never found a publisher) and then *Arabian Oil Ventures,* his quasi-official history of Aramco, which was published by the Middle East Institute in Washington. He revised all the articles he had written on Arabia and the Saudi kingdom for the *Encyclopaedia Britannica* and wrote new ones on the new oil towns such as Dhahran and Ras Tanura. He began a translation of the Koran from Arabic into English; and he revised his *Background of Islam* on the basis of a fellow scholar's redating of Sabean history. He went on the pilgrimage of 1959, spending the usual ten hours in high heat astride a bitch camel; he went with the king on a number of desert journeys, usually with his son Khalid; and he spent his seventy-fifth birthday at the hill resort of Taif, "watching the bulldozers knock down half of my property for a new road through the town."[4]

Philby resumed contact with Tom Barger, chief of Aramco's government relations, with George Rentz, chief of the Arabian Affairs Division, and with Mulligan himself.

When old man Philby took up his place at Saud's court, he found that his fears had come to pass — Saud's economy was in a disastrous state. The Saudi government's oil revenues in 1956 had reached $340 million — nearly $1 million a day — but Saud and his administration had continued to increase expenditure until now they had not the cash to meet financial obligations. This had further damaged Saudi Arabia's credit, which was only rarely good enough to enable the government to obtain loans that were not backed by guarantees from Aramco.

The government debt was $480 million at the official exchange rate, so the finance minister again went to Aramco to ask the company to underwrite loans against future royalties. Inflation was roaring along, and the free market rate fell from the official 3.75 riyals to the dollar to 6.25 riyals. Abdullah Suleiman, the financial minister with the uncanny ability to twist the arms of rich merchants and banks, was no more. Suleiman had had a nasty row with Crown Prince Faisal, and he had resigned. His replacement was one of Faisal's colleagues, Muhammad Surur Sabhan, of as yet unknown ability.

Finances were not the only problem facing the kingdom. Saud had become addicted to al-Cointreau. This threat to his health was not yet known beyond the royal family, but it would be before long. This compounded a multiplicity of ailments, not least his stomach troubles, his high blood pressure, and his sagging legs, which, because of poor blood circulation, could hardly carry the weight of his body. Moreover, Saud's poor health and his mismanagement of the government could in fact threaten the patrimony of Ibn Saud.[5] In accordance with shariah law, the family elders and the royal uncles could make appointments or force the resignation of a person in a high place in society, and they had sometimes done so. But they had to be careful in dealing with Saud. He was loved by the Bedouin. The stability of the state required that his popularity be considered before taking any such action, even if he had become corrupt as a leader.

Philby again became an important adviser to Faisal as the crown prince and the king locked horns in what became a grave crisis. At the beginning of March 1958, Philby returned to Riyadh after the Iraqi revolution. There he lashed out at an old friend and Arabist, Glubb Pasha, commander of Jordan's Arab Legion, rejoicing that "the line that divides me from your ilk is your conviction that the best interests of the Arab countries can only be served in some form of subordination to British imperial policy sweeted by lavish financial aid, whereas I am equally convinced that only in unity *inter se* can the Arabs ever realise their destiny. . . . Perhaps you will not agree with me that your cause is lost beyond recall."[6] It was. King Hussein dismissed Glubb Pasha. The Saudis liked statements like these, and once again Philby resumed his place at court, enabling him to influence one last battle for Ibn Saud's patrimony — the survival of the Saudi state.

Ever since Ibn Saud's death, King Saud and Crown Prince Faisal, a frugal man, had quarreled over the former's sumptuous self-indulgence and his corrupt administration. Neither Aramco nor the American diplomatic and consular corps in Arabia had dared to warn the king about the error of his ways, for the omnipresent menace of nationalization of Aramco was too great. Tactfully, the British diplomats had warned the king about the inevitable consequences of his conduct of the affairs of state — they had less to lose than their American colleagues.

Philby therefore came back into his own, with Faisal at least. Gradually, Faisal became determined to seize the power of the state if his half brother, the king, did not mend his ways. As Nasser's agents seemed to imperil the security of the Saud dynasty, just as they had in Iraq when the Iraqi king, the royal family, and the prime minister were all murdered in 1958, a number of the royal princes urged the crown prince to force Saud's abdication in favor of himself. Faisal declined on the grounds that Saud controlled the Bedouin of the desert, not himself. But Faisal did confront his half brother and demand that Saud hand over to himself all executive powers. In this Saud agreed, declaring that his poor health made it necessary for the younger, fitter Faisal to step in. A Puritan at heart, Faisal assumed those powers on or about March 24, 1958. Philby advised him in the constitutionality of the ultimatum, for he had been well trained in state law by the Raj in India.

Faisal had a broad spectrum of international relations problems to take stock of. The attitude of the United States toward Saudi Arabia was as ambiguous as ever. So was Saudi Arabia's attitude toward its nearest neighbors, Jordan, Iraq, Kuwait, and Yemen. Saud's relations with Egypt and Syria had been disastrous because of his purported involvement in the Serraj plot to kill Nasser. Because of his extravagance, Saud had not been able to pay a subvention to Egypt in the form of cheap oil purchasable in Egyptian pounds. Nor could it pay the Jordanians the $10.5 million due in aid money. That added Jordan to the growing list of governments disquieted concerning the worth of Saudi Arabian promises. More serious, Saud had terminated diplomatic relations with both Britain and France at the time of the Suez crisis, so that he could expect little help from those quarters.[7] The relationship with Aramco was poor, distrustful, and becoming increasingly antagonistic.

Faisal also faced daunting internal problems. He drew up a new charter for the Council of Ministers, the most trusted advisers responsible to the king for running the country. This required all council members to take an oath: "I swear by Almighty God that I shall be dedicated to my religion, then to the royal authority over me and to my country and that I shall not divulge any state secret and that I shall preserve and protect the orderliness and the welfare of the state, and that I shall perform my work with sincerity, faithfulness, and dedication."[8]

To strengthen the provisions of the oath, the new charter empowered Faisal to bring criminal penalties against any member of the council who "sold or let any property belonging to the government and bought or hired any from it."[9] Besides avoiding such conflict of interest, the charter also created a new structure for the entire government that would help define the powers belonging to Faisal and to Saud. Each minister was now responsible to the president of the council, Faisal, who in turn was responsible to the king. But the king could dismiss members only if so requested by Faisal; in turn, the president's resignation would require the resignation of the entire council. Although the new rules did not strip the king of all power, they did make the council more independent of the king's court.

The financial state of the kingdom was regrettable except in one respect — future prospects based on the Saudi Arabian oil wealth. Aramco had discovered ten major oil fields and had in production a total of 675 wells. At a time when no U.S. or Canadian well produced much more than one hundred barrels of oil a day, the Gawar field alone could produce over four million barrels a day. Most produced was high in quality: Arabian Extra Light, Arabian Light, Arabian Medium, and Arabian Heavy. Arabian Light was the most valuable, and its principal sources were 451 wells in Gawar and its neighboring field in Abqaiq. Together these wells could produce 4,960,000 barrels each day. Arabian Light was the "marker" that set the price for all other crudes.

Other figures — financial ones — gave the company room for confidence and the Saudi government room for pause in any plans it might have to nationalize Aramco. The bottom line told the story. Prior to 1950 the government received less than $150 million total royalties from Aramco. From 1950 through 1964, Aramco paid the Saudi government a total of $4.5 billion in taxes and royalty. Conservatively, the company projected that the government would now receive $1.3 billion annually (that figure soon proved to be low). There was, therefore, cause for pride and cause for concern.

The kingdom's current financial state was bleak. The new finance minister, Sabhan, had assured Faisal late in 1957 that the state's finances were sound and that the riyal had 100 percent coverage. But when Faisal visited the treasury after he had assumed full powers, he found it contained only three hundred riyals, equivalent to perhaps $100 — and Faisal needed twenty-six million riyals to meet payroll. Some four hundred million was owed to banks and merchants, all deriving from loans obtained by Abdullah Suleiman's deft machinations. One bank was on the verge of collapse, and the real coverage of the riyal was down to 12 percent, mostly in the form of gold and silver already pledged as security for foreign loans.

After only five years of Saud's rule, Arabia was virtually bankrupt. Faisal thereupon imposed Wahhabi austerity upon the kingdom that made the princes and the Hejazi merchants groan; when Faisal ordered an embargo on the import of luxury cars in June 1958, he caused much trouble for himself, for he had cut off the livelihood of important dealers. Faisal appointed an able Pakistani accountant, Anwar Ali, as head of the Saudi Arabian Monetary Agency (SAMA). Established by the U.S. Point Four program to help bring control to the kingdom's finances, SAMA had not worked in the past, owing to Saud's lack of cooperation and his habit of grabbing his purse and the special funds allocated to him — a hundred million riyals here and there — to sprinkle about in order to keep the tribes tranquil. Anwar Ali demonstrated his independence of mind when King Saud complained to him about the expensive upkeep of his palaces. What should he do? "Blow them up, Your Majesty!" Anwar Ali had replied.[10]

But despite the austerity program introduced by Faisal, Saud managed to find some money to spread about in the Nejd, the mainstay of popular support for the house of Saud. The silver riyals and golden sovereigns began again to "fall like rain during the drought of Faisal's austerity program." As Faisal's austerity program collapsed, Nasser "appealed," in August 1958, over the Voice of the Arabs radio service, to all Saudi tribes to revolt against the royal family and to form a republic. He accused the royal family of usurping the people's money, serving American imperialist interests, and assisting the Jews in founding their state in Palestine. All this certainly was a great offense to Allah.[11]

Plainly Nasser was attempting to intensify the divide between the king and his crown prince, and to some extent his campaign succeeded. Saud's physical energy restored, he wished to regain the full powers he had lost in March 1958. At the same time a revolt occurred among the Saudi princes.

Another of Ibn Saud's sons, Talal, emerged from the shadows to challenge King Saud and Crown Prince and Prime Minister Faisal. His Royal Highness Talal ibn Abd-al Aziz was said to be the thirty-fourth son of Ibn Saud, born in 1931. Another of the sleek Saudi princes in cream-colored suits and possessing an ample fortune, according to his Aramco dossier he had held a number of important posts in the government since Ibn Saud's death. His cut from oil royalties was estimated at 620,000 Saudi riyals a year in perpetuity, about $200,000, free of tax. His mother was a favorite concubine of Ibn Saud's, a beautiful Armenian known as Umm Talal. She had acquired great wealth, much of which she made over to Talal when he came of age. He had served Saud as director of royal palaces in 1953, communications minister in 1955, and Saudi ambassador to France in 1955. Saud had put him in charge of his project to restore and expand the Grand Mosque at Mecca.

In the period 1956–60 Talal was concerned with what Aramco called "business and philanthropic activities"; he had married well, to a daughter of the Lebanese prime minister, Sami Solh. He had extended his fortune by investing in real estate in Cairo, and when relations between Nasser and Saud soured, he was able to obtain a personal assurance from Nasser that his property in Egypt was safe from sequestration. Together with other evidence, this suggested that Talal had come under the sway of Nasser. Politically, therefore, he embraced Arab socialism and Arab nationalism. He clearly stated his political goals: he wished to do away with the monarch and establish a republic. Toward this end, Talal acquired a powerful ally — Abdullah Tariki, Aramco's former employee and foe. Tariki had been employed as the king's gauger, recording the amount of oil pumped out to the tankers, which the Saudi government used to estimate royalties. He had left his employment with Aramco because he was convinced that the company was cheating him.

When Tariki returned to Riyadh from Dhahran, he resumed his work as director of the Saudi government's oil and minerals office. By now an ardent Nasserite, in 1959 he attended the first Arab Petroleum Congress in Cairo as a delegate of Saudi Arabia. Quietly he inquired among other delegates whether the oil-producing countries might defend themselves against "the predators," Aramco and its parent companies, more effectively if they formed their own cartel. When he found support for such a scheme, he went to see Crown Prince Faisal, who at that moment was furious due to one of Aramco's sudden price changes. He saw merit in Tariki's plan, although he did not want to take the lead by forming the cartel in Riyadh.

Tariki went ahead with his plan with the tacit knowledge of the crown prince, as the Saudi oil industry, Aramco included, dissolved into uproar. On August 8, 1960, Exxon, the most powerful member of the Aramco consortium, found itself in an oil glut manufactured by, so it was claimed, the Russians, who had begun to use their large oil surpluses to undercut the Western oil companies. The Russians were seeking, as usual, to destabilize Europe; at the same time the Aramco consortium was keeping Europe supplied with oil in one of the Cold War maneuvers that so dominated political life at that time. Exxon cut the price it paid for Arabian oil by ten cents per barrel; the other companies followed suit. The Saudi government had not been forewarned.

Then Exxon cut its price yet again, once more without consulting the Saudis, who had embarked on costly social and welfare programs for which they had planned funds based on their estimate of incoming royalties. When the Aramco consortium cut its price, it cut the Saudi government's income as well. Some Arab governments were delighted at the Saudis' embarrassment. An Egyptian political journal rejoiced that their loss of revenue would "mean fewer Cadillacs in Arabia." So great was Saudi anger at Exxon's action — a private corporation dictating how much revenue a sovereign government should receive — that it threatened Aramco's oil concession. It was "a dangerous time in the history of the Concession Agreement."[12]

Exxon's action produced a surge of unity among all the Gulf oil states, and Aramco management began to consider how to respond if the Saudis attempted to nationalize the company. Would Aramco request the assistance of U.S. armed forces, as the Anglo-Persian Oil Company had solicited British support on the other side of the Gulf when Mossadek had nationalized the oil company in Iran? Tariki went to Baghdad, and on September 9, 1960, he met with representatives of four oil-producing countries — Iraq, Iran, Kuwait, and Venezuela. The group, which represented 80 percent of the oil then being produced in the world, established a cartel called the Organization of Petroleum Exporting Countries (OPEC). The cartel's immediate purpose was simple and straightforward:

> Members can no longer remain indifferent to the attitude heretofore adopted by the oil companies; members shall demand that oil companies steady and free prices from all fluctuation; members shall endeavor, by all means available to them, to restore present prices to the levels prevailing before the reductions.[13]

Qatar attended the conference and joined OPEC shortly afterward, and over time Algeria, Gabon, Libya, Nigeria, Ecuador, the United

Arab Emirates, and Indonesia joined. It was a militant alliance, although at first it was not powerful enough to challenge many policies of the Anglo-American companies. But such power would eventually come. Perez Alfonso of Venezuela, one of the main movers behind Tariki, was positively jaunty when he announced at a press conference that "we have formed a very exclusive club." Between them "we control ninety percent of the crude exports to world markets, and we are now united. We are making history." They were indeed.[14]

Attending the Arab Petroleum Congress in Beirut in October 1960, Tariki again attacked Aramco, this time alleging that the company was "rigging their profits to deprive the producing countries of more than two billion dollars over the previous seven years." He continued with the declaration that the oil companies would not reveal the true figures; "the truth about their Middle East profits" was "buried in their complex accounting," and therefore they "remain hidden to this day."[15] Tariki's allegations that the oil companies were concealing the facts produced a "common indignation" that enhanced the delegates' enthusiasm for participating in OPEC.

Tariki also won another point. Basic to the OPEC agreement was the stipulation that no member country should or would break rank to accept special terms from an oil company, if this move would jeopardize the profits or position of the rest of the members of "the club." OPEC's essential goal was to fix a price for oil and to force the companies to accept it worldwide. It had only one means by which to enforce this — solidarity among the oil-producing countries.

The oil companies reacted vigorously to the founding of OPEC. The declaration of an Aramco high official, Bob Brougham, characterized their general response: "We don't recognize this so-called OPEC. Our dealings are with Saudi Arabia, not with outsiders."[16]

And so it was for the first two years. Aramco and other companies involved in the Anglo-American oil industry declined to deal with the new organization. But the OPEC partners remained united. When Tariki returned to Riyadh after the establishment of OPEC, Faisal welcomed him with special warmth. The Council of Ministers immediately ratified Saudi Arabia's membership in OPEC.

The formation of the cartel provoked worldwide interest and publicized OPEC members' complaints against the Western oil companies:

> Suddenly oil became the fashion. Journalists from all over the Middle East started coming on a pilgrimage to the Riyadh office of Abdullah Tariki, and he explained to them how the Western companies were short-changing the Arabs. They paid artificially low prices for their oil, they hid their profits in the complex accounts of their tanker compa-

nies, refineries and marketing organizations, they insisted on sharing their losses by cutting prices in times of glut — but they scarcely shared the massive dividends that they reaped when prices soared in times of shortage.[17]

Tariki claimed knowledge, gathered when he worked at Aramco headquarters, that Aramco and other companies' returns on their investment were several hundred percent a year. He came up with a figure of $11 billion, which was, he said, the true profit made by the companies over the past seven years; he claimed that half of this was due and should be paid to the Arab producers. But Tariki's complaints were not confined to pricing. The two most infectious stories Tariki had to tell revealed a completely untrustworthy and cynical attitude on the part of the oil companies in their relations with Arab government. Many Saudis, in the ruling dynasty and outside it, felt that the first of these was only too believable: "That the Saudi Government was hoodwinked into giving concession rights to an enormous area for a song, because the Company was sophisticated and the Government negotiators were simple 'barefoot boys' who did not realize what they were doing."[18]

The second story was equally compelling and inflammatory. Tariki alleged that Aramco was not complying with the article in the 1933 contract obliging it to train Saudis up to the level of its American employees. He stated that Aramco's American employees had no intention of "working themselves out of their jobs" nor wished to delegate any control of the company to Saudi employees.

> In the early days Aramco was owned by the four U.S. Shareholder Companies; they controlled the amount of oil sold and the price. They paid for all of Aramco's capital investments and operating expense and took 50% of the profits as their return. The US Shareholders were paying, so the training effort was judged, to a large degree, on its economic costs and benefits to Aramco and the Shareholder Companies.[19]

Later, a senior vice president in charge of technological development would write that Aramco's training practices in the 1950s and 1960s were in fact "murky and subject to various interpretations and, in many cases, employees were not being given appropriate training opportunities." He found there were "a number of examples of new employees in their early twenties being denied or simply overlooked for training and development." There was no

> filtering mechanism to differentiate the quick from the slow, the ambitious from the satisfied, the inquisitive from the unconcerned. In the refinery we probably got a good cross section of this population. Most

of the [Saudis] were properly slotted to refinery operations jobs, but some were of superior intelligence. We had people working in refinery plants who, in a different environment, might have become doctors, lawyers or nuclear physicists.[20]

Knowing the situation only too well because of his own experience, Tariki made Saudi training and promotion a burning issue within the Saudi government. Faisal also took action, merging the ministries of finance and economy to create the Ministry of Petroleum and Mineral Resources, and then he appointed Tariki to be its director-general. By Saudi standards a brilliant theorist and an industrious technocrat, Tariki first intended that Aramco should be nationalized and become, under his management, "an integrated company" that would manage the flow of petroleum from the well to the gasoline pump. By 1960, Tariki "became such a power that he could make the nationalization of Aramco" into a cause.[21]

In December 1960, Faisal presented his budget for 1961. Revenues were up 380 million riyals to 1.7 billion riyals; Saud's privy purse was cut to 235 million riyals from the 292 million riyals in 1958. This led to a showdown. When Faisal sent the budget for Saud's approval, the king rejected it on the pretext that it was not itemized. Saud had managed to depict Faisal as a dour penny-pincher and had sown dissatisfaction with Faisal's work among many of the royal family. Faisal then wrote a note to the king, his half brother: "'As I am unable to continue I shall cease the powers vested in me from tonight and I wish you every success.'"[22] Crown Prince Faisal then withdrew from politics and left Riyadh, spending much of the ensuing seven months incommunicado at Taif. He did not speak to King Saud again until July 1961.

The royal decree announcing Faisal's "resignation" was issued by King Saud on December 22, 1960:

> We, Saud ibn Abdul Aziz al Saud, King of the Kingdom of Saudi Arabia, Having considered the request of our brother Faisal to be excused from the duties of the office of the President of the Council of Ministers, We hereby order the following:
>   1. We accept the resignation of our brother Faisal, dated December 19;
>   2. All Ministers are hereby considered resigned along with the resignation of the President of the Council of Ministers.
>   God is the grantor of success.
>
>   (s) Saud[23]

Restored to full executive powers, Saud established a new Council of Ministers. He appointed the least competent of his sons, Muhammad bin Saud, as defense minister and his heir presumptive; he gave Talal the ministries of finance and the national economy; and Tariki held the new portfolio of the Ministry of Petroleum and Mineral Resources. Talal paid an Egyptian lawyer to write a constitution for Saudi Arabia, which provided for the establishment of a national assembly. But it went nowhere. Talal handed the document to Saud, and that was the last he saw or heard of it. Saud, though promising fiscal reform, quickly reverted to his old habits. Jose Arnold — still steward of Saud's palaces — furnished new details to Aramco regarding the king's habits:

> With the austere Crown Prince safely out of the way the spending spree was on again. The flow of money into foreign countries and into the hands of the palace crowd began anew at an unrestrained and unprecedented rate as King Saud continued to put his trust in men whose only concern was accumulating fortunes for themselves.[24]

Arnold was pulled into the fray when, although his advisers had hidden the fact from him for as long as possible, Saud discovered that he had no money to pay for the supplies and services he required. He called Arnold to an audience and announced to him a new austerity plan — Arnold was to reduce the wait staff of forty by half, and also to slash the annual budget (of about $5 million) by half as well. Other staff were to receive a 20 percent pay cut.

After the king left the audience hall, Arnold recalled, "Id ibn Salim was waiting for me." He handed Arnold a piece of paper and said, "'Here is a list of stores where you are to buy the palace supplies from now on.' All of the stores on the list, I discovered later, were owned by the King's advisers or members of their family." Then Arnold faced the unpleasant task of notifying his staff, who had not been paid their wages for months, that many were to be fired.[25]

At this point Talal and Tariki produced "evidence from the files" of their respective ministries that, while prime minister, Crown Prince Faisal had accepted a bribe from a Japanese oil company that had come calling in the hope that it might buy the scraps from Aramco's table. Faisal's private office denied that there was evidence of any sort supporting this accusation. But when the allegations appeared publicly in a journal in Beirut owned in part by Talal, Faisal felt forced to utter a public denial himself. This he did on June 25, 1961:

> Some hireling newspapers in sister Lebanon have recently continued to spread biased rumors about the agreement concluded between the Government of Saudi Arabia and the Japanese Oil Company during the period when His Royal Highness the Crown Prince was President of the Saudi Council of Ministers. These newspapers were attempting

to throw a shadow of doubt on the reputation and integrity of the
Saudi regime and to accuse the Prime Minister of exploiting influence. . . . It is a childish action that aims at injuring the reputation
of the Saudi regime and those responsible for the welfare of the people. Therefore, the Office of the Crown Prince finds itself obliged to
state the bare facts [about the allegation], feeling sure that in acquainting everyone with the facts, an end will be put to these prejudiced
rumors.[26]

Faisal then plainly stated that King Saud wished to discredit him and
compel him to resign as crown prince, thus clearing the way for Saud to
arrange for his son Muhammad, the minister of defense, to become
the heir to the throne and, eventually, the revenues from Aramco.

The sequel to the allegations against Faisal were as interesting as the
plot that led up to them. On November 15, 1961, Tariki continued to
press his accusations against Faisal at a meeting of Saud's Council of
Ministers, of which he was a member. He stated that he had gained
evidence that Faisal's intermediary with the Japanese company was
Kamal Adham, Faisal's brother-in-law, and that Kamal Adham stood to
receive a large payment and 2 percent of the net profits of the Japanese
company. Since this company had gained a concession to an important
offshore oil field near Kuwait, the percentage would become exceedingly valuable. In turn, Kamal Adham had arranged that half of his
commission would go to Crown Prince Faisal and one quarter to Adham's wife, Iffat, a daughter of Faisal.

By trying to besmirch Faisal and his family by alleging their involvement in such intrigues, Tariki and Talal had unwittingly made powerful
enemies for themselves. The four scholars of the Al ash-Shaykh —
literally "the family of the sheikh, Muhammad Ibn Abd al-Wahhab," the
founder, two centuries before, of the Wahhabi movement that was now
the official religion of the Saudi dynasty and the kingdom — turned
against them. These scholars, also known as the *fatwa* committee (the
people who alone had the powers to "bind and loose"), had powers "to
elect and depose the [head of state] or delegate his powers to another
person." They were the leading figures behind the twelve divines who
formed the ulema, the mysterious council which sat in judgment on
the highest affairs of state in the kingdom. They were the "keepers
of the ideology" and had, therefore, supreme power and influence.
Faisal's mother was the leading female of the Al ash-Shaykh. Here, in
many ways, was perhaps the true power of the kingdom.

When Talal and Tariki learned that they had lost the support of King
Saud as a result of the alleged bribery story and raised the ire of the

four scholars, they suddenly defected to Nasser's Cairo. Their action produced great fears within the dynasty that the established order of Saudi Arabia was disintegrating. Talal, Tariki, and a handful of their supporters obtained political asylum from Nasser.

When Aramco learned that Tariki had defected, there was quiet jubilation. As Brock Powers, a high executive of Aramco, would state, "If Tariki had remained Minister of Petroleum and Minerals, he would certainly have tried to expropriate us, and he might have succeeded."[27]

Meanwhile, during the night of November 15, 1961 — the date on which Tariki had made his most recent, and final, charges against Faisal — Saud collapsed with acute stomach pains. Arrangements were made for him to be flown to Aramco's hospital at Dhahran. While these were being made, the king

> made an extraordinary attempt to [prove] his physical fitness to govern. He insisted on his favourite wife, the fat Umm Mansour, being brought to him. With the physical support of four slave girls he successfully had intercourse with her. The glad tidings about his virility were spread about the capital by Id bin Salem.[28]

After King Saud had been examined at Aramco's hospital, Radio Mecca issued a statement that "His Majesty, while in good health, was advised by physicians to rest until tests are concluded and until the pains in his legs, now greatly improved, disappear."[29] The physicians then decided that the king must be sent to a hospital at Boston in the United States. Shortly before he was due to leave Dhahran in an Aramco aircraft, the king called for pen and paper and wrote a decree, for the second time, establishing a regency council of five ministers to rule in his absence. He also uttered another decree restoring to Faisal the title and the functions of chairman of the Council of Ministers. It is evident that the Al ash-Shaykh had seen to it that Faisal's good reputation was preserved, and it is even possible that they ordered King Saud into exile. His collapse may have resulted from no physical illness, but from the order of the four scholars as a means to spirit him out of Saudi Arabia.

Crown Prince Faisal was back in business.

The Voice of the Arabs propaganda service marked King Saud's departure with a new campaign against the Saud dynasty's spending habits, association with U.S. imperialists, and flouting of Muslim standards of behavior and religious practices. King Saud had "concluded a secret agreement with America whereby the U.S. is granted permission to set up a secret naval base for the American fleet on Tarut Island in the Arabian Gulf."[30] It exhorted:

> O! my brother Arab! American imperialism stresses that it should remain in Saudi Arabia, and this is the price of protecting the Saudi throne from destruction. Thus Saud's throne will remain under the protection of American battleships and of the atomic base at Dhahran. But Saud should know that by this he is speeding his end. Imperialism will never save thrones from the will of the people. The people endure, but they do not forgive. The free men in Saudi Arabia do not fear any power on earth and they shall soon strike. [America,] which is controlled by Zionism, wants to liquidate the Palestine problem with the help of Saud, the criminal King and the Protector of Muslim countries. My brothers, Saud is working with the assistance of his American and Jewish friends on the liquidation of the Palestine problem. [The dynasty] of the al-Saud numbers 7,000 people. It is increasing at the rate of 25 persons per month. This family occupies our country. Every *Amir* of this family owns from 3 to 200 palaces and between 9 and 400 cars. Each *Amir* owns 17 men and each *Amir* owns 17 women. The King, who owns more than anyone, has 3,000 women. There are 45,000 servants including the *Khawiyah* [royal bodyguard], the slaves, the cooks, the royal and civil guards, and the attendants of horses, cars and cows. He also has 25,000 religious merchants who are called the Public Morality Committee. There are about 600,000 human beings sold in the roads of Saudi Arabia [sic]. The slaves are brought from the Hijaz, Najd, the Yemen, Iraq, Egypt, the Sudan, Syria, Palestine, Lebanon, Turkey, Iran, all Asia, Africa and Europe, and even Israel — for there are 15 women of the King's harem who are Jewesses from Israel, the Yemen and Europe.[31]

From these themes of satyriasis, extravagance, corruption, slavery, and misdeeds, the Voice's campaigners went on to show that Saudi society was crumbling. And behind everything lay American imperial power reposing within Aramco:

> That cursed institution, located on Saudi territory which accommodates about 10,000 American soldiers, hundreds of planes capable of carrying conventional and atomic bombs, U2 planes, 40 atomic and hydrogen bomb storehouses, the Saut al-Haqq [Voice of the Truth radio station owned by the Americans] and a training center for American spies. The latter is in addition to the "Samhah School" — the American spying outpost in el-Hasa — and the Darwish Building — the location of the American intelligence service in Damman. Besides all this, there are 850 American experts who control the Saudi army, and 7,000 Americans employed by Aramco who retain their military rank despite their civilian attire and colorful shirts.[32]

Like all propaganda, these allegations often contained a grain of truth. But there was more than mere talk emanating from Nasser's

Egypt. In October 1962, Talal announced that, first, he had abandoned his Saudi title, that of His Royal Highness Prince Talal, and that henceforward he would be known as mister. Second, he announced plans "to establish a national democratic government" in Saudi Arabia, in which the people would be left free "to choose the kind of government they prefer." The current Saudi regime was, he asserted, "steeped in backwardness, underdevelopment, reactionary individuals and tyranny." He believed that the Saudi kingdom was disintegrating into four separate entities based in the kingdom's four main regions, the Hejaz, the Nejd, Hasa, and Asir. He felt confident that his supporters in Saudi Arabia would revolt and help him bring down the state.[33]

Talal's declarations could not have come at a more dangerous time for the house of Saud, for it coincided with dramatic events in Yemen. Nasser had landed two light divisions of the Egyptian army in Yemen to support the Marxist Sallal, and the arrival of so many Egyptian troops — some say they numbered twenty thousand — touched off a severe tremor in Riyadh. Egyptian planes flew reconnaissance missions over Riyadh, Jidda, and the Hejaz with impunity; the Egyptian air force gas-bombed some Yemeni villagers. And there were fears at Aramco that, given the nature of Nasser's propaganda, the oil fields would become a target.

On December 30, 1962, Nasser's Russian IL28 bombers savaged the southwestern Saudi town of Jizan with "extensive bombing" for two days. They also bombed the inland oasis of Najran, the key to the route into Arabia for the Yemeni coffee trade. Did Nasser's attacks foreshadow an invasion of Arabia? Aramco thought so. Nasser's troops lay across the route (by way of Eritrea or Aden) that Aramco employees would take if they had to evacuate. Britain and the United States recognized the gravity of the situation. The U.S. Air Force positioned a squadron of fighters on the Dhahran airfield; Britain sent "advisers" and guns to the Yemeni royalists. And when, on January 6, 1963, the rebel leader, Sallal, announced that he now had missiles capable of hitting "the palaces of Saudi Arabia,"[34] the Saudi government established a supreme defense council, although it had precious little with which to defend itself.

Under these and other pressures, Saud's health and composure again failed him. On October 18, 1962, the royal uncles and divines again met with Saud and urged him to restore Faisal and his Council of Ministers. Saud, weak and ill, complied. Saud cabled Faisal in New York: "It is our Royal wish to entrust you with the Presidency of the Council of Ministers. . . . God grant us and you success so that you may accomplish the goals of our nation and our people. The Peace and Mercy of God be with you."[35]

Throughout the period between November 1961 and October 1963, King Saud traveled in and out of his kingdom — more often out than in — for he was under pressure from the rest of the princes to absent himself in order to let Faisal do his work. On several occasions he demanded that Faisal return to him his powers, but each time Faisal refused.

The final showdown between the king and the crown prince began in December 1963. The "December Crisis" was marked by menacing troop movements in and around the capital by the forces loyal to the king and to the king's preferred choice for crown prince. The king was supported by the sizable royal bodyguard at the palace, many sons and their adherents, and his suite. But the crisis fizzled without military action or change in the status quo. But on March 13, 1964, the conflict resumed when King Saud wrote to Faisal, requesting a reinstatement of his powers. Faisal rejected the king's request summarily:

> The present situation is the result of complete agreement on the part of the Royal Family members who feel that I should have the power because you were not able to exercise it. If you were able to, I would not stand in your way; but history and past experience have proven that you are not able. The country is now prospering; the people, the religious leaders, and all the other members of the Royal Family are happy with my rule. I will therefore hold on to this authority for the good of the country.[36]

Knowledge then reached R. I. Metz, Aramco's outstanding political agent resident in Riyadh, and his brilliant wife, the daughter of a leading ambassador, of the forces involved. A revolt then ensued, issuing from certain of Ibn Saud's sons and the old king's surviving brothers. Seventy-two of them united in what Metz reported to be "a cohesive, purposeful, dominant element of power." They intended to remove King Saud from all of his offices and to replace him permanently with Faisal. They were supported by the twelve members of the ulema, the religious scholars; and the twelve scholars were backed up by the four scholars of the Al ash-Shaykh. The four played what Metz called "the leading role" in the events that next occurred.[37]

At Riyadh, still little more than an overgrown village made of red mud bricks, tensions heightened. A plot to kill the king was rejected by Faisal's supporters; a decision in the king's camp to kill Faisal was overturned. But the scene still threatened to dissolve into widespread bloodshed and disorder. When Metz learned of the plots, he reported them to management. Aramco sealed itself off from the outside world, recalling all its parties from the desert back to Dhahran. It was said that the camp boss at Dhahran alerted Washington that it might be necessary to request U.S. troops to defend Dhahran. Meanwhile, the coup d'état seemed, to the Americans, to evolve slowly. But according to typical Riyadh standards, it progressed at "a dazzling pace."

On March 26, at about 4:00 P.M., representatives of the ulema went to Nasiriyah Palace. The mufti asked King Saud to take certain actions intended to defuse the tensions. But the king refused and immediately mobilized the Royal Guard. The guard inside the palace readied for action, and the women and children were taken from Nasiriyah Palace to the royal farm some thirty-five miles from Riyadh. Servants and some of the foreign staff were also moved out, and recoilless rifles were placed at the gates. Rumors spread that the king's sons were planning to attack Faisal's residence, which was then transformed into an armed camp by the National Guard and the army, both of whom were the Royal Guard's rivals.

Shortly after sunset and apparently after another visit to the king, the ulema came to Faisal with a proposal: the king would no longer interest himself in the business of the state provided that he remained king with government protection and that his privy purse remained intact. Faisal reportedly responded in the following manner: "The King knows, I am here to protect him, and so are his brothers. I am happy you now have proof that he is only interested in money. Thank you for your efforts but they are no longer needed."[38]

The pace of the crisis quickened in the early morning hours of March 27. A delegation of sixteen members of the royal family and the ulema called on the king and advised him that it was in his interest to accept the fait accompli that he had brought upon himself. After some pleading, the king agreed to sign a statement renouncing the throne and all its powers in favor of Faisal. But he asked that no public statement to that effect be made. The crisis eased.

Confident of victory, Faisal took a number of actions that would ensure the transfer of power from Saud to himself. He transferred the Royal Guard to the Ministry of Defense, with courts-martial for anyone refusing to recognize his authority to do so. He ordered the transfer of the king's bodyguards to the Ministry of the Interior and the National Guard, transferred the king's personal advisers to his office, ordered the Ministry of Finance to review Saud's privy purse with a view to cutting it, and finally instructed the army guard at Nasiriyah Palace to protect Saud. Then he sent word through an intermediary to Tom

Barger, by now president of Aramco, that the dispute between Saud and Faisal was settled.

The next day, March 28, the king drove some forty-five kilometers into the desert with guards, jeeps, sirens, and sons, to visit his mother. In the evening, Ronald Metz of Aramco called on Faisal, who was "relaxed and in excellent humor." Faisal stated only that "it has been difficult, but things will be all right now."[39] They were. Seven of the king's sons called on Faisal, kissed his hands, and begged forgiveness. Faisal granted them pardon and withdrew his order expelling them from the kingdom.

Faisal did not claim the title of king at this stage, preferring the less regal but still majestic style of "viceroy of Saudi Arabia." Perhaps he did not wish to provoke the king further, thereby forestalling a possible tribal rebellion. For the moment the lesser title was all that was required to rid Saudi Arabia of Saud. A number of high opinions supported Faisal. Of these, the most important document was the legal opinion of the twelve divines:

> Praise be to God, the Lord of the Worlds, and blessings and peace be upon His Faithful Messenger.
>
> In view of the differences existing between His Majesty King Saud and his brother His Highness Amir Faysal, regarding which we convened [from December 17, 1963, to January 14, 1964] we studied and reached our decision hoping . . . that it would put a decisive end to these differences; and since it has recently become apparent to us that these differences have recently widened and have almost led to the outbreak in the country of civil strife and chaos which might have led to harm and corruption on a scale that only God could comprehend; and since it is imperative that a decisive solution be found for these differences and disputes, which recur from time to time and bring nothing but harm to the people and to the country; we the undersigned have studied the situation in the light of the way events have developed, and have reviewed the state of His Majesty's health and his present circumstances. In view of the fact that His Majesty is unable to carry out the affairs of the State, and pursuant to the dictates of the public interest, we have decided as follows:
>
> 1. His Majesty King Saud shall be the King of the country and entitled to respect and honor.
>
> 2. His Highness Amir Faysal, the Crown Prince and the President of the Council of Ministers, shall carry out all the internal and external affairs of the State, in the King's presence and in his absence, without reference to the King on such matters.[40]

The four members of the *fatwa* committee who prepared and signed this decisive finding against King Saud were of considerable importance to Aramco, for until now the Aramco executive had understood that there was a body of holy men who held the supreme religious power within the theocracy but had not known who they were. They were the grand mufti of Saudi Arabia, Muhammad ibn Ibrahim ibn Abd al-Latif Al ash-Shayk; Umar ibn Hasan Al ash-Shaykh, head of the Public Morality Committees of the Nejd, Hasa (where Aramco was located), and the northern frontiers area (which included the borders of Saudi Arabia with or close to Israel, Jordan, and Iraq); Abd al-Malik ibn Ibrahim ibn al-Latif Al ash-Shaykh, chief of the Public Morality Committees throughout Saudi Arabia, the bodies known as the religious police; and Abd al-Latif ibn Al ash-Shaykh, director of the Bureau of Institutes and Colleges. Two of the four scholars were, therefore, in charge of the religious police that had caused Aramco so much trouble in the past and would continue to do so in the future. They were the watchdogs of ideology, and it is of interest and significance that a fifth member of the twelve divines was Sheikh Abd al-Aziz ibn Baz, now the vice president of the Islamic University at Medina, the xenophobe whom Barger had encountered at Layla in 1940 and who had accused King Ibn Saud in 1944 of selling the royal land to the foreigners — an accusation that almost cost the sheikh his head.[41]

This finding was then communicated by the divines to the seventy-two members of the royal dynasty and formed the basis of their decision to remove King Saud. As the royals' *fatwa* (decision) stated:

> Praise be to God, the Lord of the Worlds, and blessing and peace be upon our Prophet Muhammad and on his House and Companions. . . .
>
> In view of all this [the opinion by the twelve divines] we unanimously decide as follows:
>
> 1. To give full support to the legal opinion of Their Reverences the religious scholars.
>
> 2. We request His Highness the Crown Prince and President of the Council of Ministers, Amir Faysal, promptly to put this legal opinion into effect and to take the necessary steps to amend the regulations now in effect. . . . We pray God to grant success to all those working for the welfare of our religion and our nation. May blessings and peace be upon Muhammad, his House, and his Companions.[42]

Thus the royal family and the divines disposed of King Saud, leaving him only with his title and a reduced privy purse. Later an Aramco analyst wrote that

> several years ago few observers of Saudi politics would have included the Royal Family as a leading element of power, because The Family members did not behave as a group. They lacked a feeling of responsi-

bility towards the country and the throne. Few of them realized before 1958 that their privileged state was in danger. It took the shock treatments of [Nasser] and of Amir Talal to change their attitude. The brutal propaganda campaign conducted by [Nasser] against the Royal Family, including the King, and the subsequent defection of Talal and his brothers shook the family to its foundation. The active family members thereafter began to hold meetings, to lobby for support, to pressure the King, and to organize themselves.[43]

However, the same commentator noted that the "family's unity during the March 1964 crisis is deceptive." In Faisal "they had an acknowledged and astute leader." But "unity of purpose behind a capable leader in the future is by no means guaranteed. In fact the emergence of factions contending for more power can already be observed and may lead to a prolonged struggle with harmful and potentially disastrous results." The "question of succession to the throne remains a major source of potential strife in the family."[44]

Saud's privy purse was reduced to the equivalent of $40 million a year. Early in 1965, accompanied by a retinue of 130, which included his wives, his concubines, and his progeny, King Saud went into exile in Greece. The CIA, he alleged, had been instrumental in his deposition, and the U.S. Air Force had prevented the tribes of Hasa from coming to his rescue in 1964. Saud died on February 23, 1969, at the age of sixty-seven. Faisal sent an aircraft to fetch his body to Riyadh, and it was laid to rest in a grave near that of his father. Faisal said prayers for the soul of his brother.

Then Faisal became king and announced that his crown prince would be the third surviving son of Ibn Saud, His Royal Highness Prince Khalid. It was an interesting succession. Khalid was, Faisal's court acknowledged, a good compromise, adding that, if Khalid was not likely to do the state much good, equally he was not likely to do it much harm. Perhaps most important to Aramco, Ibn Saud's patrimony had been saved without bloodshed.

That Philby's advice played its part in the very early phases of the crisis seems to have been undoubted, if unrecorded. He proved to be again an invaluable informant to Aramco, and his support was valued by the crown prince. But St. John was not the man he once was. In 1960 he had turned seventy-six, was pot-bellied and satanical in appearance, but still respected and popular. He requested Faisal's leave to attend the Congress of Orientalists in Moscow, and Faisal agreed, bidding Hajji Abdullah to return quickly. He went first to London for the cricket and then on to Moscow. There he joined George Rentz, Aramco's chief Arabist and head of Arabian Affairs, with whom he spent the next fortnight. At the conference "he was the grand old man of the meeting — white-headed, benign, entertaining and generous with encyclopaedic information."[45]

On his way back to Riyadh in September 1960, he visited Beirut to visit with Kim, drinking Japanese Scotch at Joe's Bar and watching the belly-dancers at the Kit-Kat. He lunched with Nicholas Elliott, the chief of the British Secret Service in Beirut, and his wife, Elizabeth. The luncheon was memorable, if only because it would prove to be Hajji Abdullah's last on Planet Earth. As always, his talk enthralled. According to Elliott, St. John "left at tea time, had a nap, made a pass at the wife of the Embassy staff in a night club." Later that evening he went to a large cocktail and supper party at the home of John Fistere, the former *Time* correspondent who was now the political adviser and flack to King Hussein's court in Amman. St. John went on to the Fisteres' balcony, with its glorious view of nighttime Beirut and the Mediterranean, and there he collapsed. As in life so in extremis: there was uproar and then stunned silence. There was a story that the British ambassador in Beirut, Sir Moore Crosthwaite, tried to give St. John mouth-to-mouth resuscitation. This seems unlikely as Crosthwaite was not a man to mix mucus with such an arch-enemy of England. Isobel Fistere screeched, "Heavens alive! I've poisoned him,"[46] and thus did the legend that St. John had been poisoned richochet about Beirut.

Kim took his father to the Normandy Hotel, stopping at a nightclub on the way. A doctor was called to the hotel and he pronounced that St. John had indeed suffered a heart attack. At daybreak he suffered a second one and was taken to the American Hospital. There, St. John woke only once and announced to his son Kim: "God. I'm bored."[47]

Those were St. John's last words. He passed to Paradise late in the afternoon of September 30, 1960.

[12]

ROCK WEDNESDAY

IN 1960–61, THOMAS C. BARGER became president of Aramco. The first generation of Aramco executives had retired, leaving a new guard, most of whom had spent their careers in Arabia in the service of the company. For the next ten years Barger served as chief of a company that had emerged as yet another instance of the American genius for creating vast innovative enterprises in technology — the sustained dynamic begun in World War II that led to many accomplishments: America's two-ocean navy, an army of ten million, the Manhattan Project that created the atomic bomb, and the space program.

Barger's strength was that "unlike some of his friends he was able to adjust from the rough and ready style of pioneering activity to the far more sophisticated approach demanded of an executive in what had become the largest crude oil and natural gas liquids–producing company in the world." Of course, preserving the oil concession was one of Barger's top priorities in managing the company.

Barger's approach combined a broad vision of the company's mission and the highest standards in implementing every facet of it. His views were detailed in twelve planning papers, which he had written over the years, and together these became known as "the Barger Doctrine." In these he defined Aramco's main function in Saudi Arabia: "to preserve the Concession and optimize the returns to the Shareholders over the term of the Concession."[1]

He also felt that the company should take a socially responsible approach by providing technological and economic support to Saudi Arabia. One of his goals was to spread the economic benefits of the enterprise as widely through the local population as possible even at some extra cost by adoption of policies that direct the purchasing power of Aramco and employees to the development and support of services generally available to the public.[2]

Overall, Barger's principles of management constituted an intelligent and enlightened blend of corporate self-interest and social responsibility. They were soon to be put to the test. For when Barger took over, he inherited three great political problems. The first was the crisis brought on by the quarrel between Faisal and King Saud, but this was resolved to Aramco's satisfaction. The second was the beginning of the British withdrawal of its forces and abandonment of its bases in the Gulf — indeed, from all regions east of Suez, thus throwing the burden of Aramco's physical security upon the Saudi Arabian government and the U.S. government. The latter had established the Military Assistance and Advisory Group (MAAG) in Saudi Arabia to complement a U.S. Army Corps of Engineers mission in the kingdom; and in 1957 the MAAG was expanded to become the U.S. Military Training Mission, "the largest U.S. security assistance organization in Asia."[3] But these units could not replace the strength of the British forces in the Gulf previously available to Aramco. Washington attempted to get the British to reverse their decision to quit, but they did not succeed. India's independence in 1947 had destroyed the strategic rationale for Britain's presence in the Middle East. A British defense minister could not help but see the irony of the situation. The United States had been trying for thirty years "to get Britain out of Asia, the Middle East, and Africa." Now that Britain had decided to leave, "they were now trying desperately to keep us in."[4]

The third problem lay in the contest of wits between Frank Jungers, Aramco's chief of government relations, and Sheikh Ahmed Zaki Yamani, Tariki's replacement at the Ministry of Petroleum and Mineral Resources. The source of their conflict was the Saudi demand for greater participation in the affairs of Aramco. The struggle between these two men was to last for the next twenty years.

And it began in 1968 with Yamani's appointment to Excom, Aramco's Executive Committee (but not to Ancom, the Committee for Acquisitions and Negotiations, where the real financial and political business of Aramco was done). When Jungers and Yamani first met in Excom, OPEC had recently been established. Saudi Arabia was a founding member, thus putting Aramco on notice that it and the other member states (Iran, Iraq, Kuwait, and Venezuela) would no longer allow their fate to be passively tied to the world oil market. Rather, OPEC insisted that the member states would *participate* in pricing arrangements — a word with subtle implications that would come to mean much the same as that more explosive term, *nationalize.*

Meetings between Jungers and Yamani took place against the usual barrage of political warfare flowing from Nasser's Voice of the Arabs. From the Arab nationalist's perspective, the company represented despotism, imperialism, exploitation, and torture. Nationalists considered Saudis such as the governor of Hasa, Jiluwi, to be one of the "dung beetles which live only on imperialist generosity."[5] Yamani may have found some political inspiration in Nasserism but, unlike Tariki, he kept quiet about it. One of the slyest lawyers of his generation, he always behaved as a gentleman.

"Zaki," as he was often called, was born in Mecca on June 30, 1930, a son of a chief justice of the supreme court in the Hejaz, where Jidda and the holy cities of Mecca and Medina were located. In the first eight years of Yamani's life his father was traveling abroad, first in Indonesia and then in Malaya, as the grand mufti, the chief divine with full powers to guide Muslim practice and law. The Yamani family was forty generations old, so it was claimed, and rooted not in the turbulent tribes of the Nejd, from which the Saud dynasty drew its main strength and from which Wahhabism had sprung, but in the Hejaz, a much more cosmopolitan society. His family tribe descended from the Prophet. Judge Yamani may have embraced Wahhabism when Ibn Saud seized the province and attached it to his kingdom in the early 1920s, and young Yamani's upbringing was thoroughly Islamic. Such was his family's eminence that it had a private room for worship and contemplation in the Grand Mosque in Mecca. Yamani's first passion, after the Koran, was Meccan folk music, his second, Wagner's operas.

His education began in a Meccan school where, being remarkably bright, he usually ranked at the top of his class. At age seventeen his father sent him to al-Azhar University in Cairo, where he won his law degree at the age of twenty. When he returned to Mecca, he found a job at the Ministry of Finance. He taught Islamic law for free during his spare time. Such was his ability that the Saudi government sent him to study at New York University's Comparative Law Institute for non-American lawyers. There he studied common law and the American legal system; in Brooklyn he married an Iraqi girl.

Having won a master's degree in comparative jurisprudence, he went on to Harvard Law School to study the problems of international legal disputes and capital investment. All who met him spoke of his high ability, his calm, his quietness of manner, his use of worry beads. Yamani returned to Arabia in 1956 with a master's degree in law from Harvard to add to his New York University degree. He again served in the Ministry of Finance and also worked part-time as manager of the local Coca-Cola plant.

In due course, Yamani's reputation increased in luster. His friends called him "the greatest Arab since Joseph."[6] Crown Prince Faisal read all his articles, so Yamani claimed, and in 1957 Faisal summoned Yamani to his house in the mountain resort of Taif, behind Jidda:

> Yamani was escorted into the Crown Prince's small office.
> Feisal shook hands with him.
> Then there was a long pause.
> Feisal looked at Yamani and waited.
> Not knowing what else to do, Yamani sat down.
> Feisal just kept staring.
> So now Yamani stood up.
> "I want you to work for me as a legal adviser," Feisal said. "Have you got any conditions?"
> Yamani thought fast. "I don't think that anyone who could have the opportunity of working for you would have any conditions."
> Feisal liked that.
> And Yamani was hired on the spot.[7]

Yamani became Faisal's minister of state at the Council of Ministers, the ruling body, while Tariki was still in Saudi Arabia. Faisal's most significant appointment was his decision to make Yamani successor to Tariki in March 1962. George Ballou, a high official of Excom, remembered his first impression of Yamani during the minister's first board meeting in San Francisco:

> He wasn't anything like Abdullah Tariki. He was very quiet and very personable. The first or second night he was there someone in Aramco wondered if anybody had arranged dinner plans for Zaki. We discovered that no one had. Well, we were having a family birthday party at home but I figured I couldn't just leave Zaki on his own like that because it would have been rude. So I invited him to the party. He enjoyed himself so much he came back to the party several years in a row.[8]

It was to prove fortunate that Yamani, Faisal's minister, was received so well by Excom, for otherwise, Faisal's relations with the United States were not very good, simply because he was an Arab. Typical U.S. opinions on the Arab-Israeli conflict and the formation of OPEC did not cast Arabs in a positive light, and a generally negative stereotype was emerging.

Much was already known about Yamani at the company. He came to the attention of one of Aramco's chief lawyers, W. F. Owen, during a crisis that seemed minor but had serious aspects. In 1961, a Saudi businessman had been demanding that Aramco sell more of its oil to him, but Aramco had refused, as it was entitled to. But the merchant took his complaint to court. In the Saudi legal system, the merchant's story might have threatened or possibly invalidated Aramco's concession agreement. Aramco called Yamani in, and the matter was settled smoothly.

Then came the tussle over the case known as "the Sidon Price Claim," which began in the early 1950s and was still dragging on in the early 1960s. The Saudi government claimed that Aramco owed it $283 million in royalties on oil pumped over Tapline to Sidon. Yamani entered the legal proceedings when concerns about the stability of the kingdom during the Yemeni civil war were heightening. Without ruffling a feather, Yamani managed to obtain a settlement from the company for $180 million, plus better terms in the future.

To deal with the formidable Yamani when he became minister, Aramco appointed the equally formidable Frank Jungers to deal with the Saudi government. As Baldo Marinovic would say of his chief, he was "very aggressive, extremely bright, very ambitious, fairly ruthless, and I could almost say something like 'crafty' in making deals." Another Aramcon formed this opinion of Jungers: "He seemed to be a real cold fish." This appellation was not considered a negative criticism because "it's just the way he is, and I'm sure many people would describe him in the same way. Some people just aren't the jolly ho! ho! back-slapping type."[9]

An engineer, Jungers was born in 1926 at Regent, North Dakota. Then his family moved to Oregon, where he went to a school run by nuns and later had begun work on a preengineering course at Oregon State University when the United States entered World War II.

Jungers volunteered his way into the V12 naval pilot training program. There he remained until the end of the war. In 1947, he won a degree in mechanical engineering at the University of Washington. He then joined Aramco and soon evidenced his special gift of far-sighted political astuteness. Indeed, Jungers became the ablest of all Aramco's chief executives. He began work first at the refinery at Ras Tanura. Then he proceeded through the Aramco system from operations to management. His arrival at government relations coincided with Barger's appointment as president.

Jungers could sum up the politics of the ruling dynasty in the briefest of paragraphs. His most foundational insight about Saudi politics and Faisal's and Yamani's attitude toward the United States exemplified his precision: he spoke of the "blind, unthinking support" of the U.S. government for Israel as the only "thing that rallied the Arabs and made them a cohesive force." He believed that King Faisal was basically supportive of Americans, though he "disliked the British, he didn't want anything to do with French, but the Arabs, the other Arabs, his neighbors, accused him of being an American lackey, which he was not." It was not the Saudi people who pushed him to distance himself from the Americans, but the Iraqis, Iranians, Jordanians, and Syrians — "all of whom had different agendas, and all of whom had relatively nothing in common, except one point: the Israeli point rallied them all."[10]

From the start of his work in concession affairs, Jungers worked mainly with Yamani as his Saudi contact. Thus Yamani's push for Saudi participation in Aramco became a constant theme in their work together. Jungers thought that Yamani's motives were considered "highly suspect by all the oil companies." Because Jungers and others feared trouble would result from such participation,

> we fought the participation question as a rear guard action in which the shareholders, for all the reasons that you can think of, didn't want to go the participation route until the very last ditch. And it was sort of my job, as I saw it, to carry these arguments as far as I could, to hold the line until I truly felt that we are either going to have participation or we were going to be nationalized.[11]

Yamani achieved his important goal of insinuating himself into Excom. He had earlier been a member of Aramco's board in Dhahran, but had complained that no real decisions were made there. Company policy was set by the Executive Committee. Only there would he truly be able to influence Aramco's future direction. When Yamani spoke about Excom, it was evident that he regarded it as a perfidious body. By gaining a position in Excom in 1968, Yamani hoped to attain "inside knowledge of Aramco's and the Owner Companies' . . . marketing strategies and their policy making councils." As Jungers declared, such information constituted "the guts of their operation and was something they didn't share with any competitor" — least of all a representative of a foreign country who was also a founding director of OPEC. Yamani was especially eager to obtain information about pricing — something that Aramco was not to hand over lightly. Doing so would be tantamount to exposing its most confidential business transactions to a future competitor.[12]

Junger's fears concerning Yamani's true motives were not unfounded. That participation was to be but one step on the slippery slope to nationalization was in fact later admitted by Yamani himself. He was

> thinking from the beginning that eventually Saudi Arabia would have to own and control its own natural resources. From the first day I walked into the ministry, I believed that. Yes, I spoke of participation. But you should understand that participation was always intended to be just one step in that direction. Maybe in the beginning I didn't say it like that. Perhaps you are right to think that in the beginning I didn't make the point too clearly. . . . [Later on] I called it "complete participation."[13]

Yamani aimed for Saudi Arabia to gain complete ownership of the company *and* of the oil still in the ground, but by means other than the sort of nationalization encouraged by Nasser and his colleagues, which implied dramatic political action and possibly even military violence. He wanted full Saudi ownership to occur within ten years, but, he said later, "I was very young and, well, maybe I wanted it a bit too soon." However, he was slowly and steadily laying the groundwork for the dispossession of Aramco.[14]

Naturally, Aramco's executives resisted Yamani's pull in this direction. One observer noted that they and the other Western oil companies were "obsessed with the empire they have built. It is so vast and it took them so many decades to achieve. And now they see these newcomers, these national oil companies in the producing countries, wanting to come and take a piece of their cake, which is the last thing they want to happen."[15]

But their attitude did not slow Yamani. Because the Americans running Aramco would need to be replaced by well-educated Saudis before the company could be brought under his country's control, his earliest efforts included the establishment of Saudi Arabia's own national oil company, Petromin, and the College of Petroleum and Minerals, which was to produce "home-grown engineers, scientists and managers to suit the needs of its own national oil company." Jungers fought Yamani hard in order to prevent this. Yamani later commented that "right from the start Aramco fought me on the formation of the [College] because they saw what was coming." But still the hostility of the company surprised Yamani. "It was the idea of a change in status that bothered them. They would lose their full control. Aramco would be different."[16]

A high company executive, Bob Brougham, predicted what he

thought would be the course of participation in the long term. Though Yamani settled for 25 percent of Aramco at first, he eventually wanted 100 percent. This gradual acquisition of company control could take place without use of political strong-arming or military conflict. Thus the Saudis would gain the benefits of nationalization without the upheaval that had accompanied such actions in other countries. Yamani's strategy required patience and political wiliness. He had both qualities in abundance.

Brougham warned that if the Saudis began to call the shots at Aramco, the American staff would lose interest in their work as their stakes in the company's success dwindled. The Saudis could not afford to lose U.S. expertise and experience. Yamani countered that merely having a secure oil supply should be enough to satisfy the Americans of Aramco. On this point they disagreed. Yamani talked tough and held his ground, and participation gradually moved forward. The Americans too wanted to avoid the confrontational aspects of nationalization. Qaddafi of Libya had nationalized British Petroleum; Iraq was nationalizing the Iraq Petroleum Company. Aramco did not want to be next, so its executives cooperated. The Saudis were offered 25 percent participation in the management of Aramco.

Jungers then had the difficult task of defining and implementing this plan. It was complicated by the fact that Aramco was in fact a consortium of shareholder companies:

> We were struggling to define what participation was and what it ought to be to best suit the interests of the companies as well as the government. Participation was a difficult thing to define. Twenty-five percent of what, and under what terms? True participation, of course, meant participation in the decisions . . . to which the Saudis were not a party and couldn't be a party. That would mean being downstream with the Aramco shareholders.[17] ["Being downstream" refers to refining, shipment, and distribution of oil. Up to this point the Saudis were connected with only the mining of the oil.]

Equally, such a partnership could have well been against the U.S. antitrust laws. Jungers believed that Yamani didn't fully understand the complex market situation. Yamani's reaction to whatever alternatives Jungers offered him was "that the offer didn't constitute ownership of The Company and it wasn't therefore a politically acceptable substitute for nationalization."[18] Contending with Yamani would be a constant challenge for years to come. Thus the first chink appeared in the Americans' supremacy in managing Saudi oil. The cozily settled Aramco enclave, sheltered from the upheavals in U.S. culture in the

1960s and secure in its economic and technological success, would soon encounter new forces of change:

> Since the fifties the Aramco company town at Dhahran had grown into a settlement with every indication of permanence. Trees, gardens and two-story houses had grown up inside the barbed wire. And the "Aramcons" had become almost a separate breed. There was now a generation of employees who had been born and brought up in the desert. It had become a kind of symbol of the no-man's-land of the oil companies, belonging to no culture and no country. Visiting it, I felt as if I were inside an idealised America, like an old cover of the *Saturday Evening Post;* an America untouched by the turmoil of the sixties, by long hair or drugs, with its citizens watching old movies on Aramco TV, playing baseball or mending their cars. To the Aramco engineers the compound offered not only fat salaries and early retirement, but a kind of engineers' utopia — progress without politics, and technology without doubts. All around them the twisting pipes, the giant towers and flares were the monuments to their skills.[19]

That permanence, that security, those rewards for carrying the White Man's Burden, were to be tested in 1967. War between Israel and the Arab states was in the air, and unrest was growing in Saudi Arabia. On June 2, in Jidda, the U.S. embassy was slightly damaged by a bomb that exploded in the embassy's machine shop. A second bomb demolished a U.S. Military Training Mission vehicle near its quarters and shattered windows in the building. A third bomb damaged a print shop. Despite these incidents — all of which were kept secret — the U.S. authorities in Saudi Arabia seemed to have been reassured. For on May 27, a State Department official informed the Aramco political agent in Washington that "the Department had little apprehension about the possibility of mob action in Saudi Arabia, particularly in the Eastern Province."[20]

But Aramco itself was not so sure. The Arabian Affairs Division reported that the situation within Saudi Arabia had become "increasingly tense," as Saudi public opinion, "exacerbated by the war drums from Egypt, Syria and Iraq," had begun to "solidify" behind Nasser against Israel and the Western world. Key Saudi officials, Yamani among them, "were confident that the Arabs could defeat Israel if the U.S. and Great Britain remained outside the conflict." The Saudi government "unmistakably" warned the United States "against giving any aid or support to Israel." Yamani warned Aramco, specifically Bob Brougham, "of the consequences of US assistance to Israel"; the effect of his warning was to invoke an assurance from Washington to be delivered by Brougham that "the U.S. Government [is] doing everything possible to restrain

Israel." Yamani thought the reply "inadequate" and he asked the deputy oil minister, Hisham Nazer, in the presence of Brougham, "how Aramco should be punished for U.S. Government assistance to Israel." Nazer suggested nationalization of Aramco, to which Yamani responded ominously: "Not yet."[21]

Yamani's comment reflected a trend toward viewing Aramco and the United States with suspicion:

> In any event, feeling in Saudi Arabia, both public and private, tended to regard the US and, by association, Aramco, as villains. . . . Feeling against the regime and the House of Saud was probably stronger throughout the crisis period than ever before. The King was openly criticized by heretofore silent segments of the population for Saudi Arabia's role (or more properly, lack of a role) in the struggle against Israel. The King was personally criticized . . . for consorting with imperialists and enemies of the Arabs. . . . Saudi responses in the crisis were compared unfavorably to those of Kuwait, which took the lead in sending troops to [Egypt], cutting off oil exports to the U.S. and Britain, and in providing financial support for the Arab cause.[22]

The third Arab-Israeli war began on June 5, 1967, with Israel fighting against Egypt and Syria. During that day Radio Cairo announced Israeli air attacks on Cairo airports and Egyptian defense centers. All Arab radios carried immediate reports of widespread Arab victories and claims that large numbers of Israeli planes had been destroyed. In truth, the Israelis had destroyed the Egyptian air force as a fighting force in this early action. Then Egypt began broadcasting stories that American and British aircraft carriers had launched heavy strikes against Egyptian airfields.

Aramco's Division of Arabian Affairs circulated this summary of its intercepts and other intelligence to the management on June 6:

> Egyptian radios announced that US/UK carrier-based planes were supporting Israel. The announcement was quickly picked up by most Arab radios, although apparently Saudi Arabian radio did not carry the story. Shortly thereafter, there were a series of anti-US/UK moves in most Arab states. Egypt closed the Suez Canal, giving as its reason US/UK participation in the war on Israel's side. Iraq cut off all oil exports as did Lebanon, Syria, and Algeria; Kuwait cut off oil exports to the US and UK. Six Arab states (Egypt, Syria, Algeria, Sudan, Yemen and Iraq) broke diplomatic relations with the US and the UK.
>
> The Arab trade union federation demanded the destruction of US/UK interests in the Middle East, and Arab radios announced a boycott of US and UK planes and ships. Anti-US/UK mob violence was reported from a number of of countries. . . . Saudi Arabia, though

considering herself at war, issued no formal declaration. . . . US and UN calls for a ceasefire were rejected by the Arabs, though it was becoming apparent that the Arabs were faced with a stunning defeat. Although the US and the UK officially denied Egyptian charges of intervention, the Egyptian charges were widely believed and no Arab station carried the US/UK denial.[23]

Early on June 6, Brougham of Aramco asked Aramco's New York office to secure an immediate denial by the U.S. government of the charges that U.S. planes had participated in the war. An hour later, the U.S. ambassador in Jidda visited the Saudi foreign ministry to deliver a White House statement denying Egypt's allegations of U.S. support of Israel. But "the Saudi Government was very reluctant to take any public position on this issue. It feared to appear less militant against Israel than the other Arab states. We were assured, however, that the Government assumed full responsibility for the safety of expatriate employees and dependents."[24]

At Ras Tanura refinery and oil-loading dock, the first action against the export of oil supplies to the United States took place. Students attempted to prevent the loading of the U.S. Navy tank ship the *Manhattan*. Other attempts were made, partly by students and partly by Aramco Arab personnel, to prevent the loading of another U.S. Navy tanker, the *Cantigny*. However, both were loaded and both sailed. Later that same day, at Ras Tanura "a large gathering" made up of about 80 percent Aramco Arab personnel chanted slogans such as "Down with Johnson!" and "Stop the oil!" The mob was dispersed without violence or great difficulty.

At Riyadh, King Faisal held a mass rally at Riyadh race track and declared that

> Saudi Arabia would cut off the flow of oil to anyone who aided Israel. No mention, however, was made of specific countries. The King said: "We will regard any state or country which supports Zionist and Israeli aggression against the Arabs as an aggressor against us, and we will take action with all means and with all force against anyone who supports or provides any kind of assistance to the enemy."[25]

But this was no real cause for worry to the Americans. Aramco's political agent in Riyadh reported that the rally "was held to permit people to let off steam" and to enable Faisal to tell the people what they wanted to hear — that Saudi Arabia was at one with the Arab people in the contest with Israel. He was interrupted on a number of occasions by members of the crowd, who chanted "Cut off the oil! Cut off the oil!" At one point the crowd shouted the king down. Angered, Faisal cut the rally short. On their way home from the rally, members of the crowd passed by an Aramco office. "Stones were thrown at the glass doors, shattering them, and the Aramco-Tapline plaques outside the door were removed. Although an attempt was made to enter the building, no damage was done to the offices proper."[26]

On June 7, the third day of the disturbances,

> radio reports indicated that the Arab war effort was insufficient to stem the Israeli tide, and Israel claimed to have reached the Suez canal and to have captured Sharm ash-Shaykh. Arab radios give increasing currency to reports of US/UK intervention on the Israeli side and repeated calls for the destruction of US and UK facilities, including oil facilities. . . . Radio Riyadh announced that Saudi Arabia had cut off the flow of oil to supporters.[27]

At daybreak at Ras Tanura, on the fourth day of the crisis, crowds began forming at the bus-loading area located between Gate 20 and Radhwa Camp. By 7:30 A.M. the crowd was swelling into a mob. At this same hour at Abqaiq, Saudi workers received telephone calls from workers at Dhahran and Ras Tanura, urging everyone to come out on strike. Rumors of an impending walkout and demonstration were rife at Dhahran during the early morning hours. Contract workers did not show up for work, and it was reported that agitators were working in the lines, forming at the National Commercial Bank office near the Aramco administration building. It was Thursday, payday, and the workers were waiting in line to cash their paychecks. Aramco executives assumed that the Saudis would strike after they had received their money. They were right.

The company was facing an impressive display of group discipline among the Saudi proletariat. B. C. Nelson, Aramco's chief labor officer, related that

> when a boycott of a major facility can be placed into effect and maintained over a long period of time with no communications devices other than word of mouth and to do this without prior knowledge of the supervision of this Company or informers — you have a kind of discipline that is nothing short of phenomenal.[28]

To emphasize the strikers' unity, the gaugers — who carried out the vital task of measuring the amount of oil flowing to the tanks, which then determined how much royalty would accrue to the Saudi government — walked off the job, and the day-shift gaugers did not appear for work. One of these gaugers, a Saudi, was arrested by the Saudi authorities and was sentenced to a lashing and imprisonment. Other gaugers reported that they had set out for Ras Tanura but were unable to get to work.

That morning at 8:25 Aramco's executive management, aware that disorder was spreading, gave orders "to shut down everything except utilities and, if possible, one crude distillation unit." That morning the staff of the U.S. embassy in Jidda and of the U.S. consulate at Dhahran were advised to leave Saudi Arabia as soon as possible. On learning that the U.S. ambassador had issued a "mandatory order" from Washington for a general evacuation, a senior official at the Saudi foreign ministry asked the ambassador not to carry out these orders, explaining that he wished to discuss the matter with King Faisal. Shortly the official was back on the telephone, stating that "the King personally requested that Americans not leave the country. The Ambassador passed this information to the Department of State, with a request that he be given discretionary powers in regard to evacuation. This was duly approved."[29]

The day before, later called "Rock Wednesday," was the day in the history of Aramco when disorder turned to violence. The pace of the disturbances quickened from 8:40 A.M. onward. The Division of Arabian Affairs reported that "agitators" had gone through the General Office Building, advising all Arab employees to leave. Those who hesitated were threatened, and by 9:35 "almost all Arab employees in Dhahran were off the job." At this same time Aramco established the "Government Relations Command Center," representing the inner core of Aramco's management. Its first action was to request the amir of Abqaiq to alert the National Guard and other security agencies. The amir did so. The guard was composed almost entirely of Bedouin who were regarded rightly as being wholly loyal to the throne. There was no report that the National Guard in the other centers — Dhahran, al-Khobar, Ras Tanura, and elsewhere — were similarly alerted.

That failure became the more serious when, at 9:40 A.M., the company agent in Dammam was told by his chief that "the situation was going out of control and that immediate action was required on the part of the Amir of the Eastern Province."[30] Reports of serious disorders began to come in throughout the day from all parts of Oildom — Dhahran, Dammam, Abqaiq, al-Khobar, Ras Tanura. All Aramco's main centers of population and industry were being menaced by marching mobs. The loading of the tankers offshore now stopped completely.

In the headquarters town of Dhahran, the consul general was warned that a mob of some three hundred persons was forming at the

Aramco camp with the intention of marching on the consulate. At this time the National Guard should have been taking up its positions to protect all U.S. government property, especially Dhahran Airport (where evacuees were beginning to gather) and all the approaches to the company's buildings. But none of the Saudi officials seemed to know where the National Guard was. Despite the government's repeated assurances that Aramco and its employees would be protected, when the crisis broke out there proved to be no protection other than local police and security police — some of whom, it soon became clear, were not only in league with the mobs but were actually leading them.

When the mob arrived, chanting "Stop the oil!" the four police officers on duty joined them. The crowd did not appear to be

> in a particularly vicious mood, but they definitely were screaming about the U.S. flag and anti-American slogans were heard. . . . The mob at the consulate grew rapidly to about 1,400 persons — the police estimated 4,000 — and among them, it was noted, was the government's head gauger. He, too, was arrested and lashed with palm fronds. The mob threw rocks at the consulate. . . . The demonstrators demanded that the U.S. flag be removed. . . . Colonel Mansuri [the Saudi in charge of airport security] asked for a Saudi flag. None was available so he telephoned to have one sent. The Saudi flag arrived shortly and it was run up the flagpole.[31]

Some of the rioters began smashing the windows of official vehicles and private cars. Others removed the large plaque bearing the seal of the United States of America from the front of the building. A smaller seal over the door was removed by a police sergeant seated on the shoulders of a demonstrator. There was no intervention by any Saudi security force.

After terrorizing the consulate, the demonstrators moved on to the airport. The governor of Hasa contacted the Saudi commanding general at the airport, reporting that everything was under control. But the Aramco situation room recorded that this was not the case. Demonstrators were entering the airport. The crowd, variously estimated to be between eight hundred to two thousand persons, was being joined by the airport's Arab employees. They demonstrated at the offices of the U.S. Military Training Mission and at the TWA offices and facilities. There was a rumor that shots had been fired.

As the riots spread there was a report, almost surely correct, that the mob was being organized by the Saudi airport commander. Therefore the Saudi military would do nothing to stop the mob — in fact, the military had joined the rioters. Aramco reported on the scene at the airport: "Serious damage to vehicles, offices, homes and personal effects was done by the mob at the base. Although no one was hurt, destruction was . . . widespread . . . even cutlery and toys being bent and smashed."[32]

At Riyadh during the morning of Rock Wednesday, Yamani told the Aramco agent in Riyadh that "the people who caused trouble and damage in the Eastern Province earlier in the day would be rounded up and severely punished." But he declined to make a formal apology to the agent about the failure of the Saudi government to provide the protection it had promised. He then handed the Aramco agent a letter ordering the company "to cut off oil deliveries to the U.S. and Great Britain,"[33] although he had no authority to do so without the approval of Aramco management. As the Aramco agent in Riyadh told the situation room in Dhahran, the Saudi government was playing the intricate game of serving two masters. It had to persuade the Saudi people that Saudi Arabia was supporting the Arab cause, when clearly it had taken no direct action to do so. The government also had to make good on its promises to protect Aramco property and personnel. Balancing these two commitments was a delicate dance, and the Saudis appeared to be stumbling.

Yamani did, however, try to throw a sop to the U.S. staff of Aramco. He stated that "he did not believe the Cairo story of US/UK participation in the air attacks on Cairo airports and command centers," but that "Saudi Arabia was in no position to make statements about it yet." For the fourth time the Saudi government announced that it was sending troops to Hasa to protect Aramco. These assurances also proved hollow.

More serious news was received during the early afternoon of Rock Wednesday. Rumors were rife that a crowd was gathering to attack American homes in al-Khobar on its way to Aramco headquarters. This news was reported to Yamani in Riyadh, but again he received the report in insouciant fashion. He told Aramco that five hundred troops had left Riyadh for Hasa at noon, and five hundred more would be sent as soon as possible.[34]

The Aramco agent at Riyadh was not impressed. He warned Yamani that "at this time protection of Aramco facilities was negligible." The agent was well aware that troops were possibly not readily available to the government because of other commitments:

> The Central Government evidently [was having] great difficulty in obtaining sufficient troops. Most of the Saudi forces had previously been sent to the Yemen border and to Tabuk on their way to Jordan.

Relatively large numbers of troops were also stationed in the northern area along the Trans-Arabian Pipeline. Consequently the Central and Eastern Provinces were virtually stripped of security forces.[35]

Despite Yamani's temporizing, many Americans were asking to be evacuated. Many lower- and middle-level employees, especially those with families, were not convinced that the Saudis would protect them. But when it was learned that the al-Khobar riots had fizzled out, the evacuation was deferred. Nonetheless, the consul general was "in touch with American airlines serving Dhahran to make standby arrangements for charter aircraft to land there for the evacuation of the Dhahran area and Riyadh, if necessary."[36] By nightfall, the promised troops still had not arrived at the Aramco conurbation. At about 6:00 P.M., two Aramco aircraft arrived at Ras Tanura and evacuated some Americans there. At that hour Aramco reported that the police "stationed at most important installations both inside Aramco's headquarters area and outside had disappeared within a relatively short time after their assignment."[37]

But there was one encouraging sign at Ras Tanura. Saudi personnel arriving at the refinery announced that "they were willing to remain on the job so long as no oil was shipped." Others stated that "they were on the job in order to guard 'installations' against sabotage or damage by Americans." Otherwise news was negative. For all the promises made, by midnight the National Guard had still not arrived. Thus Rock Wednesday passed.[38]

In its news summary for June 8, the Arabian Affairs Division recorded the conflicting reports that characterized news releases relating to the crisis. Rumors and propaganda were interwoven with occasional facts:

> Arab radios reported exaggerated accounts of violence and mob action against US/UK interests in the Middle East. The Voice of the Arabs, for example, reported that 1300 American houses in Dhahran had been destroyed. Baghdad Radio reported that demonstrators in Libya had set fire to the Wheelus Air Force Base. UPI and BBC carried a Jordanian denial of US/UK aircraft involvement. This denial was not, however, broadcast in Arabic by Radio Jordan. Other major developments included reports of the indiscriminate bombing of Christian and Muslim holy places in Jerusalem by Israel.[39]

A new trend began at 1:30 A.M. on June 9, when an Aramco agent, A. M. Shihadeh, met with the deputy minister of the interior, Anqari, who had just arrived from Riyadh. He simplified the granting of exit visas for those Americans who wished to leave. That was a good start.

From Riyadh came the news that "the King was most apologetic about the Dhahran incident." By that hour "a few hundred" National Guard troops had arrived from Riyadh and took up positions around the airfield and the consulate. They had orders to shoot to kill.[40]

At 9:40 A.M. an Aramco aircraft arrived from Abqaiq, carrying personnel from the French company, Schlumberger, which worked in the offshore oil fields under contract to Aramco. The Saudi police searched them and, to their consternation, found that they were carrying explosives. As the situation room at Aramco recorded:

> The Ras Tanura Chief of Police was furious because he had not been informed of this flight. The fact that the plane was carrying explosives exacerbated the situation. The explosives were immediately impounded and the Schlumberger party was held at Gate 20 by the chief. The personnel were released shortly thereafter. However, the incident generated rumors that were not dispelled for some days that Americans were bringing explosives to Ras Tanura to destroy installations.[41]

Meanwhile, only small packets of troops had arrived to protect Aramco. Nobody knew why the dispatched forces did not appear. Fears of sabotage increased. Did this lack of protection constitute a Saudi plot to force the Americans to leave, or was it simply a case of muddled directions and incompetence on the part of government and military leaders?

New threats of mob violence arose. At al-Khobar, crowds smashed the windows of the al-Khaja hotel, the British Bank of the Middle East, and the Chevrolet agency. A small party of National Guard soldiers dispersed the mobs and arrested the ringleaders (they were found to be not Saudi Arabs, but Lebanese, Jordanians, Syrians, Adenese, and Yemenis). But, as the Aramco agent told the deputy minister of the interior, the demonstration would not have happened if there had been "five good men" in the town.[42]

Aramco had to rebuke the Saudis for several other lapses in protection and vigilance. At Ras Tanura refinery, Aramco discovered that Saudi officials were contacting Saudi supervisors "to enlist their aid in enforcing the ban on shipments of oil to certain destinations." An Aramco agent warned Yamani that "few Americans would be willing to remain in the Kingdom unless the Government took immediate action and assured them of protection." The company had evidence that the ringleaders of the attack on the consulate and the Aramco buildings on June 7 were students from the College of Petroleum and Minerals, the institution that Aramco had established for the Saudi government at a cost of $70 million.[43] Yamani and the king continued to offer assurances, but little in the way of action.

In its final report on the day, Aramco recorded that although there were supposed to be many hundreds of troops guarding Aramco's and other American installations, "there was little sign of them. About 4 A.M. on the morning of the 9th, the Local Company Representative–Dhahran located about 20 of them asleep in Aramco's Industrial Cafeteria. It was assumed at this point that the authorities were trying to give the Company the impression that the security situation was better than it actually was."[44]

By the fifth day, June 9, 1967, the most significant intercepted news report stated that Egypt had accepted a cease-fire with Israel effective at 12:20 A.M. Syria, which later accepted the cease-fire, continued fighting after the deadline. Egyptian president Nasser resigned at 9:45 P.M., to the relief of the entire Western world and the distress of most Arabs. He was overcome at so swift a defeat of his armies. But he regained his composure and, "at the demand of all Egypt," he agreed to withdraw his resignation. Reports of demonstrations against the United States and Great Britain and their purported collusion with Israel were broadcast constantly by the Arab radios.[45]

The Middle East had changed again. The Israeli army had reached the Suez Canal and had captured Jerusalem and that other great shrine of Islam — the Dome of the Rock — as well as the Golan Heights. But most shocking to Saudi Arabia was that the kingdom now had what amounted to a common frontier with Israel.

By the end of the day the tardy troops at last arrived, and all townships in the Aramco conurbation found themselves under heavy guard. Most of the forces were mobile and equipped with automatic weapons. Oil minister Yamani announced that the government would issue a public statement before oil operations were resumed. Yamani also made it known that, in his opinion, the "weakness and lack of protection had damaged the Government's reputation and he strongly recommended that the Government keep 3,000 troops in the oil area to handle such matters in the future."[46] At Aramco headquarters Yamani met in conference with senior management to express his regrets regarding this lack of security measures.

During the early afternoon the interior minister called on the U.S. consul general to express his regrets and those of the king for the demonstrations. The American flag was again flown above the consulate. The government promised to pay for repairs to facilities damaged during the demonstrations, which it did. Although some Americans were still departing in response to rumors that a number of Arabs planned to sabotage Aramco operations, the situation was stabilizing quickly. This led to the next matter of import: resuming oil production and transport.

Yamani began this discussion by suggesting the following:

> The Minister informed the Representative that: (1) He is working on a Government statement which he hopes will minimize anti-U.S. feelings. This statement, combined with the substantial number of troops in the Eastern Province would stabilize the situation and permit the resumption of operations. (2) The King has no objection to loading all tankers in Ras Tanura, irrespective of flag, so long as a Ministry of Petroleum inspector is present to ensure that the cargo is not destined for the US or the UK.[47]

However, on the morning of June 10, the Saudi government changed its tune: "Oil minister Yamani advised the Aramco resident in Riyadh that (1) the Council of Ministers had just completed an emergency meeting and had decided against making any statement in view of the current situation." Clearly the government wished to avoid sounding officially pro-American. The king's advisers also wished to limit oil shipments to those that would not appear supportive of the Western powers. Then the Saudi deputy minister of petroleum demanded "that Aramco must pay the Saudi Government for any sales lost since the shutdown, although [Yamani] felt that Aramco could take 'credit for sales not made to the U.S. and the U.K.'"[48] An argument then ensued when Brougham rejected this demand, noting that sales had been lost because Saudi gaugers had walked off the job.

The best news received by Aramco that day was that by midmorning most of the company's labor force was back at work — many of them were far too deeply in debt to stay away any longer and under far too much pressure from their wives and the debt collectors. But on June 11 the Middle East was in general still a potential powderkeg:

> Arab radios [were] reporting a general strike in Kuwait, demonstrations in Khartoum against the US and UK, the seizure of oil companies by the Government in Algeria, and a ban on demonstrations in Kuwait. News reports indicated that the curfew in Lebanon had been reduced and that Beirut Airport would resume service on 12 June. While Abu Dhabi cut off the shipment of oil, the Iraqi Government urged its citizens "to respect foreigners."[49]

Yamani had scurried off to Kuwait to meet with representatives of other Arab nations about the shipment of oil. He said that the meetings went well and that all ships, irrespective of flag, would begin loading on June 12. The captains of the ships and Aramco representatives were to sign forms guaranteeing that the oil was not destined for the United States or Great Britain. The first indication that the stoppage — which lasted from June 8 to June 12 and may have been costing Aramco and the government $10 million a day, partly because clients switched their orders to other producing countries — might be over was a telephone call by the deputy oil minister. He notified the head gauger that he should contact all his workers and have them on the job by the early morning of June 12.

Later on June 11, Yamani made a statement that the ban would not in fact affect shipments to "US/UK colonies." Later an announcement by Aramco to all Saudi officials concerning the resumption of shipments was approved by the Saudi government: "(1) The Company is acting in accordance with the Government's desires, (2) operations must be resumed as announced, and (3) Saudis who object should be counseled; those who refuse to work should be removed by force if necessary."[50]

This announcement was significant in that it implied that the company would henceforward operate under Yamani's orders. Because it seemed to mark another step on the route to nationalization, it sparked a sharp altercation between Brougham and Yamani. The wording of the first provision suggested that Aramco was acting under the government's instructions. Brougham insisted that the statement be reworded to ensure that it was clear to all concerned that Aramco remained a quite separate entity. An amendment was in fact made before the statement was publicized.

Aramco was back in business. But the disturbances had shown that the Saudi workforce was capable of disrupting Aramco's operations in a dangerous and costly manner. Aramco's extensive and expensive welfare schemes were not enough to make workers unquestioningly loyal to the company when Arab causes were at stake. They had shown themselves capable of violence on company property, thus shattering the illusion that they were not violent people. There were dissident elements among them, and many remained essentially xenophobic, despite the company's munificence.

Moreover, Yamani had skillfully used the crisis to increase his authority and had revealed that nationalization of Aramco remained his main goal. More and more, Barger and his management were forced to the defensive position in their relations with the government. Increasingly, Aramco's American labor force began to feel a change in the air as more Saudis were trained for all levels of employment at Aramco.

Was a takeover in the offing? Even some of those Saudis already in the Aramco senior staff had been involved in the riots, showing that they had no great affection for the Americans.

Rock Wednesday signified a wake-up call for the Americans who believed that their paternalism would keep the oil fields American forever.

[13]

THE GRAND CRISES

ONALD I. METZ, ARAMCO'S political agent in the capital of
Riyadh, had an interesting affinity with the devout Wahhabs. A
devout high-church Anglican, Metz's faith had a certain devotion
to the archangel Gabriel, who, in Christian tradition, was to be
the trumpeter of the Last Judgment. Gabriel, too, had his place in
Islamic theology. Gabriel revealed the Koran to the Prophet Muhammad and thereby, to Islam; thus he is hailed as the agent of truth.
Metz's religious faith gave him rare insight into the minds of devout
Wahhabs. Both Metz and his wife, Helen, daughter of a U.S. ambassador at The Hague, were Anglican, and since there was no Christian
church in Riyadh, the heart of Wahhabism, they made their devotions
in Metz's study. Later Metz became a high-church cleric in Washington,
D.C. Helen Metz became the keeper of the Islamic collection at the
Library of Congress.

Tall, ruddy, amiable, agile, perceptive, Ronald Metz was regarded as
the ablest of Aramco's political agents. He and Helen Metz lived in a
large villa of red mud brick in one of Riyadh's medieval warrens. Metz
had a very sharp ear for dynastic intelligence; and he made an important study of Faisal's regime. Some of his insights follow.

Faisal personally was only slowly "showing signs of conquering his
very suspicious nature," although he had little to fear from the intrigues of the ex-king, Saud. Saud had publicly pledged his allegiance
to Faisal and was now living quietly in Greece; his many sons were
treated like pariahs and had little hope of restoring Saud's line to
the monarchy. No, the main threat to the stability of the state arose
through Faisal's inability to delegate authority. He had retained for
himself the following titles: president of the Council of Ministers, su-

preme commander of the armed forces, president of the consultative council, chairman of the supreme committee on administrative reform, minister of foreign affairs, and de facto head of his own royal staff. The heads of the Public Morality Committees reported to him; Faisal, too, had under his wing all the key ministries, as well as the National Guard. He had a finger in every pie. The governors of the provinces were either brothers of the king or ranking members of the various branches of the royal family. The dynasty remained therefore deeply entrenched in all Saudi affairs. And, Metz noted, "It is an understatement to say that Feisal is a very busy man." Now, in 1965, he was sixty-one years old, austere, frugal, monogamist, wise, and deeply involved in all manner of political, social, and industrial reform and development programs. But although he was robust and of good Saudi-Wahhabi stock, he simply had to delegate some of his responsibilities as "he cannot physically carry his present heavy load for a long time."[1]

Nonetheless, Faisal's failure to appoint a crown prince had caused disquiet, and not only in Aramco, for it meant that the succession was not settled as shariah law required. That was a pressing political matter on which the future of a multi-billion-dollar property depended. Saudi kings lived under dangerous circumstances; during his lifetime there had been four attempts to assassinate Ibn Saud. The ex-king Saud had been overthrown three times. Might there be an attempt to kill Faisal? Civil disturbance, anarchy, rivalry among Ibn Saud's brothers (the royal uncles), or rivalry among the princes of the royal blood could undermine the stability of the Saudi state.

Differences within the royal family always threatened to wreak havoc. The "Sudairi Seven" vied for dominance within the extensive family network. The progeny of one of Ibn Saud's favorite wives, Hassa bint Ahmed al-Sudairi, the seven were born over a period of sixteen years. Able, ambitious, and energetic, according to Metz they constituted the best hope for the survival of the Saud dynasty. And they were loyal to Faisal.

In all, Metz reported, "The Sudairi Seven were hard at work to increase their power. They had succeeded in obtaining appointments for two relatives as deputy ministers — Prince Fahd al-Sudairi as deputy information minister and Prince Abdullah al-Sudairi as deputy minister at the interior ministry; and still more relatives, all royal princes, had become prominent in municipal affairs in the key triangle of urban political power and thought, Mecca, Taif and Jidda."[2]

But there were rivalries within the royal dynasty. Prince Mishal, amir of the Jidda-Mecca-Taif triangle, did not welcome Fahd al-Sudairi's appointment. Nor did his brother, Prince Mitab, formerly the deputy defense minister. Both were, Metz reported, "unhappy over the [Sudairi Seven's] successes; and none knew where these rivalries might end. The ex-king Saud's supporters continued to intrigue not for the restoration of Saud, perhaps, but for their own advancement at a time when they, as much as the ex-king, had been disgraced." Prince Talal, nicknamed "the Liberal prince" and "the Black prince," the Nasserite leader of the anti-Faisal group who defected to Cairo, was, Metz reported, "eager to regain recognition and enhance his financial position."[3] Talal had by this time recanted his Nasserite views.

King Faisal's reform programs were drawing some criticism, particularly related to Muslim standards concerning "innocent means of recreation." Traditionally, all Saudi women were bound by the laws of purdah, but new programs were exposing women to new opportunities. Radio Mecca included a women's program hosted by a Saudi woman announcer; an English-language program was also broadcasted; women's clubs had been organized in the main cities under the patronage of King Faisal's wife. Exposure to other cultures, as well as other values, was available by way of private theaters in the major cities and a film rental service in Riyadh; new TV stations were slated to go on the air in the coming spring of 1966. The Dark Ages of Saudi life appeared to be departing.

But religious fanatics within the royal family were determined to stop the king's reforms, especially the new television stations. Aside from the fact that television could be political dynamite, the introduction of technology of any sort in Saudi Arabia had had a long and complicated history. Oddly enough, the "polluting influences of the West" had in fact been sanctioned by the ulema, the Wahhabi Muslim divines, in order to resolve a problem during the reign of Ibn Saud.

In 1927, the Nejdi ulema made a ruling to allow Ibn Saud to introduce the telegraph, the radio, and the automobile into the kingdom. They did so against the menacing objections of the Ikhwan, the "Soldiers of God" whom Ibn Saud had subdued as he solidified his kingdom. Though they had not been entirely silenced, they did not have the power to go against the ulema. Thus the ulema had allowed Ibn Saud to begin the modernization of the kingdom. Permission had been extended to introduce television as well, despite the fears of orthodox Wahhabs that, as with the telephone and radio, they were devices of the "blue-eyed devils" to corrupt the established faith of Arabia. Television programs introduced the population to Western lifestyles:

The appearance of beautiful homes, fancy cars, modern appliances and beautiful dresses, in both Western and Arabic movies, instills a desire in many of the viewers to possess things which they are not able to afford. This has been excellent for business in the Eastern Province in the short term, but may cause considerable social discontent over the long term.[4]

TV caused much more than discontent; it incited protest and political action. A year after Faisal's accession, Prince Faisal ibn Musaid was age twenty-six. He was a grandson of Ibn Saud and a nephew of King Faisal. When he was at school in the United States, he had associated with the flower children of the period. He had moved from college to college, smoked pot at Berkeley, was arrested with LSD in Colorado, and became involved in a barroom brawl with a girlfriend in Los Angeles. When Prince Faisal returned home, his uncle, King Faisal, directed that he be kept in the kingdom for a time — he "had become too westernized." During his reformation, Prince Faisal had returned to Wahhabism in its most extreme form, that of the Ikhwan. The group of which he became a member was led by his older brother, Prince Khalid. It consisted of privileged youth who had formed the opinion that, through the influence of Westerners, Saudi Arabia had become a corrupted, rotten society.

When test transmissions began at Riyadh television station in mid-1965, with the assistance of technicians from one of the big networks in New York, the religious group was outraged by what it called the "new blasphemy." They decided to wreck the station. Dressed in Ikhwan shifts cut short, their beards hennaed and jutting upwards and outwards in the manner of the Ikhwan, with the black braid of the Ikhwan over their white headdresses and the black paste of antimony around their eyes, the group set out for the station, led by Prince Khalid. But the police intervened and, in the belief that they were dealing with a dangerous Ikhwan group, they opened fire. So did the princes as they retreated to Prince Khalid's palace. The head of the security police consulted King Faisal, who authorized the officer to shoot to kill, with the statement that no Saudi was above the law and that if the group fired at the police, then the police must fire back. Prince Khalid was killed in their next confrontation.

From that time forward, Prince Faisal regarded his uncle, King Faisal, as a marked man who must now, as a holy duty, pay "an eye for an eye." Such passions were ignited by the introduction of television.

Frank Jungers succeeded Barger as president of Aramco at the end of the 1960s, when Barger retired. Later Jungers would become chief executive officer and chairman of the board, one of the most powerful positions in American industry. It fell to Jungers to play a key role during the difficult years of 1969–70.

He had inherited the two main problems existing between Aramco and the Saudi government — Israel and participation. Saudi Arabia under Faisal had been, and would continue to be, "no less fervent in its defense of the rights of the Palestinians than any other Arab nation. It has honored its commitments to the Palestine Liberation Organization despite the King's known disapproval of the movement's leader, Ahmad ash-Shukayri."[5] The fact that the United States supported the creation of Israel "will remain a source of difficulty in Saudi-US relations and from time to time impose difficulties on the Company's relations with the Saudi Arab Government." Yet in spite of the Saudis' tendency to assume that Aramco always agreed with U.S. foreign policy decisions, the Palestine question had been managed reasonably well and had not created an impasse.

Participation — that Saudi term for nationalization — continued as a prickly issue. Nationalization continued to be a trend among other Middle Eastern countries. Recently Syria had nationalized oil-marketing companies, and this had affected two of Aramco's parent companies. The Arab League "may be successful in unifying petroleum policy of its members and become an organization to be reckoned with." Already OPEC "has become a force of some consequence in influencing the changing relations between governments and oil companies."[6] Still, according to an Aramco executive, there appeared to be no immediate threat of total nationalization in Saudi Arabia. The country and the company were, according to him, simply too mutually dependent to part. He anticipated that this would also be the case elsewhere:

> Whether it be joint participation in petrochemical manufactures, use of "national" transportation facilities by the oil companies, or joint exploration, producing or refining efforts, the effect is to underline the mutuality of interest between the producing companies and their concessionaires. . . . Oil companies, by involving themselves constructively in the economic destinies of the developing countries, would not only be building their growth markets of tomorrow but would also be creating a more favorable climate in which to do tomorrow's business.[7]

In 1969, R. W. "Brock" Powers arrived in New York from Aramco's headquarters to work with Excom, the body that, mainly, ran the consortium's financial affairs. Born in Boise, Idaho, in January 1926, Powers had enlisted in the Royal Canadian Air Force in World War II at the age of sixteen, his intention to become a fighter pilot with the British air force. After he was accepted his true age was discovered, and he was "booted unceremoniously one day" and then joined the U.S. Marines. After the war, in order to obtain a Marine commission, he attended the University of Southern California and graduated in twenty-eight months, majoring in advanced geology. He was interviewed for a position in Aramco by Max Steinecke, who discovered the largest oil field in the world, in Saudi Arabia. Steinecke liked Powers's credentials and bearing, and Powers preferred Aramco's salary arrangements to those of the military — $325 a month, against $50 a month in the Marines. Steinecke accepted him, upping his salary by a further $50 a month. Powers joined the exploration department when he arrived in Dhahran in 1951. He worked as a surveyor in the desert, but at the outbreak of the Korean War he was recalled for service in the Marine Corps. He did not remain there long. As a surveyor he was exempted from military service, and soon returned to Aramco. There he remained until 1964 when he was transferred from exploration to the political wing of Aramco. When Aramco sent him to the Harvard Business School for an advanced management program, it was evident that he was marked for high places. He served at a number of political desks inside Aramco until 1969, when he joined Aramco's New York office to join Excom. And, he remembered, he had barely settled in when "the oil business went berserk."[8]

Powers's work concerned the shareholding companies' nominations, a task that required much circumspection and discretion. Each nomination, meaning the amount of oil each company would require of Aramco in a given year, was regarded as a corporate secret. The nominations were taken each quarter, for a year in advance. Powers was the only person to receive all the nominations. He would then total them, and from that figure Aramco estimated what facilities would be needed to meet the shareholders' plans and what their capital requirements would be. The nomination figures could be enormous — at this time the Saudi government's royalties were increasing from $4 billion to $8 billion dollars per year.

New to higher management, Powers sometimes felt certain that the numbers were just too high and had to reflect an error:

> One month . . . I couldn't believe it. The nominations were right through the roof. They were astronomical, compared to the base we were operating on. So I looked at the numbers and I said "Something's wrong. I've got the wrong numbers." So I called everybody back and they all confirmed them. What these figures meant was what shareholders required was oil to the value of billions of dollars.[9]

When Powers presented the figures at the 1968–69 meeting of Excom, "they all looked at each other. All the members of Excom were getting the same message."[10] The figures were signaling the start of the great oil boom of the 1970s. These figures meant that Aramco would, in order to meet the shareholders' requirements, have to build facilities that could produce ten million barrels a day on a sustained basis. These would themselves cost billions of dollars, and Excom was willing to go ahead with them.

Such was Powers's competency in handling Excom that, when Jungers moved up to become president, he placed Powers as vice president of government affairs in Dhahran, where he would tangle with Yamani and oversee relations with the Saudi government. This constituted a brisk change of pace for Powers: "Government Affairs isn't dealing with rocks or minerals or anything like that, it's dealing with people, and you're constantly trying to read somebody's mind."[11]

From 1970 onward, as president of Aramco, Jungers worked to defend the company against Saudi government policy as well as that of the U.S. government under President Richard Nixon. By now Aramco had agreed to go forward with participation with Yamani and had conceded the first 25 percent of the company — in the hope that such a gesture would satisfy King Faisal and Sheikh Yamani for years to come. Jungers explained his tactic: "The important thing was to give the immediate image of being *with* the government, not trying to fight it."[12]

In the wake of the 1967 Arab-Israeli war and the decline of spare productive oil capacity around the world, the Western oil industry began to focus on the one country in which oil production appeared to be stable and superabundant. That country was Saudi Arabia. As a U.S. Senate print observed, "The increasing importance of Saudi Arabia in the world of oil in turn made the Aramco concession seem even more valuable to the four American companies which controlled it." The prospect of losing it also became ever more daunting. But the U.S. government's position vis-à-vis Israel was a continuing source of friction with the Saudi government. According to Standard Oil of California vice chairman George Keller, "We were in a situation where our government's policy in this area was causing almost intolerable aggravation from day to day in our relations with the Saudi Government." Aramco therefore "took steps to create a distinction between the company on the one hand, and the statements and actions of the U.S. Government on the other."[13]

The Aramco public relations office at Dhahran began briefings for

the many U.S. civilian officials, military officers, and corporate executives that visited Aramco each quarter, in the hope that some change
might be effected in U.S. policy and polemic. These stressed the importance of Saudi Arabia to the free world's supply of petroleum. The
briefing would then turn to the strategic importance of Saudi Arabia
to the United States. Emphasizing that through the Nixon government's policy toward Israel, the American image in the Arab world had
reached "an alarming low," the briefer would sum up Aramco's position on the matter:

> One cannot deny however that the history of our policies in the Middle
> East lends substance to the Arab charges of gross partiality and cre-
> dence to their feeling of unjust treatment at the hands of the U.S.
> We have persisted in giving offensive weapons and money to a victori-
> ous Israel and withholding assistance to the defeated. The length to
> which we have gone in giving uncritical support to the policies of the
> Israeli Government has forced even our closest allies such as Great
> Britain to chart independent and differing courses from us. As a direct
> consequence of our identification with Israel, Soviet influence in the
> Middle East — which was practically non-existent in the 1950s — has
> burgeoned.[14]

It was not difficult to prove the preferential treatment extended to
Israel by the United States. While running for office, Nixon had assured a convention of B'nai B'rith that if he was elected, he would
guarantee Israel "a technological military margin to more than offset
her hostile neighbors' immediate superiority." A month later, President Johnson, seeking support for Democratic presidential candidate
Senator Hubert Humphrey, announced that he was authorizing negotiations to supply Israel with fifty Phantom fighter-bombers superior
to any aircraft flown by any Arab state. As president, Nixon called
upon Israel to accept UN Resolution 242, requiring withdrawal inside
the state's pre-1967 boundaries. But in practice Nixon did nothing
when Israel continued to hold the Sinai Peninsula, the Golan Heights,
and the West Bank of the Jordan. To the contrary, Nixon supplied an
impressive array of jet fighters and other military assistance to the
country.[15]

Aramco's briefings would also include mention of King Faisal's
staunch opposition to Communism. This stance truly differentiated
him from other Arab leaders: "Saudi Arabia is the only country in the
Arab League which has no diplomatic relations with any member of
the Communist Bloc and King Faisal is opposed even to trading with
the Communist countries."[16]

Then a series of questions would be posed to the listener. Why should the Saudis increase oil production to meet the needs of the United States, as Washington had requested, while U.S. policy favored Israel, whose presence in Palestine the Saudis simply could not support? King Faisal's pro-American position caused him to be the butt of much criticism in the Arab world — why did the United States continue to put him, their friend, in such a difficult spot by supporting Israel? Then the sensible alternative was suggested: adopting "a neutral position in the Arab-Israeli dispute and a pro-American rather than a pro-Israel policy in the Middle East [which] would enable Faisal to argue that his pro-American policy has at last paid off by persuading the United States to drop its blind unquestioning support of Israel.... [Thus] Saudi Arabia [could] continue strengthening the economic, military and political ties it desires to have with the United States."[17]

Jungers and Powers continued to deal with Yamani in that painful and protracted issue, participation. It was not an amicable affair, and it led to the grand crisis.

After ceding 25 percent of company control, Aramco opened the second set of participation talks with Yamani. They hoped to frustrate his demands for more and more of Aramco. These meetings were held at Yamani's villa in the Lebanese hills in 1972, in the cool, clean air above steamy Beirut. The four representatives of Excom met with Yamani each morning, usually beside his handsome pool. George Piercy of Exxon found Yamani's style agreeable, but ever colored by the threat that, if they failed to make an agreement regarding participation, then the alternative was nationalization. When on one occasion the talks did break down and Piercy said no to one of Yamani's proposals, the meeting ended immediately. Next morning they resumed beside the pool. Yamani repeated the proposals he had made the day before, in the belief that Piercy had thought about the prospect of nationalization during the night. Piercy had done so and, he said, the answer was still no.

> Yamani shrugged and announced, "In that case, there's no reason to continue the meeting." Piercy's response was just to sit there and stare at Yamani. He didn't say a thing. And for the longest time Yamani just sat there and stared at Piercy. He didn't say a thing. Piercy remembers that the silence lasted several minutes. Then, without any mention of the deadlock, without any further threats to abandon the meeting, Yamani simply raised another issue.[18]

Such deadlocks and reengagements characterized the discussions. Piercy believed that, at this point, Yamani himself did not want complete nationalization, but sizable part-ownership. On October 5, 1972,

Aramco reached agreement with Yamani providing for Saudi participation in the established producing concessions. The government's ownership was to rise to 30 percent in 1979 and by 5 percent more each year until 1982; and then it would increase by 6 percent to 51 percent ownership in 1983. To the Aramco delegate this might have seemed a severe defeat, but for one remarkable fact. The oil companies could make huge profits even in adversity; and those adverse conditions accepted during the 1972 negotiations with Yamani were no exception.

Yamani's concession to the Aramco companies was a form of compensation known as "updated book value," to be paid on the oil field installations. He had managed to set in place a scheme for gaining control of Aramco while still keeping its place in the world oil market system. Aramco's parent companies would receive by direct sale a large portion of the government-owned oil, the price being determined in the future marketplace.

The document resulting from these meetings became known as the "General Agreement." The details of the transfer of ownership, the management structure of the concession, and the role of the host government would be left to lawyers to sort out.

The sting in the deal was that, eventually, Aramco would cease to own the majority of Aramco. The company was assuaged by its knowledge that, as the percentage of Saudi ownership in Aramco increased, the Aramco partners would continue to have a preferred right to buy back the Saudi share of Aramco oil. Their gain was likely to be huge, for prices were increasing all the time, and the Aramco board had already approved budgetary plans to increase production to 13.4 million barrels a day by 1976. It was, too, planning a major expansion to 20 million barrels a day by 1983.

> The Aramco partners could expect that an Aramco producing at 20 million barrels a day would so dominate the world of oil that their market shares would not only be protected but also would be increased as well — as long as they could buy back the increasing Saudi participation share of the Aramco oil. For the Aramco partners, the primary negotiating objective of the participation negotiations was ensuring their continued exclusive access to the Saudi participation crude.[19]

But the problem concerning Israel remained unresolved. War was still in the air when, on May 3, 1973, King Faisal arrived at the Hotel Intercontinental at Geneva, where Jungers and Excom were meeting with Yamani. The king's appearance, something of a surprise to Jungers, might have been related to his recent meeting with President Sadat of Egypt, at which Sadat had revealed his plans to launch the fourth

Arab-Israeli war. Without mentioning the date on which the Egyptian and Syrian armies would attack, he had requested financial assistance from Faisal.

Yamani told Jungers that the king wished to speak to him. Jungers agreed. The king appeared from the gloom of the hotel's vast marble halls, in his magnificent robes. Jungers may or may not have been surprised by the king's statement that war was coming and that he wished to protect Aramco from the inevitable Arab wrath when it did. In general, Jungers respected Faisal, but noted that the king incorrectly believed that Aramco was all-powerful in U.S. government circles. Overall Jungers thought that

> [the King] was really quite sophisticated. In the very early days, he had participated in the founding of the [United Nations]. [In the Hejaz] he had been minister of state, so he was quite knowledgeable on foreign affairs . . . but as he became more and more disenchanted on the Israeli subject, he became at times almost irrational. . . . He became obsessed with the idea that Zionism and communism were conspiring together to create the Israeli turmoil.[20]

When Jungers met with Faisal, representatives of Exxon, Chevron, Mobil, and Texaco, and Joe Johnston, Excom's secretary, were also present. They had been discussing oil prices with Yamani. With the king was a member of the Sudairi Seven, Prince Sultan, the Saudi minister of defense. Faisal expounded on his Communist-Zionist theory and then warned Excom that "only in Saudi Arabia were U.S. interests in the Middle East relatively safe," but that "even in his Kingdom it would be more and more difficult to hold off the tide of opinion" about the U.S. government's support for Israel. The king then stated that Aramco's concession would be in danger unless the United States changed its Middle East policy. As Jungers recalled, the king claimed that "the [Aramco] companies were doing nothing, and we would live to regret it."[21]

Faisal explained his reasons for taking such a strong line: the Saudis would "find themselves becoming more isolated in the Arab world and they cannot permit this to happen and therefore American interests in the area must be removed." The king concluded with the gravest words: "Action must be taken urgently; otherwise everything will be lost."[22]

Jungers took Faisal seriously. "We had to do something out of the ordinary to at least prove that we were trying. . . . I decided that I was going to go to the United States and see as many chief executives as I could, quickly." His purpose would be to influence government policy to lessen support of Israel and thereby allow Faisal to remain pro-American without incurring the wrath of his fellow Arabs.

Jungers truly went on a whirlwind tour:

> I saw, I believe, thirty-eight chief executives in a matter of days. Maybe it was more than that. We were in New York, Detroit, Milwaukee, San Francisco, Los Angeles, Dallas, Houston, and met with them. We had breakfast with Henry Ford and Tom Murphy, the chairman of General Motors; I met with the chairman of IBM. We picked the biggest banks and the biggest industrials. . . . Included were General Electric; . . . all of the banks including the Bank of America and . . . Citicorp.[23]

Most of the people that Jungers saw were sympathetic. "Many of them made statements in newspaper ads, and they took flak for it. Mobil took a very active role, and Otto Miller, the chairman of Chevron, wrote a very strong letter to all of the shareholders on this subject." Of course, "the reaction was very bad against him. . . . There were all kinds of negative reactions in the press over it." In all these efforts, Jungers tried to convey this simple message: "Oil was important to the United States" and the U.S. policy of supporting Israel was not "even-handed." Jungers's campaign "was very much pro-Arab and it was very much a protest."[24]

Meanwhile, Aramco's large public relations apparatus was at work. Directors visited Washington to present the king's message to a succession of high officials and to the president. But they failed to persuade the Washington polity that U.S. Middle East policy endangered the Aramco concession.

On his return to Riyadh, Jungers sought and obtained an immediate audience with the king. He related whom he had seen and what he had said. "How did they react?" the king asked. Jungers replied that the corporate chiefs had responded very well. He noted the efforts of the shareholder companies, especially Mobil. But Jungers noted that "the king was very probing about which ones weren't cooperative. I tried to just simply not answer that question."

> The king did get out of me who was the most cooperative and who were the least cooperative. And this trip got a lot of bad press for me and for Aramco as well. I think a lot of people, including some of our State Department friends, thought it was a poorly advised move on my part.[25]

In these circumstances, Jungers authorized his chief negotiator to ask for a meeting with Yamani to discuss the problems that existed between the Saudi government and Aramco. At those meetings in August 1973, in San Francisco, Yamani offered little encouragement. Yamani stated that the next change in the price of oil "would be a very large one." It would be "imposed rather than negotiated"; OPEC would insist "on very high prices leaving the companies no real choice" but to pay up. As if this was not threatening news, Yamani began a discussion of "the stability" of the participation agreement. He reviewed "developments" since the signing of the General Agreement in terms that suggested he was uttering a warning: stop backing the Israelis or face a shutdown in the oil fields.[26]

The renegotiations concerning participation opened in September 1973. On September 17, at San Francisco, discussions about the oil buy-back price grew complicated. But before Aramco could respond to the new prices stipulated by the Saudis, Yamani, always superb at tactics, vanished. He took off in his private jet and left the country.

The fourth Arab-Israeli war — "The October War" — broke out on October 3, 1973. To obtain maximum surprise, the Egyptian and Syrian armies attacked Israel during Ramadan, the month of prayer and fasting in the Arab states, and on the Day of Atonement, the holiest day of the Jewish calendar. The Israelis were taken by surprise. The Egyptian army succeeded in breaching Israel's defensive line in the Sinai. The Arab armies inflicted a large loss of life and equipment, and, consequently, touched off a great crisis in Israel.

On October 6, 1973, OPEC met at Vienna with Aramco and the other major Western oil companies. The Arab representatives were excited and emboldened by what appeared to be an Egyptian victory. The purpose of the meeting was to raise again the price of crude; and Aramco's negotiators, George Piercy of Exxon and Andre Benard of Shell, displayed all the unease of men dealt a weak hand. Not only were they on the defensive in regard to the price range for a barrel of oil and bruised by Yamani's sudden departure from San Francisco, but also they were aware that at any moment "the oil weapon" might descend on them. The gap between what Yamani and his colleagues in OPEC wanted, and what Aramco and the other Western majors were prepared to pay, was huge. There was no deal.

To recover something from the wreckage, in the early hours of October 12, Piercy and Benard went to see Yamani in his suite at the hotel. He was courteous enough. He ordered a Coke for Piercy, cut a lime, and squeezed it into the drink. He gave Piercy the Coke, but neither Piercy or Benard could give him anything on the price question. "They won't like this," said Yamani. He went to the telephone to talk to someone in Baghdad and spoke in Arabic for some time. When he finished he told his visitors: "They're mad at you." The session ended, and as Piercy rose to leave he asked what would happen next. "Listen to the radio," Yamani replied mischievously.[27]

They did, and they learned that OPEC in Kuwait had raised the price of a barrel of oil by 70 percent, to $5.11 a barrel — and this was only the beginning. Daniel Yergin, the U.S. oil historian, related that

> the significance of the action was twofold — in the price increase, and in the unilateral way it had been imposed. The pretense that the exporters would negotiate with the companies was now past. They had taken complete charge of setting the price of oil. The transition was now complete from the days when the companies had unilaterally set the price, to the days when the exporters had at least obtained a veto to this new assumption of sole suzerainty by the exporters.[28]

Yamani left Geneva for Kuwait and there he remarked to a colleague in OPEC: "This is a moment for which I have been waiting for a long time. The moment has come. We are masters of our own commodity."[29] Jungers was summoned to Yamani's ministry in Riyadh. Was this the moment when Yamani would announce the nationalization of Aramco? Or would he demand 100 percent participation?

Yamani had something completely different in mind. Referring to reports that the Nixon government had begun to resupply the Israeli army, Yamani announced his news peremptorily when Jungers arrived: "It's a boycott." King Faisal spelled out the reason for imposing an embargo: "In view of the increase of American military aid to Israel, the Kingdom of Saudi Arabia has decided to halt all oil exports to the United States."[30] Yamani traveled immediately to Dhahran and, far exceeding his authority, began to issue orders to Jungers. The shipment of all oil and products to the United States and the Netherlands was to be terminated, he announced. All shipments on the high seas were to be ordered to put in at other ports, which Yamani named. And as Jungers recorded the complicated arrangements that Yamani insisted on:

> At the head of the list were The Netherlands, and the United States, and so on. Then there were degrees of boycott. It got more and more complicated as the countries who were boycotted or who were about to be boycotted made their way to Saudi Arabia and pled their case and the degree of the boycott changed. We were given day-by-day instructions of what the boycott order was and who could buy what. . . . So we set up a system that determined where the oil actually ended up, every barrel . . . we knew exactly where every barrel went, and monitored it. This was under threat of complete Nationalization. There was no doubt about this. And we [obeyed] in order not to give them [the chance of nationalization]. We had no choice.[31]

At that moment the American company Aramco became the instrument of a foreign power, Saudi Arabia. Jungers complied with Yamani's wishes because "he warned that noncompliance would mean Nationalization 'at gunpoint.' Aramco acquiesced, justifying its decision as benefiting the United States since Nationalization would have jeopardized free world petroleum supply." And as Jungers argued in a memo to President Nixon, the embargo was better than nationalization, because nationalization would lead the Europeans and the Japanese "to expand their Middle East supply positions at our expense."[32]

So serious were Israel's losses in the Sinai that President Nixon authorized the Pentagon to begin a major air lift to the Israelis; and at the same time, to warn the Soviets, who were resupplying the Egyptians, Nixon placed U.S. forces on worldwide alert. That news placed a grave responsibility on Jungers.

On October 21, 1973, King Faisal extended the embargo to the U.S. Sixth Fleet in the Mediterranean. But that was not all. Soon the Saudis instructed Aramco to stop all supplies to the U.S. military. This prospect had such serious implications that Pentagon staff telephoned the managing director of the main British oil company in the Gulf, requesting that it supply the Sixth Fleet.

Jungers and his colleagues in the oil trade were now "wide open to the charge that had so often been made against them in the past — that they put profits before patriotism."[33] In New York City, official home of Excom,

> it was all too evident that Aramco was carrying out the instructions of a foreign government, and however much they insisted that they had no alternative, they had few public figures on their side. In the midst of the most Jewish city, they stood out as a pro-Arab enclave. The topography seemed symbolic: on one side of Sixth Avenue in Manhattan stood the three skyscrapers of the three TV networks — CBS, NBC, ABC — all of them sympathetic to the Israelis, and deeply critical of the oil companies: Exxon's new skyscrapers and the two floors of Aramco, at Fifty-fourth Street. . . . Aramco appeared an all-powerful supra-government, a consortium of four of the richest companies in the world in league with an alien sovereign state. But the Aramco men in New York saw themselves as persecuted and encircled; anonymous telephone callers rang up with bomb scares to make them troop out of the building, and with threats and insults against the oil traitors. There was little middle ground: each side had its own view of the priorities of foreign policy, and each had a profound distrust of the other.[34]

What Jungers never revealed was that, as the boycott operation began to get underway, he disappeared. He had been ordered to Washington.

> The boycott became a matter of concern, of course, to the Navy. The defense department approached the shareholder companies. It was then a secret that the navy needed oil and I was asked by the sharehold-

ers through [the Secretary of Excom] Joe Johnston to go to Washington to the Defense Department. The boycott was a problem and they wished to talk to me about it.[35]

Jungers met with the secretary of defense, James Schlesinger, and then he had a discussion with the deputy secretary of defense, Bill Clement. He asked Jungers whether he could think of any way to influence the Saudis to lift the embargo. Clements wished to avoid official negotiations.

Even twenty years after the fact, Jungers was extremely reticent about revealing details of his talk with Clements. But there seems to be no doubt that this meeting's focus was the menace of Russian support for the Egyptian army and the defense department's concern about the operational capability of the U.S. Sixth Fleet in the Mediterranean and the U.S. Seventh Fleet in the Pacific Ocean and Indian Ocean. Jungers did say that he flew back to Riyadh immediately and met with King Faisal:

> I explained to the king that this was a real problem and I understood his thinking, but if and when there was [to be] a shift in the Israeli policy of the United States, it certainly couldn't happen tomorrow. He was certainly aware that diplomatically these things took some time and that this was a matter that was more urgent and could be of serious consequence to the Middle East if not to the kingdom.
> The king listened carefully and he said, "Are you telling me that this approach is not instigated by the oil companies?"
> I said, "No, it's not." He well understood then that while I wasn't a designated emissary from the U.S. government, that was where it had come from.
> So he said, "Well, I really don't know how you are going to do this." And he said this in such a way that led me to believe that he wouldn't make an issue of it.
> It was up to me and [Faisal said] "God help you if you get caught, or if it becomes a public issue."[36]

Thus Jungers took it upon himself to circumvent the Saudi ban on oil to the U.S. fleets. He never revealed just how he did this. He dissembled a great deal, saying only that "we did figure out some ways to do this, and it was done. Everyone was happy and not a word was ever said and it was, of course, a secret thing for years afterward."[37]

Brock Powers, Aramco's president during the embargo period, did have more to say, although only reluctantly: "I was intimately involved with it and the decision making that went on at that time." He made this statement about the emergency shipments of oil to U.S. naval bases all over the globe:

I don't know enough about them to tell you. I know that's one thing that never surfaced. I know that the [Saudi] Government would have been highly embarrassed if it had surfaced, because here they are embargoing the United States, and still allowing shipment of fuel to the United States Navy, and on the same basis as before. There were explicit instructions; we got those instructions. They came verbally, but they came.[38]

Though shrouded in secrecy, this partial lifting of the embargo did show that Faisal did not intend to make difficulties for the U.S. Navy as it attempted to hamper Russian military operations in the eastern Mediterranean.

At that point another factor entered into the price war going on inside and outside of OPEC — the conflict between Saudi Arabia and Iran. It was an outgrowth of the sometimes violent relations between the Sunni Muslims (of Saudi Arabia) and the Shiite Muslims (of Iran). These two branches of Islam diverged in disagreement concerning who were the true successors to the Prophet Muhammad. The sectarian conflict was reflected in the antagonism between the Saudi dynasty and its king, Faisal, and the shah of Iran. The old rivalry reappeared in the form of an oil price war. As Brock Powers recorded,

There was such a tug-of-war going on between Iran and Saudi Arabia, each trying to outdo the other. . . . Out-charge, out-earn the other, not necessarily out-produce, but charge more, and of course, when Iran jacked up the prices, why, Saudi Arabia said, "Now, we've got to jack them up too."[39]

Excom unfortunately believed that Powers could intervene and prevent price escalation by talking with the Saudis. But at this point the balance of power had tipped in favor of the Saudi government, although "the oil companies refused to recognize that for literally years and years and years." "Their empire was coming apart" but "they still refused to recognize where the real power lay" — with the king, Yamani, and the supporters of participation.[40] Excom still believed it could fight off participation, though Powers and others knew that it had become simply a fact of life.

In the meantime, a fantastic boom in production had been achieved in order to meet the shareholder companies' demands for oil. Jungers managed to increase production by three million barrels a day. Aramco's field crews drilled a new well every other day. Construction teams began work on a huge new port to support Ras Tanura, soon to become the largest oil-loading dock in the world. During 1974, each

month Excom met to pay the Saudi government and the parent companies their share of the profits. Aramco's treasurer paid more than
$2.2 billion of Aramco's receipts in one month. The payment went
into Aramco's accounts at the First National City Bank, Chase Manhattan, and Morgan Guaranty, all in New York City. He also paid Saudi
Arabia's royalties and taxes into the government's accounts with the
same banks.

In reference to such huge revenues, *The Economist* of London made
these observations about OPEC:

> With their surplus of some $60 billion in 1974 they took in $164
> million more each day and $6.8 million more each hour than, by the
> best estimates, they can currently spend. At that rate OPEC could buy
> out companies on the world's major stock exchanges in 15.6 years (at
> present quotations), all companies on the New York Stock Exchange
> in 9.2 years, all central banks' gold (at $170 an ounce) in 3.2 years,
> all U.S. direct estimates abroad in 1.8 years, all companies quoted on
> stock exchanges in Britain, France and West Germany in 1.7 years, all
> IBM stock in 79 days, the Rockefeller family's wealth in 6 days, and
> 14% of Germany's Daimler-Benz in two days.[41]

Commentary in *Time* magazine placed the new wealth of the Middle
East in historical perspective:

> 1974 [was] a pivotal year that saw the decline of old powers, old alli-
> ances, old philosophies and the rise of new ones. The West's belief in
> the inevitability of human progress and material growth was badly
> shaken as inflation spread oppressively across the world, several indus-
> trial societies tumbled into recession and famine plagued a score of
> nations. There was a marked erosion in the wealth, might, cohesive-
> ness of North America, Europe and Japan. In the developing world, 40
> or more countries with few natural resources fell increasingly into
> destitution and dependency. Meanwhile, a handful of resource-rich
> nations gravely compounded the problems and challenged the vital
> interests of the rest of the world by skillfully wielding a most potent
> weapon: the power of oil.[42]

At one point, David Rockefeller of Chase Manhattan arrived in
Dhahran to discuss the world as Jungers and Aramco saw it. He asked,
"Where are we headed with this terrible thing? I think I can make
a case for saying that this was the beginning of the downfall in the
world's banking." As wealth was radically redistributed, the banks were
challenged by "the amount of money required to just move this oil
and to pay for it and to recirculate the money and get the money back
in place."[43]

As oil production increased and the price of oil rose, mammoth amounts of money were indeed changing hands monthly. Jungers gave details on how challenging it was to keep up:

> In Aramco alone our production went over 10 million barrels a day at that time. . . . The prices had gotten as high as $30 [per barrel]. . . . 10 million barrels a day times $30 is $300 million a day that had to flow to Aramco in payment for oil that was lifted offshore by the shareholder off-takers. We were on a forty-five-day payment schedule, so ten days is $3 billion, thirty days is $9 billion, and forty-five days is $13.5 billion that had to change hands all at one time.
>
> The shareholders had to pay it; which caused them large liquidity problems. We had to collect it, we had to give part of it to the government and immediately declare a dividend, and all of this had to happen simultaneously. . . . So these transactions happened quickly with everybody's banks alerted, the buyers' banks, the Saudis' banks, all were alerted, and this money had to change hands immediately and simultaneously to minimize cash movements to banks, some of which serviced more than one party.[44]

The banks were placed in a tough spot concerning the vast royalty deposits they were holding for the Saudis and other Middle Eastern parties. Indeed, the Saudis intended to use the funds for a variety of projects, but the banks had no idea how soon they would withdraw them. Should the banks invest the vast funds, or did they need to remain liquid? There was no plan in place, because such a phenomenon had not happened before. In Jungers's opinion, the banks made some poor choices, such as making overly risky loans to certain developing countries, which eventually had to be written off.

The boom in oil production and the price wars in some ways backfired on the OPEC members, despite the exponential increase in their wealth. Jungers had tried to caution the Saudis about driving up prices too quickly, warning them about the effects of inflation: "You are getting more dollars but this has got to become an inflated dollar, and you really aren't going to have any more value than you previously had; you've just raised the price of everything proportionately with oil." He also noted that the OPEC nations virtually jump-started the alternative energy industry, a direct competitor to the oil producers, and they also inspired the energy conservation movement. They had simply made oil too costly, and people naturally sought other alternatives.[45]

In Washington, meanwhile, certain parties advocated a direct means of regaining control of oil pricing and the Saudi oil fields — war. But such a plan entailed such high risks that it was never seriously considered:

There is always the danger that the Soviets would step in on the side of the Arabs — or extract a high political price from the West for staying out. Pipelines might be vulnerable to sabotage, though captured oil fields could be fairly easily protected. In any event, U.S. authorities condemn the wave of fantasizing about oil wars as "highly irresponsible." Military intervention, says a Washington policymaker, would be considered "only as a last resort to prevent the collapse of the industrialized world and not just to get the oil price down."[46]

The Saudis had heard of such plans and scorned them, though such rumors did make them uncomfortable. Yamani found the reports disturbing; it "seriously worried him that anyone could even suggest it. All the more so because desperate people sometimes do desperate things." He believed such an attempt would have been futile: "An invasion of the oilfields would have been suicide. From a practical viewpoint it was impossible. . . . If you know where the oilfields are, you know why. They are scattered in the desert with so many installations that you'd need a few hundred thousand troops to take them." But Yamani's opinion was not shared by all. According to one source, "the American military was crawling with men who not only thought that America could manage it, but were anxious to give it a try." But this opportunity would never come to pass.[47]

The worth of all this is hard to gauge. Barger, in retirement in La Jolla, California, wrote a long article for the *Los Angeles Times* — one published on its op-ed page — that showed oil fields cannot be easily destroyed on the ground or from the air — after the USAF's heavy raids, the Ploesti oil fields in Rumania were put back to work with surprising speed. Yet there may have been something to the story.

Defense Secretary James Schlesinger related how and why the war story got started:

> The Arabs were pretty pissed at me, but if you go back and read my press conferences at the time you'll see that someone asked, if the President orders you to do so, can you seize the oilfields? To such a question I would answer yes. Kissinger then got onto this business of "strangulation," if you recall. It was one of his geo-political observations. Something like, a great power cannot allow strangulation to occur by a lesser power without being prepared to take action. He told me to climb in behind him and the President and I was prepared to do so under those circumstances. But I don't think anyone else was serious about this.
>
> . . . I was prepared to seize Abu Dhabi. Something small. But nothing big. Militarily we could have seized one of the Arab states. And the plan did indeed scare them and anger them. No, it wasn't just bravado. It was clearly intended as a warning. I think the Arabs were quite worried

about it after '73. Then the whole thing receded and all that was left
was a kind of residual anger. I never detected any seriousness on the
part of anybody. I was more willing to contemplate it than others were
but it was never serious.[48]

Yet plans for military intervention were never entirely scrapped during this period. Not only might they become necessary as a stratagem
to bring Saudi Arabian oil production and pricing under U.S. control,
but also might need to be implemented if the Saudi oil fields happened
to fall into hostile hands. U.S. forces were prepared to protect U.S.
interests in Saudi Arabia by supporting King Faisal against enemies —
and he did not lack enemies. If such exigencies had arisen, it is likely
that the United States would have made a military response.

U.S. secretary of state Henry Kissinger flew to Riyadh to discuss with
Faisal the lifting of the oil embargo. This would entail, of course,
bringing up the issue of U.S. policy in Israel. Among the reporters
present were Marvin and Bernard Kalb, and they described the first
meeting between Kissinger and Faisal:

> Through the incense, Kissinger could see the King seated on his
> throne at the far end of the room. Two tall guards in black robes
> and black and white kaffiyahs [headdresses], each carrying a Saracen
> sword, led Kissinger towards Faisal. The Secretary shook his hand. The
> King smiled faintly. Kissinger sat down next to Faisal. He then noticed
> that, on both sides of the room, there were dozens of royal princes, all
> in black robes, many wearing sunglasses, some sipping coffee. Kissin-
> ger, at the King's request, got up and shook hands with every single
> Prince. Then Kissinger and the King agreed to meet privately after
> dinner. The meeting lasted two hours.[49]

Kissinger "tried to impress the King with his seriousness and sincerity." He had read, he told King Faisal, all the king's correspondence
with Presidents Kennedy, Johnson, and Nixon. Kissinger acknowledged that, on the basis of that record, the king had "good grounds
for being disappointed in American policy." Johnson had promised
the king that Israel would withdraw from the Arab lands occupied in
the 1967 war. UN Resolution 242 had urged such a withdrawal. Even
Nixon had urged it. President Nixon was "committed" to an Israeli
withdrawal, and Kissinger said he was "personally convinced" that a
settlement was now possible. He appealed for Faisal's cooperation.
Would the king support a peace conference? Yes, Faisal replied. Would
the king support a lifting of the oil embargo? That was "critically important" because its continuation would serve to "generate anti-Arab

sentiment in the United States" and complicate his "efforts to induce a gradual Israeli withdrawal from occupied lands."[50]

The king began to speak and Kissinger listened carefully. Faisal described himself as "fiercely anti-Communist and anti-Zionist." He accused the Jews of "aggression and expansionism," noting that he believed them to be responsible for the Communist revolution in Russia. Their actions in Israel were but the latest evidence of their avarice for power. But, Faisal said, he would "stop them with his oil weapon."[51]

Faisal believed that the Jews should give up all Arab lands, including Jerusalem. Faisal himself wished, before he died, to walk to the Dome of the Rock in Jerusalem (the third most holy place in Islam) without treading on Israeli-occupied territory. He told Kissinger that he wanted Jerusalem to become an Arab Islamic city again. When Kissinger noted that the Jews considered the Wailing Wall equally holy, Faisal brushed him off, stating that another wall could be built somewhere else against which the Jews could wail.

Faisal was adamant: "After so many disappointments in the past he would use his oil weapon until he compelled the Israelis to withdraw from Jerusalem." Did that mean, Kissinger asked, that the oil embargo would not be lifted until Jerusalem was recovered by the Arabs? Faisal's answer was ambiguous, and the conference came to an end. Kissinger peered again through the "cloud of incense" to admire a painting on a wall and asked, "Is that the Arabian Desert, Your Majesty?" "No," he replied. "That is our holy oasis." Kissinger apologized for the mistake. Later he said, "I guess I set back the lifting of the oil embargo by at least one month with that one comment."[52]

Although Kissinger was optimistic, as far as the king was concerned, the United States could wait for an end to the embargo until the occupation of Jerusalem was lifted. And as everyone knew, that might take forever.

[14]

REGICIDE

A T NOON ON MARCH 25, 1975, Jungers was at his quarters in the senior staff compound at Dhahran when he received a call from a protocol officer in Riyadh. The conversation was as follows:

"Frank, we need an airplane right away and we need doctors right away."
I said, "What kind of doctors? What's happened?"
He said, "Frank, think of the worst. It's happened."
I said, "Really? How did it happen?"
"He was shot."
"What kind of doctors do you need?"
"I don't know. We need them and we need them right away. And we need them over here by air."[1]

By the time the doctors arrived, it was too late. The king had died. The gunman was a nephew of Faisal. Jungers knew what to do next.

I called the protocol office again and said that I would like to come over [to Riyadh] and pay respects to the family. I realized that this would be an unusual time and there would be other heads of state and whatnot that would have to be accommodated, but I wanted to come at the most appropriate time, and would he please let me know? He said: "I sure will. I'll get with the family and we'll let you know as soon as we can."
They called the next morning and said, "Would you come over now? Be here by noon." I said, "Sure, you bet."[2]

Since the Saudi custom was to bury their dead on the day of death, Jungers expected that Faisal had already been interred and that he would be received by a member of the family, present his respects, and then leave. But it did not happen that way. Having collected his interpreter, Majed Elass, they flew to Riyadh. They were "escorted into the city square area that had been set up with tents and seating and told to wait." Soon a number of heads of state arrived. "Among them was Idi Amin, the eccentric and murderous dictator of Uganda." The Lebanese president, the king of Jordan, and representatives of Western governments also were present. The only other American on hand was the U.S. ambassador.

> We were all sitting quietly when all of a sudden the gates burst open and we went in. People were running in and the man from protocol came and grabbed me and said, "Follow me quickly. Get ahead of everybody." So I followed and came upon the slab with the king lying on it with a cloth over him. . . . They hadn't buried him. This was most unusual. Unprecedented.[3] Jungers paid his respects to some of Faisal's sons, who were weeping, and then was respectfully asked to leave. The protocol officers told him that some prayers would be said in the mosque, and that Faisal would be buried in the desert. As Jungers was not a Muslim, he could not be present at these events.

The king's death produced a worldwide investigation by the Saudis and the CIA. Rumors of an international plot to murder King Faisal circulated. The assassin, Prince Faisal ibn Musaid, had resented his uncle's rule ever since the incident related to the Riyadh television station, at which his older brother had been shot and killed by the king's security service.

On the night of March 24, 1975, Prince Faisal drank whiskey and played cards with one of his brothers, Prince Bandar, and some friends. He went to his room alone before midnight and remained there until he rose and went to King Faisal's palace at about 10:00 A.M. the next day. As a royal prince, he gained admittance and waited in an anteroom outside the king's audience chamber. A delegation that included the Kuwaiti oil minister was waiting to have an audience with King Faisal. The Saudi oil minister, Sheikh Yamani, was also present. Yamani went into the chamber to brief the king before the meeting with the Kuwaiti minister. King Faisal's chief of protocol went in with Yamani to announce his nephew's presence — it was not customary for the king to see relatives during business hours.

During that brief period, Prince Faisal found that he knew the young Kuwaiti oil minister, Abdul Mutalib al-Qasimi. He had met Prince Faisal in Colorado. When the king's chamber doors were opened for Qasimi, Prince Faisal entered with him. Yamani, who was standing next to the king, and a television crew filming the king's reception of the oil delegation were horrified spectators of the assassination. As King Faisal moved forward to embrace his nephew, Prince Faisal produced a pistol from under his robes and shot his uncle three times at short range. The first bullet entered the king's body under the chin, the second pierced one of the king's ears, and the third grazed the king's forehead. The prince then fired three more shots in the direction of Yamani, who was not hit.

The king was still alive when he arrived at the hospital, but he died there within the hour. An artery in his neck had been torn, and neither surgery nor blood transfusions could save him. When the official announcement of Faisal's death was broadcast, there was shock throughout Saudi Arabia and instant alarm abroad concerning the stability of the kingdom on which the West had become so dependent. The need to reassure the world concerning the succession was recognized by the senior members of the family. They conferred with the Wahhabi divines and then prepared their announcement.

By 12:20 GMT they had made their decision, and at that hour the proclamation was uttered. Crown Prince Khalid would succeed as king, and his crown prince would be Fahd, a member of the Sudairi Seven. Arrangements were then made for the royal family to make the oath of allegiance to the new king and crown prince, over Faisal's corpse. Jungers was present for this part of the ceremony. Within little over three hours since Faisal's death, the first of the princes of the blood had taken the oath of allegiance to Khalid:

> "I give my loyalty to you, O! Khalid, in the name of God and in the name of His Prophet."

Crown Prince Fahd then made his oath to the new king. So did all the princes, all the tribal chiefs, ministers, the civil service, the heads of the family, and the military chiefs. The burial took place on the following day as mentioned earlier.

Then the Saudis and the world community took stock of Faisal's reign. King Faisal had saved the kingdom. When he took power in 1962, the dynasty's days had seemed numbered. The talk then was all of Nasser and of republics. But Faisal had unified the dynasty, and then, with a mixture of daring, discipline, and force of character, he had united the kingdom as well. The sense of loss was very great. Faisal's "golden age" was at an end. The kingdom had lost a leader who had made the whole world tremble. Whereas Ibn Saud had created the kingdom, Faisal had made it into a modern state. And a prosperous one.

Under Faisal, the currency had been sound and the treasury in surplus. That constituted a remarkable change of pace for Saudi Arabia. In the fiscal year 1975 Aramco would pay the Saudi government $25 billion in royalties and taxes. The Saudi oil business was succeeding in every way. Profits were gargantuan, and the Saudis had gained greater control of their resources by way of participation in Aramco. Oil wealth could sustain the Saudi economy well into the future — to date, Aramco had produced a total of 27 billion barrels, which, added to the estimated reserves of 175 billion barrels, showed that all oil discoveries had totaled over 200 billion barrels.

During this time of mourning, the dynasty turned to the interrogation of Prince Faisal, the murderer. The senior princes wished to be sure that King Faisal had not been the victim of a feud or a conspiracy. Consequently, the Saudi security and intelligence authorities, with the help of the CIA, cast a wide net of inquiries. Was the prince in fact deranged? Was he merely the triggerman in a foreign conspiracy to kill King Faisal? The first announcement of the king's death had described Prince Faisal as "mentally deranged." A few days later, King Khalid, in an interview with the *Daily Star* of Beirut, said that the killing had been "an isolated act by a deranged person without any foreign scheming." Doctors in Beirut were quoted as saying that the prince had been under treatment there for drug addiction and alcoholism. Under the shariah code, if insanity was proved, then the assassin would be spared the death penalty.[4]

Prince Faisal was agitated and nervous during the first two weeks of the interrogation. He was not told of Faisal's death, and his interrogators left him with the impression that the king was still alive, recovering from his wounds. Questioning

> elicited little from the prince other than a confession, a contempt for all his uncle had stood for, not least the Islamic faith, and also an implacable resolve to kill him. Then about a fortnight after the assassination he was shown a film of the funeral. On seeing it he became completely serene and at peace with himself.[5]

The authorities were convinced that the prince had committed the murder deliberately and in his right mind. Therefore Prince Faisal was beheaded in public in Riyadh on June 18, eighty-five days after the king's murder. The execution was witnessed by a crowd of twenty thousand. The formal announcement spoke of his rejection of the true faith, and for good measure, the Saudi press agency added that the investigation had shown "no external motive for the crime."[6]

In certain circles of Washington, reservations about the qualifications of King Khalid and Crown Prince Fahd were expressed. But Aramco seemed secure. The United States had received guarantees that Saudi oil would be available to them for the rest of the century, perhaps even to the end of the twenty-first century. In May 1975, President Carter gave a White House dinner for Crown Prince Fahd, Sheikh Yamani, and other prominent Saudis. Yamani undertook to keep oil abundant and prices stable. In return Carter elevated the Saudis to the top rung of world politics when he declared that

> Saudi Arabia is a nation which has grown in many ways in the last few years in world importance. Their supplies of energy are crucial to the well-being of people in many nations. They produce their own oil for world consumption beyond which perhaps would be best for them. The wealth that has flowed to Saudi Arabia from these sales has been invested around the world in a very responsible and productive way. This responsible and unselfish action has saved the entire economic structure of the world from disruption.[7]

Not since Roosevelt's visit with Ibn Saud in Egypt in 1945 had an American president spoken such honeyed words to a Saudi Arab. In his reply to the president's toast, Crown Prince Fahd declared, "Both the United States of America and the Kingdom of Saudi Arabia follow a free economic system that seeks the well-being of man, not only in their respective countries but also in the world at large."[8]

These pretty speeches masked the conflict that still dogged the heels of U.S.-Saudi relations. The Americans and the Saudis still disagreed profoundly on the issue of U.S. support for Israel. Still, the Saudi government and Aramco were moving ahead on the largest industrial enterprise since the building of the pyramids of Egypt. With Aramco employees involved as planners, consultants, investors, and builders, the Saudi government had decided to spend $141 billion to build new ports, new refineries, new housing complexes, a new petrochemical system, and a large electrification program that would extend through the holy land from the Gulf to the Red Sea. Progress was occurring despite the unresolved problem of U.S. support of Israel.

On the morning of December 21, 1975, Yamani and the rest of the OPEC ministers arrived at OPEC headquarters on the Dr. Karl Luger–Ringstrasse, the ring road around the medieval heart of Vienna. That Sunday morning holiday lights and Christmas trees twinkled in the gloom. There were only a few cars and a few people out and about on the Dr. Karl Luger–Ringstrasse when Yamani and the other delegates bounded up the staircase to the large conference room. They had come from all parts of the world in their corporate jets. On the agenda were questions concerning price differentials and the establishment of the OPEC special fund to provide interest-free loans to developing nations.

The delegates were vigorously debating price differentials when gunshots were fired outside the conference room. There was a commotion, and six persons burst into the room. Leading them was a young man with a goatee and moustache, a brown leather jacket, and a brown beret. One of the group was a woman with a gray wool cap pulled down to her eyebrows. When another of the party, a man with a German accent, destroyed the telephone switchboard with gunfire, a police officer tried to seize his gun. The girl shouted at the officer and then put her gun under his chin. She pulled the trigger. She was identified later as the terrorist Gabrielle Krocher-Tiederman, leader of a German Marxist terrorist group. Another member of the gang began rolling live hand grenades down the staircase to keep the police at bay.

The leader ordered the conference members to lie on the floor, and Yamani and some colleagues crawled under a table. The gang leader, Ilich Ramirez Sanchez, alias Carlos, a young international assassin with a Venezuelan passport, produced a flashlight and shone it into the faces of Yamani and his group. When his eyes met Yamani's, he gave a little salute and then told his colleagues that he had found Yamani, who then realized that he was the target and probably about to die. Outside, sirens wailed as the Viennese police's antiterrorist team arrived. Carlos then deputed an Iraqi member of OPEC to act as intermediary between himself and the Austrian government.

A long siege then began. By way of the Iraqi, Carlos instructed the police to tell the Austrian chancellor, Dr. Bruno Kreisky, that he had taken the eleven OPEC ministers hostage, and had certain demands to present to the Austrian government. Kreisky was skiing in the mountains that weekend, but immediately returned to Vienna for an emergency meeting with his cabinet. Already three persons had been killed, and two wounded.

The OPEC ministers had been seized by the most wanted man in Europe. The son of a rich lawyer and leading Marxist, Carlos had been trained in revolutionary warfare by Soviet and Cuban experts near Havana. He went to university in Moscow. He had spent time in London, where he posed as a Latin American socialite, and then he went on to Jordan or Beirut for indoctrination by the Palestine Front for the Liberation of Palestine.

Carlos had undertaken at least five major operations in Europe: he had bombed Le Drugstore in Paris, killing two people and wounding thirty-four others; he had laid siege to the French embassy in Holland; he had made a bazooka attack on a DC9 at Orly Airport near Paris; he had forced his way into the London home of Lord Sieff, a leading British Zionist and head of the Marks & Spencer stores, and nearly succeeded in killing him; and he had killed three French secret service agents. He had a long list of future targets, and Yamani was one of them.

Shortly, the Saud dynasty learned why Carlos had chosen Yamani as a target. Carlos had prepared a manifesto in which he demanded that the riches produced by Arab oil be used to benefit the Arab people only. He especially condemned all those who in any way abetted Zionism. According to the manifesto, both Saudi Arabia and Iran, through their dealings with the pro-Israel U.S. government, were guilty of this offense.

In the conference room Carlos separated the OPEC people into a number of groups. One consisted of Yamani, some of his Saudi associates and their colleagues of Iran, the United Arab Emirates, and Qatar. Carlos termed these "the criminal group." The Iraqis, the Libyans, the Algerians, and the Kuwaitis they classified as "liberals and semiliberals"; the other delegates were designated as "neutrals." Carlos then wrote a note to the Austrian government, insisting that this "political statement" be broadcast by the Austrian Radio Service. If it was not, then he would start to execute his hostages, beginning with Yamani's deputy. Next he would kill the deputy of the Iranian finance minister. Third, he would kill Jamshid Amouzegar, the Iranian finance minister. Next in line was Yamani. If the Austrian government had not met his demands after these four executions, he would blow up the OPEC building. He also required that the following supplies be readied for him:

> (1) A bus with curtained windows to take him and his party to Vienna airport at 7 A.M. the following morning.
> (2) A DC9 with a crew of three must he ready, [fully] fueled to take the group and their hostages to another airport. Carlos did not say which airport.
> (3) He required 24 meters of rope, five pairs of scissors, and several rolls of adhesive tape, 100 sandwiches and as much fruit as the police could acquire.[9]

At about 3:00 P.M., Carlos led Yamani to an empty room. He told Yamani that if the Austrian radio had not broadcasted the statement by 4:30 P.M., then he would be executed at 6:30 P.M. Carlos told Yamani that "he hoped I would not feel bitterness against them because they intended to kill me, and that he expected a man of my intelligence and mind to understand their noble aims and intentions." That was indeed cold comfort.[10]

When the 4:30 P.M. deadline passed without any sign of a radio broadcast, Carlos reminded Yamani of what would befall him if the Austrians had failed to follow his orders by 6:30 P.M.

When the police sent in the sandwiches that Carlos had demanded, some of them were found to contain ham, a meat forbidden to Muslims. So the police went to the Hilton Hotel, which was about to hold a banquet for five hundred people. They persuaded the management to donate enough banquet food to feed Carlos's hostages.

At 6:20 P.M. the Austrians did broadcast the message, but in terrible French, making the original message, which was nearly unintelligible anyway, still more difficult to understand. Yamani was sure he was about to die and comforted himself by reading from the Koran. But some of the hostages, particularly the Iraqi (Riyadh Azzawi) serving as go-between with the Austrian government and the Algerian minister of energy (Belaid Abdul Salem), had been able to exert some influence on Carlos. They persuaded him that the captors and hostages should fly first to Algiers, not to Tripoli, Libya. They knew that the president of Algeria could be expected to work for the release of the hostages. This would not be so with Qaddafi of Libya. The Austrian government had stated that the DC9 would be ready at Vienna airport at daybreak on Monday, and the bus with curtained windows would arrive at the back of the OPEC building at 7:00 A.M.

Their nerves dulled by a sleepless night in OPEC's conference room, the hostages, now numbering forty, were shepherded aboard the bus by Carlos on Monday. The bus then left for the airport — but not with Carlos. He followed in an ambulance carrying the terrorist who had been wounded in the gunplay on Sunday morning. At the airport Carlos shook hands with Austrian officials and waved greetings to the television crews who were broadcasting live. Then the Austrian Airlines DC9 took off at about 9:15 A.M. It did not, it seems, file a flight plan.

By this time, news of the hostage situation had been broadcasted internationally. Frank Jungers of Aramco was so concerned that he instructed the pilot of an Aramco Lear jet to follow the hostages' plane as it took off from Vienna. The Lear jet took off and began to shadow the DC9. The trip to Algiers took about three hours. During the flight Carlos sat down beside Yamani and talked with him. Because he intended to kill Yamani, he felt free to speak openly:

> For instance, he said he thought the Syrians were deviationists and dangerous. He said that he fought in the 1970 civil war between Jordan's King Hussein and the Palestinian commandos but that he had

grown disenchanted with the Arabs. He said he could not understand how the Jordanians could love their king. He seemed very bitter about that. He told me he'd known King Faisal's grandson. You know, I still believe what he told me because it's easy to give your secrets away to someone when you know he won't reveal them.[11]

When the airliner landed, Algerian authorities sought to persuade Carlos to release all the hostages, including Yamani. In return, Carlos was told that he and his group would receive a large ransom. (It was not known who made the offer, but rumors cited either Aramco or the Saudi government.) Carlos thereupon released fifteen of the hostages, including Abdul Salem, the Algerian intermediary, but Carlos refused to release either Yamani or his Iranian colleague, Amouzegar.

Carlos later demanded that the plane depart for Libya. When the DC9 took off on the two-hour flight to Tripoli, there were twenty hostages aboard, including six oil ministers. There it landed and there it remained until the early hours of Tuesday morning, while Carlos spoke with Major Jalloud, Qaddafi's deputy, about obtaining a longer-range aircraft for the next leg of the flight; Carlos intimated that its destination would be Baghdad. But, Carlos complained, Qaddafi had double-crossed them. No such aircraft was available. Enraged, Carlos ordered the DC9 captain to fly to Tunis. But when they arrived, the authorities there refused to allow them to land and switched off all the airport lights. Carlos then ordered the DC9 back to Algiers. There Carlos left the aircraft to speak with the Algerian authorities. He was gone a rather long time.

> When Carlos finally climbed back on board, he was sporting a most disconcerting grin.
>
> Yamani immediately felt that he was hiding something unpleasant.
>
> Carlos went straight to Yamani and Amouzegar and told them both, "I do not know what I should do. I am a democrat and you two do not know the meaning of democracy. I shall have a meeting now with my colleagues and consult them on what to do about your case. I shall inform you about the decision later."
>
> Yamani and Amouzegar could only watch.
>
> When the discussion ended, Carlos came back to Yamani and Amouzegar and lied to them. "We have finally decided to release you by midday. And with that decision your lives are completely out of danger."
>
> Yamani's deputy wanted to know, "Why wait till midday?"
>
> Carlos answered, "Because I want the excitement prolonged until noon." He offered to shut off the cabin lights. "You will sleep peacefully knowing that your lives are no longer in danger."
>
> At this point Gabrielle screamed nastily at Carlos, "Fuck you."
>
> Now Yamani realized this would be his last night alive. "I was certain that they planned to execute us right there in the plane."[12]

Carlos had in fact marked 7:00 A.M. Wednesday morning as the hour for their execution. Then a remarkable intercession occurred. The Algerians had managed to bug the front cabin of the DC9, and they had overheard Carlos and his group discussing what should be done about Yamani and the other hostages. The chief of Algerian security called the plane and spoke with Carlos. He knew, he said, their intentions. He warned that if Carlos killed Yamani, the whole gang would die. Carlos refused to believe the statement, and so the security official put the president of Algeria, Houari Boumedienne, on the line. The ransom again was mentioned. Carlos was heard to say that if he released the hostages, "I won't get the rest of my money."[13]

It is not known whether Aramco's Lear jet was still shadowing the DC9, but it can be safely assumed that it was.

When the conversation with Boumedienne was finished, Carlos went to Yamani and Amouzegar and told them that they were now to be killed and that the decision was final. He then spent a few minutes insulting Yamani, Amouzegar, and the policies of their governments. Just when Yamani and Amouzegar expected to be killed, Carlos suddenly left the aircraft with his gang, announcing that the hostages were free. Incredulous, Yamani and Amouzegar rose and, spotting the Algerian foreign minister approaching, they, too, left the aircraft. It was 5:45 A.M.

Although the Aramco Lear jet's location is uncertain, it can be again assumed that it was at Algiers airport, for Yamani was immediately flown to Switzerland where his wife and two of their children awaited him. Together they were then flown to Jordan, where King Khalid awaited them with a gift of a Rolls-Royce Camargue.

Were Frank Jungers and Aramco involved in Carlos's surrender? In 1993, Jungers stated that when Yamani returned to Algiers, the Lear jet was "right there waiting for him." When Yamani was released, he "got on and got away."[14] This suggested that Yamani had escaped from the DC9 to Aramco's G2. This brush with death affected the rest of Yamani's life:

> When Yamani got back to the Kingdom, Yamani was convinced, and I think justifiably so, that Carlos would get him somehow and for some reason. So he asked for and got from the King permanent security protection when he was traveling or at home.[15]

Thus Yamani came dangerously close to death at the very time it seemed he had triumphed in his pursuit of participation — a triumph that, on closer examination, showed itself to be little more than a pyrrhic victory. After much negotiation, full participation was agreed upon in the spring of 1976. But Excom had fought hard to keep Aramco American. The agreement struck conceded 100 percent ownership to the Saudis at a date unspecified, and then only if the terms were acceptable. Therefore it was by no means absolutely certain. Also, according to the agreement,

> Aramco will continue to operate the oil installations, explore for and produce Saudi oil, and expand capacity in return for established fees. Oil lifting rights by the shareholder companies will be related to performance. Even though the total takeover has not yet occurred, decisions on oil production levels, exports pricing, and future development of reserves are now made and controlled by [the Saudi government].[16]

The Saudi government had promised that the United States would continue to receive the Saudi oil it needed to maintain its economy, but the

> ultimate responsibilities under the pending takeover remain uncertain. . . . Based on our discussions with officials of Exxon, Mobil, Aramco and the Saudi government the takeover apparently will not significantly affect day-to-day petroleum operations. Most officials believed that the revised arrangement will provide sufficient incentive for the shareholder companies to continue their exploration and development operations.[17]

Despite this official approval of participation, Excom intended to keep Aramco American and to put off as long as possible the "unspecified date" of Saudi full ownership. Moreover, Aramco and the Saudi government were stuck on a vital issue that Excom considered essential to eventual agreement: compensation to the shareholders for the "oil in the ground," Saudi Arabia's oil reserves. The shareholders' argument was that the companies' investment, not Saudi money, had brought about the discovery of Saudi Arabia's huge oil reserves. The value of the oil in the ground was "absolutely staggering." The Saudis staunchly resisted Aramco's claim to compensation.

Another factor slowed the progress of participation. The Saudi company Petromin, the entity that was probably slated to take over Aramco, might, according to a U.S. report, "eventually evolve into a fully integrated oil company and assume some functions now performed by Aramco, but it presently lacks many of the managerial and technical skills needed."[18] Indeed it did. At this point its workforce was 88 percent American and 12 percent Saudi. In 1972, Jungers had commissioned an exhaustive study of Saudi workers' competence to determine whether the Saudis would be ready to take over the company in about

1990. The findings were so negative, and therefore so dangerous politically in Aramco's relations with the Saudi government, that Jungers
ordered all copies of the report to be destroyed by fire.

Prospects for a Saudi takeover thus looked bleak. This fact frayed
relations between the Saudis and Aramco. The Saudis easily reverted
to their theme of threatening nationalization unless participation was
implemented. U.S. negotiators had to tread lightly, because of U.S.
dependence on Saudi oil. Then the Saudis began to speak ambigu-
ously about their previous guarantees to meet U.S. oil needs. Crown
Prince Fahd, the Saudis' key oil policy maker, noted that "Saudi oil is a
useful source of political and economic leverage in pursuing designated goals."[19]

In addition to the goal of participation, the Saudis also continued to
press for a change in U.S. policy toward Israel.

> The Middle East conflict is the single most important political factor
> affecting Saudi petroleum decisions. We were constantly reminded
> that a permanent peaceful settlement of the Arab-Israeli dispute is the
> key to Middle East stability and petroleum decisions favorable to oil
> consumers.[20]

If the Saudi government became dissatisfied with progress toward a
settlement, a number of unpleasant outcomes might result:

> It has several options available that could adversely affect U.S. interests,
> such as reducing oil production, canceling productive capacity expan-
> sion plans, or assuming a passive role in OPEC pricing decisions. Ac-
> cording to several U.S. Embassy officials, if another Middle East war
> flares up and direct U.S. military support is provided to Israel, [the
> Saudi government] may be pressured into joining an oil embargo if
> one is imposed by other Arab nations.[21]

Under Jungers, the search for Saudi talent quickened. The recruit-
ment of talented Saudis became more of a priority. As a requirement of
the 1933 concession agreement, Aramco had committed itself to train
Saudis to work at all levels of employment. But in the 1930s, to the
U.S. technocrats the Saudis seemed to be living in the Dark Ages, and
nobody paid much more than lip service to the notion that the Saudis
would or could take over Aramco. But times had changed.

> As the Saudi candidates became more viable, and some of them started
> moving into the management jobs, Yamani requested that we develop
> a special chart which we internally . . . called "the greening of Aramco."
> . . . We had on this chart all executive positions, general manager and
> above. The box where a Saudi was incumbent was colored green. . . .

Where we had a Saudi candidate whom we estimated would be ready in two years we'd stripe the box green. And then for the positions where we had potential Saudi candidates but we had not quite decided how far along they were, the box was rimmed green — green being the color of the Saudi national flag.

Now, . . . the chart was locked in a double safe because it was dynamite. And then, Jungers would go to Riyadh and review it with Yamani. He didn't give Yamani a copy and he brought the same original back and handed it to me. I locked it in the double-doored safe.[22]

Aramco had also made a commitment to educate Saudis who showed promise as managers and executives: We would send selected individuals to Harvard for a three-month program, to Columbia, to Stanford, to a number of universities in the U.S. We had to decide at what stage in somebody's career he would benefit most from such a general, broad educational assignment.[23]

One of those names in green — perhaps the most important one — was Ali I. Naimi. A small, neat, smiling man — he was not more than five feet and a few inches tall — Naimi came from the Bedouin tribes of central Arabia, and his career was shaped by Aramco. He was the beneficiary of Barger's dictum: "We should foster in our Saudi Arab employees as far as possible an appreciation for and knowledge of their own culture. Otherwise, we shall develop a group of intelligentsia, much like many second generation Americans who have lost the roots that their parents had and who do not yet understand America."[24]

Naimi himself described his origins and his arrival at the sheepsheds of al-Barsamah, where he asked for a job:

Sometime in 1944–45, an elder brother, who was working with Aramco, said, "Why don't you come along with me and go to the Aramco school? There are no requirements and you don't even have to work for the Company." It was very impressive. I saw this teacher, he had a huge red beard — he must have been Irish — I walked in and enrolled. No one asked any questions. I did that for two years, then my brother died. I was about 11. I took over his job as office boy. In 1947, the government passed a law which said no one below 18 was allowed to work, so I got terminated.

Not long after, I reapplied for work. I told them, "I may look young, but really I'm 20." They said, "We'll give you a chance. Go to the doctor and if he says you are 17 we will hire you." The doctor examined me and said I was about 12. I told him a sad story — I was responsible for my family — and said I was short because I was a Bedu, and he wrote down "17."[25]

Naimi became a coffee boy to the American staff at al-Barsamah. When he came of age he sought and was granted admission to

Aramco's Jebel School located in the desert near Dammam, where he won a diploma in geology. He rose to work in the stockroom. The company noticed his talent and enabled him to go to Stanford University in California. There he took an advanced degree in geology. Then he was steered, like an apprentice, from post to post through the many branches of Aramco. Naimi became an accountant at Abqaiq; from there he departed to become a foreman in a producing department. Then he ascended to the elevated post of superintendent of operations in the Abqaiq fields.

Naimi then took, and did very well on, the so-called grid test. In an attempt to clarify scientifically the potential abilities of Saudi and American workers, Jungers and two other officials had introduced an instrument officially known as the Managerial Grid, developed by two University of Texas social psychologists. Barger was chief when the test was introduced. He was "mod," he liked to try innovations — so 1,350 Aramcons submitted to the test, including the top achievers in the American and the Saudi workforce. It was a test of working style — to what extent a given employee cared about business results, about coworkers, about simply collecting a paycheck. The ideal candidate for management would show enthusiasm both for doing an excellent job and for maintaining superb employee relations.

Such psychological tests were in vogue in the 1960s and 1970s. Aramco brought in the test's developers to act as advisers during the eighteen months it took to administer the test to the staff. Although it was officially forbidden to talk about it, one main purpose of the grid was to evaluate the Saudis who had been marked for higher posts when "Saudization" of Aramco took place. Could they get along with Americans? Could Americans get along with them?

Ash Kearny, superintendent of plants at Abqaiq, "established a rule that he would only hire Saudis who tested in the top category." His efforts to train Saudis up to the higher levels of operations and administration were successful because he had taken the trouble to look out for bright Saudis and so "got the jump on other organizations by monopolizing the top talent."[26]

When in 1978 Naimi was directed to undergo the grid test, results showed that he was the management ideal. Though eventually the validity of the grid system was challenged, the smiling man behind huge spectacles could indeed live and work with Americans. He conformed to Aramco's corporate style: he was quiet, circumspect, able, attractive. He also had powerful connections to the great and the good of Riyadh's ministries. Jungers gave him a trial run as senior vice president in charge of all Aramco's oil production. Thus Ali Naimi entered the green lists of the chosen few. He became Yamani's golden lad and thereafter stood patiently in the wings, the ex-Bedouin technocrat in sandals, awaiting the summons to even higher office in Aramco.

David Holden, a leading British foreign correspondent and an authority on Saudi Arabia, was found murdered execution-style in Cairo in December 1977. The chief foreign correspondent of the *Sunday Times*, London, and formerly the Middle East correspondent of *The Times*, Holden was well regarded by Aramco, but it is doubtful that he was as well regarded by the Saudi government. In his memoirs about his work in Arabia, *Farewell to Arabia*, published in 1966, he was scornful of Saudi progress and reform and its handling of petrodollars. In 1976, he began work on a book to be entitled *The House of Saud*, a history of the Saud dynasty, relations with Great Britain, and, in its later chapters, of Big Oil, Aramco, and its relations with the Saudis. This was to be an important volume, and arrangements were made for Britain's leading ambassador in the region, Sir Humphrey Trevelyan, to write the preface. In it, Trevelyan wrote with notable circumspection that

> we shall probably never know why David Holden died. Certainly, there is no reason why he should have earned the hostility of any party in the Middle East. Nor is there any apparent reason why any group should think it to its political advantage to murder him. That he was murdered is certain. . . . He was one of the finest foreign correspondents. I saw him at work in the Middle East, always calm, always so understanding of the people, whom he knew well.[27]

In 1977 Holden went to Jerusalem to report for the *Sunday Times* on the aftermath of President Sadat of Egypt's journey to Jerusalem, one of the most important foreign political stories of the time. He went first to Egypt and then to Israel, spending two or three days on the occupied West Bank of the Jordan, before going on to Amman. It was there that something occurred to make him change his travel arrangements.

Holden was to have flown from Amman to Cairo in the company of a UPI reporter, but he felt obliged to cancel that arrangement because, as he said, he was expecting a message. Holden flew there on a later plane on December 7, 1977. The nature of the message that Holden expected was never learned, but in the newspaper business it was assumed to be an intelligence matter.

At all events, concerned that he did not report to his newspaper that he had arrived in Cairo, as was customary, Holden's newspaper began inquiries. On December 10 his body was found in a mortuary. It had been discovered in a ditch on the outskirts of Cairo, shot in the back of the neck and stripped of all means of identification. Though investigations followed, the only findings published stated that "no evidence that pointed with any conclusiveness to who his murderers might have been" had been found.[28]

Even by 1996, nothing had emerged to cause the investigation into Holden's murder to be reopened — except one tantalizing matter noted in the memoir of the superb essayist Jan Morris, a colleague of Holden and his predecessor as Middle East correspondent of *The Times*. "Our friendship," she wrote, "was that of colleagues, a background somewhat romantic and adventurous, and not without a sting of intrigue — that background through which foreign correspondents in murkier parts of the world habitually moved."[29]

Holden and Morris were in the habit of sending each other postcards when they were on foreign assignments, entertaining each other with "limericks or snatches of comic verse." He had sent her one such card on the morning of the day of his death. That card

> showed a view of the Citadel in Jerusalem [and] bore a message that seemed to me puzzling — not a mere frivolous greeting such as we usually exchanged, but one that tantalizingly seemed to convey something between its lines, if only I could read it. When the news of the murder reached me I had the card sent to Scotland Yard, in case it might afford some clue to the tragedy; but it does not seem to have helped, and I wish they would let me have it back again, for sentimental reasons.[30]

What lay behind Holden's murder? Perhaps it concerned the contents of his book, *The House of Saud*, which indicated that the man who wrote it was extraordinarily well informed, especially in matters concerning the Saudi dynasty, Big Oil, what the Saudi kings did with their royalties, and Saudi politics. This author has little doubt that Holden had received important assistance from a person or persons in Saudi Arabia. Given the exceptional sensitivity of the Saudi government to the English printed word in dynastic and religious matters — Philby was deported at least partly because of court displeasure when he published *Arabian Jubilee* in 1950, and the British ambassador Sir James Craig was declared persona non grata when the BBC aired a program concerning the execution of a Saudi princess and her Arab lover — it may well have been that an individual had cause to prevent Holden from completing his book.

THE WASHINGTON LOBBY

B Y 1978, FRANK JUNGERS was forty-nine years old and extraordinarily dynamic. He needed to be. The problems he faced were normally encountered by industrialists only in times of depression and war. In the aftermath of the oil embargo and the massive oil price increases, Yamani was in a state of revolt against the U.S. polity; oil was so identified with massive wealth and power that no less than eight investigations into the nature of the "special relationship" between the Saudi government and Aramco had begun in Washington. Participation had caused serious discord among the partners in the Aramco consortium. There were rumors of regional war in the Gulf. And Jungers had to deal with not one, but three, multi-billion-dollar industrial projects in Saudi Arabia, in addition to his main task — expanding Saudi oil production.

Jungers also had problems concerning U.S. perceptions of Aramco. On Capitol Hill, Senator Frank Church of Iowa sensed votes and declared in a speech:

> We Americans must uncover the trail that led the United States into dependency on the Arab sheikhdoms for so much of its oil. Why did our Government support and encourage the movement of the huge American-owned oil companies into the Middle East in the first place? We must re-examine the premise that what's good for the oil companies is good for the United States. . . . We must demystify the inner sanctum of this most secret of industries, especially Aramco and its four parent companies.[1]

Exxon, Standard Oil of California, Texaco, and Chevron, the parent companies, still formed the richest and the most powerful combine in the world. Together, it was alleged, in 1973 the combine made a profit of $1.2 billion on an investment of $1.4 billion. It was, said Church, obscene that these companies could make so much money when all the world, and especially America, was suffering so much as a result of their policies. Church made it quite clear whom he had in mind:

> We are dealing with corporate entities which have many of the characteristics of nations. Thus it should surprise no one, when we speak of corporate and Government relationships, the language will be that which is appropriate between sovereigns.[2]

The Department of Justice's antitrust division began to investigate the oil embargo and price increases. During the embargo, Aramco and the shareholding companies were accused by the government of having so arranged their affairs that they and the Saudis reaped immense profits from that prolonged national discomfort. Consequently, in 1977 the Justice Department filed charges against Aramco and its four parent companies, stating that the quadrupling of Arabian oil prices was due less to the actions of OPEC than to those of the consortium, "acting collectively and unlawfully to control oil prices."[3]

Additional investigations were led by the following parties:

- Henry Jackson, chairman of the Senate Committee on Energy and Natural Resources
- Benjamin Rosenthal, chairman of the House Subcommittee on Commerce, Consumer and Monetary Affairs
- Howard Metzenbaum, chairman of the Senate Subcommittee on Antitrust, Monopoly and Business Rights
- Edward Kennedy, chairman of the Senate's Judiciary Committee
- John Shenefield, assistant U.S. attorney general and head of the Justice Department's Antitrust Division
- The State Department's Bureau of Intelligence and Research

Senator Jackson intoned, "The American people want to know whether major oil companies are sitting on shut-in wells and hoarding production in hidden tanks and at abandoned oil stations." They were, he said, sick of having to line up at gas stations and worried at the new power of "camel drivers." In a report published in 1977 under the title *Access to Oil — The United States's Relationships with Saudi Arabia and Iran,* Jackson's committee warned that

> dependence on oil imports . . . is equal to dependence on OPEC oil. To date the Saudis have played a moderating role with OPEC. But the Saudis have also indicated their unwillingness to continue to stand alone in OPEC councils. They do not like to appear to be opposing other Arab regimes. They have suggested that the United States should ask its other OPEC-member friends, that is, Iran, to moderate their price positions as well.[4]

Metzenbaum asked the Justice Department to investigate reports that Aramco and its parent companies were making "up to" $7 billion by taking advantage of Saudi Arabia's lower crude prices and not passing those lower prices on to the consumer. Senator Kennedy's demand that the Department of Justice describe the relationship between OPEC and Aramco resulted in this exchange:

> *Shenefield:* It could be argued that OPEC is not a cartel and, while OPEC may set a price, the actual task of insuring that aggregate output is sufficiently small to sustain that price in the marketplace is performed by the oil companies.
> *Kennedy:* If that statement were correct, would that or would that not be a clear violation of the anti-trust laws?
> *Shenefield:* Assuming some impact on the US commerce which I think we can assume, my off-the-top-of-the-head reaction would be that it would be, yes.[5]

When Senator Church directed the Subcommittee on Multinationals to establish what "undisclosed understandings," if any, existed between Aramco, its shareholders, and the Saudis, Yamani displayed the full measure of his political power in Washington. He called the U.S. ambassador, John West, to his office and announced that

> under no circumstances will Saudi Arabia tolerate this material being made public. The files subpoenaed include Aramco documents and they are the property of Saudi Arabia. Their release constitutes an invasion of national privacy. It doesn't matter what the documents are or what the committee intends to do with the report. This is a matter of principle.[6]

Yamani provided West with his political analysis of the situation and his feeling that Saudi Arabia was being treated unfairly:

> In some countries, information about oil reserves and reservoir behaviour are not only classified but to reveal that is a crime covered by capital punishment. In this case we were singled out from all the other oil producers in the world by a group of Americans working for the Zionist lobby. Their aim was to show that Saudi Arabia is not really a country which can solve America's energy problems. Our refusal to be singled out was very clearly a matter of principle. The committee was politically motivated. So we acted in a political manner. We refused to allow a public discussion to be based on secret information about our natural resources, which would of course have been revealed to the media.[7]

But Church was relentless, and he requested that he see the 1976 agreement between Aramco and the Saudi government regarding participation, a relatively unknown concept outside the oil industry.

Yamani was unyielding in his refusal to cooperate. And he revealed something about the status of the agreement when he declared that

> it did not concern the committee. At that point there was only a draft of an agreement. It wasn't yet an agreement. It was a matter not yet approved by [the Saudi government]. It had not yet been ratified. It wasn't even for our colleagues in OPEC to see. It was only our affair. No one else's.[8]

Ambassador West took Yamani's concern directly to President Carter. The president decided that the relevant committee report, which ran to 130 pages, must not be published or circulated. Carter told Secretary of State Cyrus Vance, and Vance told Church's committee, that to publicize the report would damage the relationship between Saudi Arabia and the United States. Moreover, if the document found its way to the public, Yamani would find a way to retaliate — presumably in refusing to meet the U.S. request that Saudi Arabia increase production to 13.5 million barrels a day by the early 1980s. Yamani succeeded. Church's committee received a report on participation that had been reduced to thirty-seven pages. Topics removed included Saudi allegations that on occasion Aramco had grossly mismanaged its affairs, disputes between Yamani's ministry and Aramco officials regarding production levels, Saudi accusations that Aramco had overproduced and that the company had resorted to deceptive accounting to explain some of its reserves — serious business all.

The Department of Justice also requested that Aramco provide documentation to assist in its investigation. But Yamani gave orders within his ministry and to Aramco at Dhahran, demanding that no Aramco documents held in Saudi Arabia were to be sent to the Justice Department. In 1973 the U.S. Federal Trade Commission had accused the combine of "collusive action" to fix prices but had proved nothing. And in this later investigation the Aramco combination proved as fireproof as ever. All investigations eventually petered out.

In 1978, Jungers made Baldo Marinovic assistant to the chairman of the board, a new position in higher management. Marinovic reported to nobody but Jungers, and among Marinovic's responsibilities was supervising the work of a body called the Internal Services Group (ISG), which was, Marinovic recalled, "basically our anti-fraud, conflict of interest, embezzlement, whatnot group." The staff of ISG was made up of "gumshoes . . . former FBI or Scotland Yard types." They reported only to Marinovic. Because of the huge construction boom created by Saudi Arabia's $141 billion second Five-Year Plan, we had a hell of a lot of new people, not career Aramco people, who might be tempted to get a kickback from a contractor, and we've had a number of such cases. This group was looking into these kinds of activities. And they were reporting to me. Then if I decided that the thing had real merit, I would approach either the executive in charge of the individual or, if it was more serious, I would go to [Jungers].[9]

Less-than-professional business practices within the company grew into a large problem, and Aramco received

> complaints from local suppliers and businessmen saying that Aramco was tough to do business with. They said we were slow to pay, they said we helped the rich get richer and they complained about favoritism. So, we set up a task force to look into these complaints and, of course, we found a lot of what they said was true.
>
> We found that Aramco was slow to pay. . . . We found that our business was concentrated in the hands of a few large suppliers, but not through choice. If we wanted a General Electric product, we had to go through Ali Tamimi, the GE distributor. We didn't find any collusion and we didn't find any graft.[10]

Certain such cases proved to be politically dangerous, and one of these concerned Sheikh Abdullah Darwish, thought to be one of the richest, if not the richest, middlemen in the Gulf. It came to be suspected that Darwish and an "Arab Group" of Saudi and Gulf oil potentates might be using their great wealth to establish a lobby in Washington and New York from which to influence U.S. Middle Eastern policy in favor of the Arabs.

Born in about 1910 at Doha, the main city of Qatar, Abdullah Darwish had first worked as a massage boy to the pearl divers in the dhows plying the Gulf. He became a close friend of the ruling family of Qatar through his father's business as a trader along the Gulf coast. When his father died, Darwish and his brothers took over the firm. Through Aramco's intelligence service, much was known about Darwish and his enterprises. They had made one fortune during World War II when Abdullah's firm had "obtained contracts with the British armed forces in several parts of the Middle East, and Abdullah is said to have been impressed by British military organization methods and to have emulated them in business."[11] The brothers were also deeply involved in the speculative and often shady gold exchange market, where they were said to have made profits as high as 135 percent on some transactions.

Over time he extended his firm's operations to London; Beirut; Manama, Bahrein; and Dubai, United Arab Emirates. He also established commercial agents throughout Europe, the Iron Curtain countries, India, and the Far East. But then Darwish was forced into exile by his rivals; he went to the small port of Uqair, near the Hofuf residence of the governor of Hasa, Amir bin Jiluwi, and he worked as a merchant and contractor, mainly offering his services to Aramco. Rather quickly he gained an important measure of control over Jiluwi; and through Jiluwi he became well and favorably known to both King Saud and King Faisal. He built an elaborate palace near the Jiluwis, one of the leading families in Saudi Arabia because of their military services to Ibn Saud. Darwish entertained the higher management of Aramco on the grand scale. He became known to them as "the Pirate" because he had vision in only one eye and covered the useless one with a black patch.

Darwish's financial position was strong. His brothers in Qatar continued to run Darwish's companies to their mutual advantage. He was on good terms with Emile Bustani, the hugely rich Lebanese tycoon, and with eminent politicians of Lebanon. He maintained "an elaborate private radio service, used primarily for business, but also for monitoring Middle Eastern news broadcasting." And as an Arabian Affairs Division paper on him acknowledged, "Darwish and the business he controls appear to have unlimited prospects in the Persian Gulf."[12]

Yet for all his millions and his ability, Darwish was not reckoned by Aramco to be a good risk:

> Although Abdullah and his firm enjoy very favorable credit ratings in Europe, he has a very poor reputation in the Eastern Province. The National Gas Company has been unable to collect bills from Abdullah for several years, and Aramco has been forced to deny him credit as a result of his tardy payment of bills. Many businessmen are wary of extending him credit, since his political influence makes forcible collection measures impossible.[13]

At Aramco, Darwish associated with Tom Barger, who regarded him as an interesting informant and may have used him as an adviser. Otherwise, the relationship between Darwish and the lower levels of management had been "anything but smooth and cordial and, in general, has not been distinguished by arrangements considered profitable to both parties." Aramco's staff had had a wearying experience with Darwish when he leased an office block in Dammam from Aramco. They signed the agreement in 1951:

> The terms upon which the parties eventually agreed called for a rental of about $125,000 a year for a ten-year period, which was to amortize the building's cost in eight years. Aramco spent about $2 million a year in operating costs for most of the ten-year period, much of which was due to the poor construction and design of the building and to Abdul-

lah's failure to maintain and repair the building according to the terms of the original agreement.[14]

Burned badly, Aramco gave Darwish little business for a time but then found itself forced to use him as a contractor because of his web of contacts, through which he had cornered much of the Gulf trade in a large spectrum of businesses. His assets were thought to approximate $100 million to $150 million. Darwish's wealth enabled him

> to buy in boatload quantities, with consequent bulk and freight discounts; the opportunity to obtain the best possible credit terms directly from the manufacturer, and allowing the shortest possible period for capital commitment — 60 or 90 days as compared to payment in advance; the opportunity to speculate in foreign exchange rates, either by maintaining large supplies of various currencies or through using the advantages of the forward exchange market where commercial traders fix their receipts and obligations in their own currency in advance; the opportunity to speculate on large purchases of material at particularly favorable prices; the elimination of the need to negotiate loans or pay interest on money tied up in a transaction; the capacity to sell on credit to customers where other vendors are limited to customers who can pay cash; and the ability to stockpile goods and await favorable prices in the event of a temporarily depressed market.[15]

Darwish had also managed to run a type of business generally frowned upon in the Muslim world:

> Abdullah has also used his capital to establish himself as a notorious loan merchant. He is ruthless about foreclosing on mortgages. In a market where loans are not readily available to the ordinary merchant or government official he has found lending a particularly lucrative operation. He is careful to disguise the payment of interest to avoid the censure of religious officials by dummy purchases and resale arrangements in which prices rise but goods are never actually exchanged.[16]

Together with his ability to ingratiate himself to those in positions of power, these factors made Darwish a character to contend with.

Life on the fringes of Oildom was rewarding for Darwish because the business to be done there was indeed unlimited. The value of the goods and services purchased or rented by Aramco from Saudi businesses between 1956 and 1970 totaled $430,385,000. After 1976 that amount trebled each year. Darwish, the main merchant on the Gulf, benefited hugely. But in 1966, Darwish began to spend much time back in Qatar, from which he had been expelled in 1951. This caught the attention of the Internal Services Group, the ex-FBI and ex–Scotland Yard gumshoes at Aramco, a group with connections to various international intelligence services, all of whom were interested in economic and financial developments within the Third World.

The ISG representative in Qatar established that Darwish had become involved with a young Pakistani banker, Agha Hasan Abedi, a Shiite Muslim. Abedi intended to start a new bank, the United Bank, to serve Muslims brought into Saudi Arabia and elsewhere in the Gulf to work in the oil fields and the construction sites. This was, Abedi stressed, a new market for banking. He wished to be of service to his Muslim brothers. He would cash their paychecks and send checks to the workers' families by way of United Bank branches set up throughout Pakistan and the Gulf, including Abu Dhabi, where he already had permission to move forward. He also hoped to establish branches in Bahrein, Kuwait, Oman, Qatar, and the United Arab Emirates.

The Bank of America was interested in expanding into the Gulf and the petrodollar-world at large, and a deal was made in which the Bank of America would put up $2.5 million in return for a 25 percent share of Abedi's operations. Thus Abedi acquired something of the prestige of the Bank of America. The Bank of Credit and Commerce International (BCCI) was established and, as of 1978, its shareholders included members of the ruling families of Saudi Arabia, Bahrein, Sharja, Abu Dhabi, and Dubai, and a group of various Middle East businessmen. Together these individuals held 35 percent of the Middle Eastern holdings in a corporation called BCCI Holdings, Société Anonyme, registered in Luxembourg.

Among the Saudis with interests in BCCI were Kamal Adham, a former director of the Saudi CIA and now a prominent Saudi merchant with ties to Crown Prince Fahd and King Khalid, and Gait Pharaon, a son of the chief doctor to Ibn Saud and an adviser to the late king Faisal, and to the reigning king, Khalid. Pharaon was now a major merchant banker in Saudi Arabia; and he became the proprietor of the National Bank of Georgia, which he bought from Bert Lance, former budget director in President Carter's administration. Also listed in BCCI Holdings was Abdullah Darwish.

Under Abedi's direction BCCI became a world bank with fifty-nine branches in Europe, ninety-three in the Middle East, fifty-eight in Africa, thirty-four in the Far East and Southeast Asia, and fifteen in North America and the Caribbean. Also, BCCI had operations in Switzerland, Hong Kong, South Korea, Indonesia, Manila, Colombia, and Panama. It owned 40 percent of a bank in Nigeria, another operation in Zimbabwe, and one on the border between Swaziland and South Africa. As

BCCI expanded, it became of intelligence interest to the American and British services, particularly when it became known that BCCI had interests in the narcotics trade of General Manuel Noriega, the military dictator of Panama.

Gradually, BCCI came to the attention of the U.S. Securities and Exchange Commission, which filed a law suit charging members of the "Arab Group," including Darwish by name, for "violating U.S. securities by failing to disclose that they had secretly bought about twenty percent of the shares in Financial General,"[17] an important financial institution in the American capital.

The group had induced Washington's leading lawyer, Clark Clifford, to become chairman when it acquired Financial General, which was described as a "bank holding company that owns or controls more than one bank."[18] On October 19, 1978, an organization called Credit and Commercial American Holdings (CCAH), with offices located in the Netherlands Antilles, filed an application with the Federal Reserve in Washington seeking approval to proceed with the acquisition of Financial General. Three men would each control 24 percent of the stock in Financial General: Kamal Adham, the Kuwaiti businessman Faisal Saud al-Fulaji, and Abdullah Darwish. The chief lawyer listed on the application was Clark Clifford and his associate, Robert Altman. The Federal Reserve rejected the application. A public hearing ensued, and Clifford waxed eloquent:

> Thoughtful Americans . . . knew it was in the country's interests to bring back as many of the dollars as possible that were being sent to Arab oil nations. Here was a chance to repatriate some of those dollars by allowing Arabs to invest in American banking. They would be . . . passive investors. They would leave the banking to [Clifford] and the men who would join him on the board of directors of the new entity. Financial General . . . would grow as he and his friends brought in new business from their contacts with big American corporations.[19]

In spite of Clifford's words, Sidney Bailey, an official of the Securities and Exchange Commission, continued to view the procedure with suspicion. He had good reason to. The "Arab Group" in effect wanted a financial beachhead in the United States for both financial and political reasons — to take on the Israeli lobby in Washington. The objective became clearer when the "Arab Group" announced that it wished also to acquire Financial General's two banks in New York, the Bank of Commerce in New York City and the Community State Bank in Albany.

Manfred Ohrenstein, a state senator and leader of the Democratic

Party in New York, claimed knowledge that Arab investors were trying to "sneak in the back door" to acquire the two banks by buying Financial General. It was, Ohrenstein claimed, a "sophisticated attempt to acquire a network of banks across the Eastern seaboard and put a stranglehold on the petrodollars coming into this country."[20] The deal stalled when, through Ohrenstein, the New York State Banking Board rejected the application of the "Arab Group" on the grounds that American banks could not buy banks in Saudi Arabia. But the board was pressured to reconsider the application, and it did so in April 1982. Its decision was favorable and the Arabs won. Financial General was renamed First American, Clark Clifford was elected chairman of its board, and Robert Altman became president. But now Darwish, "the Pirate," was in trouble in Abu Dhabi. BCCI had given signs of collapsing when Darwish induced Sheikh Zaid, the ruler of Abu Dhabi, to loan BCCI first $600 million and then a further $400 million. All told, so it is said, Sheikh Zaid put $2 billion in the bank. But nonetheless BCCI crashed. There were many indictments, including those of celebrated personages Clark Clifford and Robert Altman.

Darwish's fate was not decided by the collapse of BCCI or its dependencies. Since 1975, he had invested billions of petrodollars for Sheikh Zaid, successfully by all accounts. But there was evidence that he had taken one flyer too many. That concerned an investment of $96 million in copper futures through an American broker in Switzerland. Darwish told the ruler that he had used the $96 million to buy gold, and when Sheikh Zaid discovered that all those millions had been used to buy copper futures — and worse, that he had lost all the monies — he had Darwish and his assistants arrested. He was incarcerated when the application of the "Arab Group" was at last approved by the Federal Reserve. But that illustrious body knew nothing about Darwish until the *Washington Post* published the fact of Darwish's arrest. The Federal Reserve's counsel wrote to Clark Clifford, demanding views on the arrest. Clifford replied that the *Post's* story was "inaccurate, misleading, unwarranted, and irresponsible."[21]

In 1978, at Jungers's direction, a fresh figure emerged in a new role in Washington. This lawyer, Frederick G. Dutton, was a brilliant former adviser to President John F. Kennedy, Senators Robert and Ted Kennedy, and George McGovern. Dutton was known, too, for his passionate commitment to liberal politics. After working in John Kennedy's 1960 campaign, Dutton was appointed special assistant to the president. Less than two years later, Dutton moved to the State Department as assistant secretary for congressional relations. In 1964 he resigned from President Johnson's administration and formed his own law firm. His associates were all liberal Kennedy family devotees.

In Washington, Dutton had become favorably known to Senator J. William Fulbright, chairman of the Senate Foreign Relations Committee between 1959 and 1974. It is thought that Senator Fulbright first developed the idea that the Saudis needed representation in Washington. According to Dutton, Senator Fulbright remarked to Rawleigh Warner, chairman of Mobil, one of Aramco's four parent companies, that Saudi Arabians "didn't handle themselves well in Washington, and should hire a representative."[22] Warner passed Fulbright's advice on to Riyadh, and in 1975 Dutton was offered a contract to represent Saudi Arabia in Washington.

At first Dutton hesitated because, "given the intensely pro-Israeli position of many in the Democratic Party, he feared that working for the Saudis might seem the end of his political career." Late in August 1973, the oil companies approached several Washington lawyers, but none would take the job and Dutton became the only candidate. Soon thereafter Dutton met with Mike Ameen, the Aramco government affairs agent in Washington. Dutton presented Ameen with his ideas for a "full-scale public relations effort in helping Aramco redirect positive American public opinion away from Israel." But nothing definite had been agreed upon when war broke out between the Arabs and the Israelis in October 1973.[23]

When the price of Arab oil shot up by 70 percent, to Dutton the "scent of oil blackmail was disturbing." Truly "it was clear to Dutton that this was not the best way for the Arabs to proceed, nor was invoking the oil weapon going to endear the Arabs to the American people. If anything, the Arab action would produce a nasty backlash."[24]

Dutton sent a two-page letter to Mike Ameen, warning that changes in American policy could not be accomplished by jacking up prices steeply. Turning to the topic of a tentatively planned meeting between a Saudi delegation and President Nixon, Dutton advised that the Saudis were blundering again. He then produced suggestions about how Aramco should handle the media in order to get the Arab viewpoint over to the press and the electorate. This appears to have impressed Ameen, for in late November Aramco decided not to await the outcome of the negotiation between Dutton and the Saudi government over his contract. Aramco agreed that Dutton should be made an adviser to Aramco in Washington. His duties were

> reportedly to include some of the same services he intended to provide Saudi Arabia: public relations, political intelligence and help in planning and arranging visits by Saudi officials to the United States and

by key American officials to Saudi Arabia. It was both Dutton's and
Aramco's understanding that it was only a matter of time before Saudi
Arabia would agree to a formal arrangement with Dutton.[25]

In December 1973, Dutton wrote Aramco another letter, this time
addressing the delicate matter of Aramco's loyalties. Was the company
loyal to Saudi Arabia or to the United States? Dutton wrote that it must
be seen by the Saudi Arabs that Aramco was on their side in the great
political struggle now developing. A media campaign taking the Arabs'
side must be started, and the results — press clippings, TV video film
— must be sent to them. He suggested that a "special tabloid" carrying
the Saudi message should be started by Aramco. Another of Dutton's
thoughts was that Aramco should arrange for the production of Arab-
supporting TV interviews and videotapes, along with Aramco-funded
"lectures and seminars on U.S.-Saudi relations" at "major universities
across the United States."[26]

While in Washington, Yamani, through arrangements with Aramco,
spent twenty minutes with Dutton late in 1973. Although he still had
no contract with Riyadh, Dutton sent Yamani a book of photographs of
Washington with a note saying that it was "a very small token of appreciation for all that you have done on this trip, from those who believe in
an even-handed U.S. policy toward the Middle East."[27]

It now appeared that Dutton was cooperating with Kamal Adham,
King Faisal's brother-in-law and then "head of Saudi intelligence,"
shortly to become a special friend of the CIA. Dutton was laying plans
for a complex and secret public relations operation for Aramco, in
an attempt to gain U.S. support for Saudi Arabian concerns. "Under
the aegis of a high Saudi official, the 'operation' was to depend heavily on staff personnel from Mobil, SoCal, Texaco and Exxon." Staff
would include specialists from TV, radio, and newspapers, as well as
writers and research assistants. "Senators, representatives and 'major
news people' were to be invited to Saudi Arabia. 'Targetted groups'
included the 'business community,' 'blacks,' 'environmental groups,'
'peace groups,' 'individual VIPs,' 'governors,' 'mayors,' and others."
Dutton wished to be in charge of the operation and to work directly
with Kamal Adham. Over the coming months Dutton met with Adham's nephew, Prince Turki. He was, however, unable to meet Adham,
and no contract was signed. Dutton visited Saudi Arabia in February
1974 and, in a letter of thanks to Frank Jungers for having made the
journey possible, he hoped that "a working relationship with Kamal
Adham is possible as it provides striking opportunities for getting at the
real problems of these times both here and more broadly."[28]

Expecting that the Saudi government was about ready to sign a contract, Dutton drew up a formal proposal regarding his work as a consultant. The contract was to begin on February 15, 1974, and he also declared that he should be guided by and report to Sheikh Adham and "not be assigned to work regularly under a ministry or a bureaucracy, nor under other Americans." The contract was to run for three years because of the "almost certainly protracted nature of the problem to be dealt with concerning Saudi Arabian–U.S. ties and because other sources of income and work for me will be affected by my taking this responsibility."[29]

By February there was still no contract with the Saudis — when individuals negotiated with the Saudis they sometimes had to wait months before anything happened, and sometimes they waited forever — and so Dutton was retained by Aramco. Between March 1 and June 1 of 1974 he billed them for $20,200. At the same time "he was earning a solid reputation among the Saudi elite."[30]

During this time, Jungers came under some criticism concerning the super-rich Saudi merchant Suliman S. Olayan. Olayan had begun his career with Aramco in a lowly position. He had worked his way up from the sheepsheds and had then gone into business with Aramco, but on his own account. In the 1970s, Olayan had expressed to Jungers his interest in obtaining some of Aramco's insurance business, and he was helped by Jungers. But the committee exploring possible graft or favoritism in Aramco's use of outside contractors came across Olayan's insurance file. Because the correspondence mentioned Jungers, it appeared there might be a special relationship between Olayan and Jungers, though there was no evidence of graft.

Jungers had formed a very high opinion of Olayan's abilities. He was one of the best and the brightest of the Saudi contractors who worked for Aramco. A man of ability and intelligence, he had proved a useful intermediary whenever problems developed between Aramco and the Saudi establishment. Above all, Olayan had shown that he could understand the Aramco point of view in disputes; therefore Jungers saw that he might be useful to the Washington lobby. American Express wished to appoint a prominent Saudi to its board, and Jungers instructed Dutton to recommend Olayan. In Jungers's view, Aramco needed all the friends it could get in high places.

At last, at the end of 1974, the Saudi government decided to retain Dutton "for matters concerning oil. A formal contract was negotiated, and on April 7, 1975, Dutton deposited in his bank a $100,000 fee from Petromin, the Saudi state oil agency." Dutton registered at the Foreign Agents Unit of the Department of Justice as an agent for Petromin. Dutton was not alone as a Saudi agent in the United States.

In all, there were about a dozen of them. But Dutton became known as the exemplar of the breed in Washington, "the resilient, influential core of power brokers who survive and prosper no matter who rules the White House or Congress."[31]

Public relations efforts did pay off by raising general awareness of the kingdom. In December 1977, the *Washington Post* ran a three-part survey of U.S.-Saudi relations. Before that date the kingdom had rarely made much of an impression on the U.S. media. The introduction to the series pointed up the growing importance of Saudi Arabia to the United States and the world:

> The enormous power that has settled onto the shoulders of an elderly and infirm king, his two determined but mutually distrusting half brothers and their 2,000 uncles, cousins and other male relatives is now thrusting Saudi Arabia into the front line of world politics.
>
> Taken for granted or even ignored by past U.S. administrations as a policy pygmy in its own region, Saudi Arabia and its royal family have in four years moved swiftly toward the center of American calculations and objectives abroad.
>
> The movement is beginning to affect U.S. ties to its two strongest allies in the Middle East, Israel and Iran, who now share their positions as American surrogates in the region with Saudi Arabia. The Carter administration is stepping up American reliance on Saudi Arabia in foreign policy, just as Iran and Israel are seeking for separate reasons to become less dependent on their ties to Washington.
>
> Moreover, the Saudis are using their still-growing oil wealth to counter radical trends in the Middle East, Africa and even Western Europe in ways that would have been unthinkable for the kingdom at the beginning of the decade. Increasingly, they are able and willing to act in areas where post–Vietnam America is reluctant to become more deeply involved.[32]

In a quotation from a U.S. diplomat, the article described some of the fears caused by the Saudis' enhanced powers:

> "We are reaching the point where we are more dependent upon them than they are on us," says one worried American diplomat who has much experience in the Middle East and a great deal of sympathy for Saudi goals. "No matter what good friends they are, that is an unhealthy position for us."
>
> This qualitative change may be the most vital component of the transformation of global power relationships since the oil exporting countries dictated an end to the cheap energy era in 1973. Today, Saudi Arabia's friends can argue that the U.S.-Saudi link ranks only behind the U.S.–West German alliance and Washington's ties to Tokyo in containing Soviet influence and maintaining political and economic order in the world.[33]

The Saudi dynasty did not call attention to its change of status in the world economy, for the excellent reason that its members wished to keep discussion about their finances to a minimum.

> For the Saudis, the location and amount of the tens of billions of dollars they own are as closely held as the Pentagon's information on the location of Polaris submarines in America's nuclear strike force. Saudi holdings in the United States are so sensitive that the U.S. Treasury cooperates with Saudi Arabia in keeping Americans in the dark on this subject.
>
> That highly secret figure is now between $35 billion and $40 billion. . . . For much of this year Saudi Arabia has been purchasing more U.S. Treasury bonds than the traditional big buyers like West Germany. Saudi purchases easily outstrip those of any large American corporation or bank.[34]

In all "Saudi foreign holdings exceed $80 billion." They represented what Foreign Minister Prince Saud ibn Faisal called a potential "money weapon." The funds could be used at will "to undermine the economy of the industrialized world." But such action was not likely to be directed at the United States. The Saudis were dependent upon U.S. military technology and they were prepared to make financial choices very favorable to the United States, provided they got the military equipment they wanted. Other countries were courting the Saudis and their wealth. In short, the Saudis were "spreading billions of dollars in an arc of influence that extends from Morocco eastward across Africa and the Middle East and deep into Asia."[35]

Participation was going to become a fact of life for everyone involved in the Saudi Arabian oil industry. There were many issues involved in the transfer of control. Only yesterday the Saudis had been considered mere "camel drivers." They now wished to replace the Aramcons, who had always given "every appearance of permanence and stability, with their self-perpetuating boards and bureaucracies."[36] Yet a gigantic enterprise, politics and all, was to be passed to the "camel drivers." To avoid nationalization — the abrupt and complete expropriation of the company — Aramco moved slowly ahead with the requirements of the agreement, appointing Saudis to the key jobs. But this topic raised a very delicate question: when would Saudi nationals in fact be ready to take over the management of Aramco? The pride of the Saudis rested upon their ability and preparedness to step in and take over at the appropriate time. And the length of time it took for Aramco to pass the torch — thirteen years — can be explained by this matter.

While dealing with the myriad problems involved in the transfer of power, Jungers was also confronted with the overwhelming requirements of the Saudis' $141 billion second Five-Year Plan, with its vast construction projects. And with that came another challenge. Jungers decided it was necessary to install electricity throughout Hasa, and when that was done, to complete the project by installing it throughout the country. He found it easy to justify the expense and effort:

> The power that the local power companies had was outdated, old, diesel generator sets that they tried to hook together. They weren't integrated, [it was] all localized, and it was going off all the time. The transmission facilities were terrible. So we thought of the idea of forming a consolidated power system. . . . If we could buy these individual power companies and tie them together and tie them into the Aramco system, it would make a lot of sense. The combined Aramco and newly modernized additions to the system could become a large power generation company.[37]

But at its root, Jungers's motive for providing electricity was political. According to Brock Powers, Jungers's vice chairman and heir presumptive, it was a means of "lashing [the Saudi government] to Aramco and making us dependent on each other so that nobody can ever kick us out."[38]

Jungers went to see Fahd to request a decree that would give Aramco

> the authority to buy out these power companies. We would form a Saudi Consolidated Electric Company, we would put our power into this company, we would operate the company for a fee, we would sell our power plants into that company. That company would be the vehicle that sold power to everybody, including Aramco. [Our] shareholders were not very enamored with this idea; they felt it was overcomplicating our lives. But Amir Fahd thought it was a super idea.[39]

The scheme was very practical, but how would it be paid for? Aramco could not accept financial liability for it; the shareholding companies were, as Brock Powers averred, "dead set against it" because they thought it would "diffuse our efforts from the oil and gas business."[40] But, according to Powers, Jungers managed to sell the scheme to Yamani, and through him they acquired the funds for the electrification scheme — in an extraordinary way.

Under the current operating system, Saudi oil royalties still went from Excom to Aramco, and Aramco was responsible for passing the royalties to the Saudi government. But for operating reasons, Aramco retained an important tranche of these royalties. At one stage $13 billion in royalties was held in Aramco's banks. It was from this side of the ledger that the money for the electrification scheme came. This was done with the knowledge of Fahd and of Yamani, as was the expropriation of the thirty-odd electricity companies in Saudi Arabia. They were formed into a single company, paying the shareholders of the existing companies in cash or with stock in the new company. In this way the Saudis "nationalized" the electrical power industry.

The new company was called Saudi Consolidated Electric Company. Aramco turned over all its generating facilities and some Aramcons and local Saudis to run the new company. The company then undertook the mammoth task of providing electricity to every town and village of Saudi Arabia. Nobody knew how many villages there were! The Bedouin could literally make "villages just [pop] up out of the sand," and then they would claim, "Okay, this is a village. Now we want electricity."[41]

Then money for the project started to become a serious problem, and when money became a problem in Saudi Arabia, people could lose their heads. Marinovic related that at one point Aramco "sat on" close to $13 billion. And how did Aramco avoid paying that enormous sum to the kingdom? Marinovic recalled that they invested the money to partially finance the project and thereby became "one of the biggest traders in short-term investment securities." Fahd and Yamani knew what Aramco was doing, but nobody had told the finance minister, Mohammed Aba al-Khail, or the director of the Saudi Arabian monetary agency, Mu Gosaibi. Those who knew what was happening, Marinovic remembered, "were looking with a jaundiced eye on this nest egg we had. They wanted to get their hands on it." Yamani, however, "wanted this money squirreled away by Aramco so that it would be available to Aramco for future operations."[42]

When Marinovic was pressured by the monetary agency to turn over such funds, he could state that Yamani, the minister of petroleum, approved of Aramco's practice in this matter. This arrangement in fact benefited Yamani. Because of the Aramco cash reserves, "Yamani in effect never had to go to the Council of Minsters or the king for money for his projects, for the oil projects. Every other minister had to go cap in hand and plead for allocations, for budget increases. He didn't. He had it right there stashed at Aramco."[43]

Jungers did have problems explaining his investment in electricity to the shareholders. What the hell was Aramco doing messing with electricity? It could not be long before Excom learned that there was a great deal of loose money floating around in Saudi Arabia; and it was not long before the four partners decided, as Marinovic put it, "to try and get their fists on it." The whole system within Aramco had become like Dodge City. As Brock Powers remembered, to create the petrochemical industry, Aramco had

> every pipe factory, every shipyard in the Far East doing orders for Aramco. We had, like I say, every ship, railyard, every foundry in all Japan, all the pipe mills turning out stuff for Aramco, and ships at sea — you couldn't believe the number of materials that were being fabricated to build the gas processing plants.[44]

Excom expressed its unease by forming a small technical outfit called Stemco, a derivation from *S*ocal, *T*exaco, *E*xxon, and *M*obil. Its function was to examine Jungers's projects in Arabia. From time to time in the past Excom had sent out other such teams, but none were as industrious as Stemco.

Stemco was paid by the Saudi government, but not in cash, it seems. Instead it received oil at twenty-two cents a barrel, which was then sold by Stemco for the shareholders at market price. But in effect, Stemco was a Trojan horse rolled into Saudi Arabia in order to allow the parent companies to get a piece of the profit deriving from the electrification and petrochemical projects. When Stemco staff had completed their survey, a representative of one of the shareholder companies told Abdul Hadi Taher, governor of Petromin, and a director of Aramco who was acting as a Saudi government representative, that Aramco was "spending too much, and we can do it at a fraction of that."[45] Taher then "blew the whistle" on Aramco and put a freeze on Aramco's gas project. Powers was appalled:

> We had things piling up . . . all over the world, billions and billions of dollars worth of stuff that was coming out of the foundries, the sheet metal still hot. We had to stop everything, because we were [told] that we were not to spend another penny, and because an owner company told Taher it could be done better. So a year later we had so much surplus stuff. . . . By that time we couldn't put it anywhere. . . . We were infuriated. We'd wasted roughly a billion dollars [through] that little flap. And we were a year behind schedule. And it turns out we were doing it just right, and the costs were just what we said they were going to be.[46]

The problems mounted for Jungers. To run the electrification program Jungers brought in an electrical engineer, John Kelberer, who had been running the Trans-Arabian Pipeline almost since it was built back in the 1950s — although during the 1970s it had fallen into some disuse through the introduction of supertankers. Both Jungers and Powers were impressed by Kelberer: "He knew how to work with people and manipulate them to where he got what he wanted, very good at that, very good without doing anything untoward."[47]

Nonetheless, Kelberer was the sort of character who should be watched. He was certainly being scrutinized by Excom, which began to look him over as a possible successor to Jungers, whose standing in New York was gradually being eroded because of his independent thought and action and his tendency to overextend the company. But Brock Powers thought the world of his chief. He "had more workable solutions to any problem than any man I've ever known." On the other hand he felt that John Kelberer "didn't have that talent." Even so, in a short time Kelberer began to creep up behind Jungers and Powers, who was still regarded by many as Junger's successor.[48]

Excom's dissatisfaction with Jungers grew from 1976 onward, during the beginning of the huge oil industry boom. The port facilities in Saudi Arabia became so clogged that ships had to wait up to 150 days to unload. Aramco and the Saudi government often contended over which deliveries should receive priority. Chaos and overwork characterized the boom days, yet a sense of excitement was also in the air. Executives like Marinovic found it an energizing, if trying experience. As he noted,

> The boom was something incredible. Roads were being built, bridges, ports, hospitals, oil facilities, gas facilities — I mean, bulldozers going twenty-four hours a day, cement mixers. Every big construction company in the world was there: Bechtel, Fluor, you name it. . . . And they all had to work with local partners which made the local partners very rich.[49]

Then came MORT, another of the shareholders' forays into Arabia. Its object of interest was not the electrification project, but the natural gas and petrochemicals facilities being built under the Saudi government's second Five-Year Plan. This industrial project, the largest ever undertaken by a single company, required facilities exceeding "all those installed by Aramco in all of its operations since it discovered oil in 1938." The costs would "substantially exceed that of the trans-Alaska pipeline, the highest-priced industrial effort to date." Long the world's largest oil-producing company, Aramco would "soon become one of the world's largest in gas output." On completion, the gas gathering and processing facilities "will be able to handle nearly 6 billion cubic feet of associated gas per day."[50] These projections seem, if ambitious, certainly within Aramco's goals of making profits and maintaining a strong position in Saudi Arabia. But Excom would hang Jungers for them.

The acronym MORT stood for Management Organization Review Team, a title with an ominous ring to it. Members of MORT wanted control of the gas program to be invested in the owner companies, not in Aramco. To achieve that end, they wanted to move management of the gas program out of the planning branch and into the operations branch of Aramco — an Exxon management dogma. Joseph A. Mahon, a company vice president, noted how this concept was received at Aramco:

> Although we agreed and implemented many of the recommendations of the MORT reports, we never did change our Project Management responsibilities. I don't remember talking to any executive in Aramco who thought this would be a sensible thing to do. . . . But the Excom and MORT groups weren't about to give up.[51]

Implementing such a change would have been no small matter. It would necessitate an enormous transfer of personnel, management, and equipment from one part of the bureaucracy to another. Naturally, Jungers resisted making that transfer — it might take months. But Exxon kept saying to Jungers, "you have failed to hear what we told you. We want these responsibilities in Operations. Don't come back and keep proposing something different." In 1977, the MORT team flew back to Dhahran, as Mahon put it, "to survey the damage they had done." Mahon told them that "it was clear by this time that we were going to get the new facilities built on schedule, within the money and up to standard. . . . The growing realization that this was so may have been one of the things that took the steam out of MORT's push to change Project Management."[52]

Here Jungers's mission at Aramco came to an end. Trouble developed between the Aramco management and those of the owner companies. Aramco was, they complained, only imperfectly keeping them informed about what was happening on the Gulf and was becoming not only an oil-producing company, but a civil engineering concern serving the Saudi government. That was not Aramco's business. The company's main mission was producing and shipping crude for the owner companies. They questioned Aramco's efficiency in the management of the very large but still secondary projects that Aramco had undertaken for the Saudi government.

By 1977, the difficulties between Aramco under Jungers and Excom resulted in a special board meeting at the Intercontinental Hotel in Geneva. Jungers planned to make a presentation on the company's work on oil production, electrification, and gas production, as well as that other great issue — the passing of Aramco to the Saudis. Mahon was in charge of preparing and making the presentations:

> The Board convened at 9:00 A.M. and they started arguing. They argued over the minutes of the prior meeting, about who said what and how the minutes should be written. Then they argued about how the present meeting was being run. Then they argued about a report from the Gas Task Force. . . . They went at it all day. Finally, it was 5:15 P.M. and I was still sitting there with my two presentations. I knew it would take about 3 hours to present them.
>
> I could see the Board members were tired; what they really wanted to do was knock off and go get a drink. But Frank Jungers was running the show and he kept pressing them to listen to our story. I don't think he gave a damn whether they listened to our story or not. He just wanted to be able to say that we had told them exactly what we were doing, so they couldn't complain in the future. Frank got me aside and said, "Look, cut it down and move it fast. Let's get through it." So I got up there and did three hours of presentation in two hours and we did get through it. We were done about 7:30 P.M. Half of the Board members were out of their chairs doing other things while this was going on.[53]

Little was really accomplished at Geneva and so the owners adjourned to London. Jungers lodged at Haddon Hall, that stately hotel down by the Thames. The members met in the London boardroom of Mobil, an equally stately place and noteworthy for its security — it was so tight, Mahon remembered, that it "was if nuclear weapons were stored there." It was another nervy meeting; it was suddenly terminated, and everyone was instructed to fly immediately to Amsterdam and reconvene at the airport. That is what happened. But then, again for no apparent reason, Excom suddenly changed the meeting site again — back to London. Mahon remembered, "I thought it must have to do with Mobil's security consciousness — ever since Yamani's kidnapping everyone was more careful."[54]

The meeting was as nervy as before. Jungers met some of the members of Excom's old guard at the bar of Haddon Hall. He was cheerful and confident, although one of those present thought it was a front. On the next day the meetings reconvened at Mobil's headquarters. Excom was to give a dinner that evening at a private room at the Mirabelle, perhaps the most expensive restaurant in Mayfair. As the guests dressed in black tie, the word went around: Jungers had been fired. No reason was given. The guests were advised that he would not attend, although his wife would. Dinner was, Mahon remembered, like a wake. The speeches were worse. The main speaker was Joe J. Johnston, secretary of the company in New York City for years. He broke down in tears as he made his farewell speech to Jungers.

Aramco's newspaper in Dhahran, *The Arabian Sun,* devoted a special edition to Jungers's very sudden departure from the boardroom. ARAMCO'S NUMBER ONE OFFICER RETIRES, its headline announced on January 5, 1978. There was a brief editorial:

> On January First Frank Jungers stepped down as Aramco Board Chairman and Chief Executive Officer to end more than thirty years' service with The Company. This special issue of *The Arabian Sun* marks Jungers' retirement and his relinquishment of a post that *Fortune* magazine has called "one of the most delicate positions in all industry."[55]

Business Week in New York said of him, "Jungers and the men who have preceded him have worked hard to avoid the 'Ugly American' label and have succeeded to a high degree in Saudi Arabia."[56]

Jungers went home to his new residence at Sunriver, Oregon. When he left, Mahon said, "The lights dimmed some more." Excom named John Kelberer chairman of the board. They brought Hugh Goerner in from Exxon as president. As Mahon noted, "Hugh had worked many years for Exxon and affiliates and had a very strong Producing Operations background. To me this was another indication that the Owners wanted more of an Operations orientation in Aramco."[57] Then the lights dimmed again.

[16]

THE IRAN-IRAQ FACTORS

B Y 1975–80, ARAMCO FOUND itself involved in one of the most politically precarious situations in its history. To fill the power vacuum created when Britain withdrew from the Gulf and to prevent any power such as Russia from moving in, the United States had formed an alliance with the shah of Iran, Mohammed Reza Pahlavi. Strengthened by huge American and British arms programs, the shah had emerged as the region's strongest power. He was also something of a friend. In 1973 the shah declined to take part in the oil embargo levied by the other Arab nations against the United States, Europe, Japan, and Israel. On the other hand, he did become the leader in the raising of oil prices, creating a situation that he used to enhance Iranian power abroad by becoming a creditor nation. Numerous American military, technical, and political agents established themselves in Iran, specifically to deflect the potential Russian threat to the northern mountains of Iran, but also more generally to maintain stability in the Gulf oil states.

But in 1979 a catastrophe occurred — the shah was overthrown on February 11, 1979, by the Iranian religious leader the Ayatollah Khomeini. This fundamentally religious revolution was marked by severe anti-Americanism and a return to conservative Muslim standards of behavior. The ayatollah banned Western music, compelled Iranian women to wear the veil, terminated the country's military and political relationship with the United States, and ejected Western elites from the country. On November 4, 1979, an Iranian mob led by Khomeini's mullahs seized the U.S. embassy in Tehran, taking fifty-two Americans hostage and holding them for the next 444 days. Diplomatic relations between the United States and Iran were terminated. Then, on September 22, 1980, the Iraqi army invaded Iran, beginning an eight-year war primarily over possession of the disputed area of Shatt al Arab. But religious differences also fueled the conflict — the old hatred between the Sunni and the Shiite sects of Islam. Both sides used chemical weapons.

The Iraqis opened the conflict with a sustained air assault against the refinery at Abadan, still the largest in the world, built and owned by the British until they lost control of Iranian and Iraqi oil after World War II. Saudi Arabia and Aramco began to fear for the safety of Ras Tanura, should the Iraq-Iran War draw in other parties, particularly other Arab nations sympathizing either with the Sunnis or the Shiites. And indeed, the plot did thicken. After Abadan, the Iraqi armed forces sought to devastate the whole Iranian oil industry, including all oil ports and cities. The Iranians made counterattacks against Iraqi oil facilities and persuaded Syria to cut Iraq's pipeline exports to the Mediterranean coast — this left Iraq with only one small pipeline through Turkey, drying up its oil revenues. Iran's oil output was also greatly reduced. Consequently, oil prices jumped again, to $42 a barrel. Aramco held to the prewar pricing level until the market stabilized, and when it did in October 1981, Aramco's price rose from $32 to $34 a barrel. Still, a new oil panic ignited, with dire effect on the U.S. economy. According to oil historian Daniel Yergin, the Iran-Iraq conflict threatened

> not only economic performance but the whole social fabric of the Western world. The United States Federal Reserve responded by instituting an exceedingly restrictive monetary policy that resulted in a sharp rise of interest rates, with prime, at one point, reaching the sky-high level of 21.5%. Tight money came on top of the drain of spending power from the industrial world because of the oil price increases. The combined consequence was the deepest recession since the Great Depression, with two bottoms, the first in 1980 and the second, more severe, in 1982.[1]

The situation worsened. Iraq and Iran began to attack tankers in the Gulf. The United States and its allies sent powerful squadrons of warships to defend the tankers when the ayatollah threatened to close the Strait of Hormuz, the West's only sea route from Dhahran into the Indian Ocean — a duty that culminated in a disastrous incident on July 3, 1988. A U.S. Navy warship accidentally shot down an Iranian airliner over the Gulf. All aboard were killed — some 250 passengers and crew.

President Carter's response was, in 1979, to repeat what every U.S.

president since Roosevelt had said. Saudi Arabia and the Persian Gulf constituted "an area of vital interest to the United States" and "any attempt by any outside force to gain control of the Persian Gulf" would be regarded as "an assault on the vital interests of the USA," which would be "repelled by any means necessary, including military force."[2] The United States then began to prepare to counter Russian or Iranian operations against Saudi Arabia. Indeed, the groundwork for such preparations had already been laid. The United States had taken a number of measures to ensure the safety and viability of the oil industry in Saudi Arabia:

- In 1972–88 the Army Corps of Engineers directed "five major construction projects funded entirely by the Kingdom of Saudi Arabia at a total cost of $14 billion."[3] These included the King Khalid Military City, which contained quarters for 80,000 troops and their equipment. This program included, also, airfields capable of handling B52 bombers and connected by pipelines to Ras Tanura, where jet fuel could be manufactured.
- In 1976 the United States had begun sales, training, and logistics support to establish the Saudi navy in the Suez.
- In 1977 the office of the U.S. secretary of defense conducted the "Presidential Review of U.S. Regional Security Commitments and Capabilities. It cited the need for the following forces to protect U.S. interests in Saudi Arabia: light combat forces, naval and tactical air forces, and mobile forces.
- In 1977 the United States and Bahrein concluded an agreement for continued leasing of docking and shore facilities by the U.S. Middle East Force at Bahrein Island, close to Aramco headquarters.
- In July 1978, Presidential Directive 18 designated a strike force of about 100,000 troops to respond to regional conflicts that might put Saudi oil at risk. The Department of Defense identified two army divisions, one heavy and one light, and a marine corps amphibious force to fulfill this directive. The Pentagon also was instructed to increase its strategic airlift and sealift capability so it could quickly transport these forces to potential combat zones. The strike force was to be backed up by aircraft carriers and by up to three U.S. Air Force tactical air wings, totaling about two hundred airplanes.

In 1979, the pace of military preparations quickened. President Carter stated, "As a result of the Iranian revolution and increasing tension, the Secretary of Defense increased naval task force deployments to the Indian Ocean from two every other year to four a year and gradually expanded the duration of the deployments."[4] President Carter also announced that rapid deployment forces would be used to meet contingencies anywhere in the world — particularly the Persian Gulf and Arabian theaters. Subsequent presidents took further steps regarding the protection of oil resources in the Middle East. In 1984, President Reagan stated that

> given the importance of [the Middle East] we must also be ready to act when the presence of American power and that of our friends can help stop the spread of violence. I have said, for example, that we'll keep open the Strait of Hormuz, the vital lifeline through which much of the oil flows to the U.S. and other industrial democracies.[5]

For his part, the ayatollah announced that he would seize Baghdad, revolutionize Saudi Arabia, and take Mecca. Afterward, he promised, he would make war against Israel and return Jerusalem and Riyadh to the Shiite fold. To ensure a Sunni victory over the ayatollah's forces, Saudi Arabia and Kuwait began to finance the Iraqi Sunni leader Saddam Hussein to the tune, it was said, of $38 billion. Saudi Arabia under King Khalid risked a rupture in Saudi-U.S. relations by buying "East Wind" heavy missiles from Red China. Saudi Arabia and China then established diplomatic relations, a move that in Washington was seen as yet another compromise of America's special relationship with the Saudi government. The U.S. government tried to interfere with the purchase, but the Saudis held their ground. They explained that they had bought Chinese weapons because they could not get them from the United States.

Such was the state of the Gulf when the ayatollah began his campaign to revolutionize the Shiite minority in Hasa. The area's population, about 200,000, constituted 40 percent of Aramco's workforce in the oil fields around the Shiite township of Qatif. These people were the most underprivileged in Saudi society, and by 1979 they had become disaffected to the extent that local leaders advocated the seizure of Hasa, to be followed by secession from Saudi Arabia and the establishment of a Shiite state.

The Shiite leaders at Qatif were heavily influenced by the Tehran radio station called the Voice of Free Iran, which regularly denounced King Khalid, the house of Saud, and the American component of Aramco:

> The Saudi authorities are carrying out the same treacherous role that the deposed Shah carried out in Iran. . . . The ruling regime in Saudi Arabia wears Muslim clothing, but inwardly represents the U.S. body, mind, and terrorism. . . . Funds are robbed from the people and squandered . . . for the luxurious, frivolous and shameless way of life of the Saudi royal family and its entourage.[6]

Such messages struck a chord with the Saudis of Hasa, threatening instability in the very region most important to U.S. oil interests — the location of Aramco. Peter Iseman, a leading American reporter in the Gulf, commented on the wide-ranging effects such a revolt could have:

> The West's dependence on Arabian oil is now deeply embedded, and will remain so at least until the end of this century. Renewed disturbances and tension would increase political pressure to cut back the level of oil production in Saudi Arabia and the Gulf States. This in turn would tighten world supplies and probably trigger another sharp upsurge of oil prices. An actual attack, sabotage, or even a serious political incident could interrupt oil supplies and cause widespread uncertainty and severe economic disruption. "Oilfields are extremely difficult to defend," Kuwait's Oil Minister remarked recently, "and, once attacked, are extremely difficult to operate afterward."[7]

Such an incident occurred on the morning of November 20, 1979, New Year's Day in the Muslim calendar and the first day of the fourteenth century for all Islam. The pilgrimage was taking place, and the delegation of Iranians, the largest ever sent to Mecca, talked of "exporting the revolution" to Saudi Arabia.

The first Iranian attack against the Saudi dynasty began that day, not at Qatif, but at Mecca, Islam's holiest city. At 5:20 A.M. the imam of the Grand Mosque in Mecca, Sheikh Muhammad bin Subayal, approached the microphone to begin this most special day of prayers. Just as he finished his intonations to the multitude, there was the sound of a gunshot close by. Then two more. A strange individual, Juhaiman bin Muhhamad al-Utaibi, had fired the shots, and one of the imam's acolytes lay dead. A stranger seized the microphone from the hands of the imam and shouted into it that he was the "Expected Mahdi."

In Arabic the "divinely guided one," the Mahdi is a messianic deliverer who will fill the earth with justice and equity, restore true religion, and usher in a short golden age before the end of the world — an essential Shiite doctrine. The Mahdi is seen as a restorer of political power and religious purity, and therefore the title has been claimed by a number of Islamic social revolutionaries. The most important in recent history was Muhammad Ahmad, Mahdi of the Sudan, who in 1881 revolted against the Egyptians. The British general Horatio Kitchener led a powerful force to the Sudan to put down Mahdism — an epic episode in which Winston Churchill took part. It was the last appearance of a Mahdi until 1979. There is little doubt that another will appear.

Juhaiman announced over the microphone, "The Mahdi and his men will seek shelter and protection in the Holy Mosque because they are persecuted everywhere until they have no recourse but the Holy

Mosque."[8] At that declaration the imam slipped away to call for help. As he did so a large group seemed to coalesce out of the mass of pilgrims. They included women and children, and they were all heavily armed. In a flash they had occupied the mosque and chained shut the heavy wooden doors to the vast building.

As custodian of the two holy mosques, King Khalid bore the responsibility to recapture the mosque and restore it, undamaged, to the faithful. At that moment there began for the Saudi dynasty what has been called "the two most frightening weeks since the revolt of Sheikh Feisal al-Dawish and the other rebellious Ikhwan in 1928/1929." In fact, small bands of the religiously conservative Ikhwan survived in isolated regions of the kingdom, and they leveled against King Khalid the same accusations they had brought against Ibn Saud: troubles had come to the kingdom because the royal family had permitted infidels into the holy land of Islam. And Richard Johns of the *Financial Times* reported to London: "Many observers of the scene, including Saudis, thought the revolt as ominous for the [Saudi royal family] as the great demonstrations by the Ayatollah in Teheran had been for the Shah of Persia."[9]

It emerged that Juhaiman, the leader in the insurrection at the Grand Mosque, had joined the National Guard, a military force drawn mainly from the Bedouin and regarded by the Saudi dynasty as its most reliable body of troops. He had risen to the rank of corporal but had left to study law at the university in Medina. Here he may have imbibed the fiercely conservative Islam of Sheikh Baz, a faculty member and the sheikh who had made Tom Barger's 1940 visit to Layla so unpleasant. But in 1974, after no more than two years of study, Juhaiman left Medina with ten other students.

By 1976 Juhaiman had become a preacher in Riyadh. He wrote pamphlets, for example, "Rules of Obedience: The Misconduct of Rulers," a direct attack on the Saud dynasty. He charged that the princes were corrupt and greedy and consorted with infidels. Because of the pamphlet's inflammatory nature, in 1978, Saudi security chief Prince Naif charged Juhaiman and his followers, who by then had increased to ninety-eight, with treason. Sheikh Baz was ordered to Riyadh from Medina to question Juhaiman and his friends, but he could not or would not find evidence of treason. The group was then released against a promise that they would not engage further in politics. Baz himself had been freed by Ibn Saud under similar circumstances in 1944.

Juhaiman became interested in the "doctrine of the expected Mahdi." Little was known of this doctrine to Westerners, but in Sunni doctrine he was a figure of considerable mysticism. The Mahdi would reappear "at the end of time," preceded by a Muslim Antichrist. This Antichrist would be slain by Jesus, who would restore justice on earth and establish universal Islam. And as an authority on the subject has noted, "The belief is not rooted in the [Koran] but has its origins in Jewish ideas about the Messiah and in the Christian beliefs of the second coming of Christ."[10] Juhaiman believed he had found the Mahdi, in the person of Muhammad bin Abdullah al Qahtani, a twenty-seven-year-old student at Riyadh University.

After his release from jail, Juhaiman and his entourage (which included Saudis, Egyptians, Kuwaitis, Yemenis, Pakistanis, and Americans) collected arms, mainly the AK47 of the Soviet Union. The weapons may have come from Syria or the Yemen, possibly supplied by the Russians in an attempt to undermine the Saudi dynasty.

Prince Bandar bin Sultan, the Saudi ambassador in Washington, is said to have told U.S. officials that the Ikhwan had emerged again and that they had been trained in the use of their arms in the Marxist People's Democratic Republic of Yemen. Juhaiman published another pamphlet, "The Call of the Ikhwan." Then he sent word to his followers to come to Mecca in the last five days of November 1979, the month of Muharram, and he was obeyed. At this same time, so it was claimed later, the Shiite Muslims of Qatif were to rise against King Khalid and the infidels — the Americans at Aramco and the Koreans at Jubail.

Juhaiman was accompanied on the pilgrimage by Muhammad the Mahdi, who brought with him his sister and mother; and as the month and the century drew to a close, Juhaiman's Ikhwan, numbering some two hundred people, trickled into Mecca. Some were detained by Saudi security people, but no action was taken and no alarm was sounded. By the last night of the Muslim century, Juhaiman's arms had reached the Grand Mosque, a vast building that had been refurbished by King Saud to the tune of one billion riyals. The arms had been hidden successfully in the basement along with food and water. Robert Lacey, a chronicler of the siege at the mosque, wrote that Juhaiman's and the Mahdi's planning

> showed considerable forethought, hard work and a considerable ability to reason. The fighting, when it started, showed discipline, training and a sound grasp of tactics — a tribute to the National Guard from which some of the conspirators came. But everything was dedicated to one grand irrational act, the proclamation of a Mahdi which, [Juhaiman] genuinely believed and hoped, would inspire thousands of wor-

shippers to join him and overwhelm any troops which the al-Saud might send against him.[11]

After the first gunshots and Juhaiman's introduction of the Mahdi, some six hundred men of the Saudi special forces set siege around the building. King Khalid summoned the ulema, which included Sheikh Baz, and asked for an opinion as to whether the government had the authority, according to shariah law, to attack the Ikhwan in the mosque. The divines did find that one of the Prophet's statements supported such action: "Do not fight them near the Holy Mosque until they fight you inside it, and if they fight you, you must kill them for that is the punishment for the unbelievers."[12]

At Mecca, Prince Naif, chief of the Saudi security service, was joined by the head of the Saudi foreign intelligence service, Prince Turki. Although Juhaiman was disappointed that scarcely any of the thousands at the Grand Mosque wanted anything to do with his Mahdi, his zealots were strongly placed to hold off attackers. The Grand Mosque made a fine fortress. In a long battle, the Saudi infantry recaptured the building pillar by pillar. Because Saudi troops showed some hesitation to fight within God's House and against fellow Wahhabs, the defense minister sent for the two battalions of Pakistani Muslim commandos under contract to the Saudi government "for special tasks." As Lacey wrote,

> This was Holy War. Every time the rebels saw one of the government forces fall, they cried out, "*Amr Allah!*" ("At the command of God!"). When one of their own comrades dies, they shot off his face or tried to burn it in an attempt to mask his identity. This was a task they often gave to the women and children who were with them — and some of these took to mutilating fallen soldiers for good measure. [The last stages of the siege were] fought out in the warren of cellars below the Grand Mosque's marble pavement. The Mahdi was shot and his dead body photographed after four days of fighting, proof that he was not the divinely promised one as he and his brother-in-law had claimed. But [Juhaiman] and his followers fought on. They refused appeals to surrender, for they could not expect to live very long or very pleasantly if they did not submit — and they withdrew to the basement, blackening their faces and holing up in the grubby little rooms with mattresses, their womenfolk, and what was left of their dates and water.[13]

Juhaiman was not, however, captured or killed during the first week of the subterranean fighting. But the Mahdi was killed. After about ten days, Juhaiman was cornered after the government troops had thrown tear-gas bombs, burning tires, and live electrical cables into the water that flooded the basements — an attempt to electrocute the rebels into surrender. Juhaiman's capture did not mark the end of the affair. Some of his followers continued to fight it out for four or five days. Then they surrendered before Saudi TV cameras.

Meanwhile, over a thousand miles away in Hasa, the Shiites of Qatif rose simultaneously with Juhaiman's revolt in Mecca. Doping themselves on a mixture of fermented dates and stimulating spices, they marched by the thousands through the narrow alleys of Qatif to mark the death of the Prophet's grandson, Hussein. They drove themselves into violent frenzies of flagellation and self-mutilation. The ayatollah's short-wave propaganda service began a campaign of bitter attacks against King Khalid, Crown Prince Fahd, the Saudi royal dynasty in general, and the behavior of certain princes. The ayatollah's mullahs incited them to believe, as did Tehran radio, that a general uprising had begun all over Arabia against the Saud dynasty. These crowds inflicted severe property damage in al-Khobar and Qatif — they burned cars and wrecked homes and shops, but did not disturb Aramco property.

A *Wall Street Journal* reporter stated that rumors of "impending evacuation, or American troop landings, have been so widespread that some U.S. employers have set up special hot lines to dispel them." Indeed, "the takeover of Islam's holiest mosque and the rioting in the oil-field town of Qatif have temporarily shaken the confidence of Saudis and Americans alike."

These incidents ended on January 9, 1980. Sixty-three of the Mahdi's followers were split into small groups and sent to the cities of Mecca, Riyadh, Medina, Dammam, Buraidah, Hail, Abha, and Tabuk. The accused were then beheaded in the public squares. No American participants were identified, although it was believed widely that Americans had been involved.

The Iranian threat made the Saudi government look to the purity of the faith. It uttered special decrees intended to ensure that Aramco employees observed the holy days. After January 1976, when participation became effective, the government specified how foreigners should behave on such days. For example, this advisory was issued to all Aramcons regarding the month of Ramadan:

> The blessed month of Ramadan is with us now. This is a month during which God requires Muslims to fast and one which He has preferred over all the remaining months of the year.
>
> This month is the focus of care and concern of all Muslims. Since the common manifestation of fasting is the Muslims' practice of re-

fraining from eating or drinking during the day, it certainly hurts their feelings to see other people deviate from this manifestation, even though they may be non-Muslims.

Therefore, non-Muslim residents in this country must respect the feelings of Muslims by refraining from openly eating, drinking or smoking in public places, streets and work locations. The fact that they are not Muslims shall not relieve them of this duty. This is in observance of the Islamic rites and in deference to the feelings of our citizens and out of respect for the sacred Islamic beliefs. This is also provided for in the employment contracts which require the employee to respect the sanctity of Islamic rites and comply with the regulations of the country.

As it is mandatory for all people to respect fasting during the blessed month of Ramadan, the Ministry of Interior hopes that all foreigners will comply with the contents of this statement and whoever deviates from or fails to comply with them shall be subject to such deterrent actions as may be taken by the authorities concerned, such as termination of employment and deportation from the Kingdom.

Establishments, companies and individuals must explain and convey the text of this statement to their employees, workmen and servants, and warn them of the consequences of its violation.[14]

"Immodest women" were warned that they would be punished. Still another decree announced that the religious police were authorized to arrest male foreigners with long hair, which would then be "shorn by force." All Aramcons were warned that the Committees of Public Morality were empowered to act under "High Orders issued by the King" and that they had been given "the sole authority to investigate violations of public morality and to apprehend and prosecute offenders." A fresh decree was issued relating to the use of alcohol, stating that upon "accusation or suspicion of intoxication, a doctor's certification must be obtained. The local Committee has the authority to incarcerate the accused pending trial and investigation." They had "the right to administer punishment not exceeding ten lashes or imprisonment for seven days to offenders."[15]

Aramco's response to the Iranian threat was to look afresh at the security of oil fields and their installations, which were very vulnerable to sabotage. A private California company, Vinnell, was hired to assist in the protection of the oil fields. A Vinnell vice president, Wilbur Crane Eveland, formerly a CIA contract agent in the Middle East, claimed that "Vinnell had hired a retired U.S. general and recruited Vietnam veterans to form an army of mercenaries charged with guarding the Kingdom's oil-production facilities against sabotage and foreign attack." Moreover, Eveland asserted that Vinnell "secured the contract by paying a multimillion-fee to a Saudi agent."[16]

There can be no doubt of the need for such mercenaries. Aramco considered Saudi troops unreliable. These measures were taken despite the fact that the Saudis opposed the dispatch of regular U.S. troops to Saudi Arabia except in time of war, for such troops could seem to justify the claim that Saudi Arabia had been occupied by foreign troops.

This report of security measures at Aramco was given to the U.S. General Accounting Office:

> All key installations are enclosed by high fences with elevated watchtowers strategically located and manned by Saudi Army personnel. All entrances and exits are tightly controlled; only individuals with proper passes are permitted entry. The large Ras Tanura–Juaymah complex has especially tight security controls because about 97% of Aramco crude oil is processed and exported from this location. Aramco is highly concerned with security and constantly reviews its security procedures. Nevertheless, sabotage is possible. Because of the small number of key facilities and the large volume handled by each, the impact of sabotage on production could be much more severe than in other countries.[17]

Aramco also provided evidence about how severe that damage might be. In May and June 1977, an explosion and fire broke out at Abqaiq. Had that explosion and fire occurred a few yards away, "the impact on production could have been devastating." As it was, the results were bad enough: "Although full production was restored within 6 weeks, the damage caused by these fires was extensive and repairs cost over $100 million."[18] In April 1978, explosion and fire occurred at a gas-oil separator plant north of Abqaiq. The plant was almost totally destroyed, and four employees were killed. Although this damage was not the result of sabotage, it was easy to see how readily a single fire or explosion staged by a saboteur could inflict serious loss of property and life.

Thus fears of insidious attack and the tightening of behavioral standards imposed by the religious police made Saudi Arabia an uncomfortable place to live and work for the Aramcos.

Not only were Aramco's physical facilities at risk — management personnel were also vulnerable to harassment from Saudi officials. Now that control of Aramco was passing to them, the Saudis felt compelled to prove that they were as serious about Islamic practice as the Iranians; they felt confident that there would be no U.S. reprisals as they targeted Westerners to make a show of Saudi clout. The Saudi coast guard arrested Baldo Marinovic and a number of Aramco's higher management while they were out in the Gulf on a fishing expedition. Their five boats had reached the fishing grounds when, Marinovic related, "all of a sudden the Saudi coastguard came up."[19]

When the cutter pulled up alongside his vessel, Marinovic produced his Aramco ID card and his sailing permit, and then he started to chat with the Saudi officer. He was grimly told to go to Qurrayah, the nearest coast guard station. When Marinovic began to argue with the man who gave him the order, "the fellow who was with me in the boat, our senior vice president of finance, Frank Milne," nudged him. Marinovic then noticed that another Saudi was pointing a machine gun at him. He then set course for Qurrayah, where he and his party were detained.[20]

A curious incident occurred during their detention that illustrated the peculiar dynamics of living among conservative Muslims. In Marinovic's party

> was a friend of mine who couldn't find anyone else to go with him, so he kind of conned his wife to go out with him, even though she didn't particularly like to go out in a boat. Well, they were also picked up, and they were brought to the coastguard station where a big discussion ensued among our Saudi captors.
>
> We finally figured out what was going on. There is an absolute rule that no women are ever allowed inside any military installation. So they couldn't take her into the station. On the other hand, she was a captive, so they couldn't let her go. So they had a problem. Finally, you know what the solution was?
>
> They brought him into the compound, and they left her to sit in the sand outside. She sat there for six hours. Her husband was allowed to bring her water through the barbed wire. I can assure you, she never went out in the boat again![21]

There was one significant reason for their arrest: to put the Aramcons on notice that the Saudis were in charge. Marinovic and his party were released after six hours, and they were given no reason for this harassment by the coast guard. Marinovic thought that the Saudis "were terrified that somebody was going to be a better Muslim than they were, and so at that point they started clamping down to prove that they are just as good Muslims as anybody else. Also, of course, prosperity had arrived so they felt their oats, and they started tightening up." Until that point Aramco had "almost enjoyed extraterritorial status. The Saudi police kept out of our Aramco camps, which had become small cities. We had our own unarmed security force. Women could drive inside of our camps. We had in our supermarkets a pork store where you could buy pork products." But after the Iranian revolt, "at a certain point, the police came into camp and arrested the priest at Abqaiq. He was released the same day."[22]

Gradually but perceptibly the power and control of Aramco had begun to slip away; and as it did so, another rising star of the Arab world, Saddam Hussein, president of Iraq, rose as an important force in the war between Iraq and Iran.

In 1988, General H. Norman Schwarzkopf, son of the officer who was sent to Iran in 1942 to train Iranian security forces in order to repel Hitler's Plan Orient, was appointed commander in chief of Central Command, the headquarters established by the Pentagon to deal with crises in the Persian Gulf. Schwarzkopf had spent some time with his father at the end of World War II. He claimed, therefore, some knowledge about the Persian Gulf — in addition to having lived there, he was well read in the literature of the region. Born in 1934, graduated from West Point, twice wounded in Vietnam, he had commanded the formidable Twenty-fourth Mechanized Infantry Division in NATO, and he had held a number of staff appointments when he was brought forward as the chief of plans and policy at Pacific Command. To ensure protection of U.S. interests in the Persian Gulf, U.S. forces there were expanded, beginning in 1983. Eventually, Schwarzkopf was transferred from Honolulu to head Central Command, located in Florida.

Among his tasks was the defense of Aramco and its oil fields. Iraq had begun to aim cruise missiles at ships in the Gulf, and the Reagan government offered to escort Kuwaiti supertankers under the American flag in order to safeguard the flow of oil. This escort operation, code-named Earnest Will, involved twenty-four major warships and sixteen thousand personnel. A number of naval engagements between American and Iranian warships followed.

Before departing for the Middle East, Schwarzkopf attended the Foreign Service School at Arlington, Virginia. As he wrote in a memoir, "What I encountered in Washington scared me." There were few Arabists in either the State Department or the CIA, "and at the Pentagon they were downright scarce." When he talked about "the Arabs with my fellow generals and admirals, their only question was, 'What treaty obligations do we have with them?' — meaning that since there were no treaties, the United States had no responsibilities. They were totally focused on fulfilling America's commitments to NATO, Japan, and Korea." For his part, Schwarzkopf "couldn't imagine a more important region. Oil imported from the Arabian Gulf already counted for two thirds of Japan's annual consumption, thirty percent of Western Europe's, and a tenth of the USA's. The region had sixty-five percent of the world's proven oil reserves, so it stood to reason that its importance to industrialized countries would only increase."[23]

Schwarzkopf had begun to study Saddam Hussein of Iraq. Born in April 1937, Saddam was the product of the underworld of Middle Eastern politics. He became a Ba'athist, a member of the leading political party of Syria and Iraq. He was therefore an Arab socialist, an advocate of pan-Arab unity, and a secularist. He knelt toward Mecca to say his prayers five times a day like all good Muslims, but the political world he inhabited was not characterized by religious values. When he came to the attention of the White House, Saddam had been in and out of prison for conspiracy and murder; he had escaped from prison and spent two years in Ba'athist politics; he had been wounded by gunfire in one attempted coup d'état; and he finally seized power in Baghdad, becoming vice chairman of the Revolutionary Command Council. In July 1979, having eliminated his rivals and his opponents, he became president, supreme commander of the armed forces, and secretary-general of the Ba'ath Party. Also, Saddam Hussein had amassed a remarkable arsenal:

> The Iraqi military machine — numbering more than a million men with an extensive arsenal of chemical weapons, extended-range Scud missiles, a large air force and one of the world's largest armies — emerged as the premier armed force in the Persian Gulf region. In the Middle East, only the Israel Defense Force had superior capability.[24]

That data made an impression on the U.S. military, especially when, in the late 1980s, it seemed that the United States would have to fight Saddam to defend Saudi Arabia and Aramco. Such concerns were heightened when, at an Arab summit in May 1990, Saddam Hussein's attitude was only too apparent. His "haughty appearance gave a clue to the state of his mind — bitter, vainglorious, intent on revenge, a man with a strong sense of being wronged who was no doubt preparing to take by force what he considered his due."[25] But for all his poverty — war debt intensified by the severe crash in oil prices by 1984–85 — Saddam's army was still the most powerful in the Arab states, and the fear developed that, to restore his economy, he would seize and then milk the rich oil-bearing states of Kuwait, Abu Dhabi, and Saudi Arabia. Saddam would resolve his financial troubles by making his creditors his clients.

The Iraqis had long held that Kuwait was Iraq's nineteenth province; certainly Saddam agreed. Furthermore, its riches aside, Kuwait was also arrogant about its wealth and was pressuring Saddam to repay the war loans that, with Saudi Arabia, it had made to Saddam to protect Sunni Kuwait against Shiite Iran. Thus Kuwait became Iraq's target.

Regarding U.S. involvement in the ensuing conflict, it was alleged that Ambassador April Glaspie had been authorized to advise Saddam that the United States had no interest in Iraq's border dispute with Kuwait, thus encouraging Saddam to occupy Kuwait. Some have also speculated that the United States and Saudi Arabia had wearied of Saddam's "mad dog" menaces in the Gulf and together conspired to tempt Saddam into a trap to destroy him. Was Saudi Arabia ever in danger of Iraqi attack? According to the opinion of James E. Akins, former U.S. ambassador to Saudi Arabia, it was not:

> I have never believed that Saddam intended to invade Saudi Arabia. He knew it would bring him into instant war with the United States and, while he might have some initial success, it is unlikely that he could have sustained long transportation lines across the desert . . . through Kuwait to the Saudi capital at Riyadh or to the oilfields of Damman. In any case, American bombers would [have] quickly [destroyed] Baghdad.[26]

All the same, defensive measures were taken during the Gulf War to protect Aramco from possible attack by way of the highway on Jubail, a main port and center of the industries created by Saudi Arabia in its second Five-Year Plan, which could then spread to the Aramco installations and oil fields at Dhahran, Ras Tanura, and Qatif.

[17]

THE ARAMCO WAR

FTER THE SHIITE REVOLT at Mecca and riots at Qatif, there came dynastic trouble. King Khalid fell ill. He had undergone open heart surgery and the insertion of a pacemaker in Cleveland in 1972, hip surgery in London in 1977, and more heart surgery in Cleveland in October 1979. He had sustained a "minor heart attack" in February 1980. During the crises in Iran, Iraq, and Arabia, therefore, Khalid reigned but left much of the management of the kingdom to Crown Prince Fahd. Khalid died shortly afterward, on June 13, 1982, and Crown Prince Fahd succeeded. Analysts considering Fahd's fitness to rule Saudi Arabia and its oil industry concluded that Fahd was capable but had weaknesses. He had, with U.S. assistance, ably administered the second Five-Year Plan. But his diabetes constituted a health problem, his spending another:

> He squandered millions of dollars as a young man. But now, except by [that of] the Sultan of Brunei, his wealth may be unmatched in history. He has seven huge palaces in Saudi Arabia and a conservative estimate of their value would be $11 billion. In addition to the palaces in his own country he has a 100-room palace at Marbella, another fitted out for eighteenth-century French kings outside Paris, a third with 1500 telephone lines in Geneva and a huge house near London which cost £30 million to refurbish. Of course, there is his flying palace, a Boeing 747 fitted with a sauna, a lift, chandeliers and gold bathroom fixtures, and his equally lavish $50 million yacht. He uses gold-plated tooth-brushes and his beach buggy is a Rolls Royce Camargue converted for the purpose by the British firm of Wood and Barrett. Fahd's personal wealth, excluding his palaces, is estimated at $28 billion.[1]

In dynastic affairs, it was observed, Fahd's blood lines included those of the Sudairi tribe, the clan from which sprang Ibn Saud's favorite wife. Such was Saudi society that a man who had Sudairi blood had enough. Fahd's reputation for competence also owed much to the reports of journalists and diplomats, which "endowed Fahd with a non-existent talent." The journalists began to call him "amiable and talented," "a workaholic," "modern and liberal thinking" — an estimate now considered a "public-relations lie" that hid a "lack of character" that "goes beyond his love of money, women, gambling and alcohol to affect the way he runs the Government."[2]

Disregarding King Faisal's reforms related to the powers of the monarchy, Fahd had seen to it that the full powers of the state were returned to him. His roles included head of the royal family, prime minister, chief government executive, supreme religious imam, commander in chief of the armed forces, and chief justice. As a Palestinian writer commented,

> With this type of unchecked control, the country's huge oil income is totally in Fahd's hands. Apart from the perfunctory need to appease the religious leaders, there are no executive, legislative or judicial authorities to question his decisions. And because he controls the country's income and his position as head of the family comes first, describing Saudi Arabia as the world's largest family business becomes axiomatic.[3]

Yet despite Fahd's independent ways and grasping of the reins of government, the Aramcons had confidence that they would yet prove indispensable. After all, Yamani was still in place as minister of petroleum, and despite his wily maneuvering, the Aramco executives knew how to work with him.

Then King Fahd sacked Yamani in 1986. Despite nearly twenty years of service, Yamani was an inconvenience to Fahd, who wished to determine oil policy himself. Fahd was head of the Supreme Petroleum Council, which determined

> future oil production levels, investments in the petroleum industry, oil pricing and other marketing questions, the Aramco takeover, participation agreements and implementation of economic development plans. The Crown Prince formulates the major oil policy decisions, based on the discussions and recommendations of the Council, and provides guidance to the ministries for carrying out daily operations.[4]

Yamani's ministry was located directly under the council, and it is easy to see how the two may have come into conflict. As one report noted, Yamani "establishes production levels, sets prices, and determines how petroleum revenues should be budgetted for oil operations and capacity expansion." Fahd may have been jealous of his many

accomplishments: he negotiated with Aramco to implement participation to the Saudis' advantage and acted as Saudi Arabia's spokesperson
on the topic of oil. He "acted as the chief Saudi representative at the
OPEC meetings," where he was influential "in determining oil pricing
decisions."5 To gain the full power Fahd desired in matters relating to
oil, he had to dismiss Yamani.

One observer told an interesting story of Fahd's reaction to an incident during Vice President George Bush's visit to Aramco in the spring
of 1986. Bush

> began telling Fahd what a good meeting he'd had with Sheikh Yamani
> the day before in Riyadh. Acknowledging Yamani's presence a few seats
> away from Fahd, Bush lavished praise on the oil minister, extolling his
> virtues. It was too much for Fahd to bear. He flared into a rage. His
> hands trembled. One of the Americans present says that Fahd made
> Bush understand in no uncertain terms, "When you want to talk to
> someone in Saudi Arabia about oil, you come to me. No one else."
> Fahd told Bush, "I am the one who makes the decisions, not Yamani."6

There were other reasons for Yamani's slide into obscurity. He was a
Hejazi cosmopolitan, whereas most of the Saudi establishment were
dour Nejdis. The latter regarded the Hejazis as city slickers, less than
dedicated Wahhabs, and not always reliable. On the other hand, the
Hejazis regarded the Saudi dynasty's hometown, Riyadh, as "that primitive hick town up there on the desert plateau."7 Yamani's main patron
in the dynasty, the late King Faisal, had spent many years as viceroy of
the Hejaz and could judge Yamani not by his origins but by his ability.
King Fahd and the Sudairi Seven, with their Wahhabi orthodoxy, could
hardly tolerate the media superstar Yamani, a man who wore Cardin
suits, Gucci booties, and floral American ties.

The seven failed to prove anything criminal against Yamani, but
certain problems in the oil market were blamed on him. In 1981, the
oil price had begun to crash, and members alleged that he had been
talking the price down to benefit the United States. By 1982, the price,
hitherto around $40 a barrel, crumbled to $32. Iran accused Yamani
of undermining the price in order to acquire special surveillance aircraft from the United States. As OPEC itself began to crumble, Iraq
alleged that Yamani had become an American agent. An oil glut began. The price dropped below $27 a barrel. Yamani tried to stop the
declines, but he failed. In 1984 Saudi revenues fell to $36 billion, and
in 1985 to $25 billion. Spending on the Five-Year Plan was cut back
though not abandoned, and the kingdom began to run a budget deficit. In June 1985 Saudi oil output sagged as low as 2.2 million barrels

a day, little more than a fifth of what the kingdom had produced and sold five years earlier. Exports to the United States, which had been as high as 1.4 million barrels daily in 1979, slumped to a mere 26,000 barrels a day in June 1985.

This sharpened Fahd's dislike of Yamani, and to the surprise and regret of many Aramcons, Yamani was fired in 1986. Then Fahd put his own designee into the ministry and, at last, proceeded to take full control of Aramco.

On November 8, 1988, King Fahd uttered a royal decree announcing the sale of the Arabian American Oil Company to the Saudi Arabian government. He gave the company a new name: the Saudi Arabian Oil Company.

Aramco's era of "enlightened self-interest" passed into history when Fahd's decree defined the new venture as "an integrated international oil company which is to engage in all activities related to the oil industry, on a commercial basis and for the purpose of profit." It had been eighteen years since the participation talks had begun in 1970; twelve years since 1976, when Aramco had agreed formally to transfer Aramco to Saudi Arabia when the Saudi government had paid for it, and eight years since title had formally passed to the Saudi government. A dour crowd, the Saudi management held no celebration when the decree was promulgated.[8]

The sum paid for Aramco by the Saudi government was not revealed publicly. But in January 1976, when Aramco and the Saudis had reached agreement on the terms through which the company would pass to Saudi Arabia, an elaborate media statement was prepared and approved by all parties. Although it was not used, the terms in this statement formed the basis for the transfer of power:

> The Council of Ministers of the Kingdom of Saudi Arabia today announced ratification of agreements providing for the ownership by the Government of 100% of Arabian American Oil Company's producing and refining assets, and 50% ownership of Aramco's gas liquids facilities. Agreement in principle had been reached on (date) at (location) by the Saudi Arab Minister of Petroleum and representatives of the Aramco owner companies, Exxon, Mobil, Standard of California, and Texaco.[9]

The agreement read as if the greatest fire sale in history had just occurred. It compensated Aramco for "the net book value" of the assets and provided "that Saudi Arab oil will continue to be made available to world consumers through the U.S. owner companies in substantial

volumes at prevailing market prices." Total compensation to be received under "all prior and current agreements approximates $2.8
billion." This included "approximately $1.5 billion payable under the
current agreements for crude oil assets" — the "oil in the ground"
discovered in Excom-financed exploration and hitherto a source of
dispute and controversy between the parties — and $450 million for
refining and natural gas liquids assets.[10]

Did "net book value" include the true value of the wells, refineries,
pipelines, roads, housing estates, port facilities, aircraft, airfields,
ships, office buildings, vehicles, repair shops, rigs, radio and television
stations, telephone networks, sewage plants, water wells and water desalting systems, hospitals, schools, and all the other facilities constructed by Aramco? The Aramco announcement of 1976 covered
that aspect of the deal with a statement that, although diplomatically
worded, nonetheless suggested regret:

> Net book value alone for properties with a high producing potential
> clearly is less than any realistic worth which would be reflected in an
> arm's length deal. However, we consider the overall agreements to be a
> settlement package in which Aramco is exchanging its concession and
> property rights for compensation, receiving fees for services, and ob-
> taining a long-term crude supply.[11]

At first sight this proposal does seem to have been niggardly for
what was called, accurately enough, "the largest oil company in the
world" — and what the Saudi newspaper *al-Bilad* called "this gigantic international oil company." Nor was compensation for "oil in the
ground" overly generous. Marinovic, Jungers's first lieutenant and formerly the treasurer of the company, had described the value of the
reserves as "staggering." In the 1976 statement, Aramco claimed that
"oil in the ground" reserves totaled 175 billion barrels, which may
have been a very conservative estimate — Robert L. Maby, Jr., a leading
geologist familiar with Saudi oil reserves, estimated on the basis of
1980 data that the reserve totaled 258 million barrels, with 600 billion
"privately assessed" by parties neither of the government nor Aramco.
There were, Maby claimed, enough proven reserves in the ground
in Saudi Arabia to supply the United States with oil not for just the
twentieth and twenty-first centuries, but even into the twenty-second
century.[12]

If Maby's figure was true, then the worth may be estimated at
$121.26 billion, or $282 billion if the "privately assessed" figure applied. Yet Aramco received $1.5 billion, at best a low-end figure. But, as
Aramco's statements disclosed, the company would receive other com-

pensation as part of the package deal, including fees for operating the installations and oil fields and for its work on the Five-Year Plan:

> Under the terms of the agreements, Aramco's producing and refining assets will be transferred to the Government. The four shareholder companies will continue to provide manpower and substantial technical and managerial services to the operations and will fund and conduct an exploration program.
>
> In return for services provided, the successor organization will receive a fee . . . per barrel based on production and subject to certain minor adjustments. This fee is net after payment of Saudi Arab taxes.
>
> The successor organization will also fund and conduct a substantial effort in the search for new oil reserves in Saudi Arabia. . . . It is anticipated that the combination of the producing fee and the exploration incentive fee . . . per barrel based on production.[13]

Otherwise, the government would, from the effective date of the agreement, "provide all capital required in oil production and refining. The [Saudi] successor organization will provide half of the operating funds for the currently existing natural gas liquids facilities, and will wholly fund the exploration program." The American successor organization would have access to seven million barrels per day of crude oil at current market prices — $329 million in oil each day at the rate of forty-seven cents per barrel, or $130.2 million each year — a truly vast sum in guaranteed revenues. In other words, the American successor organization could expect to "export from Saudi Arabia a base volume of approximately 7 million barrels per day for some years to come. This compared with approximately 7.5 million barrels per day of crude oil which they exported in 1976." Furthermore, the Saudi government seemed willing to make more oil available for direct purchase.[14]

Thus the Saudi government remained a horse worth backing.

The fee for Aramco's participation in the gas program would be $10 billion and for Jungers's electrification program, some $4 billion. But there was much more behind the agreement. In all respects, Saudi Arabia would remain one of America's most important markets for industrial and military goods. Furthermore, Fahd had asked the United States to establish military bases in the holy land. In an emergency, these would provide the United States with centers in Saudi Arabia from which to defend oil supplies in Hasa, Kuwait, and Bahrein, and to enable it to contest Iranian expansionism.

Thus the United States took both gains and losses as the Saudis took ownership of Aramco. The U.S. companies retained 50 percent ownership of the gas production facilities, yet turned over the Ras Tanura refineries entirely. Tapline, which extended through Jordan, Syria, and Lebanon to an outlet on the Mediterranean, remained a property of Aramco. The company would continue to assist in oil exploration, and the 1,609 U.S. employees in Saudi Arabia (of 19,012 total employees) were expected to continue work there.[15]

Lastly, the plan did provide Aramco with an opportunity to remind the media and the public of its achievements in social and economic services. It had undertaken large projects, at its own expense, to improve the lives of the population of Hasa. Their efforts included the following programs:

- Aramco had constructed fifty-four schools for boys and girls, spending $79 million on this project.
- Aramco had provided extensive training for its Saudi employees and subsidized their full-time attendance at educational institutions, mainly in the United States. In 1975 alone, three hundred employees benefited from this program.
- Aramco supported a scholarship program for sixty government-selected students enrolled in universities in 1975.
- Saudi employees and their dependents were eligible for free care at Aramco's extensive medical facilities. In 1975, they made over 500,000 visits to clinics, and hospital care was provided to a daily average of 240 people.
- Aramco's home ownership program had, by 1975, helped eighty-six hundred Saudi employees purchase homes.
- During 1975 alone, Aramco and its expatriate employees spent over $1.1 billion in the local economy. In the same year, the company paid to the government some $25 billion in royalties and taxes.

Documents relating the details of the Saudi takeover stated this conclusion:

> In short, Aramco has been deeply involved in the entire fabric of life of the Eastern Province of Saudi Arabia. Under 100% government ownership, there will inevitably be changes in the projects, plans and programs initiated by Aramco. The extent to which such changes occur cannot be known at the present time. However, it is expected that under the new arrangements, the American oil companies which created this unique enterprise will continue to contribute to progress for this vital area of the world.[16]

The great game was over; the White Man's Burden was lifted, or so it seemed. If "the creation of wealth" defined American capitalism, then Aramco had been the most successful exponent of the ideology. Since its 1933 up-front payment of about $250,000 to the Saudi government, Aramco had earned billions of dollars. The Saudi government had in turn received billions of dollars. The Saudi rulers had been catapulted

into the ranks of the major financial powers, while Aramco had induced the U.S. government to assume Britain's former place as the
major political and military power in the Middle East and the Gulf,
which had contributed greatly to America's newfound status as the
world's first major superpower after World War II. The "indissoluble
marriage" between the Saudi government and Aramco had, remarkably, survived despite old man Philby's warning that "the idiosyncrasies
of this country and its people are indeed like [those of] nobody on
earth!"

The Californians and the Texans had survived in that harsh, arid,
dour world of the Wahhabs, and the company had prospered greatly.
They had discovered and profited from the world's largest, richest oil
field and made Saudi Arabia rich. Although the two parties had really
been held together by their common interest in money, that in no way
depreciated the immensity of their achievement. It was a saga of success, due at least in part to the triumphant realization of Tom Barger's
wide-ranging vision for the company. Its tenets might usefully be applied to the business enterprises of post-Communist capitalist societies:

- To preserve the Concession and optimize the returns to the Shareholders over the term of the Concession
- To maximize Saudi participation in the economic support of the
  enterprise
- To ameliorate the impact of [the] enterprise on Saudi society
- To provide technological and managerial assistance to the society and
  economy of Saudi Arabia, especially in the Eastern Province
- To carefully evaluate side effects of Aramco's actions, before they take
  place, and insure that expenditures of money do not outweigh returns expected
- To spread the economic benefits of the enterprise as widely through
  the local population as possible even at some extra cost by adoption
  of policies that direct the purchasing power of Aramco and employees to the development and support of services generally available to
  the public
- To set standards of behavior that are in accordance with the best
  industrial practice in the United States, and standardize conduct of
  affairs of the Corporation in respect to the treatment of employees,
  and relations with the Government and public that Corporate actions
  can be always justified to a reasonable Saudi acquainted with business
  practices elsewhere
- To ensure the provision in the Corporation of competent technical,
  managerial, administrative and craft skills
- To keep abreast of technological advances in oil fields bearing on the
  business of the Corporation and apply new techniques as they can
  contribute to the efficient operation of the Corporation

- To do what we reasonably can to obtain better mutual understanding between Saudis and Americans
- To plan facilities so as to ensure reasonable protection against unforeseen contingencies, industrial or political
- To be informed and alert to social and political change in order to adapt the Corporation's activities, but not to direct or influence other than normal industrial necessities.[17]

In the wake of ratification of the 1976 General Agreement, Ali I. Naimi, the pint-sized ex-Bedouin coffee boy, became the first president of Saudi Aramco. Now in his late fifties or early sixties, Naimi had worked for Aramco for over forty years, and he had been well trained. He spoke excellent English, he was familiar with Aramco's special lingo, he knew his business, and he was liked and respected by his American counterparts. He was a royalist, a Wahhab, and a technocrat to his fingertips. But although he enjoyed complete executive authority, he worked with a strong American component. When he became chairman of the board, three of nine members were Americans: Clifford Garvin, former chairman of Exxon; Harold Haynes, former chairman of Chevron; and Rodney Wagner, vice chairman of the Credit Policy Committee of Morgan Guaranty, the banking house in New York City. Also, more than one thousand American specialists were responsible to Naimi's management for, mainly, high-tech work.

Thus the Americans could claim that, to a degree, they still ran Aramco. Furthermore, the Americans had left Saudi Aramco in good condition — except for some problems with pollution of the environment. In March 1970, Brock Powers, then vice chairman of Aramco, began to receive complaints about the blighted condition of the environment in and around the oil fields. The government and the public joined in decrying a pipeline break that in April 1970 affected much of the Saudi shoreline of Tarut Bay. A Saudi petroleum ministry official led a drive to obtain compensation from Aramco for the damage done to the rich tidal fisheries. At least two, and possibly three, claims against Aramco succeeded, and damages totaling between $22,000 and $24,000 in each case were paid to the fishermen. Moreover, Aramco had received a number of government letters complaining about various types of pollution — from sewage disposal in Tarut Bay to poisonous fumes being vented from the oil fields. Government ministries opposed a water injection system by which some of the fields' crude was forced, under water pressure, to the surface. The program "posed a threat to the purity of the country's water resources."[18]

Jungers appointed J. A. Mahon to chair an investigatory commission, and he reported the following conclusion:

> These signs of increasing Saudi awareness of pollution problems, coupled with recent international and regional legal developments, indicate that Aramco may be faced with legislated controls in the not too distant future. While [the Saudi government] has begun to demonstrate concern over atmospheric pollution, Government action against pollution of the sea by oil may be expected to come first.[19]

Mahon's committee, which completed its study in June 1974, produced a worrisome report. Aramco's onshore facilities, which included industrial sites, towns, and ports, were all seriously polluted. Garbage dumps produced noxious smoke and odors and were hazardous to the population: "Men, women, and children scavenge not only for salvageable junk, but for food as well. The goats and sheep live on waste material which can be toxic and there is no way of preventing such sick animals from being slaughtered and sold."[20]

Jungers established a group of sixty specialists in industrial pollution to clean up the Gulf coast, and by the time of the handover of Aramco, the oil fields were clean.

Naimi's workforce numbered 57,500, mainly Saudis and a few Americans. Its marketing unit, Saudi Petroleum International, had offices in New York City, London, Tokyo, and Singapore; and in due course it owned a shipping company, Vela Marine International, which became the world's second-largest owner of tankers. Very commercially minded, Naimi took on large joint ventures in Korea and in the Philippines, with another in China in the offing.

Excom's constituent companies continued to operate and manage the kingdom's oil fields as contractors for the Saudi government. But the strong common front earlier presented by Excom had been fractured by internal stresses, which serve to demonstrate the old saw that in oil, as in politics, there are no long-term friends and no long-term enemies, only long-term interests.

In what was not quite a double-cross, Mobil, short of crude, entered into negotiations with Saudi Aramco independent of the other affiliated companies to obtain extra guaranteed allotments of oil at a special price. Texaco facilitated the Saudis' old dream of obtaining "downstream rights" (marketing rights) in North America. Much to the chagrin of the rest of Excom, Texaco arranged its affairs so that it and Saudi Aramco divided profits fifty-fifty to supply the Red Star filling stations of the American Northeast; together the two thus became the sixth-largest importer of oil in the United States and the largest "down-streamer" in the twenty-six eastern and southeastern states and Washington, D.C. Naimi was ambitious and he moved quickly.

The Aramcons who remained to work under Wahhabi management at first found the experience onerous. The Saudis asked many to remain, mainly project managers who were too valuable to lose. The Wahhabs in the workforce were zealous for Islam, much influenced by the personality of the new grand mufti of Saudi Arabia, Aramco's old "friend" Sheikh Abd al-Aziz ibn Baz, the Wahhabi fanatic who had appeared in Saudi politics repeatedly to protest the westernization of Saudi Arabia. Baz was now the ideological watchdog of the kingdom. His religious police had become still more watchful and intrusive under a regime of white-hot Wahhabism.

A correspondent in Dhahran described the change in atmosphere:

> Human rights and conventional civilized practices are now taking a back seat to the over-zealous Muslim religious and national movement that affects everyone's daily life. Hit broadest by this movement are (1) Christian church gatherings; (2) women; (3) westernized Muslims; and (4) westerners and Filipinos. . . . Crucifixes, holy water and church bulletins are no longer permitted at R.C. Masses.
>
> Ten Fellowship [low-church Protestants] members were recently deported for conducting religious services in private homes in Riyadh. . . . What a difference a few miles makes — in Bahrein the Christian presence is publicly accepted, welcomed, and acknowledged.
>
> In regard to women, recent [Saudi government] edicts spell out new regulations (1) disallowing women from working alongside men [and] (2) making it mandatory for single women to live in security-controlled housing unit compounds. . . . Some women job concessions made in conjunction with the King's May 1983 visit to Aramco were: (1) Males replace all females who held receptionist type positions in major office complexes [and] (2) Males replace all female teachers.
>
> Another regulation now calls for returning student daughters to be met and accepted by their father at Airport Passport Clearance Office. . . . Also their driving in camp privileges may soon be revoked. Westernized Muslims are now back in Muslim dress with prayer beads.[21]

The religious police caught up with Westerners indulging in outlawed forms of recreation, and many spent two or more years in prison for offenses relating to alcohol consumption and pornography. But despite the constraints of living in Saudi Arabia, many Americans chose to stay.

Life in Dhahran became onerous. The élan had departed. Service to a foreign monarchy was not as it was in the days of Aramco. Life under

Saudi Aramco had become time-service, with one eye on the pension. As Baldo Marinovic described the new world: "If you had a cocktail party at home, you did not sit outside in plain view with glasses; you had the party inside or in an enclosed patio, where you had privacy. Generally, things became more and more unpleasant. The pressure was on, and the feel of total freedom just vanished." He went on wistfully:

> When I came out . . . you had this feeling of absolute security. I would take the boys and we would drive out in the desert 150 miles and camp somewhere. And all of a sudden, out of the sand would pop up some Bedouins. We would invite them over, and they would have tea with us, and then they would invite you to their tent. You felt so absolutely safe and secure.
>
> I always kept all my doors open. I don't think we had a key to our house. You would drive down to the local town, and you would park as near the store as you could. You would leave the key in the ignition, the windows were all rolled down. Then you would go into the store, buy whatever it is, walk by your car, toss the package through the windows on the seat and walk on, go on shopping. And I still have not quite adapted to a different reality, I often still leave my front door open.[22]

Marinovic described life at the office:

> The personal relationship with Saudis at work varied. I had individuals working for me that came to me with all kinds of personal problems, and I was their big father, in a certain way. There were individuals that worked, said hello and were very nice, worked well, and went home. I didn't know much about them. There were some Aramco individuals, not many, who did establish some kind of a social interchange with Saudi employees and their families, but it was very few, and it wasn't a very profound or deep relationship. The cultural barriers simply made it impossible. One of the biggest problems, of course, is the status of women. You always had stag parties. You could not ask a typical Saudi to bring his wife. Now, gradually, you had a number of Saudis who were quite sophisticated, educated abroad, contractors, bankers, and so on. With that particular group, you had a more normal social interchange. But it was purely work-related. In other words, they would invite you, you would invite them, because somehow you were connected through work. There was no real personal relationship. Of course, even though Aramco made tremendous efforts to teach its American employees Arabic, I don't think I know a single American employee who really was fluent in Arabic. Gradually, as the general well-being spread and the Saudis became richer and richer, and they started making more money than their U.S. counterparts at the same level, relationships tended to change. At that point, quite a few of our U.S. employees became nervous about their positions, about their careers, and so on. So we intro-

duced a system where people who were replaced by Saudis and lost their jobs, and there were no other jobs for them in The Company, but who had done a real good job in preparing Saudis to take over the job, were given very generous allowances.[23]

The British, with their greater experience of the sadness that most expatriates experience when their careers ended and it was time to go home, knew how to leave. The flag was lowered at sunset, a band played "Greensleeves," there was a great party in full dress on the greensward, and a toast first to the queen and then to the local potentate. Swords flashed in the sunset, and the national anthems of the two sides were played. Salutes were exchanged. There was good humor, and the tribulations that had led to their departure were dismissed as part of life and politics. Often as not, a member of the royal family was present. When the Anglo-Iranian Oil Company folded its tents at Abadan on the other side of the Gulf, there was a cruiser alongside the refinery, dressed overall. Finding themselves nationalized out of existence as the Anglo-Iranian management came aboard, the company had the marine band on the quarterdeck play "Colonel Bogey," that stirring Victorian tribute to that imperial figure who was steady but never brilliant. The British developed the pangs of nationalization and departure into an exhibition of sweet sorrow — a reminder that they might be back again, in one form or another, as they sometimes were.

The American departure was very different, even though President Bush sent half a million troops to safeguard Saudi Aramco a little later. For some time the last remnants of American industrial genius in Arabia dribbled down to the airport, argued with the religious police, took up their economy-class seats, and staggered aboard the westbound TWA, glad to be gone. Marinovic, that cheerful figure of management, decided simply that that was that. The time had come to go home. Marinovic decided to retire. As he said, "All of a sudden, I saw this confluence of things. I was going to be sixty within a month of having thirty years of service with The Company. So that was it."[24] Marinovic wrote his letter of resignation to his immediate chief, Kelberer, the chairman of the board. "Officially, I am now resigning as of such-and-such date, and so on." But — typical of this stage of Aramco's life — nothing happened. Marinovic's resignation was not accepted. It was ignored. Kelberer could not bring himself to part company with his trusted friend and colleague.

After a fortnight or so, Marinovic mentioned his decision to Kelberer, with whom he had excellent relations, but still nothing happened. So when Kelberer was absent, Marinovic went to his desk, found his resignation letter, placed it on top of the pile, and put a sticker on it saying "Urgent." But still nothing happened. So he wrote formally:

> The Chairman of the Board,
> Arabian American Oil Company,
> Dhahran:
>
> Dear Sir:
>   As assistant to the chairman of the board, I feel it is my duty to point out to you that you may be albeit unknowingly breaking one of the laws of the Kingdom of Saudi Arabia, our host country, whose laws we are bound to respect. You may not be aware of the fact that His Majesty King Khalid signed on such-and-such a date a Royal Decree outlawing slavery. Accordingly, I urge you to conform to the laws of this country and sign my letter of resignation.[25]

Next day Kelberer came to Marinovic's office, uttered an unprintable word, and signed the letter. The fact was that, as Marinovic said, "Kelberer wanted me to stay one more year as he was planning to stay on another year." As a courtesy Marinovic went to see Ali Naimi, the Saudi president, to tell him that he was retiring. Naimi's reaction was "somewhat unexpected." Naimi said to Marinovic: "You know, this is not the time to go. You are showing lack of confidence in this process of Saudization, you're a key man in this whole process, and now you're leaving. This is not acceptable." Marinovic replied: "Ali, look. I can stay another three months, six months, so what? What difference does it make? When you make up your mind to go, you go." Marinovic noted, "I didn't want to linger on, and I'm glad." It was 1985 and the joy and the purpose he had felt being in Aramco's experience had gone. He had worked his way out of his job. So he went. For him, the White Man's Burden was over. And so he went home with his wife, his dog, his cat, in a company private jet provided by Naimi. It was almost as casual as checking out of the Holiday Inn.[26]

It was one of the curiosities of Aramco life that no one could say what the bottom line was, how much money the company made. Not even Frank Jungers. Speaking from his office in Portland, Oregon, he thought at first that the company had made "many millions." Then he thought it might be "many billions." Lastly he thought that the original investment of £100,000 gold might have realized "a trillion or two" — in the United States that means a thousand billion. It seemed impertinent to remark that Aramco was now at one with Nineveh and Tyre, those vanished imperial trading cities of prehistory. Jungers was thinking in the universal dimension. He had made a speech to the Aramcons, he said, in which he described Dhahran as the last of the great private endeavors. There could never be another like it because Big Oil had become a matter between governments, not between individuals and commercials. He paused. Then he said: "The only place left where we could do it again is in Space." Yes, he said, he had been thinking about that while in Oregon. "It was," he thought, "doable," adding: "And what sport that would be!"

The Aramcon spirit was still alive.

ACKNOWLEDGMENTS

The documentation for this volume is based mainly on the papers of William E. Mulligan, who spent his last years in New Boston, New Hampshire, after a career in government relations and the Arabian Affairs Division of the Arabian American Oil Company. These entities were primarily responsible for political relations between the oil company and the Saudi Arabian government. The documents were discovered by this author in the basement of Mulligan's residence during a visit in July 1990. As a foreign correspondent for a major London daily newspaper in the Middle East between 1956 and 1961, the author had had much to do with Aramco, and therefore he saw the papers' value immediately: Aramco was well known for its secrecy, and its labyrinthine inner politics was largely unknown to the Western press corps in the region.

The author found filing cabinets containing a large collection of five hundred folders grouped in eighteen boxes. They encompassed the history of that extraordinary company from about 1934, when the company obtained the concession to Saudi oil, until the early 1980s, when it assigned its interest to the Saudi government.

It emerged that during his career with Aramco, Mulligan had collected every piece of company paper that came his way, his purpose to write the history of Aramco when he retired. When he did retire, he found that he was not able to do so because of serious illness. Consequently he invited me to undertake the task. I agreed, and found the papers to be exceedingly rich in content, especially in the area of Aramco-Saudi politics and problems.

Born in 1918, Mulligan received a B.A. from Gonzaga University in Spokane, Washington, and spent much of World War II as a corporal in a U.S. Air Force communications squadron based in the British crown colony at Aden, the British base at the point where the Red Sea meets the Indian Ocean. In that position he began what became his life's work. When he joined Aramco at the end of World War II, the company sent him to study classical and Islamic studies at the Hartford Seminary Foundation in Connecticut, where he studied Arabic under the venerable American Islamicist and Arabist Dr. Edwin Calverley. Mulligan then returned to Aramco, joined government relations in 1946, and worked extensively with

George Rentz, Aramco's principal Arabist and Islamicist. Over the years, he became accepted as an expert in his subject, and as a close friend of Rentz, he was accepted into the circle of those other experts in Arabian matters, H. St. John B. Philby, Thomas C. Barger, Violet Dickson, David S. Dodge, and Parker T. Hart. He wrote numerous papers about the origins and personalities of the Saudi royal family, Saudi-American diplomacy, and men such as Sheikh Ahmed Zaki Yamani, Suliman S. Olayan, Adnan M. Kashoggi, and others. Since the history of modern Saudi Arabia is intermeshed with the history of Aramco, the Mulligan papers form an important source of information about that remote and secretive kingdom.

So important did the papers become that after they came into the author's possession the Saudi government displayed some anxiety about the contents of some of the files, particularly those having to do with relations between the Saudi royal dynasty and the British government, the main foreign power in the Middle East and the Persian Gulf during much of the period of Pax Americana there. The papers were never "weeded" by either Aramco or the U.S. government and, indeed, it does seem that neither was aware that Mulligan's papers existed until they were lodged in the Special Collections Department of Georgetown University Library in Washington, D.C. Both entities may well have wished that they had known, for the documentation included a great deal about the inner politics of the establishment and functioning of the Saudi government, the establishment of Israel, boundary disputes, and the tumultuous politics of the Middle East. In short, Aramco's government relations took on many of the aspects of a private intelligence service working in the interests of "the sovereign state of Aramco," as it was known by the press corps and the State Department, foreign diplomatists, and their intelligence services. The correspondence between Mulligan and the main personalities referred to in this book was regarded as being especially revealing, and as a high official of Aramco told the author: "They blew Aramco's cover. And they also blew the Saudis' cover."

I would like to thank a number of persons who have assisted me in this work. Willa Baum, the head of the oral history department of the Bancroft Library at the University of California, and Carol Hickey rendered an important service in making available to me their interviews with many of the leading lights of the company, particularly during the dangerous period of the 1970s and 1980s. This project owed much to the chairman and chief executive officer of Aramco, Frank Jungers. Mrs. Shirley Mulligan, Mulligan's widow, and Mrs. D. T. Gallagher, lately of Aramco, gave me much of their time concerning the transfer of H. St. John Philby's literary estate to the company — an estate that was and is a unique and very large and valuable library and document collection concerning the Saud dynasty. My thanks are due also to Ruth Baacke of the Middle East Institute in Washington, D.C.; E. J. Applewhite, formerly station chief of the CIA in Beirut; Ray Close and his colleague Stanley H. Bedlington; Richard Beeston, of *The Times* of London, a colleague during my years in the Middle East; John Farmer, of the British Secret Service in Beirut during my time; my good friend Larry Collins, the American novelist who was *Newsweek*'s man in Beirut; Mrs. Sylvia Crane, Charles R. Crane's literary executrix; James Critchfield, the CIA's station chief in Oman; Major W. O. Little, the British government's intelligence officer during the Buraimi incident; Carleton Coon of Princeton, who gave me much help regarding the relationship between St. John Philby and the Saudi dynasty; Nicholas Elliott, the famous British spy in Beirut during the Kim Philby period; Mrs. France Farmer, who knew much about Kim Philby's activities; Robert Headley of the CIA and the Aramco political staff during the 1950s and '60s; Harry Hopper of the CIA in Rome during the Philby incidents; James Morrison, the U.S. television producer who saw much of the Philbys while working with Lowell Thomas in Arabia; John Taylor, the excellent archivist at the National Archives; Robert Norberg of the Aramco staff in Washington; Helena Naylor, Kim Philby's sister and St. John's English literary executrix; Sophie Rentz, George Rentz's widow and keeper of the Rentz papers; Ms. Gillian Grant, an archivist at the Middle East Institute at Oxford, England; George Kennedy Young of the British Secret Service; and, perhaps above all, my old friend at Special Collections in the Littauer Library at Georgetown, Nicholas B. Scheetz. In my experience there are many excellent research libraries, but two excel. One is the Eton College Library, where the librarian serves sherry before luncheon to his researchers; the other is Nicholas Scheetz's system at Georgetown University Library. He is usually good for luncheon at The Tombs.

I am grateful to all those named above. They have all rendered me important services over the long history of this volume. So have my long-suffering editor, Marc Jaffe; Ms. Susanna Brougham, the manuscript editor; and Ms. Mindy Keskinen, who did so much of the administrative work that led to this volume.

NOTES

Prologue

1. David Holden and Richard John, *The House of Saud* (London: Sidgwick & Jackson, 1981), p. 64.
2. H. St. John B. Philby, "Report of Najd Mission, 1917–1918" (Baghdad: Government Press, 1918), in the W. E. Mulligan papers, Special Collections, Georgetown University Library, Washington, D.C.
3. Interviews with W. E. Mulligan at New Boston, New Hampshire, July 1990.
4. Anthony Sampson, *The Seven Sisters: The Great Oil Companies and the World They Shaped* (New York: Viking, 1975), p. 37.
5. Ibid.
6. J. H. Colton, *Geography* (New York: Ivison, Phinney, 1863) (n.p.), cited in Mark Sullivan, *Our Times: America Finding Herself* (New York: Scribner's, 1932), p. 91.
7. H. St. John B. Philby, *Arabian Oil Ventures* (Washington, D.C.: Middle East Institute, 1964), pp. 4–7.
8. Ibid.
9. Mulligan interviews. The treaty is in treaty files, Mulligan papers. See also Elizabeth Monroe, *Philby of Arabia* (New York, 1973), pp. 58–61.

Chapter 1: The Setting and the Stage

1. Eighty-second Congress, Second Session, Committee Print No. 6, *The International Petroleum Cartel* (Washington, D.C.: U.S. Government Printing Office, 1952), p. 51ff. This document is also in the Mulligan papers.
2. Ibid.
3. Ibid.
4. Ibid.
5. Ibid.
6. Ibid., p. 71ff.
7. Ibid.
8. Ibid.

9. Philby, *Arabian Oil Ventures*, p. 98.

10. Ibid.

11. Ibid.

12. British Legation, Jidda, to Khan Tasaddul Husain, Intelligence Department, Home Department, Government of India, November 3, 1930, FO 967-38, Public Records Office, London. (This was Philby's file at the British missions in Jidda.)

13. Monroe, *Philby of Arabia*, p. 165.

14. H. St. John B. Philby, "Why I Turned Wahhabi," *Egyptian Gazette*, September 26, 1930.

15. Ibid.

16. *Saudi Gazette* newspaper article, September 24, 1978, in Mulligan papers, newspaper files.

17. Ibid.

18. Ibid.

19. William J. Kennedy, ed., *Secret History of the Oil Companies in the Middle East*, vol. 3, *Ibn Saud–Philby Relations* (Salisbury, N.C.: Documentary Publications, 1979), pp. 12–15. This is a collection of reprinted State Department documents at the National Archives, Washington, D.C. The author is grateful to Dr. Glenn Brown, lately of the U.S. Geological Survey in Saudi Arabia, for having provided these and other volumes. The editor is an analyst formerly with the CIA.

20. *Saudi Gazette*, September 24, 1978.

21. Ibid.

22. John O. Crane to Walter Rogers, January 22, 1929, Special Collections, Georgetown University Library.

23. Philby, *Arabian Oil Ventures*, pp. 73–74.

24. Ibid.

25. Ibid., pp. 74, 176.

26. Ibid.

27. Charles R. Crane to John O. Crane, March 6, 1932, Special Collections, Georgetown University Library.

28. Georges Antonius, "An Account of the Experiences of Charles R. Crane in Jidda" in the Sylvia Crane Papers at Woods Hole, Mass.

29. Philby, *Arabian Jubilee*, p. 165.

30. Correspondence of Charles R. Crane. In the care of Mrs. Sylvia Crane, Woods Hole, Mass.

31. William J. Donovan papers, Operation Torch files, U.S. Army War College, Fort Carlisle, Penn. See also Saudi Arabia Reports of Carleton Coon and Anthony Cave Brown, *Treason in the Blood* (Boston: Houghton Mifflin, 1994), pp. 370–71.

32. Philby, *Arabian Oil Ventures*, p. 27.

33. Ibid. Also Philby papers (correspondence files), Middle East Institute, Oxford: correspondence file from Philby to wife Dora.

34. Ibid.

35. Ibid.

36. Karl S. Twitchell, *Saudi Arabia* (privately published, 1975), p. 148ff.

37. Charles R. Crane to Ibn Saud, September 9, 1932. In possession of Mrs. Sylvia Crane, Woods Hole, Mass.

38. Interviews with Dr. Glenn Brown, Reston, Va., June–September 1990.

39. Philby, *Arabian Oil Ventures*, p. 77.
40. Ibid.
41. Ibid., p. 79.

Chapter 2: Pax Aramco

1. From a photostat of Philby's original manuscript concerning the negotiation, Mulligan papers.
2. Ibid., pp. 79–80.
3. Ibid.
4. Ibid., p. 80.
5. Monroe, *Philby of Arabia*, p. 206.
6. Philby photostats, Mulligan papers, p. 80.
7. Ibid., p. 81.
8. Ibid.
9. Ibid.
10. Ibid., pp. 81–82.
11. Ibid., p. 83.
12. Ibid.
13. Ibid.
14. Ibid.
15. British Legation, Jidda, to Khan Bahadur Tasaddui Husainy, Intelligence Department, Home Department, Government of India, Simla, in file FO 967/38. November 14, 1930, entitled "Mr. Philby," Public Records Office, London.
16. *Sir Andrew Ryan: The Last of the Dragomans* (London: Bles, 1951), p. 266.
17. Ibid.
18. Anglo-Persian Oil Company to Sir Andrew Ryan, January 3, 1933, FO/371/16870, in file 139, Public Records Office, London.
19. Joseph W. Walt, "Saudi Arabia and the Americans: 1928–1951" (Ph.D. diss., Northwestern University, 1960), p. 96.
20. Dan van der Meulen, *The Wells of Ibn Saud* (London: Murray, 1957), p. 115ff.
21. *T. E. Lawrence: Revolt in the Desert* (New York: Garden, 1926), p. 1.
22. *Sir Andrew Ryan*, p. 290.
23. Monroe, *Philby of Arabia*, pp. 204–5.
24. Ibid.
25. Information personal to the author.
26. "Arbitration between the Government of Saudi Arabia and the Arabian American Oil Company: Memorial of the Arabian American Oil Company," Annex, p. 348. Hereafter cited as Aramco Memorial. Mulligan papers.
27. Ibid.
28. Philby, *Arabian Jubilee*, p. 116.
29. Monroe, *Philby of Arabia*, p. 136.
30. Ibid., p. 98.
31. Philby photostats, Mulligan papers.
32. Ibid.
33. Ibid., p. 99.

34. Ibid.
35. Ibid., p. 40.
36. Ibid.
37. Aramco Memorial, Annex 1, p. 120; Annex 1, 1.13.
38. Philby photostats, Mulligan papers.
39. *Sir Andrew Ryan*, pp. 297–98.
40. Philby photostats, Mulligan papers.
41. Ibid.

Chapter 3: On Dammam Dome

1. Affidavit of Fred A. Davies, in Aramco Memorial, p. 108, Annex 5.
2. Ibid.
3. Michael Sheldon Cheney, *Big Oil Man from Arabia* (New York: Ballantine, 1958), p. 69.
4. Phillip C. McConnell, *The Hundred Men* (Peterborough, N.H.: Currier Press, 1985), p. 29.
5. van der Meulen, *The Wells of Ibn Saud*, p. 11.
6. "Study of Official Attitude Towards Alcohol" in Customs folder index, Mulligan papers. And see note 7 for the rest of the text.
7. It was related that the caliph Umar once went out at night to observe the drinking of alcohol in Medina, the second holy city of Islam. He saw a man sitting and drinking alcohol:

   > In the morning he called on him and said to him, "Has not God ordered you not to drink alcohol?"
   > "Yes, indeed!"
   > "But why did you drink last night?"
   > "How did you know? You weren't my companion!"
   > "I saw you personally!"
   > "But I was in my room!"
   > "I jumped into the yard and saw you through the window."
   > "Well, Caliph, you have broken three rules of the Quran, while I have broken only one."
   > "What do you mean?"
   > "God says, 'Do not spy,' but you did so; God says, 'Do not go into a house without its owner's permission,' and you broke into my house without my permission; and God says, 'Enter houses through the doors,' and you jumped over the fence."
   > "Well, please forget all about it and go in peace."

8. McConnell, *The Hundred Men*, p. 31.
9. Aramco Memorial, Annex 6, p. 116ff.
10. Ibid.
11. Ibid., p. 11.
12. Yet the king did offer a form of protection from the religious police. One of Ohliger's staff, Phillip C. McConnell, would write:

   > King Ibn Saud and his close associates were more amenable to the practices sought by the Americans in their private lives than were the religious leaders of

that large portion of the public who looked to those leaders for guidance. In the early years of the American operation, the King frequently was accused of catering to the wishes of the foreigners and infidels by adopting practices and permitting actions not authorized by the Koran. As a devout Moslem, he wished to support those teachings. But he also recognized that certain adjustments [must be made] for these strangers from the west, if harmony was to be maintained. However, he insisted that the adjustments must not come so rapidly as to cause major resentment by the public. [McConnell, *The Hundred Men*]

13. Aramco Memorial, Article 22.

14. Ibid.

15. Aramco Memorial, p. 16 of the Agreement; Letter, L. N. Hamilton to Abdullah Suleiman, May 29, 1933, see p. 16 of the Agreement.

16. Wallace Stegner, *Discovery: The Search for Arabian Oil* (Beirut: Middle East Export Press, 1974), p. 32.

17. Unpublished diaries of J. W. Hoover, Saudi Arabia, August 22, 1933–December 30, 1935, Mulligan papers.

18. Ibid.

19. Recollections of B. C. Nelson, Mulligan papers. See Labor Relations file identified in Georgetown index.

20. Stegner, *Discovery*, p. 72.

21. Ibid.

22. Ibid., p. 54.

23. Joy Winkie Viola, *Human Resources Development in Saudi Arabia* (Boston: International Human Resources Development Corporation, 1986), p. 5.

24. Ibid.

25. Stegner, *Discovery*, p. 70.

26. Ibid.

27. Ibid.

28. Ibid., p. 84.

29. Aramco Memorial, p. 110.

30. Stegner, *Discovery*, p. 91.

31. Ibid.

32. Phillip McConnell, "Strangers from a World Unknown," *Aramco World Magazine: A Celebration*, May–June 1984.

33. John Spyros Salapartas, "The Open Door in the Middle East: The Anglo-American Oil Agreements" (master's thesis, University of Wisconsin, 1964).

34. Stegner, *Discovery*, p. 98.

35. Ibid., p. 99.

36. van der Meulen, *The Wells of Ibn Saud*, p. 131.

37. Stegner, *Discovery*, p. 126.

38. Ibid.

39. Ibid.

40. Ibid.

41. Ibid.

42. Ibid.

43. Ibid.

44. Ibid.

45. McConnell, *The Hundred Men*, p. 31. Emphasis per original.

46. Ibid.

47. Ibid.

48. Royal Institute of International Affairs, *Chronology of the Second World War* (London: RUSI, 1947), entry for September 11, 1939.

Chapter 4: Plan Orient

1. Judge Bert Fish, "Some Notes on the Present Government of Saudi Arabia (March 11, 1940)," in *Saudi Arabia Enters the Modern World*, edited by Ibrahim al-Rashid (Salisbury, N.C.: Documentary Productions, 1980), vol. 1, p. 39.

   Fish was the State Department's agent in Jidda. The work cited is a collection of State Department documents.

2. *Documents on German Foreign Policy*, series D, 5.6, *The Last Months of Peace, March–August, 1939* (Washington, D.C.: U.S. Government Printing Office), p. 743 (document 541).

3. Ibid.

4. Ibid.

5. Memo on Saudi Arabia, October 17, 1941, Diplomatic Branch document 890F.00/75, National Archives.

6. Philby correspondence, letter to Dora, January 10, 1940, St. Antony's College, Oxford.

7. Ibid.

8. U.S. Senate Hearings, "Petroleum Arrangements with Saudi Arabia," 25426 and 25071.

9. Winston Churchill, *The Grand Alliance*, vol. 3, *The Second World War* (London, Cassell, 1950), pp. 490–91.

10. Ibid.

11. McConnell, *The Hundred Men*, p. 61ff.

12. Stegner, *Discovery*, p. 136.

13. Ibid., p. 138.

14. Ibid.

15. Correspondence with Antonio Cumbat of Rome, November 1975, Mulligan papers.

16. Walter Warlimont, *Inside Hitler's Headquarters: 1939–1945* (London: Weidenfeld & Nicolson, 1964), p. 131.

17. Ibid.

18. So xenophobic was it, indeed, that when Ajib Khan, a company interpreter, visited the palace in Riyadh and encountered the king's sister, Nura, she warned Ajib "to be very careful not to fall into evil ways through his association with Christians and to strictly follow the principles of Islam, as she realized the association with Christians would lead to temptations in violation of the Faith." ["Report of Aramco Rep on Attitude of Fanatical Wahhabis of the Interior of Saudi Arabia (Jidda, April 11, 1945)," in al-Rashid, *Saudi Arabia Enters the Modern World*, vol. 1, 800F.00/-1145].

19. McConnell, *The Hundred Men*, p. 162.

20. "Complaints by Certain Arabian Fanatics That Ibn Saud Is Surrendering His

Land to Unbelievers, December 4, 1944," in al-Rashid, *Saudi Arabia Enters the Modern World*, vol. 1, 890F/001 Abdul Aziz/1-4-444.

21. Monroe, *Philby of Arabia*, p. 86.

22. Tom C. Barger, *Out in the Blue: Letters from Arabia*, p. 220. This collection of letters from Tom Barger to Kathleen Barger is unpublished.

23. al-Rashid, *Saudi Arabia Enters the Modern World*, vol. 1, p. 201.

24. Barger, *Out in the Blue*, p. 220.

25. Ibid.

26. Ibid.

27. Ibid., p. 223.

28. al-Rashid, *Saudi Arabia Enters the Modern World*, vol. 1, p. 245.

29. McConnell, *The Hundred Men*, p. 138.

30. Ibid.

31. Ibid.

32. Ibid.

33. T. H. Vail Motter, *The United States Army in World War II: The Persian Corridor and Aid to Russia* (Washington, D.C.: Office of the Chief of Military History), p. 170.

34. Churchill, *The Grand Alliance*, chap. 14.

35. McConnell, *The Hundred Men*, p. 54.

36. Ibid.

37. Ibid., pp. 55–56.

38. Warlimont, *Inside Hitler's Headquarters*, p. 226.

39. Maurice Matloff and Edwin M. Snell, *Strategic Planning for Coalition Warfare: 1941–1942* (Washington, D.C.: Office of the Chief of Military History), p. 250ff.

40. Ibid., p. 252.

41. Martin Gilbert, *Winston S. Churchill*, vol. 7, *Road to Victory* (London: Heinemann, 1986), p. 163.

42. F. W. Deakin, *Brutal Friendship* (New York: Harper & Row, 1962), pp. 21–22.

43. This order of the day was written by two U.S. secret agents, Carleton Coon and Gordon H. Brown, both of the Office of Strategic Services (OSS), at work in the Atlas mountains of Morocco. The text was created at the request of Roosevelt through the chief of the OSS, Major General William J. Donovan. Coon recounted that when they had written the order in English, they gave it to one of their spies, an Arab code-named Pinkeye, and he began to read it aloud in the manner of a holy man reading the Koran. Struck by the lyricism that crept into the text as he declaimed it, the agents decided to use not their own text, but a revision based on Pinkeye's rendition. The text is now in the Donovan Operation Torch files at the U.S. Army War College, Fort Carlisle, Penn.

Chapter 5: Colonel Eddy

1. Bascom N. Timmons, *Jesse H. Jones: The Man and the Statesman* (New York: Holt, 1956), p. 236; Senate Hearings, Petroleum Arrangements with Saudi Arabia, 25435, 25426.

2. Timmons, *Jesse H. Jones,* p. 236.
3. Transmission of Translations of a Speech by His Majesty Abdul Aziz Ibn Saud and of an Interview of Abdullah Suleiman, Saudi Minister of Finance, January 11, 1943, Diplomatic Branch document 890F.00/79/PS/BMB, National Archives.
4. Ibid.
5. Ibid.
6. Ibid.
7. Ibid.
8. J. C. McIntosh, U.S. Legation, Jidda, letter dated December 10, 1942, Special Collections, Georgetown University Library, Washington, D.C.
9. "Imperial Security in the Middle East (July 2, 1945)." Cabinet Paper Cab/66, Public Records Office, London.
10. Ibid.
11. Ibid.
12. "Strategic Aspects of the Discussion on Oil Policy: Report by the Chiefs of Staff," April 5, 1944, War Cabinet paper W.P. (44)187, Public Records Office, London.
13. Daniel Yergin, *The Prize* (New York: Simon & Schuster, 1990), p. 396.
14. Memorandum from Halifax to Foreign Office, February 19, 1944, F0371/42688, Public Records Office, London.
15. Yergin, *The Prize,* p. 396.
16. Senate Hearings, Petroleum Arrangements with Saudi Arabia, Executive Session, 1:3–4; 6:662–63, Exhibit 27: DeGolyer Report.
17. Yergin, *The Prize,* p. 393.
18. Warren F. Kimball, *Churchill and Roosevelt: The Complete Correspondence* (Princeton, N.J.: Princeton University Press, 1984), vol. 2, pp. 734–44. See C-583 and R-474.
19. Ibid., R-474.
20. U.S. Senate print, "Multinational Oil Corporations and U.S. Foreign Policy" (Washington, D.C.: U.S. Government Printing Office, 1975), p. 38.
21. Ibid.
22. Note entitled "Secretary of State Hull and the British Ambassador, Lord Halifax," Diplomatic Branch document 890F00/6-2642 OS, National Archives.
23. Ibid.
24. Laurence Grafftey-Smith, *Bright Levant* (London, 1970), pp. 257–58.
25. Ibid.
26. Ibid.
27. Kennedy, *Secret History of the Oil Companies,* vol. 6, p. i.
28. "Memorandum of Conversation — Crimean Conference — Dinner given by the Prime Minister, February 10, 1945," FDR Library, Hyde Park, N.Y.
    For confirmation that the quotation in text represents the exact wording of the president, see also at Hyde Park Mr. Charles Bohlen's minutes in the Map Room Papers of the Roosevelt–Stalin–Churchill meetings.
29. Letter, Eddy to Secretary of State, March 3, 1945, Diplomatic Branch document 890F.001 Abdul Aziz/3-345, National Archives.
30. Ibid.
31. Ibid.

32. Ibid.

33. Ibid.

34. Harry Aldrich to William J. Donovan, March 26, 1945, Microfilm, OSS Ops, Mediterranean Theater of Operations 128, OSS director's files, Donovan papers, U.S. Army War College.

35. Ibid.

36. Ibid.

37. Ibid.

38. Ibid.

39. Ibid.

40. Dispatch, Colonel Eddy to OSS, "Remarks Made at Presentation of Airplane," April 14, 1945, Diplomatic Branch file 890F, National Archives.

41. Ibid.

42. Ibid.

43. "British Policy in the Middle East," July 12, 1943, War Cabinet paper 66, Public Records Office, London.

44. Kim Philby, *My Silent War* (London: MacGibbon & Kee, 1968), pp. 98–99.

45. Philby correspondence, letter to Dora, February 21, 1947, St. Antony's College, Oxford.

46. Donald Downes, *The Scarlet Thread* (New York: British Book Centre, 1953), pp. 32–33.

47. Donald Downes to Colonel Ulius C. Amoss, July 24, 1942, Downes OSS papers, National Archives.

48. Joseph Charles to Near East Section of the State Department, June 16, 1944, RG226 document XL995, National Archives.

49. "Special Report for General Donovan's Eyes Only," September 22, 1944, Intelligence Service file 15,409,22, Donovan papers, National Archives.

50. Memorandum on the oil concession in the Arab Sheikhdoms of the Persian Gulf, FO/371-6377, Public Records Office, London.

51. Ibid.

52. Ibid.

53. Ibid.

54. al-Rashid, *Saudi Arabia Enters the Modern World,* vol. 1. See "General Observations Regarding Dhahran and Bahrein," December 20, 1946, by Parker T. Hart.

55. Ibid.

56. Ibid.

57. Personal information.

58. Mulligan interviews.

Chapter 6: The Company Town

1. Cheney, *Big Oil Man from Arabia* (New York: Ballantine, 1958), p. 1.

2. Ibid., p. 7.

3. Ibid., p. 9.

4. Ibid., p. 10.

5. Ibid., p. 12.

6. Ibid., p. 13.

7. Ibid., p. 14.

8. Ibid., p. 18.

9. Ibid., pp. 19–20.

10. Ibid.

11. Ibid., p. 29.

12. Ibid.

13. Ibid., p. 30.

14. Ibid.

15. Ibid., p. 57.

16. W. F. Owen, Aramco oral history project. See p. iv for full citation.

17. Cheney, *Big Oil Man from Arabia,* p. 149.

18. Kennedy, *Secret History of the Oil Companies,* vol. 2, pp. 254–55. The report is dated December 12, 1948, and entitled "Conflict within the Aramco Organization."

19. Ibid., p. 384ff.

20. Ibid.

21. Ibid.

22. Ibid.

23. Ibid.

24. Ibid.

25. Ibid., vol. 1, pp. 164–65.

26. S. T. Kimball, "American Culture in Saudi Arabia" (paper presented at a meeting of the U.S. Anthropology Section of Oceanography and Meteorology, February 27, 1956), Mulligan papers.

27. Ibid.

28. Ibid.

29. Ibid.

30. Ibid.

31. Ibid.

32. Ibid.

33. Ibid.

34. Ibid.

35. Peter and Ellen Speers, Aramco oral history project (interviews beginning in May 1993).

36. Ibid.

37. Ibid.

38. Ibid. With the passing of years, all the housing was upgraded. Ellen Speers noted that "all the miserable places were knocked down and there was no longer such a [discrepancy among] the types of housing." [Ibid.]

39. Ibid.

40. Ibid.

41. Ibid.

42. Ibid.

43. Ibid.

44. Ibid.

45. Ibid. Also, in the 1960s, boys began to wear their hair long, and in some cases they were seized and shorn by the Committees of Public Morality.

46. Ibid.

47. B. C. Nelson, "Employee Relations in Aramco, Then and Now" (paper presented to Aramco's Management Development Seminar, Dhahran, Saudi Arabia, March 6, 1965), Mulligan papers.

48. In September 1964 an announcement by the newly formed Palestine Liberation Army revealed that its new commander was a certain Lieutenant Colonel Wajih Hussein Madani, who had been employed by Aramco from July 13, 1949, to August 31, 1950. Well educated by the British in Palestine, he had become a commissioned officer in the British army. After the war he had been an interpreter-instructor with the British military mission to Saudi Arabia and later a staff captain in the Arab Legion, the British-officered Arab army in Jordan. An experienced officer in military transportation, he was offered the post of clerk in Aramco's transportation department; subsequently he was transferred to the exploration department. But on August 31, 1950, he suddenly resigned. From Aramco he went on to become a captain in the Syrian army and a lieutenant colonel in the Kuwaiti army.

Why had he accepted the humble job of clerk with Aramco? Having spent a year in Aramco's transportation department, and speaking excellent English, he must have learned much about Aramco's activities of interest to the PLO. Was anyone he had known in the company involved in the covert wing of the PLO? Such possibilities awakened Aramco management to consider that there might be spies in their ranks.

49. George Lenczowski, *Oil and State in the Middle East* (Ithaca, N.Y.: Cornell University Press, 1960), p. 285.

50. Kennedy, *Secret History of the Oil Companies,* vol. 2, p. 13.

The document cited is "Saudi Government Representatives Suggest 'Fair Solution' to Grievances of Arabian American Oil Company Saudi Laborers," dated September 15, 1945.

51. Ibid.

52. Ibid.

53. Ibid.

54. Nelson, "Employee Relations."

55. Ibid.

56. Ibid.

57. Ibid.

58. Peter Speers, Aramco oral history project.

59. Cheney, *Big Oil Man from Arabia,* p. 227.

60. File 43, Mulligan papers.

61. Cheney, *Big Oil Man from Arabia,* p. 232.

62. Ibid.

63. Ibid., p. 217.

64. Ibid., p. 218.

Chapter 7: Almighty Excom

1. Kennedy, *Secret History of the Oil Companies,* vol. 2, pp. 81–83.

This document, "Disagreement between Aramco and the Saudi Arabian

Government Concerning the Interpretation of the Gold Clause of the Concession Agreement," originated at the U.S. legation at Jidda on February 26,
1947.

2. Ibid.

3. Ibid.

4. Kennedy, *The Secret History of the Oil Companies*, vol. 2, p. 67.
    This document is a letter from W. Leonard Parker to Marcel E. Wagner,
president, American Eastern Corporation, and to Loy Henderson, director, Office of Near Eastern and African Affairs, State Department, June 6,
1946.

5. Aramco Memorial, p. 49.

6. "Report Together with Individual Views to the Committee on Foreign Relations, United States Senate, by the Subcommittee on Multinational Corporations, January 2, 1975." Hereafter cited as Multinational Report.

7. Ibid.

8. *The Petroleum Times,* London, May 2, 1936. Cited in the Federal Trade Commission Report, 1952, p. 115; Multinational Report, p. 46.

9. Multinational Report, p. 48.

10. Williams, Aramco oral history project.

11. Mulligan interviews.

12. W. F. Owen, Aramco oral history project.

13. Baldo Marinovic, Aramco oral history report.

14. Ibid.

15. Ibid.

16. Ibid.

17. Ibid.

18. Ibid.

19. Ibid.

20. Ibid.

21. Philby, *Arabian Jubilee,* p. 129.

22. Ibid.

23. Kennedy, *The Secret History of the Oil Companies,* vol. 3. See report of Dr. E. A.
White, the U.S. legation doctor.

24. Ibid.

25. Philby correspondence, St. Antony's College, Oxford.

26. Ibid.

27. Ibid.

28. *Aramco World,* July 1951.

29. Ibid.

30. Ibid.

31. Ibid.

32. Ibid.

33. Ibid.

34. Ibid.

35. Kennedy, *The Secret History of the Oil Companies,* vol. 3, pp. 94–95. The document is a letter to President Truman from C. W. Barthelmes, February 27,
1947.

36. Ibid.

37. U.S. Senate Committee print, February 16, 1948.

38. Ibid.

39. Ibid.

40. Ibid.

41. Ibid.

42. Ibid.

43. Ibid.

44. Ibid.

45. Ibid.

46. Roy Lebkicher, George Rentz, Max Steineke, and others, *Aramco Handbook* (Arabian American Oil Company, 1960), pp. 150–53.

47. Ibid.

48. Kennedy, *The Secret History of the Oil Companies,* vol. 3. See Childs reports collection.

49. Ibid.

50. Ibid.

51. Ibid.

52. Lenczowski, *Oil and State in the Middle East,* p. 156.

53. W. F. Owen, Aramco oral history report.

54. Ibid.

55. Ibid.

56. Ibid.

57. Ibid.

58. Ibid.

59. Ibid.

60. Ibid.

61. Ibid.

62. Ibid.

63. Lebkicher et al., *Aramco Handbook,* p. 153.

64. W. F. Owen, Aramco oral history project.

Chapter 8: The Palestine Crisis

1. Norman Rose, *Chaim Weizmann* (New York: Viking, 1986), p. 345.

2. Philby correspondence, January 10, 1940, St. Antony's College, Oxford.
   Philby's own account of this situation is as follows:

   Time dragged on with never a sign from the King, and on a certain occasion when Yusuf Yassin and I were alone in the desert I ventured to broach the subject to him. As I expected, he was hostile, but, so far as I know, he kept my confidence and I heard no more of the incident. Still later, under similar conditions of confidence, I told Bashir Sadawi [another of the king's advisers] the general outline of the plan, and found him unexpectedly favourable; but within the hour he had told the King of our conversation, and, when I walked into the audience chamber that afternoon, the King summoned me to his side. "Didn't I tell you," he said, "not to talk to anyone about that matter?" I made some very lame excuse, saying that I thought he may have forgotten all about it, and that there was no harm in discussing it as an academic proposition. Well, remember, he said; don't do it again! . . . In May I decided to press the King for an answer, but, as I anticipated, he put me off again — though without one single word of reproach.

3. Ibid.
4. Ibn Saud–FDR correspondence file, FDR Library.
5. Ibid.
6. Philby, *Arabian Jubilee*, p. 216.

Philby offered this version of the circumstances in which he presented the play to Ibn Saud:

> January 8, 1940 — a few days after my return to Arabia. There was nothing whatsoever to prevent him telling me then and there that it was an impossible and unacceptable proposition — in which case I should have informed Dr. Weizmann accordingly and dropped the whole thing. But the King did not tell me that. He told me, on the contrary, that some such arrangements might be possible in appropriate future circumstances, that he would keep the matter in mind, that he would give me a definite answer at the appropriate time, that meanwhile I should not breathe the matter to anyone — least of all to an Arab — and finally, that if the proposals became the subject of public discussion with any suggestion of his approving them, he would have no hesitation whatsoever in denouncing me as having no authority to commit him in the matter. I was perfectly prepared to accept that position, and the King knew that I would communicate his answer to Dr. Weizmann. He did not forbid me to do so! [St. John Philby to Chaim Weizmann, November 17, 1943. FDR Library]

7. Memorandum for the president from H. B. Hoskins, September 23, 1943, PSF file on Saudi Arabia, FDR Library.
8. Ibid.
9. Ibid.
10. Memorandum from S. I. Rosenman to the president, March 8, 1944, PSF file on Saudi Arabia, FDR Library.
11. St. John Philby to Chaim Weizmann, November 17, 1943, PSF file on Saudi Arabia, FDR Library.
12. Ibid.
13. Ibid.
14. Ibid.
15. Philby correspondence, letter to his wife Dora Philby, St. Antony's College, Oxford.
16. W. F. Owen, Aramco oral history project.
17. Ibid.
18. Kenneth W. Condit, *U.S. Joint Chiefs of Staff History, 1948–1950* (unpublished manuscript).
19. Kennedy, *The Secret History of the Oil Companies*, vol. 3. See Childs reports collection.

Childs also made the following comments:

> I do not foresee any tangible action detrimental to our interests as likely to emerge in Saudi Arabia, for the instant or in the immediate future, as a result of the decision of the United Nations in favor of the creation of a Jewish State achieved, in the opinion of the Arabs, so largely through American influence. I do believe, however, that a great deal of the friendly confidence in us has been broken. . . .

They have, as is known, a very deep distrust of the Soviet Union; they have maintained, and will continue to maintain, friendly relations with Great Britain, while observing considerable reserve in view of a distrust of the political motives of the British. They have had an almost childlike belief in their ability to count upon a most disinterested friendship on the part of the United States. . . . It appears likely to me that we shall now be lumped with the British as a Power with whom intimate contacts must be maintained, but for reasons of self-interest only. [December 1, 1947, Diplomatic Branch document 890F.00/12-147, National Archives]

20. Ibid.
21. Ibid.
22. Diplomatic Branch document 890F.00/12-147, December 1, 1947, National Archives.
23. Ibid.
24. Ibid.
25. Memorandum from Loy Henderson to Assistant Secretary of State Armour, December 15, 1947, document 890F.0012-1547, National Archives. The document includes text of a telegram from Moore in Dhahran to Aramco in Washington, D.C.
26. Top secret telegram from Jidda to OSS, December 15, 1947, document 890F.00/12-1547, National Archives.
27. Memorandum for Rentz's file, entitled "Trip to Riyadh with E. A. Locke," February 8, 1948, Mulligan papers.
28. Ibid.
29. Ibid.
30. Ibid.
31. Ibid.
32. Howard M. Sachar, *A History of Israel: From the Rise of Zionism to Our Time* (New York: Knopf, 1976), p. 311.
33. Grafftey-Smith, *Bright Levant*, p. 252.
34. Kennedy, *The Secret History of the Oil Companies*, vol. 3, p. 175. The document is a memo from Loy Henderson to George C. Marshall, May 26, 1948.
35. Ibid.
36. Condit, *U.S. Joint Chiefs of Staff*, p. 112.
37. Ibid., p. 116. Condit cites a State Department bulletin of June 5, 1950.
38. Ibid.
39. Ibid.
The committee observed that Ibn Saud's fears were somewhat unfounded: "Apprehensions are exaggerated because of the King's advancing age and the manner in which he obtained control of Saudi Arabia. It is felt these fears may be gradually removed by the creation of stable conditions in the Near East and by greater reliance on the effectiveness of the United Nations. Saudi Arabia does not fear direct attack by Israel but is apprehensive that Israel may make aggressive moves in the immediate regions surrounding Palestine." [Ibid.]

40. Ibid.
41. Ibid.
42. Ibid.
43. Multinational Report, p. 141.

44. Philby, *Arabian Jubilee*, pp. 219–20.
45. Ibid.

Chapter 9: The King Dies

1. Philby correspondence, August 10, 1953, St. Antony's College, Oxford.
2. Ibid.
3. Bergus, Jidda, to OSS, September 1, 1948, Diplomatic Branch document 890F.00/9-148, National Archives.
4. Ibid.
5. Dean Acheson, *Present at the Creation* (New York: Signet, 1969), p. 241.
6. Philby, *Arabian Jubilee*, p. 222ff.
7. Ibid.
8. Ibid.
9. Ibid.
10. Ibid.
11. Ibid., p. 230.

There was a single exception, Philby wrote, and that was the finance minister, Abdullah Suleiman.

From the beginning he had stood out among his colleagues as a man of great capacity and originality, with a genius for leadership, and supremely confident both in the soundness of his views and in his ability to translate them into action. Physically a frail little man of "uncertain age," but with something of the inspiration of the prophets in his soul, and endowed in full measure with the native intelligence of the desert, he entered upon his new task as Finance Minister as to the manner born more than twenty years ago, and has gone from strength to strength: concentrating his attention on the problems confronting him like a boxer in the ring, and risking the occasional frown of Fortune in his fanatical determination to win through. Respectful, and even humble, in the presence of the king, always sitting on the floor while folk of less distinction loll on chairs or brocaded benches in the assembly, he always seemed to stand out in any company. . . . And the king himself recently put the matter in a nutshell. He was laying down the law on some subject or another, when he suddenly appealed for support to Abdullah Suleiman, who was sitting some distance away, and who enjoys the advantage of a real or assumed hardness of hearing. "I didn't hear," he replied, as if waking from a daydream. "No!" retorted the king, "Ibn Suleiman listens to no man, but everyone listens to Ibn Suleiman!" [Ibid., p. 230]

12. Ibid.
13. Ibid.
14. Ibid.
15. The United States persuaded the British not to launch a military operation and, instead, the British Secret Service, using the CIA as cover for its activities, overthrew Mossadek in August 1953 and replaced him with a "reliable" Iranian general, Fazollah Zahedi.

But there was a price to be paid by the Anglo-Iranian Oil Company for American collaboration in the restoration of the shah. The company changed its name to British Petroleum and was awarded a 40 percent share of Iranian oil; Shell got 14 percent; the Compagnie Française des Pétroles, 6 percent; and four American majors (including Standard Oil of California) got the remaining 40 percent. At last, Britain's absolute primacy in the Gulf was broken. But that did not worry the British government greatly. Britain had begun to discover large oil resources in the North Sea, off the east coast of their islands. Also, the British government was considering an evacuation of British military forces from the Middle East, leaving the defense of the region to the United States and thereby immensely cutting its defense budget. But the intrigues of the U.S. ambassador in Tehran did leave a bad taste in Britain.

The tussle with Mossadek, the Israeli question, and the surging Arab and Muslim nationalism throughout the Middle East and southwestern Asia all contributed to rising antagonisms for the "blue-eyed American infidels" in the Saudi holy land.

16. Kennedy, *The Secret History of the Oil Companies,* vol. 3.

17. Mulligan papers. See Georgetown University catalogue for Aramco in memoriam.

18. Kopper to Jones, "Staff Meeting Discussion" and "Ibn Saud Sends Ultimatum to Aramco," Diplomatic Branch document 786A00/12-1051, National Archives.

19. Philby correspondence, letter to Dora, St. Antony's College, Oxford.

20. Personal statement to author by an Aramco employee who was present.

21. Robert Lacey, *The Kingdom* (London: Hutchinson, 1981), p. 309.

22. Philby correspondence, letter to Dora, St. Antony's College, Oxford.

23. Robert Rhodes James, *Anthony Eden* (London: Papermac, 1986), p. 506.

24. These conversations took place in great secrecy and indeed remained secret until the Mulligan papers were discovered in 1993.

25. Interview with William E. Mulligan, Dartmouth, New Hampshire, January 1992.

26. "Aramco's Donations, Contributions, and Assistance to Saudi Arabia, 1933–1970," Mulligan papers.

27. Leonard Mosely, *Dulles: A Biography of Eleanor, Allen, and John Foster Dulles and Their Family Network* (New York: Dial, 1978), pp. 348–49.

28. Alistair Horne, *Macmillan: 1894–1956* (London: Macmillan, 1984), vol. 1, pp. 378–79.

29. Ibid., p. 270.

30. Ibid., p. 271.

31. Harold Macmillan, *Riding the Storm* (New York: Harper & Row, 1971), pp. 270–77.

Macmillan set out the difficulties in his message:

> I made it clear that although the present insurrection had obviously been organized and armed from outside, we proposed to say as little as possible about the Saudis in our statements and to press forward with an attempt to bring the Sultan and King Saud [Ibn Saud had died in 1953] into better relations. Our duty was clear, both from the narrower and the broader aspects.
>
> The Sultan has appealed to us to help him, and the obligations of friendship seem to us to demand that we do not desert him in times of trouble. Moreover, there must be a risk that if the troubles in Muscat are not both contained and disposed of as soon as possible, they may spread. I hope that it will be possible

to restore the Sultan's authority quickly, by dealing with the help of limited air support from us, a speedy blow at the confidence and prestige of the rebel leaders. . . .

There was a lot of telephoning, over a message from the President, announcing the arrival of Foster Dulles in London on Monday. I was very anxious about what might be read into this, and rather annoyed at the abrupt way it was all done. However, we straightened it out all right, and I think the public will accept that he is coming here to talk about disarmament (which will be good) and *not* about Muscat (which will be very bad). [Ibid.]

32. Ibid.

Macmillan wrote in his memoir:

One member asked whether there was anything to suggest that the rising had been supported or inspired by the Government of Egypt, or the Government of Saudi Arabia. The Foreign Secretary wisely replied that he had made no allegations against specific Governments. Nevertheless it was "evident that these anti-tank guns and machine guns were not produced in Central Omam itself." It was now clear that so long as the operation was successfully and rapidly carried out, we had little to fear in Parliament. [Ibid., pp. 272–73]

33. H. C. Mueller, "Protection of Southern Borders, February 7, 1956, Mulligan papers.

34. Lenczowski, *Oil and State in the Middle East.*

35. "Presentation to Use Before Special Committee," February 5, 1958, Mulligan papers.

36. Memorandum to W. L. Owen, "Exploration Activities," from Dammam, September 17, 1955, Mulligan papers.

Mulligan's papers contained further evidence of the size of his operation in support of the Saudis' case. These consisted of the numbers of translations of press and radio news and feature stories reviewed that month. By Mulligan's count (he was an advocate of time and motion studies to estimate the efficiency of his staff): 120 press articles went through the Aramco system, for a total of 223 pages of text and 400 news items culled from 26 radio channels during the month of April 1956. The stations monitored by Aramco's monitoring system were in Baghdad, Bahrein, Beirut, Cairo, Damascus, India, Jerusalem, London, Mecca, Moscow, Cyprus, Omdurman in the Sudan, Pakistan, Sana in Yemen, and Tehran. And when Mulligan was asked by Aramco's general counsel, W. F. Owen, why Aramco was so interested in so remote a part of the world as Buraimi, Mulligan replied, "The Company is interested in any show of oil anywhere in the Arabian Peninsula." [Ibid.]

37. Macmillan, *Riding the Storm,* pp. 276–77.

38. Hansard, November 1, 1957.

Chapter 10: Double-Cross

1. Lenczowski, *Oil and State in the Middle East,* pp. 335–36.

2. Ibid.

3. Horne, *Macmillan,* vol. 2, p. 41.

4. Ibid.

5. Ibid.

6. Dwight David Eisenhower, *The White House Years,* vol. 2, *Waging Peace* (London: Heinemann, 1956), pp. 15–16.

7. Denis Healey, *The Time of My Life* (London: Michael Joseph, 1989), p. 218.

8. Horne, *Macmillan,* vol. 2, p. 93.

9. C. 1958, Special Committee Report, Mulligan papers.

10. Ibid.

11. Ibid.

12. Aramco Memorial, p. 13.

13. W. F. Owen, Aramco oral history project, 1993.

14. Arbitration Between the Government of Saudi Arabia and the Arabian American Oil Company, *Aramco Memorial,* Mulligan papers.

15. W. F. Owen, Aramco oral history project.

16. Ibid.

17. Aramco Memorial.

18. Ibid.

19. Nicholas Fraser, Philip Jacobson, Mark Ottoway, and Lewis Chester, *Aristotle Onassis* (New York: Lippincott, 1977), pp. 133–34.

20. W. F. Owen, Aramco oral history project.

21. Ibid.

22. Fraser et al., *Aristotle Onassis,* p. 141.

23. Aramco Memorial.

24. Fraser et al., *Aristotle Onassis,* p. 141.

25. Ibid.

26. Ibid., p. 112.

27. Aramco Memorial, pp. 112–13. The affidavit was dated July 25, 1955.

28. Ibid., p. 116ff.

29. Fraser et al., *Aristotle Onassis,* p. 145.

30. Ibid.

31. Ibid., p. 147.

32. Ibid., p. 148.

33. Ibid.

34. Ibid.

35. Ibid.

36. Jose Arnold, *Golden Swords and Pots and Pans* (New York: Harcourt, Brace & World, 1963), pp. 163–65. And see Mulligan papers, Arnold PF.

37. Ibid.

38. Ibid.

39. Arnold, *Golden Swords,* pp. 163–65.

40. Ibid.

41. Ibid, p. 113.

42. Ibid., pp. 44–45.

43. Ibid., pp. 51–52.

44. Ibid.

A fleet of air-conditioned passenger cars, in which the king, his advisers, and his guests traveled, made up the last section of this fantastic expedition. At the end of each day the king, returning from the chase refreshed, would summon the court jesters. Arnold recorded:

He enjoyed their antics and sometimes even took part himself in the slap-stick performances. The jesters' favorite frolic was a wild form of tag in which the pursuers attempted to flail the pursued with a piece of knotted rope. Whenever one would tire of running, he would crawl under King Saud's chair, which was the only official haven, and peep out through the folds of the King's robes to make faces at his tormenters. Occasionally, when the game got out of hand, King Saud would take up a rope and join the chase, bearing down sternly on the more unruly participants. At other times, the jesters would run through a routine of jokes and pantomimes that ranged from farcical to obscene. [Ibid., p. 67]

45. State Department document 786A.11/4-1553 LWC, April 15, 1953, National Archives.
46. Ibid.
47. Ibid.
48. Ibid.
49. Ibid.

Chapter 11: Abdication

1. Monroe, *Philby of Arabia,* pp. 285–86.
2. Ibid.
3. Ibid.
4. Philby papers, St. Antony's College, Oxford.
5. Holden and Johns, *The House of Saud,* p. 200ff.
6. Philby papers, St. Antony's College, Oxford.
7. When in 1959 the Saudi government became seriously alarmed that Iraq was lapsing into Communism and anarchy, Saud sent to Prime Minister Macmillan of Britain "a passionate appeal for Anglo-American armed intervention." Macmillan could only reply that "a return to normal diplomatic relations between Britain and Saudi Arabia, which had been broken off at the time of the Suez operations, would facilitate mutual consultations." [Macmillan, *Riding the Storm,* p. 353]
8. Philby Manuscript, p. 39, Mulligan papers.
9. Ibid.
10. Ibid.
11. Here is some of the text from the Voice of the Arabs radio announcement:

My Arab brother, where did King Saud get his money? It is the people's money, the money from oil which is monopolized by America and takes it and gives King Saud and his harem gifts, the money which is spent on consuming goods for the pleasure of the ruling family. We ask that this money go to the people in order to realize a true renaissance toward Muslim socialism. . . .

Oh! my brother Arab, American imperialism stresses that it should remain in Saudi Arabia, and this is the price for protecting the Saudi throne from destruction. Thus Saud's throne will remain under the protection of American battleships and of the atomic base in Dhahran. But Saud should know that by this he is speeding up his end. Imperialism will never succeed in saving thrones from the will of the people. The people endure, but they do not forgive. The freemen in Saudi Arabia do not fear any power on earth and they shall soon strike. . . .

O! My brother Arab, America, which is controlled by Zionism, wants to liquidate the Palestine problem with the help of Saud, the criminal king and the protector of Muslim countries. My brother, Saud is working with the assistance of his American and Jewish friends on liquidation of the Palestine problem. . . .

The Saudi Arabian Government issued a statement denying that there is socialism in Islam and that socialism is a denial of God. The heathens and unbelievers who fought the Prophet Mohammed are nearer to Islam than the al-Saud and their religious men who are corrupt and who spread corruption. How can a family who stole the petroleum royalties and stole the gold from al-Mahd and made of it the "bed of pleasure" which was manufactured for the King by a Jewish firm in Baden Baden, West Germany. It cost half a million pounds. Even the shoes of the harem are made of gold. Furthermore, billions of silver riyals were shipped to Israel by the royal family in 1959 through the imperialist company Aramco in Dhahran. The silver was sold in Israel. [Mulligan papers]

12. Anthony Sampson, *The Seven Sisters: The Great Oil Companies and the World They Shaped* (New York: Viking, 1975), p. 161.
13. Ibid.
14. Ibid.
15. Ibid.
16. Ibid.
17. Lacey, *The Kingdom,* pp. 333–34.
18. William E. Mulligan, "Aramco's Changing Relations with the Saudi Arabian Government" (paper presented at the Management Development Seminar, March 6, 1956), Mulligan papers.
19. Joseph A. Mahon, Aramco oral history project.
20. Item 45, Joseph A. Mahon papers, Special Collections, Lauinger Library, Georgetown University.
21. Ibid.
22. Holden and Johns, *The House of Saud,* p. 212.
23. "The Transfer of King Sa'ud's Powers to Crown Prince Faysal" (Aramco, October 1964), Mulligan papers.
24. Arnold, *Golden Swords,* pp. 222–23.
25. Ibid., p. 224.
26. William E. Mulligan to G. E. Mandis, June 27, 1961, Mulligan papers.
27. Brock Powers, Aramco oral history project.
28. Holden and Johns, *The House of Saud,* p. 218.
29. Aramco Chronology of Events Involving His Majesty, King Saud, November 16, 1961–October 11, 1962, Mulligan papers.
30. Mulligan papers.
31. Ibid.
32. Ibid.
33. Ibid.
34. Ibid.
35. "The Transfer of King Sa'ud's Powers to Crown Prince Faysal," October 1974, Mulligan papers.

36. Ibid.
37. Ibid.
38. Ibid.
39. Ibid.
40. Ibid.
41. Ibid.
42. Ibid.
43. Ibid.
44. Ibid.
45. Monroe, *Philby of Arabia,* p. 294.
46. Storm interview, Mulligan papers.
47. Letter, Kim Philby to George Rentz, Mulligan papers.

Chapter 12: Rock Wednesday

1. Thomas C. Barger, "Planning Guides for Aramco as a Corporation," Mahon papers.
2. Ibid.
3. Healey, *The Time of My Life,* p. 214.
4. Ibid.
5. See file dealing with Nasser propaganda, Mulligan papers.
6. Jeffrey Robinson, p. 48.
7. Ibid.
8. George Ballou, Aramco oral history report.
9. Baldo Marinovic, Aramco oral history project.
10. Peter Speers, Aramco oral history project.
11. Frank Jungers, Aramco oral history project.
12. Ibid.
13. Robinson, p. 60.
14. Ibid.
15. Ibid., p. 61.
16. Ibid., p. 62.
17. Frank Jungers, Aramco oral history project.
18. Ibid.
19. Sampson, *The Seven Sisters,* p. 235.
20. "The June 1967 Riots — Chronology," Mulligan papers.
21. Ibid.
22. Ibid.
23. Ibid.
24. Ibid.
25. Ibid.
26. Ibid.
27. Ibid.
28. Report by B. C. Nelson, Mulligan papers.
29. "The June 1967 Riots — Chronology," Mulligan papers.
30. Ibid.
31. Ibid.

32. Ibid.

33. Ibid.

In Dhahran, meanwhile, the amir of Hasa had appeared at the U.S. consulate. The consul general, who had just learned that the Dhahran telephone exchange had been badly damaged, received him and noted: "The Amir was obviously taken by surprise and rather shaken. . . . He exhibited a great reluctance to take a close look at the damage caused by the rioters. In fact, it was only after repeated demands by the Company Representative–Dammam that the Amir reluctantly agreed to get out of his car and see the damage in the Telephone Exchange. It appeared that the Amir wanted to get away from it all as quickly as possible." [Ibid.]

34. "The June 1967 Riots — Chronology," Mulligan papers.

35. Ibid.

36. Ibid.

37. Ibid.

38. Ibid.

39. Ibid.

40. Ibid.

41. Ibid.

42. Ibid.

43. Ibid.

44. Ibid.

45. Ibid.

46. Ibid.

47. Ibid.

48. Ibid.

49. Ibid.

50. Ibid.

Chapter 13: The Grand Crises

1. R. I. Metz, interview and report, Mulligan papers.

2. Ibid.

3. Ibid.

4. Ibid.

5. Report by Homer Mueller, Mulligan papers.

6. Ibid.

7. Ibid.

8. Brock Powers, Aramco oral history project.

9. Ibid.

10. Ibid.

11. Ibid.

12. See his briefing manuscript, Mulligan papers.

13. Ibid., p. 141.

14. Ibid.

15. Lacey, The Kingdom, p. 410.

16. Ibid.

17. Ibid.
18. Robinson, p. 68.
19. Multinational Report, p. 136.
20. Frank Jungers, Aramco oral history project.
21. Ibid.
22. Multinational Report, p. 142.
23. Frank Jungers, Aramco oral history project.
24. Ibid.
25. Ibid.
26. Ibid.
27. Ibid.
28. Yergin, *The Prize,* p. 606.
29. Ibid.
30. Ibid.
31. Frank Jungers, Aramco oral history project.
32. Ibid.
33. Sampson, *The Seven Sisters,* p. 255.
34. Ibid.
35. Frank Jungers, Aramco oral history project.
36. Ibid.
37. Brock Powers, Aramco oral history project.
38. Ibid.

It was no secret that Israeli armed might was absolutely dependent on U.S. aid. As Jungers said,

> They have the equipment that we give them; they don't buy it, we give it to them in doses of billions of dollars' worth. It was during this period that Bill Chandler, president of Tapline, wrote an article. . . . It was titled, "Israel, the 51st State," and it presented the premise, which was quite true and plausible, that if we made Israel a state, it would cost us a lot less and nobody would attack the 51st state. . . . Of course, [the Israelis would refuse this offer] because they want the money. As a state, they wouldn't get any kind of aid. They'd have to stand in line with the Detroits and Los Angeleses of this country and beg for money like everybody else. We treat them better than we treat our own Americans, on a per capita basis. The article caused a lot of fuss in a lot of places, but it was a well-written article and there was a hell of a lot of truth in it. The Israeli press and the American press were up in arms over the oil company kowtowing to the Arabs like that. [Ibid.]

39. Ibid.
40. Ibid.
41. Mulligan papers.
42. Frank Jungers, Aramco oral history project.
43. Ibid.
44. Ibid.
45. Ibid.
46. Ibid.
47. Robinson, p. 101.
48. Ibid.
49. Marvin and Bernard Kalb, *Kissinger* (Boston: Little, Brown, 1974), p. 515.

50. Ibid.
51. Ibid.
52. Ibid.

Chapter 14: Regicide

1. Frank Jungers, Aramco oral history project.
2. Ibid.
3. Ibid.

Other commentators reported on the death of Faisal:

> The burial took place on the [day following Faisal's death], with the Arab heads of state present and as many world leaders as could get to Riyadh in time. Crown Prince Fahd led the procession from the al Raisa, the state residence where Feisal's body lay in state, to a small mosque where, it was estimated, 100,000 persons were gathered. At the obsequies the congregation intoned the interment prayers. "It is the decree of God," they intoned. King Khaled, now the chief member of the dynasty, replied, using words laid down to protocol: "I am pleased with the will of God." Feisal was then taken by ambulance to the dynasty's stony and bleak cemetery outside Riyadh and, close to the places where Ibn Saud and ex-king Saud were buried, Feisal was buried with his face turned towards Mecca. Afterwards, one of the princes stated, "We had a hundred nervous breakdowns. For a week everyone went to bed at eight o'clock in the evening." [Holden and Johns, *The House of Saud*, pp. 382–83]

> No one could make sense of the killing: a mixed-up assassin thrown off balance by the temptations of the West, an ancient impulse for blood revenge, the memory of the television station riots, the *majlis* tradition of open access to the ruler: the circumstances of Feisal's slaying were queerly strung with the same elements of old and new that the king had tried to weave together in his eleven-year reign. Saudis could only shrug their shoulders and sadly accept the will of God. [Lacey, *The Kingdom*, pp. 426–27]

4. The investigations did produce evidence that Prince Faisal had been rather close to the family of the late King Saud, and that his father, the fifteenth son of Ibn Saud, had lived in a palace adjacent to Nasiriyah, Saud's residence in Riyadh.

Some evidence was uncovered to bring King Saud's family further into the orbit of Prince Faisal: he had become engaged to one of King Saud's daughters, Sitta bint Saud, and only recently his mother and father had gone to Beirut on his behalf to make arrangements for their wedding. Some authors found reason to explore the international aspect of the king's death:

> The assassination led to speculation, some of it mischievously inspired, about international conspiracies. Arab attention focused on the CIA — inevitably, given the general preoccupation with the Agency. It could be and was tortuously argued that it was in the interests of the U.S. to remove a king who was so intransigent on the question of Jerusalem and replace him with a more amenable leadership. Such conjecture could only be reinforced by language such as the *Washington Post* used in its editorial commenting on Feisal's death.

It said: "Feisal probably did more damage to the West than any other single man since Adolf Hitler." The fact that many Westerners referred to him as a "friend" or moderate was a "revealing measure of his power." No credence, however, was given by the Saudis to widespread rumours that the CIA had been at work on Kissinger's instructions following his last frosty interview with the late King. [Holden and Johns, *The House of Saud*, p. 382]

5. Ibid.
6. Ibid.
7. Ibid.
8. Ibid.
9. Ibid.
10. Ibid.
11. Robinson, *Yamani*, p. 164.
12. Ibid., p. 168.
13. Ibid.
14. Frank Jungers, Aramco oral history project.
15. Ibid.
16. Report and Chronology on Participation, Mulligan papers.
17. Ibid.
18. "Critical Factors Affecting Saudi Arabia's Oil Decisions," report to Congress published by the comptroller general of the United States, May 12, 1978, Mulligan papers. Hereafter cited as GAO Report.
19. Ibid.
20. Ibid.
21. Ibid.
22. Baldo Marinovic, Aramco oral history project.
23. Ibid.
24. Robert L. Norberg, retired Aramco agent in Washington, D.C., mentioned this in a talk on Aramco at Sweet Briar College, December 1, 1995.
25. Ibid.
26. Mahon papers.
27. Sir Humphrey Trevelyan, Introduction to Holden and Johns, *The House of Saud*.
28. Jan Morris, *Pleasures of a Tangled Life* (New York: Random House, 1989), pp. 154–56.
29. Ibid.
30. Ibid.

Chapter 15: The Washington Lobby

1. Anthony Sampson, *The Seven Sisters*, p. 273ff.
2. Ibid.
3. Ibid.
4. Robinson, *Yamani*, p. 222.
5. Ibid.
6. Ibid., p. 221.
7. Ibid., p. 222.

8. Ibid.

9. Baldo Marinovic, Aramco oral history project.

10. Joseph A. Mahon, Aramco oral history project.

11. Biographical sketch of Abdullah ibn Darwish, c. July 16, 1962, Mulligan papers.

This text continues with a physical description of Darwish:

> [He] is a relatively tall, fleshy man whose weight belies his tremendous energy. He has a large nose and an opaque right eye. He genuinely prefers the traditional Arab dress and customs. He beiches, picks his teeth, scratches his body, and converses in a manner startling to a westerner. He is reportedly a sodomite and acts as though every western woman has her price. These habits and attitudes may not be representative of the highest ideals of Persian Gulf Arabs, but it should be said in all fairness to Abdullah that they are not uncommon. [Ibid.]

12. Ibid.

13. Ibid.

14. Ibid.

15. Ibid.

16. Ibid.

17. Ibid.

18. Ibid.

19. Ibid., p. 71.

20. Ibid., p. 73.

21. Ibid.

22. *New York Times,* April 2, 1978; Steven Emerson, "The Arabians' Knight: The Transformation of Fred Dutton from Liberal Warrior to Foreign Agent," *Common Cause,* January/February 1986.

23. Ibid.

24. Ibid.

25. Ibid.

26. Ibid.

27. Ibid.

28. Ibid.

29. Ibid.

30. Ibid.

31. Ibid.

32. Jim Hoagland and J. P. Smith, *Washington Post,* December 20, 1977.

33. Ibid.

34. Ibid.

35. Ibid.

36. Sampson, *The Seven Sisters.*

37. Frank Jungers, Aramco oral history project.

38. Brock Powers, Aramco oral history project.

39. Ibid.

40. Ibid.

41. Ibid.

42. Baldo Marinovic, Aramco oral history project.

43. Ibid.

44. Ibid.
45. Ibid.
46. Ibid.
47. Ibid.
48. Brock Powers, Aramco oral history project.
49. Ibid.
50. Ibid.
51. Mahon papers.
52. Ibid.
53. Mahon papers, interviews.
54. Ibid.
55. *The Arabian Sun,* January 5, 1978.

Chapter 16: The Iran-Iraq Factors

1. Yergin, *The Prize,* p. 717.
2. Department of Defense, "Final Report to Congress: Conduct of the Persian Gulf War, April 1992." See chronology in appendix D, p. 368. Hereafter cited as Final Report.
3. Ibid.
4. Ibid.
5. Ibid.
6. Article by Peter Iseman, *The Nation,* April 19, 1980.
7. Ibid.
8. Ibid.
9. Report by Richard Johns, *Financial Times,* London, undated, Mulligan papers.
10. Ibid.
11. Lacey, *The Kingdom,* p. 484.
12. Ibid.
13. Ibid., p. 486.
14. Proclamation by the Saudi Government, Mulligan papers.
15. Ibid.
16. Wilbur Crane Eveland, *Ropes of Sand: America's Failure in the Middle East* (New York: W. W. Norton, 1980), p. 338. Eveland claimed to be a relative of Charles R. Crane. None in the Crane family had ever heard his name.
17. GAO Report.
18. Ibid.
19. Baldo Marinovic, Aramco oral history project.
20. Ibid.
21. Ibid.
22. Ibid.
23. Norman H. Schwarzkopf, *Schwarzkopf,* pp. 324–25.
24. Final Report, pp. 8–9.
25. General Prince Khaled bin Sultan, *Desert Warrior: A Personal View of the Gulf War by the Joint Forces Commander* (New York: HarperCollins, 1995), p. 157.
26. James E. Akins, talk given at a seminar on the Gulf crisis, University of Michigan, November 1990.

Chapter 17: The Aramco War

1. Said K. Aburish, *The Rise, Corruption and Coming Fall of the House of Saud* (London: Bloomsbury, 1994), p. 56.
2. Ibid., pp. 57–58.
3. Ibid., p. 68.
4. Ibid.; GAO Report.
5. Ibid.
6. Robinson, *Yamani,* pp. 182–83.
7. Ibid., p. 173. Robinson is citing the former British ambassador at Jidda, Sir James Craig.
8. Lacey, *The Kingdom,* p. 492.
9. Aramco press kit, January 1976, Mulligan papers.
10. Ibid.
11. Ibid.
12. Robert L. Maby, Jr., "Reserves, Resources, and Harbingers," Mulligan papers.
13. Aramco press kit, January 1976, Mulligan papers.
14. Ibid.
15. Ibid.
16. Ibid.
17. Ibid.
18. Ibid.
19. Files on environmental problems, Mahon papers.
20. Report on environmental affairs coordination to R. W. Brock, June 30, 1974, Mahon papers.
21. Anonymous correspondent with Mulligan, Mulligan papers.
22. Baldo Marinovic, Aramco oral history project.
23. Ibid.
24. Ibid.
25. Ibid.
26. Ibid.

INDEX

264 – No name – no order mentioned. Remarkable !